DEPENDENCY AND NON-LINEAR PHONOLOGY

CROOM HELM LINGUISTICS SERIES

Dependency and Non-Linear Phonology

EDITED BY JACQUES DURAND

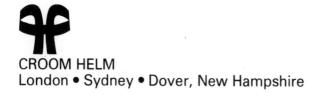

CROOM HELM
London • Sydney • Dover, New Hampshire

© 1986 Jacques Durand and contributors
Croom Helm Ltd, Provident House, Burrell Row,
Beckenham, Kent BR3 1AT
Croom Helm Australia Pty Ltd, Suite 4, 6th Floor,
64-76 Kippax Street, Surry Hills, NSW 2010, Australia

British Library Cataloguing in Publication Data

Dependency and non-linear phonology. — (Croom
   Helm linguistics series)
   1. Grammar, Comparative and general — Phonology
   2. Dependency grammar
   I. Durand, Jacques
   414   P217.3

ISBN 0-7099-0894-6

Croom Helm, 51 Washington Street, Dover,
New Hampshire 03820, USA

Library of Congress Cataloging in Publication Data
Main entry under title:

Dependency and non-linear phonology.

   (Croom Helm linguistics series)
   Bibliography: p.
   Includes index.
   1. Grammar, Comparative and general—Phonology—
Addresses, essays, lectures.   I. Durand, Jacques,
1947–   .   II. Series.
P217.D46   1986   414   85-24265
ISBN 0-7099-0894-6

315841

Typeset in 10pt Times Roman by Leaper & Gard Ltd, Bristol, England
Printed and bound in Great Britain by Mackays of Chatham Ltd, Kent

CONTENTS

This book is dedicated
to the memory of David Kilby

EDITORIAL STATEMENT

CROOM HELM LTD publish a Linguistics Series under the chief editorship of John Hawkins (Max-Planck-Institut für Psycholinguistik and University of Southern California).

The series does not specialise in any one area of language study, nor does it limit itself to any one theoretical approach. Synchronic and diachronic descriptive studies, either syntactic, semantic, phonological or morphological, are welcomed, as are more theoretical 'model-building' studies, and studies in sociolinguistcs or psycholinguistics. The criterion for a work's acceptance is the quality of its contribution to the relevant field. All monographs published must advance our understanding of the nature of language in areas of substantial interest to major sectors of the linguistic research community. Traditional scholarly standards, such as clarity of presentation, factual and logical soundness of argumentation, and a thorough and reasoned orientation to other relevant work, are also required. Within these indispensable limitations we welcome the submission of creative and original contributions to the study of language.

The editor and publisher wish to draw this series to the attention of scholars, who are invited to submit manuscripts or book-proposals to:

Professor John Hawkins, Max-Planck-Institut für Psycholinguistik, Berg en Dalseweg 79, NL-6522, The Netherlands *or* Department of Linguistics, University of Southern California, Los Angeles, CA 90089-1693, USA; *or to* Jonathan Price, Linguistics Editor, Croom Helm Publishers, Provident House, Burrell Row, Beckenham, Kent BR3 1AT.

INTRODUCTION

Dependency and Non-linear Phonology is a collection of articles by the following linguists: John Anderson (Edinburgh), Mike Davenport (Odense) & Jørgen Staun (Copenhagen), Jacques Durand (Essex), Colin Ewen (Leiden), Heinz Giegerich (Edinburgh), Charles Jones (Durham), Ken Lodge (East Anglia), John Rennison (Vienna) and Nigel Vincent (Cambridge). In the last few years attention in phonology has shifted away from segment-sized units and operations on these to the nature of sequences above the segment (syllable, foot, tone group) and the interplay between intrasegmental and suprasegmental structure. Instead of the fairly unified theory based on Chomsky and Halle's *The Sound Pattern of English* which dominated phonological practice until comparatively recently, there has been a vast increase in competing models of phonology (autosegmental phonology, metrical phonology, CV phonology, dependency phonology, three-tiered phonology, grid-only phonology, etc.). All these models can be described as NON-LINEAR by opposition to standard generative phonology where a phonological representation is simply depicted as a LINEAR arrangement of segments (even though each of these segments is composed of simultaneously occurring features) and where phonological rules operate on such strings (they delete, insert or permute segments, or change their feature values). Despite undeniable differences in outlook between the current alternative systems of phonological description, there are many lines of convergence and basic agreement on what an adequate theory of phonology should account for. They all share the belief that phonological representations need to be much more articulated than traditionally assumed and that a number of phenomena (in particular, but not exclusively, stress and pitch contours) cannot be appropriately dealt with if phonological representations are limited to string-like arrangements of segment and boundaries.

The purpose of this volume is to explore in depth one such model — DEPENDENCY PHONOLOGY — and to examine its connections with other non-linear proposals. Ever since its inception in the early seventies, research in dependency phonology has been animated by the conviction that both the internal structure and the external structure had to be more richly articulated than was commonly assumed. This two-pronged attack on the requirements of phonological representation is one of the hallmarks of dependency phonology *vis à-vis* rival proposals where intrasegmental structure and suprasegmental structure have often received separate treatments. Another central aspect of dependency phonology is the proposal that a basic element in the characterisation of both kinds of structure is the eponymous relation of dependency, such that segments in sequence and components of segments may exhibit variable relative salience. In other words, DEPENDENCY is taken as the core formal relation underpinning the model and constituency is argued to be derivable from the more basic concepts of dependency and order. Although dependency phonology has already been used in the description of a variety of languages, the major published application of this system has so far been in the field of English historical linguistics (Anderson & Jones's *Phonological Structure and the History of English*, North-Holland, 1977). The present collection offers the first comprehensive exposition of this model and tests it against a wide set of phonological problems. But the volume does not stop there, and one of its merits is to offer a discussion of the relative scope of dependency-based and constituency-based representations and to allow readers to make up their own minds by giving them treatments of comparable phenomena within competing frameworks. To this effect, it provides original articles on suprasegmental structure and intrasegmental structure within rival notational models and the articles written in the dependency framework contain copious references to alternative solutions outside dependency phonology. The book should therefore be of interest to all phonologists in that it provides a novel integrated treatment of phonological structure clearly set against alternative approaches.

Dependency and Non-linear Phonology opens with Anderson & Durand's 'Dependency Phonology' which is intended to provide a detailed introduction to this framework. All the central concepts and notational conventions used in dependency phonology are carefully defined and Anderson & Durand attempt within the space available to point out the major differences between dependency phonology and rival systems of representation. The introduction is self-contained and does not presuppose any knowledge of dependency phonology. It provides the most complete overview to date of the central tenets of this system of phonological representation.

Following on from Anderson & Durand, there is a detailed article by Anderson, 'Suprasegmental Dependencies', which is a major exposition of the treatment of suprasegmental categories within dependency phonology. The internal structure of the syllable, the need for categories such as the foot and the tone group are all considered in turn and with specific reference to the stress patterns of English. Anderson's article is directly complemented by three papers: Vincent's 'Constituency and Syllable Structure', Giegerich's 'Relating to Metrical Structure' and Ewen's 'Segmental and Suprasegmental Structure'. Vincent discusses the evidence for the syllable in phonological theory and examines the relative merits of some recent approaches to syllable structure (in particular CV phonology and constituency-based proposals which assign rich internal structure to the syllable). His conclusion is that a hierarchical model of syllable structure as advocated, for instance, by Selkirk in a variety of recent articles (and by Anderson in this volume) is required to capture a number of significant generalisations. Giegerich, for his part, offers a thorough overview of the metrical model and a discussion of aspects of English stress (comparable to those dealt with by Anderson) within this framework. He also considers in detail whether a hierarchical representation of suprasegmental structure could be replaced by an approach based on the notion of 'grid'. His conclusion is that grids are artefactual upon metrical structure and have a smaller range of application than metrical trees. Colin Ewen's paper contains a comparison of metrical and dependency structures (as well as grid representations) from the point of view of dependency phonology. It provides a useful comparative synthesis of some of the issues raised by Anderson, Giegerich and Vincent. At the same time, it discusses the nature of the internal structure of segments and argues that the richer internal structure assigned to segments in dependency phonology renders unnecessary the positing of tiers basic to CV phonology. This article provides a good transition to the papers in the rest of the volume.

Of the other papers, Durand's 'French Liaison, Floating Segments and Other Matters in a Dependency Framework' is the one that is more specifically concerned with suprasegmental structure. It is the first treatment of a sizeable portion of the phonology of

French within a dependency framework and shows how insights normally associated with metrical and autosegmental phonology can find a natural integration within this model. The papers by Jones and Lodge are both about English and stress the link between intrasegmental and suprasegmental structure. Jones's 'A Dependency Approach to some Well-known Features of Historical English Phonology' argues that by using a model such as dependency phonology which allows greater componentiality than hitherto available, it is possible to make quite general statements about historical processes which are normally treated as disparate. This article re-examines some of the questions which are illustrated at greater length in Anderson & Jones's *Phonological Structure and the History of English* — a work which has provided much of the impetus for current research in the dependency model. Lodge, in 'The English Velar Fricative, Dialect Variation and Dependency Phonology', provides a clear discussion of the fate of the velar fricative in the history of English, its reflexes across modern English dialects and its putative status in synchronic grammars of English. He shows how the loss of the velar fricative is a weakening process which must be referred both to syllable structure and to the internal structure of segments and he explains how the two are interrelated within the dependency framework.

The article by Mike Davenport & Jørgen Staun ('Sequence, Segment and Configuration: Two Problems for Dependency Phonology') provides a theory-internal discussion of intrasegmental structure. Davenport & Staun address two main questions. First of all, how should affricates be represented? Secondly, how do components expressing glottal stricture and airstream mechanisms fit into the notion of gesture central to the dependency proposal? On the basis of representative cross-linguistic data they suggest ways in which the standard dependency account of the above could be improved. Their article should particularly be compared with the suggestions concerning infrasegmental structure made by Colin Ewen in this volume. Finally, the article by Rennison — 'On Tridirectional Feature Systems for Vowels' — puts forward a system where the basic components for the description of vowels are related to the dependency primitives but in a binary notation. The work is based on a careful cross-linguistic survey of vowel systems and should be carefully compared with the treatment of vowels discussed in Anderson & Durand's 'Dependency Phonology'.

Many of the articles in this volume were presented in preliminary form at the Dependency Phonology Conference organised at the University of Essex in September 1983. All the contributors, however, have striven to produce articles which would lead to a coherent volume on modern phonology and some of the articles were written afresh after the Conference to allow for a more integrated publication.

I wish to thank Jenny Potts and Wyn Johnson for carefully checking the manuscript of *Dependency and Non-linear Phonology*. All remaining imperfections are to be imputed to me. My wife, Jane Durand, provided invaluable support during the preparation of this volume.

Jacques Durand
Essex

NOTATIONAL CONVENTIONS

The main notational conventions followed in this volume are given below. The reader is referred to Anderson & Durand (this volume) for more detailed explanations and further conventions.

→ is used for the dependency relation: a→b is to be read as 'a governs b' or 'b is a dependant of a'.

⟹ is used as the familiar rewrite symbol of generative grammar; ⟹ is also used for diachronic change: a⟹b is to be read as 'a rewrites as b' or as 'a changes into b'.

⟶» is used for subordination: a⟶»b is to be read as 'b is a subordinate of a'.

< is used for immediate strict precedence: a < b is to be read as 'a bears a relation of immediate strict precedence to b'.

; is used for the dependency relation between components and is equivalent to →. Thus a;b is to be read as 'a governs b' and is equivalent to a→b.

: is used to express mutual government between components: a:b is to be read as 'a governs b and b governs a' or 'a and b mutually govern each other'.

, is used to express the simple combination of components or when the distinction between simple combination and mutual government is not relevant to the discussion. In the first interpretation, a,b is to be read as 'a and b enter into a relation of simple combination'.

. can also be used to denote simple combination, particularly where it is desirable to show explicitly that a simple combination rather than mutual government is involved.

| | verticals are used to enclose components.

/ / and [ ] have their standard phonological interpretation (underlying vs. surface representation).

The system of phonetic transcription used, with occasional exceptions, is the IPA.

CONTRIBUTORS

John Anderson

Department of English Language
University of Edinburgh
George Square
Edinburgh EH8 9JX
Scotland

Mike Davenport

Engelsk Institut
Odense Universitet
Campusvej 55
5230 Odense M
Denmark

Jacques Durand

Department of Language and Linguistics
University of Essex
Colchester CO4 3SQ
Essex
England

Colin Ewen

Vakgroep Engels
Rijksuniversiteit te Leiden
Postbus 9515
P.N. van Eyckhof 4
2300 Leiden
The Netherlands

Heinz Giegerich

Department of English Language
University of Edinburgh
George Square
Edinburgh EH8 9JX
Scotland

Charles Jones

Department of English Language and Medieval Literature
University of Durham
Elvet Riverside
New Elvet
Durham DH1 3JT
England

Ken Lodge

School of Modern Languages and European History
University of East Anglia
Norwich NR4 7TJ
England

John Rennison

Institut für Sprachwissenschaft
der Universität Wien
Liechtensteinstraße 46A
A-1090 Wien
Austria

Jørgen Staun

Engelsk Institut
Kobenhavns Universitet
Njalsgade 84, Trappe 8
2300 Copenhagen S
Denmark

Nigel Vincent

Department of Linguistics
University of Cambridge
Sidgwick Avenue
Cambridge CB3 9DA
England

1 DEPENDENCY PHONOLOGY

John Anderson & Jacques Durand

1. Dependency Phonology and Structural Analogy

With respect to its conception of phonological representations, CLASSICAL GENERATIVE PHONOLOGY can be characterised as *structurally minimalist*. No intermediate phonological units are posited as intervening between the minimal unit, or segment, and the 'phonological phrase', the maximal domain for phonological processes. And although segments are not atomic and indivisible, they are simply conceived as unordered sets of component properties ('distinctive features') which are limited to two values (+ or −). This is the only structural variable except for that represented by possibly multivalued suprasegmental features of stress and/or tone, which are also associated with particular segments. Thus, as is familiar, the structure of any 'phonological phrase' is characterised phonologically as a matrix wherein each cell is given the value for a particular feature (on the paradigmatic dimension) with respect to a particular segment (on the syntagmatic).

In recent years, various 'frameworks' have developed whereby this minimal two-dimensional, or 'linear', conception has been enriched in two complementary respects. In the first place, phonological constituents such as the syllable have been invoked ('syllabic phonology'), or prominence and other relations have been extracted from segmental representation ('grid phonology', 'autosegmental phonology'), or both ('metrical phonology', 'CV phonology', 'dependency phonology'). Secondly, it has been proposed that different and/or additional structural properties, constant and variable, enter into the characterisation of the segment ('particle phonology', or 'autosegmental phonology', 'dependency phonology'). To some extent, these developments recapitulate aspects of earlier, 'pre-generative' frameworks (such as Firthian prosodic analysis). However, it is not our concern here to give an historical account, and still less an evaluation of the current situation with its fast-changing and multifarious trends.

1

Rather, we shall try to define the central core of properties that can be said to characterise DEPENDENCY PHONOLOGY (DP) and situate the various articles contained in this volume in relation to it. This is not intended as a comprehensive and definitive version of dependency phonology but as a condensed overview of this framework and a guide to the rest of the volume. We begin with the notion of dependency which is the cornerstone of the whole system.

Perhaps most central, and obvious, in the DP framework is the claim that the binary non-symmetric relation of DEPENDENCY is crucial to the notation and permits (in conjunction with precedence and association — see below) an adequate representation of both supra- and intrasegmental structure. The notion of constituency which is basic to much modern work in phonology and syntax is here assumed not to be primitive but to be derivable from the dependency relation (or its transitive closure: SUBORDINATION) and (linear) PRECEDENCE. The sets of elements at different levels of phonological representation are given partial orderings by the relations of subordination and precedence. We return below to the character of different levels and their ASSOCIATIONS. But before that it is worth pointing to an important 'hyperphonological' aspect of DP.

It can be claimed that the dependency, or head-modifier, relation is also crucial to the characterisation of syntactic and morphological structure. Thus, for example, syntactic constructions are distinguished primarily by the identity (word class) of their head, which constitutes the obligatory atomic nucleus of the construction; and secondarily by the direction of modification (on what side does the modifier lie?). So that in (1):

(1)   The farmer killed the duckling

the construction *killed the duckling* is distinguished as having a verb head, *killed*, its obligatory, atomic, element modified to the right by *the duckling. The duckling* in turn has a noun head modified to the left by *the*. However, *killed* is also the head of the whole construction represented by (1); this construction is distinguished by direction of modification: the less inclusive construction headed by *killed* (the verb phrase) has only right modifiers; *killed* as head of the sentence has *the farmer* as a modifier to the left. It is inappropriate to pursue these aspects of syntactic structure here (see Anderson, to appear a,b). What is most significant in the present context is the relevance of the dependency relation to other levels of linguistic description.

The relevance of dependency throughout the linguistic description is in accordance with what has been called the STRUCTURAL ANALOGY assumption (Anderson, to appear a). This is simply the assumption, familiar from much post-Saussurean work, that we should expect that the same structural properties recur at different levels. Structural properties which are postulated as being unique to a particular level are unexpected and suspicious if unsupported by firm evidence of their unique appropriateness in that particular instance. Thus, arguments for the appropriateness of the dependency relation at different levels — and within different aspects of phonological representation — are mutually supportive. It can indeed be argued that structural analogies between different levels are much more detailed than simply involving recourse to the dependency relation (see in particular Anderson, to appear a). We shall point out such analogies as our exposition proceeds.

1.1 *Levels of Representation*

In a wide sense, DP is essentially a notational proposal, in particular concerning the structural relations entered into by phonological categories (see Anderson & Ewen 1980: 10-12, on 'notational models' vs. 'phonological theories'). As such, the dependency assumption has consequences for other aspects of notation, specifically the nature of the categories of phonology. For instance, as we shall see, no non-atomic units (syllable, etc.) need explicit labelling; and no 'relational; categories (strong vs. weak, for example) are invoked. Also features, called components in DP, are optimally UNARY: as once more we shall see, the problems arising from binary and multivalued feature systems can be avoided if the dependency relation is invoked. But, clearly, any choice of notation has wider repercussions, specifically with respect to the relationship between different levels of representation. Let us at this point, therefore, be a little more precise about the notion of level.

Each utterance is associated with several distinct representations of structure. Some of these representations belong to distinct PLANES: they are constructed out of disjoint sets of basic categories. Syntactic and phonological categories are heteroplanar; given the structural analogy principle, they share structural properties but the basic alphabets of categories do not overlap. Homoplanar representations may belong to different levels: categories are shared, but not necessarily all; and different principles of combination are involved. Within phonology we can distinguish between a lexical level and an utterance, or phonetic level. Phonetic representations not merely introduce some categories absent from lexical (e.g. aspiration of plosives in English) but they also differ e.g. in that regularities appertaining thereto are not sensitive to morphological structure, but rather to syntactic, informational and rhythmic (see 2.3). Within each level proper we can distinguish a suprasegmental and a segmental SUBLEVEL. Suprasegmental structure is an unlabelled projection of the partial sequence of segmental representations which specifies the heads and modifiers of the constructions into which segments enter (syllables, feet, etc.).

We can distinguish within segmental structure various subsegmental groups, or GESTURES, which are collections of basic components which behave systematically as a unit. Some of these groupings are universal such as the CATEGORIAL vs. ARTICULATORY gestures distinguished below (3.1). And in the simplest cases, gestures enter into a one-to-one relationship. However, for example, a single articulatory gesture may be shared between distinct categorial, as typically in nasal + plosive codas. And in, for example, cases of vowel harmony a non-universal subgesture (some articulatory component) is shared between vowels in the same word (see Anderson & Ewen, to appear: Ch. 8).

We illustrate these distinctions, within the phonological plane, in (2), which characterises the phonological structures assigned to *Get to Maisie!*.

Later sections will spell out in more detail the conventions used here. Let us simply note at this stage that the different levels (sublevels, gestures) are related by lines of assignment, or ASSOCIATION, which is a transitive symmetric relation. Dependency relations in the segmental sublevels are indicated by semi-colons (for unilateral government) and colons (for mutual dependency). A;B means 'A governs B' (or 'B is dependent on A') and A:B means 'A and B mutually govern each other'. Dependency relations above the segment are expressed by solid lines joining nodes where the higher node is the governor or head. The representations in the categorial gesture (combinations of |V|, vocalic, and |C|, consonantal) specify the major class of the segment. The

(2)

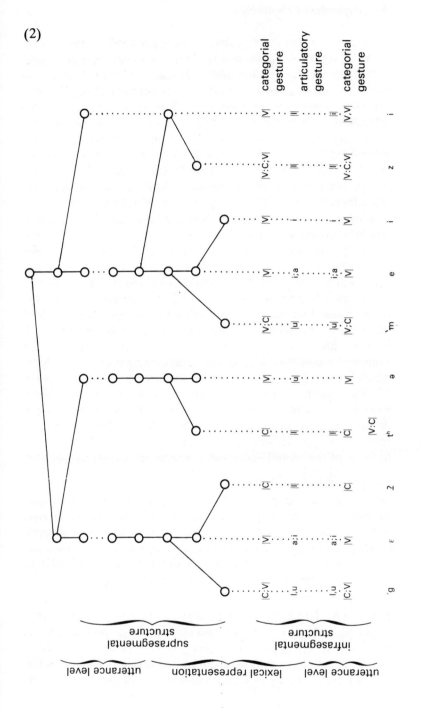

components within the articulatory gesture (namely, in this case, |i|, |a|, |u|, |l|) distinguish place of articulation. Roughly, |u| is peripheral (grave), |i| palatal, |a| low and |l| lingual. The utterance representation simply gives some idea of one possible realisation of the sentence. Here, for example, the final plosive in *get* is de-articulated (notice the loss of the |l| component at the phonetic level), the following plosive is aspirated, the full vowel of *to* is de-articulated (i.e. reduced to [ə] — for the representation of schwa, see 3.3.3), and the final vowel of *Maisie* is tensed (i.e. |V| ⟹ |V,V|). For clarity, a narrow phonetic transcription incorporating these features is provided underneath the relevant segments.

Most of what follows is an attempt to explicate the categories, dependency relations and associations presented baldly in (2). We do not pursue in any detail the character of the appropriate rules of association: see, however, Anderson (this vol.) for some of the rules which, for English, associate both lexical and utterance suprasegmental representations with lexical structures. This means, in particular, that we shall not explore the wider consequences of adopting the notation proposed with respect to the relationships between levels of representation. Anderson (to appear c), for example, argues that dependency representations favour analyses which are strongly concrete (see too Anderson & Ewen, to appear: Ch. 8). Until now, however, many studies within the DP framework have been relatively neutral on the abstractness-concreteness debate and some of the articles in this volume will be felt by the reader to be quite far apart from this point of view. Let us continue to focus on the central notational assumptions underlying DP.

1.2 *The Responsibility of Notation*

Before proceeding with a more detailed examination of the notation offered by dependency phonology, it behoves us to give some consideration to what one might expect of a phonological notation. Our basic assumption, which we take to be relatively non-controversial, is embodied in the NATURAL RECURRENCE assumption. This, as formulated in Anderson (1980: 165), slightly revised, reads as follows:

NATURAL RECURRENCE (NR):

(a) phonological groupings (paradigmatic and syntagmatic) are not random; certain groupings recur;

(b) phonological groupings and the relationships between them have a phonetic basis; they are natural.

On the basis of this we take it that the components and structural properties embodied in any phonological notation should in principle be phonetically identifiable. We say 'in principle' in view of the fact that many phonological constructions, such as the sonority hierarchy, which are well supported on grounds of recurrence and applicability to different domains, are nevertheless poorly understood in relation to phonetic properties (cf. e.g. Ohala & Kawasaki 1984). Articulatory and acoustic properties do not as such determine the nature of phonological constructs. This is unsurprising given the range of physical variables that may correlate with phonological distinctions. However, there must be in principle some phonetic basis for any posited phonological property. This imposes a particular requirement on the character of phonological notations. We embody this requirement in the NATURAL APPROPRIATENESS assumption:

NATURAL APPROPRIATENESS (NA):
A phonological notation is such as to optimise the expression of phonological groupings and relationships which are natural and recurrent.

(This collapses the componentiality and constituentiality assumptions of Anderson 1980, and Anderson & Ewen, to appear: Ch. 1). The notation should render the expression of natural and recurrent situations simpler than that of the idiosyncratic and non-occurrent.

To the extent that the binary feature notation of Chomsky & Halle (1968) permits the capturing of 'natural classes' that notation conforms with NA: clearly the class of vowels denoted by [+high] is recurrent and natural, as is its relationship with [+high] consonants. However, as we shall argue below, not all natural groupings are amenable to such a notation. Moreover, syntagmatic groupings, constituency and other syntagmatic properties remain unexpressed. If these latter are recurrent and natural, then the notation of Chomsky & Halle (1968) fails totally in this respect with regard to NA. Observe that we do not regard 'markedness theory' as a solution either to this inadequacy or to the failure in expressing a large number of natural classes and processes. We consider 'markedness theory' as a *post hoc* adjustment to a notational system which fails to ensure NA (for discussion, see Lass & Anderson 1975; Lass 1976, 1984; Anderson 1980; Anderson & Ewen, to appear: Ch. 1). Further, the notion of constituency, as opposed to recurrent sequences, remains unexpressed even by the marking conventions.

Dependency phonology involves a contention that not merely constituency but also the dependency relation (in terms of which constituency may be defined) is crucial to the expression of recurrent syntagmatic groupings. And, further, the expression of 'natural classes' requires the positing of intrasegmental dependency relations of the type embodied in (2) above, which we spell out more fully in later sections. We turn now to a consideration of the motivation for such claims as part of our exposition of the notational system of DP.

2. Suprasegmental Dependencies

Various phonological constituents can be established as domains for phonological regularities of different sorts. It has been claimed within the framework of DP that above the syllable one need recognise only the foot and the (tone) group. Further, this same hierarchy is displayed both within words (i.e. lexically) and in the structure of utterances (recall (2) above). Within the syllable, constituent structure more detailed than the division into onset and rhyme is not universally appropriate, but in English, we shall suggest, some further refinement is warranted.

2.1 *Lexical Constituents and their Headedness*

The syllable is the basic domain for the statement of phonotactic constraints. Thus, for instance, the fact that English lacks word or morpheme initial /tl−/ is not to be attributed to word (or morpheme) position as such. Simply, /tl−/ is not a permitted syllable onset in English; and thus medial /−tl−/ sequences are necessarily heterosyllabic. This is reflected in the phonetic differences between pairs like the one in (3):

(3)   (a) Atlantic   (b) attraction

In the (a) example, the /t/ belongs with the first syllable and is unaspirated and glottalised; in (b), on the other hand, the /t/ is aspirated (this being reflected in the devoicing of /r/) and non-glottalised, as befits a syllable-initiating plosive. The appropriate generalisation is not that /tl−/ is inadmissible as a word (or morpheme) initiator; rather /tl−/ is not a permissible syllable onset and its absence at the beginning of words is contingent on this.

More general motivations for the syllable are noted in many of the articles in this volume and the work alluded to therein. This is not the place to dwell on these. Our concern is to point out the headedness of the syllable as a construction: it is characterised by the presence of an obligatory atomic element, the syllabic peak, in whose absence there is no syllable. Examples (3)(a) and (b) have three syllables and each of these is characterised by the presence of a syllabic element. Note in fact that the first syllable of (3) consists of the syllabic alone (but cf. Anderson this vol., to appear d; and Giegerich, this vol., on empty onsets). Each syllabic constitutes a peak of prominence. Whatever the controversies concerning the phonetic basis for the syllable and concerning its demarcation, the syllabic peaks are clearly identifiable. The syllable thus meets the distributional criteria for having a head; and relative prominence is its substantive manifestation.

This is similarly the case with the foot, whose head is a stressed syllabic and its modifiers any unstressed syllabics to the right. Again the head is (substantively) more prominent and (distri-butionally) atomic and obligatory.

In utterance structure the foot is the basic unit of timing. This means that in certain circumstances certain lexical feet may be suppressed in utterances. However, they also constitute lexically the domain for various regularities, including, again, phonotactic. For instance, in English we find only long vowels finally within monosyllabic feet:

(4)   buy, bias

(And in final position within the syllable, in many varieties of English, we find that with the exception of [ə] only tense — but not necessarily long — vowels occur: *pity, solo,* etc.)

The phonological hierarchy in lexical structure is a grammatical-isation of the utterance hierarchy. Therefore, in particular utterances, the substantive correlates of the phonological structures attributed to words may not materialise; they are not given utterance status. Thus *princess* is lexically two-footed; but given the utterance circumstances either foot may be suppressed, as in (5):

(5)   Princess Di isn't a real princess

in which, in the two respective instances of *princess*, the second and first syllables respectively are de-footed. This is perhaps even more strikingly the case with lexical group structure.

We can associate with each (non-compound) word a group structure in which the head of the group is the syllabic which bears the tonic (tone shift) when the word is said in isolation: it is again atomic, obligatory and more prominent. However, not all words are associated with an utterance tonic: e.g. the first occurrence of *princess* in (5) forms an utterance group with the following word, which bears a tonic. And, typically, grammatical words, like *a* in (5), are both de-footed and de-grouped.

2.2 *Dependency Representations*

In the above sections we have briefly defined the need for a number of suprasegmental categories in phonology and argued that dependency systems afforded us a suitable notation. In this section, we therefore offer a condensed semi-formal introduction to the graphs and relations used in DP. As we said above, dependency models are based on the concept of (linear) precedence and of dependency. Let us take as our starting-point a syllable such as *set* where the head of the construction is the syllabic element, i.e. the vowel /e/. Let us, for the moment, assume that a syllable has no more internal structure than the presence of a syllabic flanked by optional dependants — a position defended at length in Clements and Keyser (1983) within the framework of CV phonology and which has been adhered to in much DP work. In that case, the string /set/ would be structured as follows:

(a) GOVERNMENT RELATIONS
s ← e → t (i.e. /s/ depends on /e/, or alternatively /e/ governs /s/, and /e/ governs /t/, or alternatively /t/ depends on /e/)
(b) PRECEDENCE RELATIONS
s < e < t (i.e. /s/ bears a relation of 'immediate strict precedence' to /e/ which, in turn, bears the same relation to /t/. Notice that 'strict precedence' — i.e. s << e, s << t, e << t — is formally the transitive closure of immediate strict precedence.)

One way we can express these relations in the form of a graph is by associating a node or vertex with each segment and connecting the nodes by directed lines or edges, i.e. arcs, such that the arc initiates in a head node and terminates in a modifier of that head (see (6)).

(6)

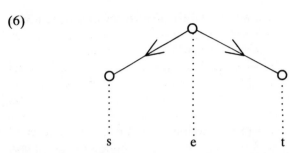

Conventionally, the head is placed higher than its modifiers. Since, however, the higher position of the node corresponding to the head codes the same information as the arrowheads marking the edges in (6), the standard convention in dependency grammars is simply to represent the directional dependency relation by placement on the vertical axis, in the same way as precedence relations are expressed on the horizontal plane. Thus (6) would be simplified to (7):

(7)

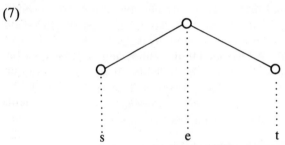

This type of representation is also used in syntax. The reader will perhaps be familiar with graphs such as the following:

(8)

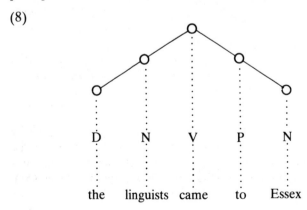

or, alternatively, (8'), wherein labels are attached directly to nodes:

(8')

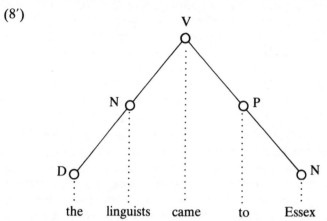

Note that the representation of (8) with its hierarchy of dependency relations is not without analogue in phonology. It is commonly argued that an adequate phonological notation should be able to integrate the sonority hierarchy (cf. Kiparsky 1979; and see below 3.4 on the way this hierarchy is derived from more basic primitives in DP). All we need to do is allow internal dependencies of the type exhibited in (8) within syllables. If we take an example such as *blimp* the dependency graph will be as in (9) with /b/ dependent on /l/ which in turn is dependent on /i/, the latter governing on its right /m/ which in turn governs /p/.

(9)

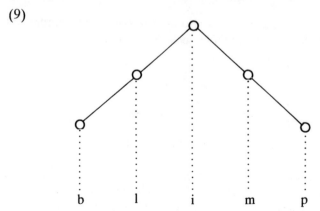

No special set of labels (such as strong-weak) is required to characterise the sonority hierarchy. Its incorporation into the model falls out naturally from assumptions about how to express governor-dependent relations within constructions. Moreover, it often turns out that we need to have access to the information that a particular unit is indirectly governed by another unit (i.e. there is a descending path of arcs connecting them). We shall therefore draw a terminological distinction between government and subordination. Informally, a category is GOVERNED by, or is a DEPENDENT of, another category if a single arc connects the two relevant nodes. The symbol which is used in this volume for government is a single arrow →. On the other hand, a category is a SUBORDINATE of another category (e.g. /b/ in relation to /i/ in (9)) if a continuous descending sequence of arcs connects them. Subordination is represented by a double-headed arrow: —». (Readers should therefore not interpret → in the articles contained here as the rewrite symbol of standard generative phonology. For this a double-bodied arrow will be used ⟹. Much work in DP uses a double arrow ⇉ for the dependency relation. While the reader ought to be aware of this convention, we have not followed it here for reasons of typographical convenience.)

Standard accounts of dependency grammar outside DP and work in case grammar associated with it (cf. for instance, Matthews's comparison of dependency and constituency models in his *Syntax*, Ch. 4) assume that all representations are of the same format as the examples quoted in this section. Both dependency and precedence are binary, asymmetric, irreflexive relations and well-formed dependency graphs conform to the following informal characterisation:

(10)   STANDARD DEPENDENCY GRAPHS
   (a)   there is a unique vertex or root
   (b)   all other vertices are subordinate to the root
   (c)   all other vertices terminate only one arc
   (d)   no element can be the head of two different constructions
   (e)   no tangling of arcs or association lines is allowed.

What we wish to argue is that (c) is too strong to accommodate the generalisations an adequate system should be able to express; and (d) is unnecessary, given that its motivation is to enable us to keep different constructions distinctively labelled (as containing distinct heads). But constructions may share a head and be distinguished in other ways. Again, our system should be able to express the notion 'sharing a head'.

First of all, there is solid evidence that segments must be allowed to be ambisyllabic (see Anderson & Jones 1974, 1977; Anderson & Ewen, to appear; and Clements and Keyser 1983 within the framework of CV phonology). Thus the medial /t/ of *pity* can be argued on a variety of grounds (both phonological and phonetic) to belong at once to the first and the second syllable of the word. In other words, dependency graphs of the following sort, where a vertex terminates two arcs, must be allowed:

(11)

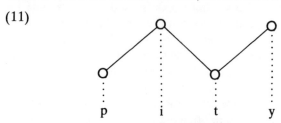

Further evidence concerning ambisyllabicity is adduced in this volume by Anderson on English, Jones in his discussion of consonantal metathesis in the history of English (see his 5) and Durand on French (see his 3.5).

Secondly, one element can be the head of different constructions, as indeed we have already argued in presenting a given syllabic as successively the head of a syllable, a foot and a tone group. This would be the case in the lexical structure of the word *intercede*: the final vowel *e* is in turn the head of the last syllable, of the second, monosyllabic foot and of the whole tone group. We code this by allowing the construction of nodes which are not adjoined to other nodes (i.e. linearly to the left or the right of them) but subjoined to them (i.e. nodes which are related by government but are equal in precedence). Thus a partial representation of *intercede* would be (12):

(12)

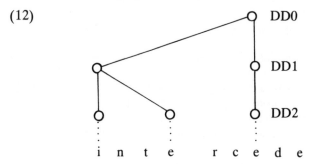

The node of dependency degree 0 is ungoverned (the group head). On the next level down, at dependency degree 1, we have two nodes governed by the DD0 node representing respectively the first foot (*inter*) and the second foot (*cede*). The first node is adjoined to the DD0 node, the second one is subjoined. Finally, on the bottom level, at DD2, the nodes represent the three syllables of which this word is comprised. These latter nodes are in turn governed by the nodes at DD1 and once again related to them by either adjunction or subjunction. In other words, the precedence relation must at least be allowed to be antisymmetric: symmetry, i.e. the existence of both $a_i \leq a_j$ and $a_j \leq a_i$, where $\leq$ indicates non-strict precedence, implies $i = j$, i.e. reflexivity. We will, however, suggest below that the internal representation of segments requires precedence relations which are merely non-symmetric: the existence of a symmetric relation between two components does not imply their identity.

Generalising from (12) above, we can say that the supra-segmental structure of words is given under the form of unlabelled proper trees which are oriented by the dependency relation: as required by (10)(a), one node is ungoverned (the group head); and, as required by (10)(b), all others depend on one head. Word-trees, we assume, also conform to (10)(e), such that arc and association lines intersect only at vertices.

The identity of the head and thus the construction follows from its placement in the hierarchy: therefore NO LABELLING IS NECESSARY (contrast e.g. Selkirk 1980a). Moreover, as we move towards the root of the tree the direction of modification reverses at each stage: if a modifier is present, the group head is left-modified, the foot head is right-modified and, as we shall see, this pattern of modification can also be argued for within syllables (with the onset as a left-modifier and one level down the rhyme as a right-modifier). This ensures the determinacy of each construction, and is not disturbed by the positing of complex feet of various types (see Anderson, this vol.).

We have pointed out above that in standard versions of dependency theory the type of representation given in (12) — with the added labelling of nodes in syntax — would be prohibited by a uniqueness requirement on heads: a particular category may be the head of only one construction-type. This is to ensure determinacy of construction-type. But constructions may be distinguished in other respects, such as by direction of modification, as we suggested in 1 to be true of the categories sentence and VP in syntax. A tree such as (13) below, with its hierarchy of nodes and its systematic reversal makes labels such as VP and S unnecessary. These categories are uniquely reconstructible from the configuration of nodes and arcs, and the syntactic categories associated with the graph.

(13)

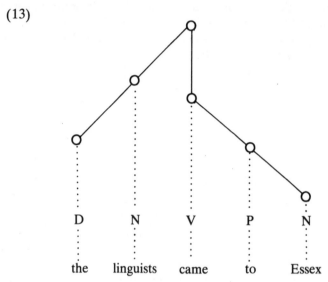

D	N	V	P	N
the	linguists	came	to	Essex

Let us now return to the internal structure of syllables. Each head in the construction discussed so far is more prominent than its modifier(s). In the case of the syllabic this prominence is in part associated with relative inherent sonority: the syllabic is more sonorous than its modifier(s). If we assign dependency relations within the syllable in accordance with relative sonority, then the typical pattern is the one that we find for *blimp* as represented in (9) above. That is, dependency relations mirror the sonority hierarchy such that to each side of the syllabic the graph is monotonically projective, with degree of subordination uniformly increasing with distance from the syllabic. Such a profile we take to be universal, though exceptions must be noted for particular languages. However, some exceptions are so prevalent, for instance [s] + plosive clusters, as to suggest that a distinct universal principle is involved. We return later to the characterisation of the sonority hierarchy, which is associated with infrasegmental dependencies.

Notice now, however, that the construction in (9) does not conform to the pattern of binary reversals we have suggested as appropriate for suprasyllabic constructs. In (9) the head is bilaterally modified. In itself, of course, this may be no great objection, given the distinct basis for assignment of dependency: relative inherent sonority. But other considerations also suggest that (9) is structurally underdifferentiated for some languages at least, and possibly all languages whose syllables have codas; specifically, that we should recognise within the syllable a rhyme constituent of the character suggested in (14):

(14)

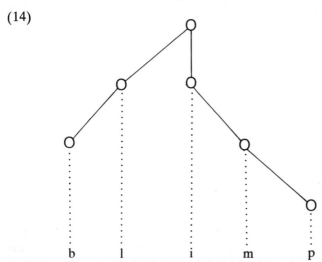

The onset-rhyme division incorporated in (14) is supported, for example, by evidence that this transition is perceptually 'salient' (cf. e.g. Ohala & Kawasaki 1984) as well as by evidence of its comparative non-permeability to phonotactic constraints. On this latter aspect, see particularly Anderson (this vol., to appear a) and Vincent (this vol.), where further details of syllable structure are also explored.

2.3 *Suprasegmental Associations*

The phonological structures assigned to words determine in part the structure of utterances. The rules associating the sequences of word structures with an appropriate utterance representation also take into account the organisation of the utterance in terms of syntactic structure and information ('pragmatic') structure, as well as rhythmic templates and tempo requirements. In principle, however, utterance suprasegmental structure is determinate with respect to these various factors.

The role of some of the determining factors is illustrated in (2). Given a slowish tempo each lexical syllabic therein is associated with an utterance syllabic. The group head in a non-grammatical word is normally also an utterance foot head, but the grammatical word *to* is de-grouped and de-footed and is attached in utterance structure to the preceding foot head. The group head of the last word in a syntactic phrase which is not immediately part of another phrase is typically an utterance group head, i.e. is the tonic, as with *Maisie* in (2). However, informational considerations — e.g. emphasis on the imperative verb in *GET to Maisie* — gives an alternative placement of tonic. Alternative utterance associations deriving from the rhythmic factors (some of which go under the name of 'iambic reversal') are illustrated by (5) above. As represented in (2), utterance suprasegmental structure is expressed in terms of the same hierarchy of constructions as is the lexical structure. However, there may be different constraints on their combination: see again Anderson (this vol.).

Just as utterance suprasegmental structure is assigned in accordance with lexical structure and other properties attributable to utterances, so lexical suprasegmental structure itself is a projection of the infrasegmental structure and the morphological properties attributed to words. As we have seen, dependency relations within the syllable reflect relative sonority, with the addition of the syllable-rhyme hierarchisation. Prominence in words above the syllable is determined by a combination of syllable structure properties and morphological properties, including word class. This is evident from a range of recent work in metrical, autosegmental and dependency phonology; and we shall not attempt to illustrate the nature of these associations here. A discussion would involve distinct complex matters such as 'cyclicity' or 'extrametricality' which would take us too far afield at this stage.

The particular segmental-suprasegmental associations appropriate to (2) are rather trivial: the first two words are monosyllabic and thus the single syllabic is both foot and group head; the final word has a weak final syllable (short vowel and no coda) which is therefore ineligible for foot headship, the latter going automatically to the preceding syllabic. A more complex example of phonological word structure is given in (12) or in (15):

(15)

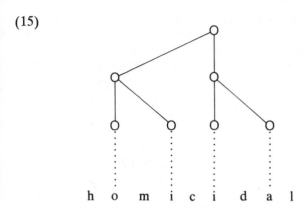

h   o   m   i   c   i   d   a   l

with two feet and tonic on the second, which as disyllabic is not weak (cf. once more Anderson, this vol.).

3. Infrasegmental Dependencies

In the above sections we have sketched out our conception of suprasegmental structure and examined the main features of the DP notation in this domain. One of the central claims of DP, how-ever — and perhaps the one that sets it apart from most current models of phonological representation — is that the internal structure of segments must be considerably richer and more articulated than in classical generative phonology or, indeed, elaborations of the latter that we are aware of. In particular, as we shall see, a basic element in the characterisation of infrasegmental structure is once again the eponymous relation of dependency which allows the expression of relative degrees of salience among the components of segments. We begin by examining in 3.1 a first enrichment of the standard system before envisaging a more radical departure from widely accepted assumptions in this area.

3.1 *Gestures*

The distinctive feature system offered in most systems devised in the wake of Chomsky & Halle's *The Sound Pattern of English* (SPE) can be characterised as minimally componential. As we have pointed out in 1.3, the features that a segment comprises in the SPE tradition constitute an unordered set and, furthermore, a set which is unpartitioned. While reference is made to the possible desirability of organising the features 'in a hierarchical structure' which would incorporate notions like 'major class features' or 'cavity features', these concepts are used in SPE 'for purely expository purposes' (1968: 300). By contrast, DP assumes that the expression of certain recurrent phenomena requires that a further structural property be attributed to segments. Certain groups of features, or components in DP terminology, belong together both phonologically and phonetically. This is particularly striking in examples of homorganic assimilation which requires agreement between certain systematic groups of features ('place of articulation') rather than between random subsets of these. To illustrate our claim, consider the recurrent phenomenon of nasal assimilation whereby, under varying conditions across languages, nasal consonants assimilate to the place of articulation of the following obstruent. What we would like to be able to state, as Hyman (1975: 91) does, is something along the following lines:

$$(16) \quad [+\text{nasal}] \implies [\alpha \text{ place}] \: / - \begin{bmatrix} -\text{sonorant} \\ \alpha \text{ place} \end{bmatrix}$$

but the standard formalism forces a schema like (17) on the analyst:

$$(17) \quad [+\text{nasal}] \implies \begin{bmatrix} \alpha \text{ ant} \\ \beta \text{ cor} \\ \gamma \text{ back} \end{bmatrix} \: / - \begin{bmatrix} -\text{sonorant} \\ \alpha \text{ ant} \\ \beta \text{ cor} \\ \gamma \text{ back} \end{bmatrix}$$

The drawback of (17) is obvious: homorganicity is not about pairwise agreement between individual features, but about identity of articulation of segments as wholes. The solution adopted in DP consists in positing submatrices called gestures (following Lass & Anderson 1975; Lass 1976) which can be invoked as units. The three gestures posited in standard formulations of DP are the CATEGORIAL, the ARTICULATORY, and the INITIATORY (cf. now the excellent summary in Lass 1984: 282-93). In terms of classical parameters the content of the gestures can be conveniently summarised as in (18):

(18) CATEGORIAL GESTURE

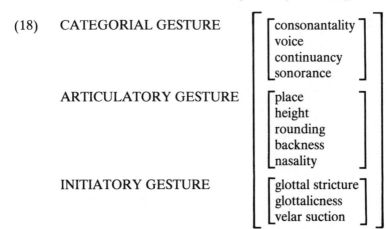

$$\begin{bmatrix} \begin{bmatrix} \text{consonantality} \\ \text{voice} \\ \text{continuancy} \\ \text{sonorance} \end{bmatrix} \\ \begin{bmatrix} \text{place} \\ \text{height} \\ \text{rounding} \\ \text{backness} \\ \text{nasality} \end{bmatrix} \\ \begin{bmatrix} \text{glottal stricture} \\ \text{glottalicness} \\ \text{velar suction} \end{bmatrix} \end{bmatrix}$$

ARTICULATORY GESTURE

INITIATORY GESTURE

The standard formalism has to be extended so that a variable can range over not just a feature but a whole matrix, covering any combination of feature values within it — so long as they agree with those of some other relevant submatrix invoked in the formulation of the rule. Rule (17) could now be simply reformulated as (19):

(19) $[\text{+nasal}] \implies [\alpha \text{ ARTIC}] \; / - \begin{bmatrix} [\text{−sonorant}] \\ [\alpha \text{ ARTIC}] \end{bmatrix}$

Current work in DP however involves a careful re-examination of some of the consequences of the above claims. Thus Davenport & Staun (this vol.) question the assignment of glottal stricture (the |0| component) to the initiatory gesture and argue that it should be part of the categorial gesture. In addition, they assess the possibility of allowing inter-gestural dependencies (as in Ewen 1982) and reject it in favour of an analysis where gestures (and subgestures if (20) below is accepted) are simply discrete, separable submatrices of segments. On the other hand, Ewen (this vol.) argues for a regrouping along slightly different lines which reduces the gestures to two — the CATEGORIAL and the ARTICULATORY — which are themselves divided in two further subgestures (see Anderson & Ewen, to appear, for detailed argumentation). The internal structure of segments would be as in (20), still formulated with the same parameters as above:

(20)   GESTURES AND SUBGESTURES

<table>
<tr><td rowspan="3">CATEGORIAL
GESTURE</td><td rowspan="2">PHONATORY
SUBGESTURE</td><td>consonantality</td></tr>
<tr><td>voice
continuancy
sonorance</td></tr>
<tr><td>INITIATORY
SUBGESTURE</td><td>glottal stricture
glottalicness
velar suction</td></tr>
<tr><td rowspan="2">ARTICULATORY
GESTURE</td><td>LOCATIONAL
SUBGESTURE</td><td>place
height
rounding
backness</td></tr>
<tr><td>ORO-NASAL
SUBGESTURE</td><td>nasality</td></tr>
</table>

In the rest of this presentation, however, we shall adhere to the organisation of gestures summarised in (18) since this constitutes the backdrop of many of the discussions in this volume.

One important further consequence of the decomposition of segments into submatrices of various types is the formal possibility that a particular submatrix might be unspecified for certain categories. This is particularly appropriate for [h] and [2] which are analysed (following Lass 1976) as the minimal fricative and stop respectively — i.e. segments which are unspecified with respect to the whole of the articulatory gesture while being specified as a voiceless fricative and stop within the categorial gesture. Thereby, a satisfactory explanation can be given for widely attested processes of weakening where, for instance, a fricative is first of all reduced to [h] on the way to zero (as in dialects of Spanish where a word-final /s/ has first of all been reduced to [h] before being totally deleted). A change such as [s] $\implies$ [h] $\implies$ Ø can be much more satisfactorily formalised as follows:

(21)

$$
\begin{bmatrix} \begin{bmatrix} +\text{cont} \\ -\text{voice} \end{bmatrix} \\ \begin{bmatrix} +\text{ant} \\ +\text{cor} \\ +\text{cont} \\ +\text{strid} \end{bmatrix} \end{bmatrix}
\implies
\begin{bmatrix} \begin{bmatrix} +\text{cont} \\ -\text{voice} \end{bmatrix} \\ \begin{bmatrix} \varnothing \end{bmatrix} \end{bmatrix}
\implies
\begin{bmatrix} \begin{bmatrix} \varnothing \end{bmatrix} \\ \begin{bmatrix} \varnothing \end{bmatrix} \end{bmatrix}
$$

where we once again use standard distinctive features but exploit the subgroupings given in (18). In the same way that [h] and [ʔ] are treated as the reduction fricative and the reduction stop respectively, schwa can also be represented as a reduction vowel — i.e. a segment which is categorially a |V| but without articulatory content — whenever this is motivated on phonological grounds (see Durand, this vol., on schwa in French). Examples of de-articulation by loss of the articulatory gesture have been given in (2) where the underlying /t/ in *get* is realised phonetically as a glottal stop and where the underlying /u/ in *too* is realised as a schwa. (For further discussion of weakening by gesture-change, see Lodge, this vol.).

3.2 *Componentiality and Infrasegmental Dependencies*

In the SPE tradition, not only are features simply co-present but they are also assumed to be binary in their abstract classificatory function and in the expression of phonological processes unless these are late detail rules. The main, and apparently the only, reason put forward by Chomsky & Halle for adopting binary features *in lexical representations* is that 'the natural way of indicating whether or not an item belongs to a particular category is by means of binary features' (1968: 297). The use of the latter in rules is clearly motivated by the fact that processes make reference to natural classes which can be captured by opposite values of single features or varying combinations of these. The use of binary features to distinguish segments and to express natural classes are in fact two facets of a single characteristic of such features, the capacity to permit a simple bifurcation. But, as we shall exemplify at several points in our exposition, binarity is not a *sine qua non* of segmental distinguishability or of the expression of natural classes. Given that Chomsky & Halle appear in SPE to have jettisoned most of the Jakobsonian motivation for binarity (e.g. its use in decoding speech, its biological roots, its psychological salience: see Jakobson & Waugh 1979), the conciseness of binarity has to be weighed against other considerations. In particular, many phonological regularities do not involve simple bifurcation but are hierarchical. Thus, in lenition processes (see 3.4 below) there is a hierarchy of segment-types with respect to their susceptibility to weakening and to possible deletions. Similarly, vowel height is conceded by Jakobson, Fant & Halle (1952) not to be a dichotomous scale: compactness and diffuseness which are normally the positive and negative value of A SINGLE FEATURE become for vowels the opposite poles of a single scale arbitrarily limited to three values: [−compact,+diffuse], [−compact,−diffuse], [+compact,−diffuse] but not *[+compact,+diffuse]. And natural phonologists (cf. Donegan 1978) have described relative height in terms of an increase in the strength of vowel COLOURS of palatality (strongest in [i] and labiality ([u]). However, in both cases, the binary notation obscures the scalar relation involved (see 3.3.3 below). Of course, integer-based non-binary features can provide for such scalar relations, but at the cost of the aspect of expressibility that is most characteristic of binary features and which justifies their use in SPE, the simple bifurcation (see Anderson 1980; Anderson & Ewen, to appear).

Preferable to either feature proposal is a notation employing unary components which may individually be absent, present, in simple combinations, or, if in combination, either of equal or unequal strength. In this notation, two components, say A and B, may define a hierarchy as in (22) by their potential for combination.

(22)   1   2   3   4   5
      A > Ø   A > B   A = B   A < B   Ø < B

where Ø is the identity element. The relations from 1 to 5 show decreasing strength or prominence of A and, correlatively, increasing strength or prominence of B. But, the bifurcations can still be specified in such a way that their expression is simpler, under a straightforward counting of symbols, than that of the individual symbols or of unnatural groupings: the notation can therefore capture the notion 'natural recurrent class'. The class 1-4 is that containing A; 1-3 is that in which A≥, or in which ~(<B) (where tilde represents negation); 1-2 is that in which A>. On the other hand, a grouping which involved the two poles of our scale, 1 and 5, would require the disjunction (A > Ø) v (Ø < B). In the following sections, we suggest, in conformity with structural analogy, that the non-symmetric relation which can hold between components is simply the dependency relation and we attempt to illustrate the expressibility of the DP notation.

3.3 *Articulation: the Vowel Components*

3.3.1 *Combinatorial Possibilities.*   In the above paragraph, we

refer to a system based on unary components which can be combined in a variety of ways. We shall first of all explore some of the main possibilities available in the system before turning to a concrete application with respect to vowel components.

Unary components may either be absent or present. If two components — a and b — are part of a gesture (or subgesture), they may enter into simple combination (symbolised by comma) as in (23):

(23)   a   b   a,b

But they may also enter into contrastive dependency relations whereby a governs b (a → b), or b governs a (b → a), or a and b mutually govern each other (a ↔ b) as in (24):

(24)

Instead of arrows or graphs, which can prove cumbersome, government in the case of components is often symbolised in the DP literature by semi-colon for unilateral government (a;b and b;a respectively for the first two directed graphs of (24)) and by colon for mutual government (a:b for the last one). On the analogy of (22), the maximal set of possibilities of combination for two components is given in (25):

(25)   a

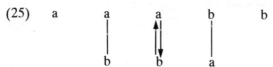

Before examining the conventions for the expression of natural classes, let us now turn to the characterisation of vowels.

3.3.2 *The Vowel Space.*   The vowel space is characterised by four components, as in (26):

(26) |i| — palatality or acuteness/sharpness
       |a| — lowness or sonority
       |u| — roundness or gravity/ flatness
       |ə| — centrality

These properties — enclosed between verticals — are RESONANCE or VOWEL COMPONENTS (cf. e.g. Donegan 1973; and Schane 1984a,b, who uses similar primitives under the name of 'particles'). They correspond to the features in the articulatory gesture (apart from nasality) of vowels and other segment-types whenever relevant (e.g. in the characterisation of secondary articulation).

Vowel systems of the /i, a, u/ type, which are widely attested and constitute the simplest possible vowel systems (on the assumption that Kabardian and Trubetzkoyan linear systems can be reinterpreted: see Crothers 1978: 108-9), will be characterised as follows:

(27)   {i} /i/   {u} /u/

        {a} /a/

where the symbols between slanted brackets have no systematic import but abbreviate the description on the left. On the other hand, if we wanted to describe a system of the /i, e, y, ə, a, o, u/ type (e.g. Albanian: see Crothers 1978: 42), we would adopt a representation such as (28):

(28)   {|i|}   /i/   {i,u|}   /y/   {|u|}   /u/
        {i,a}   /e/   {ə}   /ə/   {u,a}   /o/
                        {|a|}   /a/

The reader will notice that, whereas in (27) all vowels are characterised by the presence of one component, in (28) some vowels require more complex specifications than others. In particular, the vowels /y, e, o/ are treated as 'mixed' vowels (as they have often been called), that is to say as vowels which have two components of equal strength. In addition, another convention has been introduced. When components within curly brackets are flanked by verticals, this indicates that the segment is characterised phonologically (as far as the articulatory gesture is concerned) by the presence of just that component or that particular combination of components. Finally, in a system such as the one in (29) below, which characterises, for example, standard Italian, it will be noticed that simple combination of components will not suffice and that the dependency relation has to be invoked:

(29)   {|i|}   /i/   {|u|}   /u/
         {i;a}   /e/   {u;a}   /o/
         {a;i}   /ɛ/   {a;u}   /ɔ/
                          {|a|}   /a/

Two things should be pointed out at this stage. First of all, the notation captures directly the concept of markedness. The more complex the system the more combination of features will have to be allowed (cp. (27), (28) and (29)). The more marked the segment (along (post-) Jakobsonian lines), the more complex its representation. Thus, the segment /y/ in (28) is assigned a more complex internal structure than either /i/ or /u/. This, for instance, would correlate with its relative rarity *vis-à-vis* these other segments in the languages of the world and with the fact that it is acquired later in well-studied languages such as French which have the series /i, u, y/. Secondly, notice that our choice of |i|, |a|, |u| (and |ə|) as primitive components is reasonably grounded in phonetic theory. The vowels [i], [a], [u] which are uniquely characterisable in terms of these primitive components are quantal vowels in the sense of Stevens (1972). All three vowels are acoustically stable: they have well-defined spectral properties which do not change for small errors in articulation. And [i] and [u] have also been argued to play a role in the calibration of speech (cf. Lieberman 1975: 76-81; 1984: 159-66). By contrast, the mixed vowels can be said to be indeterminate: different speakers use different articulatory manoeuvres to generate the acoustic signal corresponding to them. In the words of Lieberman, 'the indeterminate vowels of a particular speaker essentially "float" with respect to the acoustic space specified by the determinate vowels' (1975: 80).

The |ə| component on the other hand is required to represent central and centralised vowels. We assume that central vowels such as [ə], which are quite common in the basic inventory of languages of the world, are not appropriately dealt with in a system which forces the analyst to classify them as [+back] or [−back]. The |ə| component appears to be as fundamental as the other three and it is interesting to notice that the vowel [ə] which it helps represent is described by Lieberman as 'perhaps the "simplest" and most basic vowel sound': it corresponds to an idealised neutral position since 'the area function for this vowel is acoustically equivalent to a uniform tube open at one end' (1975: 62). It should, however, be borne in mind that, like standard distinctive features, the components function as abstract phonological markers and that whenever they are used in the analysis of a language they do not correspond to precise articulatory manoeuvres or acoustic values. Thus |ə| could appropriately be used for four-vowel systems surveyed by Crothers (1978) which have /i,a,u/ plus some kind of central vowel which can be realised as [ə] or [ɨ] or even [ɯ]. Notice too that at some level of phonological representation some vowels which may surface phonetically as [ə] may be better handled as vowels unspecified for the articulatory gesture (cf. 3.1). Finally, when we said above that [ə] could be used to represent centralised vowels we had in mind the possible analysis of, say, the short vowels of RP in the following terms (see Ewen 1981):

(30)   /ɪ/   {i;ə}   /ʊ/   {u;ə}
          /e/   {i;a}   /ə/   {|ə|}
          /æ/   {a;i}   (ʌ /   {a;ə}   /ɔ/   {a;u}

Given the four vowel primitives so far defined the question arises of how to represent back unrounded vowels. A vowel like [ɯ] appears to lack all these components, and particularly if we think of them in articulatory terms: it is not front, not round, not low, and not central. In the terminology of natural phonology, it is 'colourless' or 'achromatic'. In earlier work in DP, [ɯ] is in fact characterised negatively as in (31) where tilde denotes negation:

(31)   {|~{i,u}|}

and, correspondingly, /ɤ/ and /ʌ/ (with their IPA values) were represented as {|~{i,u}; a|} and {|~{i,u}:a|}. While such a method of representation can be used to characterise systems and processes which involve back unrounded vowels (see e.g. Ewen's 1980a elegant treatment of Turkish vowel harmony), it raises a number of difficulties discussed by Lass (1984: 277ff) and by Rennison (this vol.). In treating these vowels negatively we are creating an asymmetry in the system, since all other vowels are defined positively, and adding to our formal machinery, since (a) the negation operator is otherwise only required for the expression of natural classes (see 3.3.3) or for archisegmental representations; (b) we allow for [ɤ] and [ʌ], as characterised above, the combination of a purely negative content |~{i,u}| with a positive component |a|. The solution advocated by Lass within DP consists in going back to a more traditional solution where the single component |u| is replaced by a backness component |ɯ| and a labiality/rounding component |ω| (and the reader will notice that this is very much Rennison's position here within a binary framework). The main difficulty with this is that the claim that complexity is mirrored by the notation has to be jettisoned. In fact, in a system like Turkish with /i, y, u, ɯ/ Lass would have to adopt the following characterisation:

(32)   /i/   {|i|}   /y/   {i,ω}   /ɯ/   {|ɯ|}   /u/   {ɯ,ω}

where the vowel /u/ has a more complex representation than /ɯ/. This seems to us to undermine quite seriously much of the basis for the DP notation. The alternative pursued in Anderson & Ewen (to appear) and partly based on *acoustic* properties of back unrounded vowels, consists in using the centrality component to characterise this set of sounds. Thus [ɯ], [ɤ] and [ʌ] would respectively be analysed as {|ə,i,u|}, {|ə,i,u;a|} and {|ə,i,u:a|}. The reader is referred to this work (6.3) for a detailed discussion of back unrounded vowels.

3.3.3 *The Expression of Relations, Natural Classes and Processes.*
One of the most striking differences between binary distinctive features and DP components is that the latter allow a clear expression of privative vs. equipollent vs. gradual oppositions (in Trubetzkoy's sense) whereas the standard SPE notation conflates privative and equipollent oppositions and does not allow for gradual oppositions except as phonetic scales. Thus, in (28) above, the opposition between /i/ and /y/ is formally shown to be privative and that between /i/ and /u/ is shown to be equipollent. In (29), on the other hand, the set /i, e,ɛ, a/ forms a gradual opposition with two polar extremes |i| and |a|. Of course, it is possible to express gradual oppositions by allowing, beside binary features, multivalued scalar features (cf. e.g. Ladefoged 1971, 1980; Lindau 1975, 1978). We could for instance adopt (33) below for the system presented in (29).

(33)   /i/   /u/   4 high
        /e/   /o/   3 high
        /ɛ/   /ɔ/   2 high
                /a/   1 high

There are, however, a number of problems with such scalar features. First of all, whereas the choice between the two polar extremes of a scale in DP is motivated, it is not clear formally why one should consider low vowels — *vis-à-vis* high vowels — as the first rung of the ladder (value 1) in the scalar notation. Secondly, the positing of a multivalued scalar feature constitutes a weaker hypothesis concerning natural languages than the corresponding characterisation in DP. If we consider vowel height, the DP notation makes the prediction that only FIVE degrees of vowel height are possible *phonologically*. Limiting ourselves to front unrounded vowels, the maximum set would be of the following type:

(34)   i   e   ɛ   æ   a
             |i| |i;a| |i:a| |a;i| |a|

in which three different combinations of |i| and |a| occur; two in which the components are related by unilateral dependency and one in which they are mutually dependent. By contrast, in positing a multivalued scalar feature, one of two courses is open to us: either we leave the range of values unspecified; or we state the upper limit as the highest observed value. Neither solution makes a strong prediction as to what constitutes a possible phonological system with respect to the parameter under analysis. Thirdly, while the statement of certain processes is better expressed by having recourse to multivalued scalar features than to binary features, the expression of natural classes and the bifurcations made possible by the binary notation are no longer perspicuous in this type of notation. Suppose that in a system like (33) the following changes occur concurrently:

(35)   (a) u $\Longrightarrow$ o   (b) o $\Longrightarrow$ ɔ

Now, this type of lowering process, while well-attested synchronically and diachronically (see e.g. Hyman 1975: 123, for a synchronic example occurring in closed syllables in Feʔfeʔ-Bamileke), is quite complex to state with standard features. The simplest statement appears to be (35′):

(35′) $\begin{bmatrix} V \\ \alpha\,\text{high} \\ -\text{low} \\ +\text{round} \end{bmatrix} \implies \begin{bmatrix} -\text{high} \\ -\alpha\,\text{low} \end{bmatrix}$

which requires paired variables and disjunctive ordering of its subparts, and is, in terms of feature counting, costlier than the

statement of a process which would have the following effect: (a) e
$\Longrightarrow$ o; (b) ε $\Longrightarrow$ ɔ. The latter within the system under discussion
would be simply statable as (36):

(36)
$$\begin{bmatrix} V \\ -\text{high} \\ -\text{back} \end{bmatrix} \quad \Longrightarrow \quad [+\text{round}]$$

Why, for instance, this latter change should be more highly valued
than a lowering (or conversely a raising) process of the type
formalised in (35′) is not at all clear. And, indeed, the problem is
even worse, in this respect, within Rennison's tridirectional system
(this vol.). The latter uses primitives similar to the DP components,
but within a binary notation, and has to rely crucially on the
feature ATR (Advanced Tongue Root) for systems such as (29/
33) where the back unrounded vowels would have the following
classification:

(37)

/u/		/o/		/ɔ/	
+U		+U		+U	
−A		+A		+A	
−I		−I		−I	
+ATR		+ATR		−ATR	

The statement of a unitary process such as (35) would now require
to be split into two independent rules: u $\Longrightarrow$ o is [−A] $\Longrightarrow$ [+A];
whereas o $\Longrightarrow$ ɔ is [+ATR] $\Longrightarrow$ [−ATR]. This is, as is well known,
where the use of scalar features allows for a more insightful for-
mulation since, instead of (35′), it would be sufficient to state:

(38)
$$\begin{bmatrix} V \\ n\ \text{high} \\ +\text{round} \end{bmatrix} \quad \Longrightarrow \quad [n-1], \text{ where } n \geq 3$$

The $n \Longrightarrow n-1$ part of the formulation is satisfactory, but what is
now in question is the expression of the class [−low] as $n \geq 3$.
How do we know, given this notation, how this class compares
with $n \geq 1$ or $n \geq 2$? Thus $n \geq 1$ encompasses the whole dimension
of vowel height and yet has seemingly the same 'cost' as any other
formulation which will use the symbol n followed by $\geq$ (or its
converse $\leq$) and by a random number. It is our contention that the
DP notation allows for a natural expression of processes such as
(35) while retaining the expressibility afforded by binary features.

The notational conventions used so far allow us in fact to
capture the natural subclasses of (29/33) — taken as a representative

example — in a natural way. Thus the class of palatal vowels
(/i, e, ɛ/) will be defined as {i} — i.e. all segments which contain
the |i| component; the class of round vowels (/u, o, ɔ/) as {u}; the
class of non-round vowels (/i, e, ɛ, a/) as {~u}; the class of non-
high vowels as {a}, and so on. On the other hand, a more complex
grouping such as the class of non-low round vowels (/u, o/) would
have to be specified as {u;} (or equivalently {u → }) — i.e. the class
of vowels where |u| preponderates. (Recall that |u| is formally
equivalent to {u → ø}, where ø is the identity element.) And as a
final example, the set of mid vowels (/e, ɛ, o, ɔ/) would have to be
specified as {a,~a} — that is to say, the set of vowels which contain
|a| in combination with some other component.

We can now turn to the lowering process of (35). This would
quite simply be formulated as:

(39)   V ⟹ |a|
       where V = {u;}

This rule stipulates that a component of |a| is to be added to the
representations of /u, o/. This is interpreted by universal conditions as converting the vowel affected into that vowel which
differs from it in terms of minimal increase in the preponderance of
|a|. In other words: (a) {|u|}⟹{|u|, |a|}⟹{u;a}; and (b) {u;a} ⟹
{u;a,|a|} ⟹ {a;u}.

Lack of space prevents us from exploring further the treatment
of processes involving vocalic systems. What we wish to note, however, is that processes which shift the vowels up and down the
height dimension are well attested diachronically (cf. e.g. the Great
Vowel Shift or Middle English Open Syllable Lengthening) and
synchronically (cf. e.g. diphthongisation and lowering in Malmö
Swedish: Lindau 1975: 8-10). They find a natural interpretation in
DP. But the advantages of the DP notation do not stop there.
There are cases, which have been much discussed in the DP
literature, where the changes involved do not readily make sense if
the vowel space is envisaged as quadrangular — whether with
binary or scalar features. One example which we will not discuss
in detail or attempt to formalise here (see Anderson & Jones
1977), is Old English I-Umlaut (OEIU) or i-mutation. This
change is conveniently summarised by Quirk & Wrenn as follows:

> *i*-mutation, shared in varying degrees by all Gmc languages
> except Gothic, had been completed in OE by the time of the

earliest written records. It is closely related to the raising of *e* to *i* (207) inasmuch as it is the direct result of the influence of *i* or *j* on the vowel in an immediately preceding syllable. By *i*-mutation, Pr. OE ă (before nasals), *ĕ, ā, ŏ, ŭ* are fronted or raised to mid or high front vowels:

OE *a* before nasals (Gmc *a*) > *e*, as in *menn*, n.a.pl. of *mann* (*monn*) 'man';

OE *æ* (Gmc *a*) > *e*, as in *bed(d)* 'bed', Gmc **badja* (cf Go. *badi*)

OE *ā* (Gmc *ai*) > *ǣ*, as in *hǣlan* 'heal' ...

OE *o* (sometimes Gmc *u* analogically lowered; cf 207) > œ [œ] > *e*, as in *ele*, Lat. *olium*, and *exen*;

OE *ō* > *ǣ* [ø:] > *ē*, as in *gēs* 'geese', sg. *gōs* (...);

OE *u* > *y*, as in the verb *trymman* (< **trumja*n) 'strengthen', beside the adj. *trum* 'strong';

OE *ū* > *ȳ*, as in *rȳman* 'make space', beside the adj. *rūm* 'spacious' (1959: 151-2).

While Quirk & Wrenn, like other scholars, point out that this is a unitary change, a glance at what happens from a quadrangular perspective:

(40)

−back −round	−back +round	+back −round	+back +round
i	y ⟵		u
e	ø ⟵		o
æ ⟵			a

(NB: ǣ is not affected.)

will show that, given standard assumptions, the above change would have to be treated as two unrelated subprocesses of fronting and raising in the context of /i/ or /j/ in the next syllable. By contrast, given a DP interpretation, as outlined in (41), where length is once again left out:

(41)

{|i|}	{|i,u|}	⟸	{|u|}
{|i;a|}	{|i,u;a|}	⟸	{|u;a|}
{|a;i|} ⟸ {|a|}			

the whole process can be seen to be transparent. The |i| component characterising the trigger-vowel in the right-hand syllable (/i/ or /j/) is purely and simply added to the class of vowels where |i| is not preponderant, which can be symbolised as {~i→}. They all move by universal condition to the nearest slot in terms of minimal increase in the preponderance of |i|. (For a more detailed account of i-mutation and a formulation thereof, cf. Colman, to appear. See too the discussion of bidirectional vs. tridirectional vowel features in Ewan and van der Hulst 1985.)

3.4 *The Categorial Gesture*

Two components are used for the characterisation of the categorial gesture. They are |V|, a component which can be defined as 'relatively periodic', and |C|, a component of 'periodic energy reduction'. These two components are closely related to the Jakobsonian features [vocalic] and [consonantal], but unlike the latter are not binary. The presence of, say, |C| in a segment does not imply that the segment is in a simple binary opposition to an otherwise identical segment which does not contain |C|. Like the vowel components examined earlier, |C| and |V| can either occur alone or in various dependency combinations. (42) sets out part of the universal inventory of categorial types:

(42)
$$
\begin{array}{cccc}
\text{V} & \begin{array}{c} \text{V} \\ | \\ \text{V,C} \end{array} & \begin{array}{c} \text{V} \\ | \\ \text{C} \end{array} & \\[2ex]
\text{vowels} & \text{liquids} & \text{nasals} & \\[3ex]
\begin{array}{c} \text{V:C} \\ | \\ \text{V} \end{array} & \begin{array}{c} \text{V:C} \\ | \\ \text{V} \end{array} & \begin{array}{c} \text{C} \\ | \\ \text{V} \end{array} & \text{C} \\[2ex]
\begin{array}{c} \text{voiced} \\ \text{fricatives} \end{array} & \begin{array}{c} \text{voiceless} \\ \text{fricatives} \end{array} & \begin{array}{c} \text{voiced} \\ \text{plosives} \end{array} & \begin{array}{c} \text{voiceless} \\ \text{plosives} \end{array}
\end{array}
$$

Instead of (42), which provides mainly a graph characterisation of the categorial gesture, we could also use the conventions established earlier and represent the above segment-types as in (43), which gives two equivalent notations for each categorial type:

(43)
$$
\begin{array}{ccc}
\{|V|\} & \{|V;V,C|\} & \{|V;C|\} \\
\text{or } \{|V|\} & \{|V \rightarrow V,C|\} & \{|V \rightarrow C|\} \\
\text{vowels} & \text{liquids} & \text{nasals}
\end{array}
$$

$\{\|V,C;V\|\}$	$\{\|V:C\|\}$	$\{\|C;V\|\}$	$\{\|C\|\}$
$\{\|V,C \rightarrow V\|\}$	$\{\|V:C\|\}$	$\{\|C \rightarrow V\|\}$	$\{\|C\|\}$
voiced	voiceless	voiced	voiceless
fricatives	fricatives	plosives	plosives

From (42)/(43), it should be clear that vowels and voiceless plosives are maximally opposed, with the other segment-types showing varying intermediary degrees of preponderance of |C| or |V|. There are, however, constraints on possible combinations. In particular, a maximum of two occurrences of each component is allowed in the representation of a particular segment-type, and, if a component occurs twice, the two instances have to be related by dependency. These constraints may have to be relaxed at the phonetic level. Thus, in diagram (2), we have allowed the characterisation of the last tense vowel of *Maisie* as |V,V| at utterance level.

As was the case for vowels, the representations above are intended to reflect the relative complexity of segments. Thus vowels and voiceless plosives, which are maximally different paradigmatically, and constitute the unmarked syllable type when combined syntagmatically, have the simplest representations. On the other hand, if we expand our range of types of segments, the most complex representation would be given to voiced 'strident sonorants' such as the fricative trill of some Scottish accents or Czech /ř/ of which Jakobson (1968: 58) says that 'it is one of the rarest phonemes that occur in language, and hardly any other phoneme of their native language presents such major and persistent difficulty to Czech children'. Jakobson notes, for instance, that Czech settlers in Russia tend to lose this phoneme and substitute [ʒ] for the voiced allophone of /ř/. A possible representation for this type of sound is that in (44):

(44) $\{\|V:C \leftrightarrow V\|\}$
       fricative trill

which places fricative trills half-way between liquids and fricatives. The substitution of [ʒ] for [ř] is structurally one of the two optimal moves in the direction of a less complex sound: bilateral dependency is replaced by unilateral dependency with |V:C| in governing position. The other move, which is predicted by our representations, would also reduce bilateral dependency to unilateral dependency, but, this time, with |V| in governing position: the fricative trill [ř] would be reduced to a simple liquid. This arguably corresponds to a subportion of the changes described in Romaine's (1978) work on Scottish /r/. Notice too that the common Czech pronunciation of *Dvořak* as [dvorʒak] supports the representation in (44): the fricative component that we have built into (44) is segmentalised. The complexity of the segment is undone via sequencing of subparts of its representation.

Once again, the representations in (42)/(43) permit the characterisation of a number of natural classes. Thus vowels can be defined as {|V|}, i.e. the class of segments which contain |V| alone. Sonorants are {|V|→}, i.e. the class of segments containing |V| in governing position. Obstruents are {C→}, i.e. the class of segments which have (at least) governing |C|. Voiced obstruents show in addition dependent |V| and are {C→V}. Other groupings can be similarly defined.

The notation we have adopted has two advantages over standard proposals. First of all, it allows the expression of hierarchical relationships holding between various segments. Thus processes of 'strengthening' and 'weakening', for which no device is available within the SPE framework (cf. Chomsky & Halle's remarks, 1968: 401), and the recurrence of which has led phonologists to postulate a variety of strength scales external to the notation (with the notable exception of Foley's work: e.g. Foley 1977), can be captured in DP as changes leading to more |C|-ness (strengthening) or to more |V|-ness (weakening).

As an example, consider a lenition process such as the one in (45) (borrowed from Lass & Anderson 1975: 158):

(45)   pre-OE   OE   ME   late ME
        /-g-/ ⟹   [-ɣ-] ⟹   [-w-] ⟹   ([-u-] ⟹   Ø
        [*aagan] [aaɣan]   [ɔɔwən]   [ɔɔn]

This series of changes can be characterised — with respect to the consonant-type undergoing deletion — as in (46):

(46) |C;V| ⟹ |V,C;V| ⟹ |V;V,C| ⟹ |V| ⟹ Ø

where each step represents an increase in |V|-ness until the segment is weak enough to be deleted. We are not claiming here that the increase in |V|-ness is generally achieved in a simple uniform manner, since it may result from (a) addition of single V; (b) alteration of dependency relationships so that the new segment contains the same basic elements as before, but is V-er than before; or (c) deletion of single C. Nor are we claiming that there is only one single weakening hierarchy since in fact that hierarchy is a complex one with various branches. Rather, we are claiming that the DP notation allows us to relate a series of changes which are at best handled by strength hierarchies whose explanatory power does not extend beyond the phenomena at hand (see e.g. Ewen 1977, 1980a: 6.4; Anderson & Ewen, to appear: 4.5).

The second, related, advantage of our proposals concerning the categorial gesture is that it makes redundant a sonority hierarchy external to the representations. Sonority hierarchies such as the informal one in (47):

(47)   SONORITY HIERARCHY
        vowels glides liquids nasals obstruents

are often set up to account for the preferred, unmarked position of segments within syllables. The claim embodied in (47), and supported from a wide variety of languages, is that in syllables which have complex rhymes the natural ordering of segments should conform to the left-to-right ranking of (47) with vowels as ideal peaks. As is well known, the sonority slope is reversed within the onset with obstruents now as favourite initial elements. A syllable such as /blimp/ (example (14) in 2.2) exemplifies this ideal pattern. But, it should be obvious that our characterisation of the categorial gesture in (42) also defines a sonority hierarchy. As we move from {|C|} towards {|C|} sonority increases. Given a sequence of segments forming a syllable, relative sonority can be simply read off the categorial characterisation of the segments.

It is perhaps worth pointing out that a recent proposal by Selkirk (1984a) goes some way towards conceding the claim made repeatedly in DP that SPE-type major class features (e.g. [sonorant]) need not be part of our primitives but can be derived from more basic elements of the notation. Selkirk's solution, which consists in positing a scalar feature [sonority], falls, from our point of view, under the same general objections as were formulated against the scalar treatment of vowel height (cf. 3.3.3).

3.5 *The Characterisation of Consonants: Articulation*

In this section, we examine briefly the treatment of the notion of 'place of articulation' for consonants. The reader is referred to Anderson & Ewen (to appear: Ch. 6) for detailed discussion of these matters. One component that plays a major role in the characterisation of place of articulation is once again |u|. It will be recalled that this component can be defined as 'gravity'. It therefore seems appropriate to use it, following Jakobson, to define labials and velars vs. dentals, alveolars and palatals. Secondly, we shall adopt a component of linguality, |l|, which characterises dentals, alveolars, palatals and velars (i.e. all sounds produced with the blade or body of the tongue). The evidence for this component is surveyed in Lass (1976: Ch. 7, 1984: 11.5) who lists a wide array of phenomena in the history of English which can be optimally explained by reference to such a component. This gives the representations in (48):

(48)   {|u|}   {|l|}   {|l,u|}
         labials   dentals/alveolars   velars

On the other hand, palatals are characterised as in (49):

(49)   {|l,i|}
        palatals

where the |i| component, introduced in 3.3, expresses palatality; although in view of the marked status of palatals a representation such as {|l,i,u|} might prove more appropriate.

We shall also postulate a component of apicality, |t|, and a component of dentality, |d|, to differentiate various classes of dental and alveolar consonants. The apicality component combines with |l| to allow a distinction between tongue-blade, tongue-tip, and sublaminal (retroflex) consonants. A maximum of three possible configurations is allowed:

(50)   {|l;t|}   {|t:l|}   {|t;l|}
         laminals   apicals   retroflexes

But since, as far as we know, only a two-way PHONOLOGICAL opposition is attested, the distinction can always be captured in terms of {|l;t|} and {|t;l|} which will then have a more abstract systemic interpretation than the one given in (50).

We also adopt a component of dentality, |d|, which allows the distinctions made in (51):

(51)   {|u|}   {|u,d|}   {|l,d|}   {|l|}
        labials   labio-dentals   dentals   alveolars

Uvulars can be dealt with along the same lines as other tongue-body consonants, by use of the corresponding vocalic components. (52), below, seems to us appropriate:

(52)   {|l,u,a|}

On the other hand, as in various other treatments of distinctive features, we would invoke a component of tongue-root retraction, |r|, to characterise pharyngeal consonants. Like uvulars, we suggest that pharyngeals are both grave and cognate with low back vowels, and offer (53) as a tentative characterisation:

(53)   {|r,u,a|}
        pharyngeals

Two further components are required to complete our survey: |λ|, a component of laterality, and |n|, a component of nasality. (But recall, in connection with |n|, the discussion of gestures and sub-gestures in 3.1 and see Ewen, this vol.) These two components allow the following distinctions to be made.

(54)   {|l|}   {|l,λ|}   {|l,n|}
        non-lateral   lateral   nasal
        alveolar   alveolars   alveolars
        liquids

Although the space available precludes further exploration of this area, there is one controversial point we wish to discuss briefly: viz., the absence in our system of a feature of lip-rounding which is criticised by Rennison (this vol.). *Prima facie,* our system faces similar objections to the ones which have been raised to Jakobson's use of the feature [grave]. What we want to observe here is that secondary articulation can generally be handled by subjoining components of place of articulation to the primary articulation. Thus palatalisation, velarisation and pharyngealisation can respectively be represented as {|X:l,i|}, {|X;l,u|}, {|X;r|}. Along the same lines, the distinction between rounded and unrounded labials — which would otherwise be problematic for us — can be made as in (55):

(55)   {|u|}   {|u;u|}
        labials   rounded labials

3.6 *The Initiatory Gesture*

In this section, in order to sketch the background to the discussion of this topic by Ewen (this vol.) and Davenport & Staun (this vol.), we offer a traditional account, within DP, of initiation as a separate gesture.

We shall distinguish two major parameters within initiation — (a) a parameter of glottal stricture; (b) airstream mechanisms — and start with (a). We propose a component of *glottal opening,* |O|, which characterises only degrees of glottal opening, and leaves the states of the glottis out of account. The |O| component is, in particular, required to cater for languages which oppose more than two phonation types. Thus, in Hausa a contrast is made between voiceless, voiced and creaky (laryngealised) consonants. If we allow the |O| component to enter into dependency relationships with the categorial gesture, then the plosives of Hausa can be characterised as in (56):

(56)

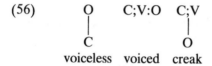

$$\begin{array}{ccc} \text{O} & \text{C;V:O} & \text{C;V} \\ | & & | \\ \text{C} & & \text{O} \\ \text{voiceless} & \text{voiced} & \text{creak} \end{array}$$

In addition, the |O| component can be used to characterise the opposition between voiced and voiceless sonorants. We assume, as is traditional, that sonorants are naturally voiced and that a system, such as Burmese (cf. Ladefoged 1971: 11), making a contrast between voiced and voiceless nasals and laterals is somehow marked. This complexity can be captured notationally by allowing the |O| component, for languages of this type, to interact with the categorial gesture in the representation of voiced and voiceless sonorants, as in (57):

(57)

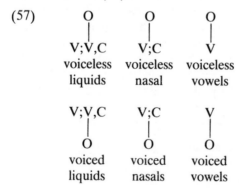

$$\begin{array}{ccc} \text{O} & \text{O} & \text{O} \\ | & | & | \\ \text{V;V,C} & \text{V;C} & \text{V} \\ \text{voiceless} & \text{voiceless} & \text{voiceless} \\ \text{liquids} & \text{nasal} & \text{vowels} \end{array}$$

$$\begin{array}{ccc} \text{V;V,C} & \text{V;C} & \text{V} \\ | & | & | \\ \text{O} & \text{O} & \text{O} \\ \text{voiced} & \text{voiced} & \text{voiced} \\ \text{liquids} & \text{nasals} & \text{vowels} \end{array}$$

Finally, the |O| component could plausibly be used to characterise oppositions of aspiration, since some phoneticians, like Kim

(1970) or Catford (1977), have claimed that there is a direct correlation between the degree of glottal opening and aspiration (see Ewen 1980a: Ch. 9; Anderson & Ewen, to appear: 5.3).

Let us now turn our attention to the components characterising airstream mechanisms. If a language has recourse only to the pulmonic egressive (or pulmonic pressure) airstream mechanism, we shall assume that this fact does not require to be coded in phonological structure. But, as is well known, language use, distinctively, other airstream mechanisms beside pulmonic egressive: namely, glottalic egressive (or glottalic pressure); glottalic ingressive (or glottalic suction) and velaric ingressive (or velaric suction). It is usual to separate within airstream mechanisms the initiator, on the one hand, and the direction of initiation, on the other. We characterise glottalic initiation via a component of glottalicness: |G|. We express direction of initiation by making |G| a governor or a dependent of the categorial gesture of the relevant segment as in (58), where place of articulation features are left out:

(58)   {G → C}   {|C|}   {C → G}
          /p'/   /p/   /p̰'/

The examples of (58) show a set of voiceless glottalic stops: for ejectives such as /p'/ (glottalic egressive stops) |G| is a governor whereas for glottalic ingressive stops, such as /p̰'/, |G| is a dependent. Normal pulmonic egressive stops obviously lack the component |G| and, if we wanted to express notationally the fact that they involve pulmonic initiation, we could achieve this by subjoining the |O| component to the categorial component. Voiceless glottalic egressive stops are, however, very rare (Catford 1977: 71, mentions only Tojolabal, a language of Guatemala, as exhibiting such sounds). Commonly, glottalic ingressive consonants are voiced. This can be represented by combining the |O| component with |G| to indicate the fact that the glottis is to some extent open in the production of such stops. (It will be recalled that Ladefoged, in various writings, says of the glottis that it functions as a 'leaky piston' in the production of voiced implosives.) Thus, the segment /ɓ/ of e.g. Uduk will be represented as in (59):

(59)   C;V
          |
        O,G

The representation of clicks, which are velaric ingressive segments, can be simply expressed by recourse to a component |K|, velaricness, since no language is known to oppose velaric suction and velaric pressure phonologically. Thus, the voiceless click /ʇ/ would receive the following representation (where once again, articulation is left out):

(60) |C,K| (/ʇ/)

If, however, we wanted to represent a velaric egressive sound, such as the so-called 'raspberry', by opposition to clicks — say in an account of the paralinguistic behaviour of many French speakers — we could do so once again by invoking the dependency relation: {K;C} would represent 'velaric pressure' and {C;K} 'velaric suction'. The complexity of representations once again varies according to the precise linguistic status of the phenomena described.

An important question discussed in this volume is that of the adequacy of representations such as (56)-(60) above, which allow dependency relations to hold between the |O|, |G| and |K| components, on the one hand, and the categorial gesture as a whole (specified by combinations of |V| and |C|), on the other. Such interaction of gestures as wholes is indeed argued for in Ewen (1980a: 7.4.5, 9.5.2, 9.5.3). There are, however, a number of problems inherent in such an approach explored by Davenport & Staun (this vol.). One solution, in line with our discussion in 4.1, is to limit dependency relations to holding only between subgestures, or between components of subgestures, assuming the structure for segments given in (20) and defended by Ewen (this vol.).

3.7 *Complex Segments*

In the construction of word trees each (non-prosodic) categorial gesture is associated with a suprasegmental node. Typically, too, each categorial gesture is associated with one articulatory gesture and vice versa. Departures from such a situation have, however, been argued for in the literature on DP.

In particular, one-to-many associations seem to be appropriate in the case of long vowels:

(61)   {|V|} {|V|}   = /a:/

          {|a|}

wherein the presence of two successive categorial gestures is associated with the attribution to such vowels of two suprasegmental nodes. Arguably, too, intrasegmental structure may be further complicated by a dependency relation holding between successive gestures of the same type. To the extent that affricates such as /t͡s/ are to be analysed as mono- rather than bisegmental, then a representation such as that in (62) is called for:

(62)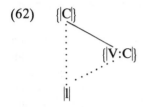

such that the entire configuration is associated with one suprasegmental node (with the proviso that only non-dependent categorial gestures are so associated). In (62), the basically plosive character of the complex segment is represented by the governing position of the {|C|} subsequence. So too with 'short diphthongs' — i.e. diphthongs which are grouped phonologically with short monophthongs:

(63)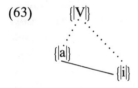

which will, once again, be associated with a single suprasegmental node. The dependency relation in (63) indicates a falling diphthong.

If, as seems likely, such dependency relations are non-contrastive, then, of course, they may be introduced by general convention rather than being included as part of individual lexical entries. That is, lexically, we have in such instances too simply one-to-many association: within segments, dependency relations between successive instances of the same gesture-type are derivative only.

It should, nevertheless, be pointed out that the status of affricates, at least, is controversial. Thus Ewen (1980a: 7.4, 1982) argues that what distinguishes these and other instances of doubt-ful segmentality is a violation of the association between sonority and dependency: in the structure associated with the sequence /ts/ the less sonorant element governs. And he attributes the various peculiarities found with initial /s/ + plosive clusters in such languages as English with an analogous violation: in this case the governor, /s/, is further from the syllabic than its dependent plosive (see the discussion of the very same issue in Davenport & Staun, this vol.). However that may be — and notice, for instance, that the non-segmentality of /s/ + plosive seems much better motivated than such a status for affricates — it appears to be clear that no non-derivative dependency relations between gestures need be posited, thus severely constraining the character of segmental structure.

Observe finally that if one and only one suprasegmental tier may be associated with each (non-dependent) categorial gesture, then we can obviate the need for a distinct CV tier (Clements & Keyser 1983) empty of segmental content. The categorial gesture serves both to provide part of the internal specification for each segment and also to determine what syllable structure is to be erected for each lexical item (see Ewen, this vol.: 3).

3.8 *Dependency Preservation*

The description of complex segments brings us naturally once again to the question of the relationship between suprasegmental and infrasegmental structure. Throughout section 3, we have been arguing that the dependency relation is also central to the modelling of the internal structure of segments. Support for this position can be drawn from the literature on historical changes: the unmarked situation is for changes to preserve dependency relations, and we tacitly appealed to this idea in dealing with processes affecting vowel systems in 3.3.3. It is not our purpose to chart the whole range of historical changes to show the validity of the concept of dependency preservation. Rather, we shall content ourselves here with an example of historical development which involves a change in segmentality and shows a typical transfer of dependency from the suprasegmental level to the infrasegmental level.

Consider a language system which exhibits a contrast between high-mid and low-mid among its vowels. If, in such a system, an /ai̯/-type diphthong monophthongises, it will emerge as a low-mid rather than a high-mid vowel:

(64)

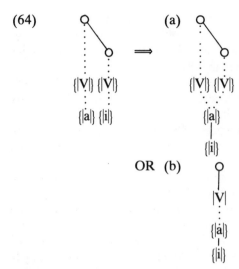

(a)

OR (b)

Whether or not length is preserved ((a) vs. (b)) depends on the character of the system which pertains at the point at which the change is carried through. Length is preserved in the Middle French change of /ai/ $\implies$ /ɛː/ instantiated by *vrai*, for instance. And this seems typical. In either case, the suprasegmental dependency between [a] and [i] is preserved, under monophthongisation, at the segmental level, by virtue of the dependency relations holding between the components |a| and |i| in the articulatory gesture.

4. Dependency Phonology and Other Frameworks

4.1 *The Distinctiveness of DP*

What most clearly differentiates DP from other recent, and not so recent, proposals concerning phonological notation is its explicit implementation of the structural analogy assumption. In particular, as has been shown in the preceding sections, representations are constructed out of atoms related by the relations of dependency, precedence and association, as they are also on the syntactic plane; and more detailed analogies presuppose this general analogy.

Structural analogy, obviously, also characterises representations at different levels within the phonological plane. In particular, both supra- and infrasegmental structure involve the dependency relation, differing as to whether nodes are unlabelled or not. This too is not characteristic of previous proposals concerning phonological representations. But only such an assumption permits the formulation of general conditions of the character of dependency preservation discussed in 3.8.

Clearly, DP does share a number of local assumptions with other frameworks. For instance, 'metrical' structures (cf. Liberman & Prince 1977; Giegerich, this vol.) attribute an asymmetrical relation (s/w) to the members of phonological constructions. In DP, this is assumed to be merely *one* manifestation of the dependency relation. And, the characterisation of such asymmetrical relations by quasi-categorial labels is rejected as inappropriate. (On this, and the question of binarity, compare Ewen, this vol., and Giegerich, this vol.) Nor, too, are non-atomic categories labelling nodes (as in e.g. Selkirk 1980a,b, 1982; see Vincent, this vol., for exemplification) necessary in a framework in which constructions, as in the syntax, are defined by dependency and precedence (cf. 2.2 above).

As regards the atoms of phonological structure, these have consistently been assumed within DP to be unary features or components, so that segments structure is principally characterised by the presence and absence of components and the presence and absence of dependency relations between them. This again has not been typical, until recently, of proposals within other current notational frameworks. But it is characteristic of some recent, but mostly as yet unpublished, work in the non-linear tradition (by e.g. Goldsmith; Kaye & Vergnaud), including particle phonology (Schane 1984a,b). We illustrate below how the unary feature assumption, as well as resolving many of the problems associated with non-unary treatments of segmental phonology, also permits formulations of suprasegmental regularities which are maximally general and concrete.

It is not so obvious that other assumptions usually made in DP are as intimately connected with the positing of the dependency relation as basic. For instance, the notion of gesture or subsegment can indeed be implemented in relation to segmental representations constructed out of distinctive features (recall our formulation in (21) of the s $\implies$ h $\implies$ Ø trajectory where we used standard DF's for convenience: cf. 3.1); but then the composition of gestures is arbitrary with respect to other aspects of the notation. On the other hand, in DP, gesture boundaries can naturally be constructed in relation to units characterised by dependency relations: components which never enter into a dependency relation either with each other, or both with some third, do not belong to the same gesture. Thus, |i| and |C| do not meet this condition, and so belong to distinct gestures; by contrast, |i| and |a| are often linked by dependency and are therefore co-gestural.

Structural analogy is satisfied by the characterisation of supra-segmental structures as unlabelled projections of strings of segments associated with particular domains, words (giving word structure) or utterance (giving utterance structure): syntactic structure is just such a projection of strings of categories. The highly structured character of the suprasegmental representations proposed within DP also follows from the assumption that these involve dependency relations, relations whose substantive manifestation is relative prominence (just as infrasegmental dependencies are manifested by relative preponderance of the components so linked).

We conclude this section with an illustration of the intimate interaction of supra- and infrasegmental structure permitted by DP, as well as the crucial role of the dependency relation. The example we shall consider (see Anderson & Jones 1977; Jones 1978, for detailed accounts) involves Old English Back Umlaut (OEBU) and a subpart of Old English Breaking (OEB). Our contention will be that these two sound changes, which are both epenthetic and involve the introduction of an identical vocalic segment, are usually treated as disparate phenomena in the absence of analytic tools complex enough to relate them. Restricting ourselves to the range of phenomena covered in Jones (1978: 162ff), both pro-cesses can be argued to involve the insertion of a [+back] vocalic element between a stressed front vowel and the two apparently unrelated environments:

(a) $\quad - \quad \begin{bmatrix} +son \\ +back \\ -nas \end{bmatrix} \quad C$

(e.g. æld $\Longrightarrow$ æuld) OE ‹eald›

(b) $\quad - \quad C \quad \begin{bmatrix} V \\ +back \\ -stress \end{bmatrix}$

(e.g. gæ tu $\Longrightarrow$ gæutu) OE ‹geatu›

so that [i] ⟹ [iu], [e] ⟹ [eu] and [æ] ⟹ [æu], where the height
of the epenthetic vowel is subsequently adjusted in the direction of
the syllabic segment. While the backness feature of the epenthetic
segment is clearly relatable to that of a following segment, it is
difficult to see in the standard framework what these two environments have in common. Why should a back sonorant immediately
adjacent to the affected vowel and a back unstressed vowel located
in the next syllable have the same effect? And why should the
epenthetic segments be vocalic in both cases? The beginning of an
answer to these questions is to be found in the suprasegmental
structure that we would assign to our representative examples.
Thus *æld* and *gætu* would be given the following (partial) representations (where the top node is the foot node and where for
clarity the syllable is given 'flat' internal structure):

(65)

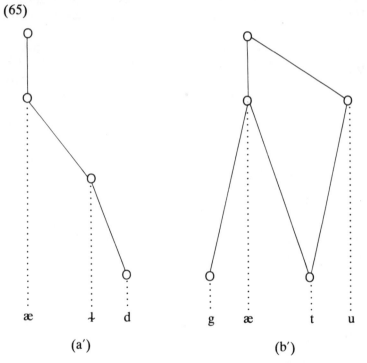

(a′)   (b′)

In these two representations the segment which provides the backness component is in fact an immediately adjacent right-hand
dependent within the foot as upper bound category (in (a′) at
syllable level; in (b′) at foot level). The rest of the answer lies in

the infrasegmental structure of sonorants and vowels. Recall that in section 3.4 vowels were given as {|V|}, categorially, whereas liquids can be characterised as {|V;V,C|}). The right-hand trigger-segments of (a) and (b) can therefore be conflated as {|V|(→V)}, i.e. the class of segments which contain |V| alone with an optional dependent V (an environment high in periodicity). The insertion of a vocalic segment is not arbitrary but can be naturally interpreted as the copying of the governing |V| in the categorial representation of the trigger-segment. On the other hand, its backness is a copy of the articulatory [u] component which would be part of the repre- sentation of the relevant liquids and vowels ([ɨ] and [u] in (65) above). OEBU and OEB can both be argued to be instantiations of a general recurrent process of vowel strengthening in English

(66)

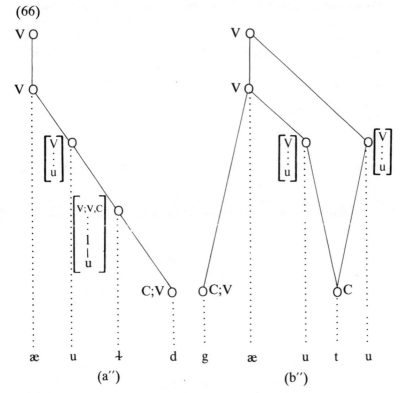

(a'')   (b'')

and other languages whereby a strong governing vowel is further strengthened in the context of an immediately adjacent right-hand side dependent which is high in |V|-ness (see too within DP Ewen

1978 on Dutch; ÓDochartaigh 1981, on Gaelic; and Jones, this vol.). Clearly, an adequate expression of this process appears to rest on the interaction of supra- and infrasegmental structure in ways which go well beyond standard assumptions concerning phonological structure. We shall refrain here from a formalisation of this process of strengthening, referring the reader to Anderson (this vol.) and the references above for possible specification of such strength schemata. Let us content ourselves in this intro-duction with the graphs showing the output of OEB and OEBU, where *for convenience* we label the nodes with informal speci-fications of the segments involved (see (66) above).

4.2 *Dependency Phonology and Autosegmental Phonology*

As should be clear from the above, DP suprasegmental structures are more highly articulated than those associated with typical proposals in autosegmental phonology (from Goldsmith 1976 onwards). We shall attempt to show that this enables us to propose a significant constraint on the character of associations between nodes, which we give as (67):

(67)   The unmarked association is one-to-one

Associations whereby a node is linked with more than one node at another level are claimed to be untypical. Thus, accounts of particular phenomena which involve widespread violation of (67) are suspect. Let us now try to illustrate the consequences of this for descriptions of vowel harmony. At the same time, we shall demonstrate the appropriateness of the deployment of unary com-ponents in relation to suprasegmental phenomena.

Given the limitations of space, we consider here only the much discussed vowel harmony of Hungarian (see e.g. Vago 1980a,b; Ringen 1980). The basic observation concerning this phenomenon is that certain combinations of vowels are incompatible in native Hungarian words. Thus, roots may contain vowels either belonging to the set /y(:), ø(:)/ or the set /u(:), o(:), a(:)/ but not a mixture of the two:

(68)   (a) Város-nak, 'city' (dative)   /a: − o − a/
        (b) öröm-nek, 'joy' (dative)   /ø − ø − e/

and the vowels of suffixes agree in backness with the root. With respect to these sets, roots (and words) are either back or front. However, roots containing only /i(:)/, /e:/ and possibly /e/ −

vowels which are usually labelled 'neutral' — may be associated
with either a front or a back vowel suffix:

(69)   (a) szín-nek,   'colour' (dative) /i: — e/
        (b) cél-nak,   'aim' (dative) /e: — a/

Roots containing a back vowel and a neutral vowel take only back
suffixes:

(70)   (a) tányér-nak, 'plate' (dative) /a: — e: — a/
        (b) béká-nak,   'fog' (dative)   /e: — a — a/

while those containing only front vowels, neutral and non-neutral,
take a front suffix:

(71)   tömeg-nek,   'crowd' (dative) /ø — e — e/.

Preverbs do not participate in harmony:

(72)   (a) át, 'over'
        (b) jön, 'come'
        (c) átjön, 'come over)

and compounds are harmonically autonomous with the character
of any suffix being determined by the immediately preceding root.
This suggests that the domain of harmony is not the word but the
foot, whose head is the first syllable of the root.

    This range of phenomena is straightforwardly described on the
assumption that Hungarian has five long-short pairs of lexical
vowels characterised as in (73):

(73)   {|u|}   {u,a}   {|a|}   {i,a}   {|i|}
        /u/   /o/   /a/   /e/   /i/

and a lexical prosody |i| optionally associated with each root. Thus
the root in (68b) is lexically:

(74)   i
        |V| C |V| C
        ⋮   ⋮
        u,a   u,a

where consonantal specifications are not given, as irrelevant, and |i|
is unattached (prosodic) and unsequenced; whereas the lexical
specification for (68)(a) lacks the |i|-prosody. |i| is a quasi-gesture in
the sense of Anderson & Ewen (to appear: Ch. 7) — that is, a
language-particular gesture.

After erection of the word-tree, |i| is associated with the (super-) foot head:

(75)

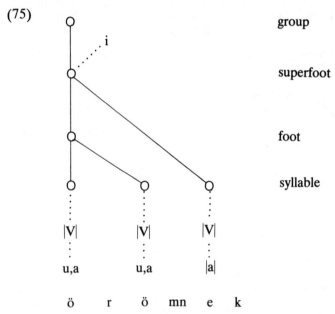

(where syllable internal structure is ignored). By contrast, (72c) would be analysed as in (76):

(76)

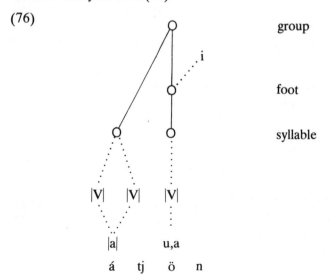

where again the prosody is associated with the foot head and so is not manifested in the phonetic realisation of the vowel of the preverb. (68a), of course, has no foot-level prosody.

The roots in (69a) and (71) are also clearly lexically specified for the |i| prosody:

(77)　(a)　i

C　　|V|　　C

|i|

sz　　í　　n

　　(b)　i

C　　|V|　　C　　|V|　　C

u,a　　　　i,a

t　　ö　　m　　e　　g

whereas it is lacking in (69b) and (70); and the back vowels emerge as back and the neutral vowels, as in (69a) and (71), as front. The neutral vowels need not be marked as not participating in vowel harmony. It is simply that their phonetic realisation, given that they are lexically front, does not reflect the presence (vs. absence) of the |i| prosody; this is manifested elsewhere in the word; as in (69a) and (71).

This sketch is necessarily incomplete. But even so, three conclusions may safely be drawn:

(a) Both the abstract analysis of the neutral vowels criticised by Kiparsky (1973) and the use of diacritic features is avoided. (See Anderson (to appear d), on the concreteness of DP representations.)

(b) The adoption of unary features or components allows a much simpler specification of the Hungarian vowel system than, say, the proposal made by Goldsmith (to appear), which utilises features of different status.

(c) Vowel harmony here involves the association of a quasi-gestural vowel component with a single node, the foot head. We assume this to be typical of 'prosodic' phenomena (vowel and tone harmony, for instance): in conformity with (67) above, the prosody is associated with a single node in phonological or morphological structure. This has long been recognised by analyses within the tradition of 'prosodic analysis' (cf. Palmer 1970; and for some discussion Anderson, to appear d). In this respect, DP can be seen as a continuation of that tradition.

Acknowledgement

We wish to thank Colin Ewen for kindly looking at this overview of dependency phonology and making suggestions for improvements. He is, however, absolved from responsibility in connection with all remaining errors. His influence on the course of dependency phonology will be obvious from the references.

2 SUPRASEGMENTAL DEPENDENCIES

John Anderson

Perhaps the most distinctive characteristic of the phonological representations assigned within the framework of dependency phonology is that the structural relation of dependency is attributed both to supra- and to infrasegmental structure (see Anderson & Jones 1974; Anderson & Ewen 1980, to appear: 3.4; Anderson & Durand, this vol.).* Here, however, I shall be concerned almost entirely with suprasegmental structure; one of the things I shall be trying to show is that even within this more restricted domain the deployment of dependency representations enables distinctive claims concerning phonological structure to be made, claims which are appropriately expressive and restrictive, and thus worthy of further investigation.

DEPENDENCY is a non-transitive, binary, 'inequality' (non-symmetrical) relation, like IMMEDIATE PRECEDENCE. Whereas immediate precedence is to be interpreted as (correlating with) relative priority in time, dependency introduces a non-temporal priority. Also, dependency holds only between the atoms or basic elements in the appropriate domain; in the present case, only between SEGMENTS. The structure assigned to a sequence of segments involves only pairs of segments, one member of which is dependent on the other, or is GOVERNED by it. CONSTITU-ENTS are defined in terms of the dependency relation: a constituent is formed by a segment and all those segments which are SUBORDINATE to it, where subordination is the transitive closure of dependency. The designated segment is the HEAD of the construction; its dependents are MODIFIERS.

The priority introduced by the dependency relation is manifested in two ways. The prior element, the head, is CHARACTERISTIC of the construction: it is obligatory to the construction; without it there is no such construction. For instance, in the absence of a syllabic element there is no syllable. Priority is also manifested as the head's greater STRENGTH in some substantive property relative to its modifier(s). Again, in the case of the syllable, the syllabic is more PROMINENT than an associated

55

non-syllabic. These two aspects constitute, if you like, the 'syntax' and 'morphology' of headhood.

In what follows, I turn firstly to a brief review of some of the evidence that favours an interpretation of suprasegmental structure as dependency stemmata; and I shall at that point offer a preliminary characterisation of suprasegmental structure in such terms (sections 1-3). I shall then propose (4) a distinction between INTRALEXICAL or word phonology and EXTRALEXICAL or utterance phonology. This is motivated not merely by a difference in domain (the word vs. the utterance) but also systematic differences in how structures are assigned (including what factors are relevant thereto) and perhaps by differences in general constraints that govern the form of constructions. Sections 5-16 are concerned with various aspects of intralexical structure in English and its assignment, in an attempt to show the appropriateness of a dependency interpretation of a relatively rich set of data (though this is limited by the confines of the present exercise). Section 17 provides a short programmatic sketch of extralexical phonological structure, particularly of those respects in which it differs from intralexical, and of its interaction with word structure; thus correcting the preliminary characterisation offered in what immediately follows.

1.

Evidence for a dependency interpretation of suprasegmental structure is provided by the establishment of the appropriateness for the expression of phonological regularities of groupings of segments with one (obligatory) strong (atomic) member. In the first place, let us note those groupings for which there exists a range of evidence; then we can proceed to examine the relevance of dependency to them. My survey is brief: constituency in itself does not require a dependency interpretation, though it does follow from such; moreover, arguments for phonological constituents are already familiar from a number of sources (including many of the works in my bibliography).

Much discussed as a unit, indeed, has been the SYLLABLE, which I take to be a syllabic plus optional margins. (We approach a more precise characterisation below.) This is in the first place the appropriate domain for the statement of (non-morphological) conditions on morpheme or word structure: words are sequences of well-formed syllables (cf. e.g. Kahn 1976; Anderson & Ewen, to appear: 2.2). The most basic constraint of all in English is that each word is at least one syllable. Certainly, word position is relevant to some restrictions; specifically, in English certain sequences (as in *text, sixths*) are possible only word-finally (and we return below to the description of these). But otherwise the most general formulation of word structure constraints is permitted if words are regarded as sequences of syllables and the constraints are formulated with respect to syllable structure.

It seems clear too that many phonological processes have the syllable as their domain. Consider for instance Saib's (1978) discussion of spread of pharyngealisation in Berber, from which it emerges that the spreading pays attention both to syllable boundaries and to the structure of the syllable involved (for further discussion see again Anderson & Ewen, to appear: 2.2.2). Or take glottalisation of voiceless stops in English, which occurs only syllable-finally, as in the examples in (1):[1]

(1)   pi*ck*, Dere*k*, a*c*rid, Me*cc*a

but not in the non-finals in (2):

(2)   *k*in, a*cc*ount, Ait*k*en

Similarly, short [i] in English is able to tense only syllable-finally, as in (3):

(3)   Rotar*i*an, As*i*atic, modest*y*, bur*y*, p*y*jamas

but not (4):[2]

(4)   b*i*t, *i*ntend, Asiat*i*c

Repeated reference to the syllable as a domain is unaccounted for in phonological representations which lack the syllable as a unit.

We also have evidence that, within the syllable, the syllabic and CODA constitute a unit which excludes the ONSET. This is suggested by traditions of rhyming verse. But also characteristic of the RHYME are mutual restrictions between the syllabic as NUCLEUS of the rhyme and the coda which are not paralleled by onset-syllabic restrictions. Thus, in English the nucleus /au̯/ cannot in general be followed by non-coronal consonants as a coda. Consider the distribution illustrated by (5):[3]

(5)   (a) brown, */−au̯m/, */−au̯ŋ/
        (b) loud, */−au̯b/, */−au̯g/

    (c) lout, */−aʊp/, */−aʊk/
    (d) mouth, mouse, slouch, */−aʊf/
    (e) mouth (*verb*), rouse, gouge, */−aʊv/

Further, as is well established, and as we shall return to, considerations of syllabic weight are almost entirely a question of the internal structure of the rhyme.

I leave aside for the moment the status of onset, nucleus and coda as constituents.

Syllables are grouped into feet. The FOOT I take to be the basic unit of rhythmic organisation, constituted by a stressed syllable and any unstressed to its right (Abercrombie 1965b). But the foot is also a domain for distributional restrictions. For example, in English no short vowels may appear finally in the first syllable of a foot. Thus, *buy, knee, bias* and *neon* are not paralleled by forms in which the (first) syllable is terminated by a short vowel. Long vowels, on the other hand, are limited to the first syllable of a foot.[4] /h/ in English is limited to foot- or word-initial position: *history, hysterical, Jojoba* [hə'həɯb]. But (fast-speech) weakening of stops in English is excluded from foot-initial position, as in (6):

(6)   ['træxɪŋ 'deɪʂə]   tracking data

but not from word-initial, if it is not also foot-initial:

(7)   [ɸə'lɪtɪkl̩]   political

(examples, and transcription, from Brown 1977: 74). Similarly, flapping of /t,d/ is foot-medial.

It is also arguable that the preference for enclisis over proclisis in language is related to foot structure: clitics prefer to attach themselves to the same foot as the cliticee, which requires postposition.[5] Thus, in Buryat unstressed pronouns have encliticised themselves to the verb, even though, as Comrie (1978) has shown, the language has been syntactically verb-final as far back as we can reconstruct. Further, proclitics tend to lose syllabicity as a means of attaching themselves to the cliticee. Contrast the behaviour of the Middle English proclitic *ne* in (8):

(8)   nolde 'didn't want to', nat 'didn't know', nis 'isn't'

with Modern English enclitic *not*:

(9)   shouldn't, hasn't, doesn't, wasn't

which typically (despite *won't, shan't, aren't, can't,* for which there are particular explanations) retains syllabicity. Given the (stress-initial) structure of the foot, enclitics require less radical structural change, if any, to attach themselves to the same foot as the cliticee.

Feet are grouped into TONE GROUPS, the stretch associated with a major tone shift. These constitute the maximal domain for assimilations and deletions in casual speech. For example, in English fast speech syllable-final /t/ and /d/ are omissible between consonants when syllable-final no matter where in the foot they occur:

(10)   ['kDnflɪkstɪl]   conflict still
        ['ɪntres'reɪts]   interest rates
        [ðə'fækðət]   the fact that

(Brown 1977: 61), but not across a tone group boundary. Compare the Gorgia Toscana, the weakening of voiceless stops between vowels in this dialect, which cannot occur across a tone group boundary:

(11)   //Le case carine//costano molto care in America//
        'Cute houses are very expensive in America'

The double slashes enclose tone groups, within whose domain the underlined intervocalic plosives may be weakened, even across a foot boundary, as with *molto care.* However, the initial *c* of *costano* doesn't weaken, since the preceding vowel is in a separate tone group. This phenomenon is discussed by Nespor and Vogel (1982: 2.3.2; from which my example is taken), as is also nasal assimilation in Spanish (4.1), which also has the tone group as its domain.

Tone groups are assembled into utterances — what I shall term below second level groups (G^2), or what for Halliday (1967) constitutes a 'tone group'. Halliday distinguishes a 'pre-tonic' and a 'tonic segment' within the 'tone group'. The relative independence of these is recognised within the present framework in terms of the status of each as a group. The hierarchisation between 'pre-tonic' and 'tonic' is characterised by the dependency relations proposed in what follows; specifically, that holding between the G^2 head and an associated group head. With Halliday, I take the G^2 (utterance) construction to be the appropriate domain for 'tune-text association' (Liberman 1975; Ladd 1978). I do not, however, pursue this complex matter here (but on the formation of G^2 see 17 below, in particular). My aim at this point is simply to illustrate the appropriateness of such constituents as rhyme, syllable, foot and group.

2.

Each of these successively more inclusive groupings — rhyme, syllable, foot, group — is motivated by a range of phonological phenomena. Let us now try to establish that each is also a grouping with one (obligatory) strong member.

In most languages only one segment is obligatory to the rhyme, viz. the nucleus;[6] the coda may be absent. And in many languages the coda is very limited. The nucleus is also more prominent than the coda. It is therefore plausible to suggest that the rhyme is a right-modified structure with the nucleus as its head.

Again, within the syllable we typically find only one obligatory element, one in whose absence there is no syllable, the SYLLABIC segment, which as head is also more prominent than any of its subordinates. The modifier of the syllabic, the onset, is on its left; the syllable involves left- rather than right-modification.

On the interpretation just offered, the strong members, or heads, of the rhyme and the syllable, the nucleus and the syllabic, respectively, are constituted by the same segment: [ɪ] in *bit* is head of both rhyme and syllable. The only structural difference between the rhyme and the syllable is the DIRECTION OF MODIFICATION and their relative placing in the HIERARCHY OF INCLUSIVENESS: the left-modified syllable includes the right-modified rhyme, and never vice versa.

In most interpretations of dependency grammar the head of each construction is unique to that construction; what identifies the construction is the category of the head: a noun phrase is simply a phrase with a noun head. But constructions still remain distinct, without recourse to constituency labels, if they nevertheless share the same head but differ systematically, for example, in direction of modification. Thus, it is arguable that verb phrase and sentence share the verb as their head and differ only in direction of modification: in a SVO language, sentence is a verb-headed construction with a left-modifier (the subject); verb phrase has a right-modified verb head.[7]

I am suggesting that the situation with syllable and rhyme is identical in showing constructions differing only in direction of modification, and in obligatory inclusivity. Further, not only do nucleus and syllabic not differ in category label; no category label at all need be invoked.

This situation is characterised by the dependency stemma in (12):

(12)

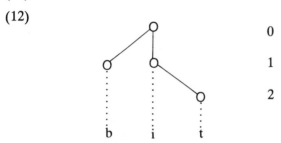

which expresses graph-theoretically the relationships of (13):

(13) (a) $/i/_0 \rightarrow /i/_1$, $/i/_0 \rightarrow /b/$, $/i/_1 \rightarrow /t/$
       (b) $/b/ \leqslant /i/_0$, $/i/_0 \leqslant /i/_1$, $/i/_1 \leqslant /i/_0$, $/i/_1 \leqslant /t/$

where $\rightarrow$ is the asymmetric dependency relation and $\leqslant$ the anti-symmetric relation of immediate precedence. The graph ASSOCIATES each of the segments in the string /bit/ with a node linked to other nodes by dependency ARCS. There is one node which is not a dependent, the root: it has a degree of dependency of 0 (as indicated on the right in (12)). Dependent on it is the node (hence of degree 1) associated with /b/. Also dependent on the degree 0 node is another node which, however, unlike that associated with /b/, does not differ in precedence from the degree 0 node and thus is associated with the same segment /i/, which thus is associated with two nodes differing only in degree of dependency. /b/ is said to be ADJOINED to $/i/_0$; $/i/_1$ is SUBJOINED to $/i/_0$. Thus in (13), whereas $/i/_0$ both governs /b/ and is preceded by it, it governs $/i/_1$ but is identical in precedence with it ($/i/_0 = /i/_1$). /t/ in turn is adjoined to $/i/_1$ (hence is of degree 2) and is preceded by it.

The syllable is the construction headed by $/i/_0$, which is left-modified. The construction nevertheless includes the whole string in (12), since a construction comprises not just a head plus its modifiers but a head and all its subordinates: both /b/ and /t/ are subordinate to $/i/_0$, though only /b/ modifies it. The rhyme is the construction headed by $/i/_1$, which is right-modified.

The foot is again right-modified. The head of the foot is the syllabic of the first syllable in the foot. This is the only obligatory element, and it is more prominent than any other syllabic in the foot. This is characterised in (14):

(14)

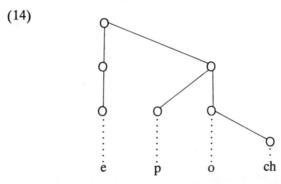

                    e   p   o   ch

wherein *e* is successively head of a rhyme, syllable and foot. The foot differs from the syllable in direction of modification and in being more inclusive; it differs from the rhyme in being more inclusive, with the syllable intervening. The constructions remain distinct despite their sharing a head.

Similarly with the tone group: the head of the rightmost foot in the group is the group head: i.e. the group head is left-modified. It is the only obligatory foot head, and it is more prominent by virtue among other things of being the locus for a tone shift. A tone group may consist of a single nucleus which is successively head of a rhyme, a syllable, a foot and a group, as *I!* The tone group differs from the foot and rhyme in direction of modification and in being more inclusive; it differs from the syllable in inclusivity.

3.

Both the tone group and the syllable are left-modified; the foot and the rhyme are right-modified. Each grouping is obligatory in English and has a fixed place in the hierarchy. Thus each is distinct, without recourse to labelling (even of the head). Given that each construction is obligatory, we can distinguish a foot as the right-modified construction whose head is the third node from the bottom associated with the nuclear element, as revealed in a representation such as (15), which contains two feet:

(15)

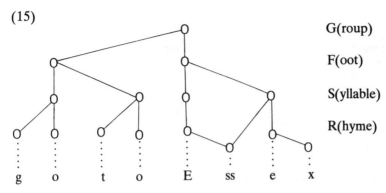

G(roup)

F(oot)

S(yllable)

R(hyme)

g   o   t   o   E   ss   e   x

(I ignore for the moment the structure of clusters (x) and the ambisyllabicity attributed in (15) to the medial consonant in *Essex*.)

Suprasegmental representations are thus label-free. Constructions, heads and modifiers are distinguished by the configuration of arcs and nodes alone (and, as we shall see below, the identity of the sequence of segments from which they are projected). Not even atomic category labels like syllabic are required. Certainly, there need be no recourse to non-atomic, higher-level category labels like 'syllable', etc.: the labels on the right in (15) simply abbreviate the information available from the stemma itself. Nor, for that matter, need there be recourse to 'relational' quasi-categories like S(trong) and W(eak) (cf. e.g. Ewen, this vol.). Constituency, constituency-type and relative strength are defined by the dependency graph.

The upper constructions, group and foot, also differ from the lower in the nature of the segments with which their modifiers are associated. Group and foot always involve a vowel governing a vowel: they are HOMOGENEOUS. With syllable and rhyme a vowel governs a consonant: they are HETEROGENEOUS. I ignore here syllabic consonants: for English, at least, they are arguably always derived — see section 10 and note 12 below. Even admitting syllabic consonants, we can still make an analogous distinction: the modifiers in a syllable and rhyme are necessarily consonantal. No other elements in these constructions are so restricted.

Homogeneous constructions are also ITERATIVE. As we have seen, one tone group head may be subordinated to another, second level, head, as represented in (16):

(16)

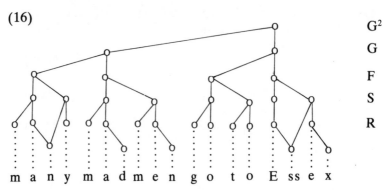

(17) shows foot-to-foot subordination, which occurs under 'de-accentuation' (Ladd 1978), whereby the group head is not the head of the final foot in the group (the 'tonic' falls on *Bobby*):[8]

(17)

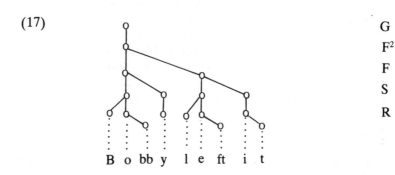

(18) shows both group-to-group and foot-to-foot subordination:

(18)

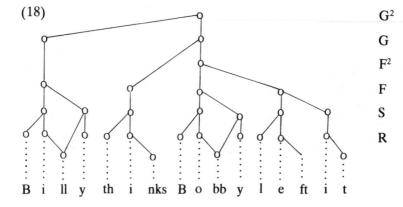

Given that only feet and groups are iterated, the identity of construction-types remains determinate.

4.

A consideration of the immediately preceding examples also makes it clear that the foot and group structures associated with a particular string of segments may vary (even if the overt morphosyntactic structure remains constant): for instance, the headship of G^2 in (18) may alternatively be associated with *thinks*. Thus, as is well known, group structure cannot be entirely predicted from the sequence of syllables that constitutes an utterance. It depends in particular on the information structure associated with the utterance: what is being presented as new, contrastive, parenthetical, etc. Foot structure is also affected as a consequence ('de-accentuation').

Foot structure is also sensitive to rhythmic requirements, as is evidenced by STRESS-REVERSAL (or 'iambic reversal' or whatever). Compare (19):

(19)   (a) //Thirt_ée_n//cáme to d_í_nner//
        (b) //B_í_lly//persev_é_res in it//

(with foot heads marked with an acute and group heads underlined) with (20):

(20)   (a) //Thírteen l_í_nguists//cáme to d_í_nner//
        (b) //B_í_lly//pérseveres gl_á_dly//

in which the foot heads in *thirteen* and *persevere* are shifted to the left away from an adjacent group head to the right. An adequate characterisation of this and related phenomena depends on an explication of the relationship between intralexical and extralexical structure. I offer some suggestions in this direction in section 17.

Section 17 examines also some of the phonological and syntactic factors that interact with information structure and rhythm (and tempo) in determining extralexical foot and group (and syllable) structures. In what intervenes, however, I want to contrast with these extralexical structures the 'frozen' foot and group structures assigned within words in the lexicon. I am going to suggest that the same hierarchy of constructions as we have just surveyed is assigned to words. Word structure shows the hierarchy we have established for utterances, but clearly it is determined by other factors: it is not sensitive to information structure, but simply to the phonological character of segments and the morphological character of the words in which they appear.

Languages vary in the constraints they impose on lexicalised foot and group structures. For instance, Hayes (1980) in his typology of intralexical feet distinguishes quantity-sensitive assignment of foot structure from non-quantity-sensitive and bounded from unbounded — English being quantity-sensitive and bounded. Languages also vary in the 'prominence' they accord to the foot word-internally: foot-prominence is evidenced by 'initial-stress' languages; lack of it by 'final-stress'. (On the initial/final dichotomy see e.g. Dogil 1981.) English is relatively foot-prominent.

Let us turn now to a consideration of some of the crucial constraints on the intralexical phonological structure of English. Central to these are rules which build up word-trees by making dependency assignments. I am assuming that no suprasegmental structure is stored as such in the lexicon. Each word is represented as a sequence of morphologically bracketed segments only.

Segments are internally complex, however: in that the components or features that characterise them are grouped into two or more gestures or subsegments (though these groupings are themselves predictable) — specifically, for our purposes, a categorial gesture (which specifies major class/manner of articulation/phonation-type) and an articulatory gesture (which specifies place of articulation/vowel-dimension); and in that they may display internal adjunctions (as in the case of affricates, pre-/post-nasalised stops or diphthongs that are not contrastively long).

Intralexical suprasegmental structure is a projection of such representations whereby each segment is associated with one or more nodes in a word-tree built up out of the constructions we have surveyed. The existence of exceptions (a large proportion of which seem to be American place-names) to the regular processes of word-tree formation (cf. e.g. note 23 below) does not disguise the essentially projective character of this relationship, nor does it require the storage of suprasegmental structure as such, even in the case of the exceptions.

Extralexical structure is in turn a set of alternative projections of sequences of word-trees determined by factors such as syntactic and information structure and rhythm. The account of phonological structure outlined in the immediately preceding sections crucially over-simplifies, among other ways, in neglecting the interaction between word and utterance structure.

5.

We have associated with headship of phonological constructions the properties of obligatoriness to the construction ('no syllabic, no syllable') and (relative) prominence *vis-à-vis* modifiers. In the case of the rhyme and the syllable, prominence goes along with greater inherent sonority: the element which is head outranks its modifiers in this respect (however it is characterised).

Accounts of syllable structure in the framework of dependency phonology that I am aware of (e.g. Anderson & Jones 1977; Ewen 1977, 1980a) and many 'metrical' proposals (e.g. Kiparsky 1981) assume a correlation between relative sonority and relative strength within syllabic structure. Roughly, the internal structure is a bidirectional projection of the sonority hierarchy, with (on Kiparsky's account) language-particular exceptions. In dependency phonology sonority is a function of the preponderance of the $|V|$ ('vocalicness') component in the categorial gesture. Determination of syllable structure simply involves rendering less sonorant segments, i.e. segments with less $|V|$, dependent on segments with more, provided that each dependency arc does not infringe projectivity (arcs and association lines meet only at nodes).

We might thus offer (21) as a first approximation to the determination of syllable structure, on the basis of this assumption:

(21)   DEPENDENCY ASSIGNMENT (DA) 1: SYLLABLE
         FORMATION:
         Given two segments a, b, where $a < < b$, a $\rightarrow$ b
         iff b is weak, i.e. $\{V\}_a \supset \{V\}_b$. Otherwise, b $\rightarrow$ a.

If the proportion of $|V|$ associated with a segment which precedes — not necessarily immediately ($<<$) — another is greater than that associated with the other, then the former will govern the latter; otherwise, vice versa.

(21) gives the dependency assignments in (22) with respect to the word /stɪŋk/:

(22)   (a) s → t   (b)
        s ← i
        t ← i
        i → ŋ
        ŋ → k

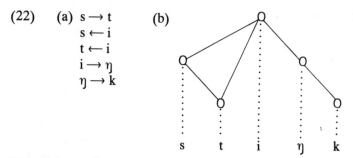

Non-projective assignments (i.e. where dependency and/or association lines cross) are discarded: e.g. /t/ ← /ŋ/, /s/ → /k/; also eliminated are dependency arcs which coincide with a path of arcs: so **/i/ → /k/, given /i/ → /ŋ/ → /k/.

(22b) makes apparent a general match of sonority and thus degree of dependency with distance from the syllabic. The /s/ + plosive cluster is thereby distinguished as odd, which is on other grounds appropriate. Consider, for example, the distinctive behaviour of such clusters in early Germanic alliteration and reduplication — *st-* alliterates only with *st-*, whereas, e.g. *sn-* alliterates with *s* + vowel, etc.; and the association of such an /s/ with a distinct chest pulse (cf. Anderson & Ewen, to appear: 3.2.2). /t/ also emerges as ambidependent, unless further restrictions are imposed on (21) or the representations assigned by it: we return to this shortly.

Application of (21) does not distinguish a rhyme constituent; nor does it ensure an obligatory status for either syllable or rhyme: no dependency assignments are made to a one-segment string. We can establish a rhyme if the 'otherwise' in (21) is interpreted as imposing a conjunctive ordering on the two subparts of syllable formation. And the obligatory status of the syllable is ensured if the relation between a and b in (21) is one of immediate precedence:

(23)   DA 1′: SYLLABLE FORMATION:
        Given segments a, b, where a ≤ b:
        (i) a → b iff b is weak, i.e. $\{V\}_a \supset \{V\}_b$.
        (ii) otherwise, b → a.

This gives (24) after the application of DA 1′ (i):

(24)

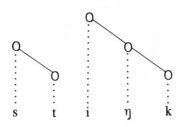

s   t   i   ŋ   k

and (25) after DA 1′ (ii):

(25)

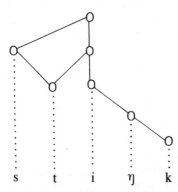

s   t   i   ŋ   k

on the assumption that each application of DA 1′ confers a distinct head: /i/ is assigned headhood three times, given that it governs three different segments. If, however, only one instance of head-hood may be acquired per subpart of DA 1′, then the extra layer of (25) can be eliminated:

(26)

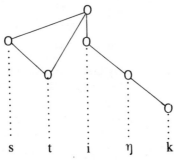

s   t   i   ŋ   k

with the consequence that the onset involves no longer just a single modifier of the syllabic.

(21) had to be formulated in terms of precedence ($<<$), not

immediate precedence ($\leqslant$), in order for non-adjacent segments like /s/ and /i/ in (22) to be related by DA 1. In (23) immediate precedence can be invoked, in that the segments to be related belong to adjacent constructions: since the /st/ construction is formed by application of DA 1′ (i), then /s/ and /i/ are the heads of immediately adjacent constructions and so may be related by DA 1′ (ii). This is in conformity with the HEAD CONVENTION of dependency grammar, given informally as (27):

(27)   HEAD CONVENTION:
        A regularity that mentions the head of a construction is interpreted as invoking the construction as a whole unless a subordinate of the head is mentioned by the same instance of that regularity.[9]

a in (23) is thus to be interpreted as the construction headed by a at that point.

(23) also allows a = b. In that case DA 1′(i) will not apply, since the preponderance of |V| of a and b is necessarily identical. But by DA 1′(ii) any element that does not meet the condition for DA 1′(i) will be assigned an extra head. Usually this headship will be eliminated by the convention that gives us (26) instead of (25). But if the element is the only non-dependent member of the syllable, the extra head will remain, as with a word like *ass*:

(28)

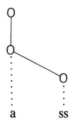

ss is made dependent on *a* by DA 1′(i), and the additional head is introduced by DA 1′(ii). This ensures that the syllable will have a head even when there is no onset: the syllable is obligatory.

DA 1′ does not, however, require that rhymes be obligatory; they thus have in this respect the same status as consonant clusters (see below). Despite the contrary assumption implicit in the previous discussion, this might be appropriate: languages may lack rhymes, or clusters, but not syllables. The hierarchical determinacy of construction-types is not thereby impaired. On the other hand, the role of rhymes in English does seem to be rather different from that appropriate to consonant clusters: consider, e.g. the requirement that in a stressed syllable the rhyme cannot consist of a simplex nucleus alone.[10] However, this does not appear to constitute sufficient motivation for proposing a universal obligatory status for the rhyme.

The representations assigned by DA 1′ retain the ambidependency of an element like /t/ in /stiŋk/ that followed from DA 1: recall (26). We derive some support for this from the properties of three-segment onsets such as that in /strip/. DA 1′ assigns the structure in (29) to such a string:

(29)

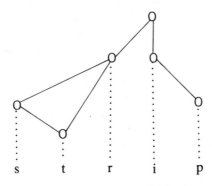

s   t   r   i   p

One motivation for constituency is the limitation of the domains within which mutual restrictions between segments hold (cf. e.g. Selkirk 1980a, b). Mutual restrictions cannot be reduced to pairwise constraints involving adjacent segments. For example, in English although both /st/ and /tw/ are viable onsets (*stink*, *twirl*), /stw/ is not. Moreover, not all adjacent pairs show restrictions: onset and syllabic are typically independent in this respect (though see below on /ju:/).

An appropriate limitation of the domain of such restrictions is made possible with respect to the dependency structures proposed here in terms of what I shall call the NEUTRALISATION CONDITION:[11]

(30)   NEUTRALISATION CONDITION:
        Restrictions between contrastive segments hold only among n-tuples of segments which uniquely share a construction.

In these terms, onset restrictions like */tl/, */dl/ are to be expected, as are */sb/ etc. And these are maintained in the sub-onsets in (29): */stl/, */sdl/, */sbr/. The restrictions are generalisable only if the plosive in (29) belongs to two constructions at once. However, there is also a construction consisting of all of just /str/ etc., the onset; and here too constraints hold, such as that banning */stw/. And we find similar restrictions within the rhyme, both between the consonants that constitute the coda (*/mt/, etc.) and between the nucleus and its coda (*/uŋ/). But onset-syllabic constraints are only marginally attested, given that they do not form a construction that does not include the coda. Rather, we find constraints on overall syllable shape, such as the avoidance of syllables with complex onsets and codas of identical content (allowing for the difference in the 'sonority slope'), e.g. */ClVlC/ — though such constraints may be violated in the interests of 'expressiveness' (Fudge 1970).

The paucity of onset-syllabic restrictions in English provides some support for an obligatory status for the rhyme in that language, at least. Otherwise, a coda-less syllabic could be said to belong uniquely with the onset to a single construction, the syllable. In that case, we could not relate the absence of mutual restrictions to the neutralisation condition (30).

Such a configuration as is given for the onset in (29) also enables us to generalise Kiparsky's (1981: 248) constraint on codas in English, that they 'can contain at most two segments'. (This, of course, assumes the 'extrametricality' of the final coronals in *sixths*, etc. — see further below.) If we reformulate this in terms of dependency structure, we can generalise the constraint as in (31):

(31)   SYLLABLE DEPTH CONDITION:
       No segment in English is more than two degrees of (adjunctive) dependency from the head of an obligatory construction.

which will apply both to rhymes (including coda), provided rhymes are obligatory, and to syllables (including onset), and in particular to trisegmental onsets such as that in (29).

I shall assume, along the lines suggest by Fudge (1969: 268), Fujimura & Lovins (1978) and Kiparsky (1981: 253-4), for example, that obstruent coronals[12] may constitute a HYPER-METRICAL or 'extrametrical' extension to the rhyme. This prevents erroneous, or at least unwarranted, parsing by DA 1′ (23), or parsing failure, in the case of sequences of consonants of equal sonority (32a) or with 'reverse slope' (32b) or showing both these characteristics (32c):

(32)　(a)　act, licked, slugged
　　　　(b)　tax, eighth, bits, adze, bids
　　　　(c)　text(s), sixth(s), acts

(32c) also infringe Kiparsky's coda length restriction, as well as requiring unmotivated internal structures on the assumption that DA 1′ applies to such sequences. It is inappropriate to suggest, e.g. that *tax* displays simply the reverse of the structure assigned to initial /s/ + plosive sequences, in that final /ks/ sequence displays none of the distinctive properties or restrictions associated with the latter — apart from the reversal of the 'sonority slope'. For the same reason, it is equally inappropriate to propose that inital /s/ before plosive is hypermetrical.[13]

I shall assume, then, that any non-initial coronal obstruent in a word-final sequence of obstruents is hypermetrical with respect to DA 1′(i). Instead it is assigned a place in structure by the STRAY SEGMENT CONVENTION (SSC), which is able to apply after DA 1′(i):

(33)　STRAY SEGMENT CONVENTION:
　　　Given three segments a, b, c, where a $<$b$<$c, a $\rightarrow$ c iff a $\rightarrow$ b.

Application of SSC creates in this case a SUPER-RHYME, as represented in (34):

(34)　(a)　　　　　　　　　　(b)

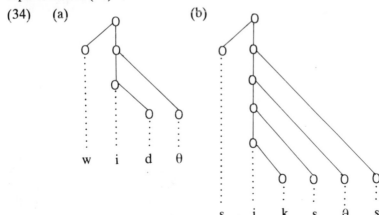

In (34b) application of SSC is reiterated. I assume, however, that all super-rhyme head nodes should by convention be collapsed into one.

6.

The formulation DA 1′ given in (23) depends on equating head-hood within the syllable uniformly with relative inherent sonority. However, apart from in the case of the syllable and possibly the rhyme heads, there is no distributional motivation for this: there is no reason to prefer /ŋ/ over /k/ as the head of the final cluster in (26) and the like — independently of the sonority assumption. Thus, the equation of greater sonority with syllable and (perhaps) rhyme heads (i.e. where the head is a vowel) is supported by the obligatory status of the syllabic and the nucleus. But in consonantal clusters such as /ŋk/, /ŋ/ cannot be said to be any more essential than /k/. Why not, then, take the head of consonant clusters to be the most consonantal segment? In this section I should like to explore this alternative conception: that strength in the case of consonant clusters is to be measured in terms of the relative preponderance of the |C| component.

Such a revision of the strength measure requires that we substitute for (23) some such formulation as (35):

(35)   DA 1″: SYLLABLE FORMATION:
         Given segments a, b, where a ≤ b:
         (i) a ⟶ b iff b is weak, i.e. a ≡ {|V|}, or, if not, {C}ₐ ⊃ {C}ᵦ;
         (ii) otherwise, b ⟶ a.

This gives (36) after the application of DA 1″(i) with respect to /sprint/:

(36)

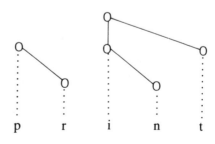

s   p   r   i   n   t

and (37) from DA 1″(ii):

(37)

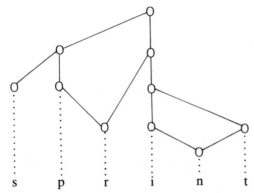

s   p   r   i   n   t

or rather, on the assumption that only one instance of headhood may be acquired per subpart (cf. the discussion of (25) above), (38):

(38)

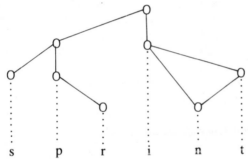

s   p   r   i   n   t

DA 1″ still creates a number of ambidependencies. These can be eliminated if we restrict the paths from a head to a subordinate to only one, the longest. This is required by the SINGLE PATH CONDITION (SPC):

(39)   SINGLE PATH CONDITION:
        Retain only whichever of several paths with the same initial and terminal contains the greatest number of adjunctions.

This requires that (38) be simplified as (40):

(40)

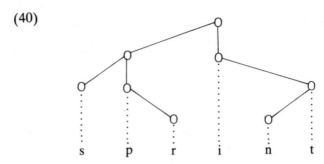

s   p   r   i   n   t

However, it is not clear on what grounds, other than simply the elimination of ambidependency, application of SPC here might be motivated. We return to this question in the following section and subsequently.

DA 1″ is more complex than DA 1′. But it has some advantages. It still provides a characterisation of the fact that the /p/ in /sprint/ or the /t/ in /strip/ belongs to two different constructions, without sacrificing the syllable depth condition (31), and without appeal to ambidependency. But it also makes possible a more perspicuous statement of the conditions governing alliteration and reduplication in the early Germanic languages: given the representations provided by DA 1″, we can say that alliteration involves all the uniquely left-subordinates of the syllabic, including null (vowel alliteration), i.e. left-subordinates of the syllabic that are not right-subordinates of anything. With respect to DA 1′, we have to say that alliteration involves the leftmost subordinate of the syllabic, including null, and any right-dependent of it.[14]

A further consideration concerns complex segments like affricates or pre-/post-nasalised obstruents. Say we characterise these as suprasegmentally simplex (they are assigned a single node in the word-tree) but as involving infrasegmental adjunction (cf. Anderson & Ewen, to appear: Ch. 3), as, say, in (41), representing /t͡s/:

(41)

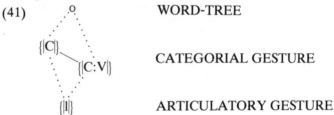

WORD-TREE

CATEGORIAL GESTURE

ARTICULATORY GESTURE

where the categorial gesture involves an adjunction, but the articulatory (1 = lingual; {ll} indicates not palatal, velar or dental) does not. The status of head for the plosive part of the complex is motivated by the fact that in most respects affricates pattern with the plosives (Herbert 1977: 163-4); frequently they develop historically from (simple or geminate) plosives. However, affricates are also often the historical consequence of the collapse of two segments: e.g. instances of English /t͡ʃ/ like that in *attitude*. In such a development the internal adjunction simply preserves the suprasegmental dependency relation, in conformity with the DEPENDENCY PRESERVATION CONDITION (DPC), which requires that changes in segmentality preserve individual dependency relations, where possible.[15] The dependency relation is preserved in this case only if suprasegmental structure is of the character specified by DA 1″ rather than that assigned by DA 1′ (plosives govern both supra- and infrasegmentally).

Most importantly, perhaps, the representations provided by DA 1″ relate much more directly to the unmarkedness of plosive + vowel as a syllable type (cf. Cairns & Feinstein 1982 — though it does not seem to me that their argument provides support for Chomsky & Halle's (1968: Ch. 9) 'theory of markedness' as such). Given that in a language the existence of onsets consisting of /s/ + plosive or of clusters with initial plosive presupposes single-plosive onsets and that the existence of other single-consonant onsets presupposes single-plosive onsets, an onset consisting solely of a plosive is unmarked with respect to other types.

It is, moreover, arguable that in English onsets are obligatory and that the minimal onset consists of a plosive. This appears to be at odds with many English words, such as *odd, eat, act, I* .... However, in some varieties of English such words are initiated by [ʔ] (cf. again Lass 1983), which can be characterised as a plosive lacking an articulatory gesture. Further, as suggested in Anderson (1969), the distribution of [h] in English suggests another parallel between apparently onset-less syllables and those initiated by plosives. The word- and foot-initial positions that are associated with [h] (recall section 1) are also loci for aspiration of voiceless plosives. Say we posit a plosive as underlying phonetically empty onsets (sometimes realised as [ʔ]); then [h] is simply the aspirated congener of this plosive. So we have the proportion: [b]:[p^h]::[0]:[0^h]; manifested as *bit:pit::it:hit*, for example.

Whereas [b] and [pʰ] are distinguished by other properties also, [0] and [0ʰ] differ only by virtue of aspiration. Where aspiration is lacking, as in syllable-final position, the latter contrast is absent, and we simply have no coda. /0/ ≠ /0ʰ/ is also not manifested foot-medially, except marginally for speakers who distinguish the medial transitions in *neon* and *Meehan,* and in *Graham* and *mayhem* (if indeed the latter is single-footed). But for many speakers the alveolar plosives are neutralised in this position also, as a flap. The opposition is also neutralised in clusters, though earlier in the history of English there would appear to have existed a contrast between e.g. [0l-] and [0ʰl-], once [h] could no longer be regarded as a variant of /x/ — i.e. in the Middle English descendants of Old English forms like *hleapan* 'jump', cf. *leap* 'basket'; and some accents preserve a contrast between /0w/ and /0ʰw/, as in *witch* vs. *which,* parallel to that between the onsets in *twirl* and *dwarf.* After /s/ there is also neutralisation, but so too with full plosives (*bit/pit/spit,* etc.). I suggest it is not implausible, then, that the onset in English is obligatory and that its head is a plosive which may be phonetically unrealised; further, that the /0/ ≠ /0ʰ/ contrast is neutralised foot-medially and in most clusters, and realised as [0]. If this contrast is simply absent as such in codas — neither /0/, /0ʰ/ nor their neutralisation occurs there — codas are not obligatory, which seems to be appropriate.

A primary status for plosive onsets is also suggested by the prevalence of fortition rather than lenition or at least resistance to lenition in word- and foot-initial position. Thus, initially, Indo-European [bʰ] develops, possibly through [β], to [b] in Old English, for example; whereas medially between voiced sounds we get [v], unless the [b] is 'protected' by another (i.e. except in gemination): cf. *beam* [b-] 'tree', *giefan* [-v-] 'give', *hebban* [-bb-] 'heave'. See for details Lass & Anderson (1975: Ch. V, 2). Notice, however, that, unlike them (Ch. V, 1.3.1), I regard aspiration and affrication as manifestations of strengthening: the only way to strengthen voiceless stops is to create complex segments. These may eventually, it is true, be simplified as the corresponding fricatives; but this is particularly associated with medial position, whereas affrication and aspiration as such are typically position-free or characteristic of initial position (as in English) — cf. Zabrocki (1951) on e.g. Armenian (Ch. V) and Lass & Anderson (1975: Ch. V, 1) on various developments in the Indo-European, Uralic and Dravidian groups. Again, plosives are the preferred onsets.

DA 1″ also creates stemmata which, with the exception of the (on any analysis) aberrant initial /s/ + plosive clusters, conform to the alternating pattern of direction of modification we have established for constructions from the rhyme upwards. Consider the tabulations of (42) in this regard:

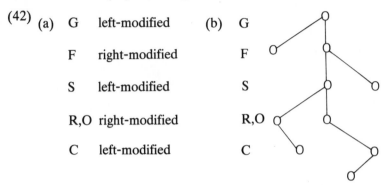

(42) (a) G   left-modified   (b) G

     F   right-modified   F

     S   left-modified   S

     R,O right-modified   R,O

     C   left-modified   C

(O = onset, C = coda). At each successive level the direction of modification switches. I have characterised the group and foot as homogeneous (section 3), and the syllable and rhyme as heterogeneous. The onset and coda are intermediate in this respect: both head and modifier are a {C} segment; but the modifier must have less {C}.

7.

We have thus far failed to consider nuclei which are themselves complex, in involving a long monophthong or diphthong. The existence of restrictions operative in the structure of long vowels (e.g. in English: */ɛ:/, */uɪ/ provides motivation for a constituent within the rhyme which excludes the coda. I shall consequently assume for English a dependency assignment which precedes DA 1 (of any variety) and creates complex nuclei. At first glance the formulation of this appears to be rather simple; perhaps of the character of (43):

(43)   DA 0: NUCLEUS FORMATION:
        Given two vowels a, b, where a < b, a → b.

Since DA Ø requires the presence of two distinct vowel segments (a<b), it does not involve a claim that the nucleus is an obligatory construction.

The derivation for e.g. *pipe* thus emerges as in (44):

(44)   (a)

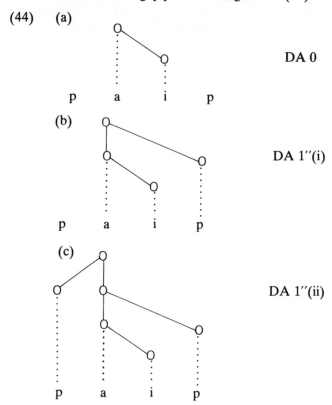

This derivation assumes that /i/ fails to govern /p/ (by DA 1″(i)) and thus create ambidependency on the basis of the convention suggested in (45):

(45)   MODIFIER CONVENTION:
        A modifier is not available for headhood to be sub-
        sequently conferred on it.

We return below to a consideration of the appropriateness (or otherwise) of such a convention. Such configurations as are assigned in (44) are supported by the existence both of constraints holding of intra-nuclear constructions and of constraints holding between the coda and the nucleus as a whole: recall e.g. the restrictions on /aṷ/ tabulated in (5) above.

However, it may be that we should allow for pre- as well as

post-nucleic modification. — I shall designate the head of the
nucleus the NUCLEIC segment. What I specifically have in mind
is the status of [ju:] in English, which suggests just such an interpretation. Say this sequence is represented lexically as /iuu/, i.e.
as a sequence of three vowels, further differentiation being
redundant. Then the modification to DA 0 incorporated in (46):

(46)   DA 0′: NUCLEUS FORMATION:
        Given two vowels, a, b, where a < b:
        (i) a → b iff b is weak, i.e. ~ ∃ vowel c (≠ b), b → c;
        (ii) otherwise, b → a.

will provide a derivation for, say, *cute* as in (47):

(47)   (a)

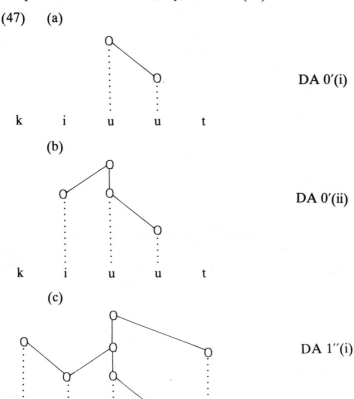

(d)

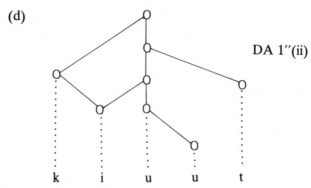

DA 1″(ii)

k　　i　u　　u　t

The ambidependency which (46) creates in the case of /i/ in (c/d) is appropriate, given that this /i/ is involved in restrictions with both the following nucleus (only /u:/ may follow) and the preceding onset (*/ʃi-/, */ʒi-/) — and indeed many varieties of English reject any preceding coronal: */di̭-/, *ti̭-/, etc.; thus *duke, tune,* etc. lack a /-i-/. However, /i̭/ in (c) can be made dependent on /k/ only if it is a non-vowel (cf. (35)). Thus, consequent upon the application of DA 0′(ii) the /i/ must be reinterpreted as a sonorant consonant, which like pre-nuclear sonorant /u/ in e.g. *quiff,* is eligible for dependency on a preceding more consonantal segment:

(48)　　{|V|} $\Longrightarrow$ $\left\{ \begin{matrix} |V| \\ | \\ C \end{matrix} \right\}$ $/ - \overset{\leq}{\leftarrow}$ {|V|}

i.e. it is reinterpreted immediately before a governing vowel. This replicates many historical changes, and indeed in large part the redundancy rule which applies to other instances of pre-vocalic /i/ and /u/. Before /u:/ the rule is simply delayed until the vowel

(49)

G
F
S
O,R
e-N,C
N

following /i/ is made to govern it.[16]

These nuclear structures maintain the pattern of reversal of direction of modification we have already established, as shown diagrammatically in (49) (where N = nucleus, e-N = extended nucleus).

Both the head and the modifier in (e-)nuclear structures are vowels: so the constructions are homogeneous. But, unlike the group and the foot, they are not obligatory constructions; and they occupy the other pole of the hierarchy.

The separability of nucleus formation suggests that the formulation of syllable and rhyme formation might be improved upon — at least, rendered more transparent — if we separate off cluster formation, as DA 0.2 (taking nucleus formation (46) to be DA 0.1, given that they are mutually exclusive):

(50)　(a) DA 0.1: NUCLEUS FORMATION: = (46).
　　　(b) DA 0.2: CLUSTER FORMATION:
　　　　　Given consonants a, b, where a < b:
　　　　　(i) a → b iff b is weak, i.e. $\{C\}_a \supset \{C\}_b$;
　　　　　(ii) otherwise, b → a.
　　　　(where we can provide for an obligatory status for onsets by allowing a = b)
　　　(c) DA 1‴: SYLLABLE FORMATION:
　　　　　Given segments a, b, where a ≤ b:
　　　　　(i) (rhyme formation) a → b iff b is weak, i.e. a ≡ $\{|V|\}$;
　　　　　(ii) otherwise, b → a.

This allows for derivations such as that for *strike* presented in (51):

(51)　(a)

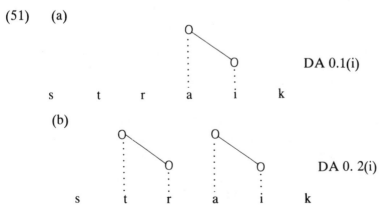

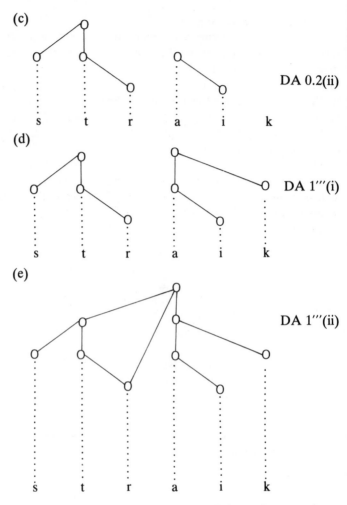

(c) ... DA 0.2(ii)

s   t   r   a   i   k

(d) ... DA 1'''(i)

s   t   r   a   i   k

(e) ... DA 1'''(ii)

s   t   r   a   i   k

(DA 0.1(ii) is inapplicable.) Application of dependency assignment rules like (50a) rests on the assumption that they cannot
reverse previous dependency assignments. This follows from the
DPC, given here as (52):

(52)   DEPENDENCY PRESERVATION CONDITION:
        Dependency relations are preserved, where possible,
        throughout a derivation (and in diachronic changes).

Thus, the /t/ → /s/ dependency established by DA 0.2(ii) cannot
be reversed by application of DA 1'''(i).

Ambidependencies are again created by unrestricted application of the DA rules, as in the case of /r/ in (51e); i.e. if we assume the non-applicability of the SPC (39). There is no strong motivation for the /a/-/r/ dependency. However, an alternative to appeal to SPC would be to eliminate such dependencies by a generalisation of the modifier convention (45), as in, say, (53):

(53)   MODIFIER CONVENTION (GENERALISED):
       A modifier is not available for subsequent dependency assignment.

whereby a modifier is exempted from application of any subsequent DA rules. This would ensure that only the heads of consonant clusters participate in rhyme and syllable structure as dependents.

But we now have a motivation for retention of ambidependency in the form of the characterisation of the distribution of the /i̯/ in (47), etc. On the other hand, this is clearly a rather special case, given that /i̯/ must change its categorial status via (48) in order for both DA 0.1 and DA 0.2 to apply. And the configuration resulting from unrestricted application of DA 0 and DA 1''' is quite distinctive:

(54)

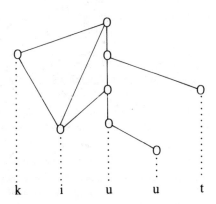

```
k       i       u       u       t
```

/i̯/ is dependent to its right by application of DA 0.1(ii), to its left by DA 0.2(i) and to its right again by DA 1'''(ii). This last dependency, the right-dependency of /r/ in (51e) and the left-dependency of /n/ in (38) are eliminated by either SPC or the generalised modifier convention. Exemption of the results of applying both DA 0.1 and 0.2 with respect to the /i̯/ of (54) can be associated with its change in categorial status.

However, some fresh considerations relevant to the status of ambidependency are introduced by a contemplation of syllables in sequence, to which we now turn.

8.

In polysyllabic words unrestricted application of DA 1''' (or, for that matter, DA 1') creates ambidependency, specifically ambisyllabicity, like that in (55):[17]

(55)

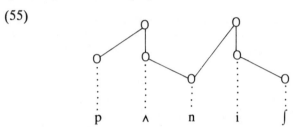

p   ʌ   n   i   ʃ

At this stage SPC is inapplicable. If we assume DA applies simultaneously to all syllable-forming sequences in a word, the modifier convention (53) could be used to eliminate ambisyllabicity — but, as we shall see, inappropriately.

Moreover, avoidance of ambisyllabicity would complicate the rules of syllable structure. Adoption of medial syllabifications whereby the initial cluster in a syllable is maximal at the expense of the preceding syllable (/n/ in (55) belongs uniquely with the second syllable), i.e. INITIAL MAXIMALIST SYLLABIFICATION, or of the reverse (/n/ belongs uniquely with the first syllable), i.e. FINAL MAXIMALIST, complicates the formulation of the constraints on syllable structure. Either word-final codas (even laying aside hypermetrical coronals) are more complex than medial ones (given the initial maximalist assumption) or word-initial onsets are more complex than medial ones (given final maximalism). Allowing the ambisyllabicity resulting from the GENERAL MAXIMALIST assumption and predicted by DA 1''' permits the most general statement of syllable structure constraints: all syllables without hypermetricality conform to a single pattern.

Anderson (1975), Anderson & Jones (1977) and Jones (1976) argue further that this ambisyllabicity is appropriate to further generalisations; specifically that such representations are crucial to the characterisation of the notion 'weak cluster', which is relevant to, among other things, the determination of the intralexical foot head.

Application of the modifier convention (53) would eliminate the right-dependency of /n/ in (55): i.e. all medial syllables would be final maximalist. This would be quite inappropriate: quite apart from the evidence that pre-foot-formation syllabifications are general maximalist, post-foot-formation syllables are, as we shall see, either also general maximalist or initial maximalist (the syllable ends where the next begins, where each initial is maximal). I shall be suggesting below on other grounds that we abandon (53) in favour of SPC: its inappropriateness here lends further support for this decision. However, we can anyway prevent (53) from applying at this point if we exempt ambidependencies where the governors do not belong to the same construction. But, on the other hand, the failure of SPC to apply here follows from the nature of the condition itself: there are no multiple paths; no additional restriction is required. We return below to consider what happens when foot structure is assigned. Let us at this point briefly review the 'weak cluster' argument for pre-foot-formation ambisyllabicity.

A consideration of familiar verb forms like those in (56):

(56)   (a)   punish, hurry
        (b)   maintain, lambaste
        (c)   agree, attend

suggests that a formulation of foot-formation such as (57) might be appropriate:

(57)   DA 2: FOOT FORMATION:
        Given syllabics a, b, where a ≤ b:
        (i) a → b iff b is weak, i.e. b is head of a rhyme of the form |b (→ [C])| #;
        (ii) otherwise, a = b, b → a.

In (i) b is weak if the rhyme consists only of b or optionally a dependent consonant preceding a word boundary, thus allowing for the penultimate stress in (56a). By (ii), the final syllables in (56b/c) form a foot on their own. We return below to the pre-final syllables in such forms; by DA 2(ii) as it stands they should all form feet, but only those in (b) do.

In nouns and derived adjectives, as again is well known, a final syllable that does not have a complex nucleus is 'ignored' by the foot-forming rule: it is hypermetrical. Contrast (58a) with (b/c):

(58)   (a)   degree, terrain
        (b)   repentant, alliance
        (c)   cinema, anathema

In (58a) the final nucleus is complex, and thus the syllable is not hypermetrical but is assigned headship of a foot by DA 2(ii). The other examples have simplex final nuclei, the final syllable thus being hypermetrical; and headship is therefore conferred on the penultimate (b) by DA 2(ii) or the prepenult (c) by DA 2(i). Observe that this is rather different in one significant respect from Hayes's (1982) account, whereby final stress is allowed on (58a) by virtue of ordering assignment of 'extrametricality' after assignment of stress to final complex nuclei. I am assuming that such extrinsic ordering devices should not be available to the phonology on account of their undesirable power. The account suggested below does not require appeal to the 'extrametricality' of such syllables.

Consider now the syllabification. The penult of (58c) is weak: given the 'invisibility' of the final syllable, it will indeed meet the criterion for weakness suggested in DA 2(i), whether the /m/ follows or precedes the syllable boundary, or if it is ambisyllabic. Similarly, the penultimate in *alliance* is unproblematically strong. But in order for *repentant* to have a strong penult, that syllable must contain both consonants following the nucleus. This is allowed for on a final maximalist assumption or if we assume ambisyllabicity of the /t/. But on neither assumption, apparently, do we account for the fact that the penultimates in (59) are strong:

(59)   pentathlon, interregnum

in that only one of the consonants following the penultimate nucleus is tautosyllabic with it. How are we to resolve this discrepancy?

A consideration of the syllabifications in (60):

(60)   (a)   cin-em-a
        (b)   rep-ent-ant
        (c)   alg-eb-ra
        (d)   pent-ath-lon
        (e)   as-best-os

and (61):

(61)   (a)   ci-ne-ma
        (b)   re-pen-tant
        (c)   al-ge-bra
        (d)   pen-tath-lon
        (e)   as-be-stos

which are based respectively on final maximalist and initial maximalist assumptions, reveals that they yield classes which include the relevant set of weak rhymes but are over-inclusive. Only the penults in (a) and (c) function as weak; but in (60) these are grouped in terms of syllabification with (d) and in (61) with (e), which are both strong, in attracting stress. And the initial maximalist syllabifications of (61) are incompatible with the characterisation of weakness given in DA 2 (57). In neither case do we seem to have appropriate definitions of 'weak cluster', as one rejecting stress on the preceding nucleus.

   If, however, we assume ambisyllabicity, such that both initials and finals are maximal, then we characterise the weak syllables in these forms as those whose rhyme contains only a dependent consonant which is also dependent to its right, as revealed in (62):

(62)   (a)

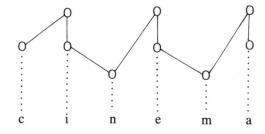

c   i   n   e   m   a

        (b)

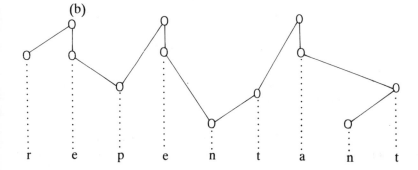

r   e   p   e   n   t   a   n   t

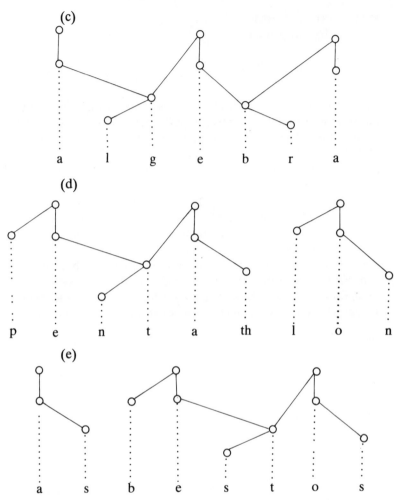

(c)

a l g e b r a

(d)

p e n t a th i o n

(e)

a s b e s t o s

in which this condition is met only by the penults in (62a) and (c). This suggests that we should modify DA 2 (57) as in (63):

(63) DA 2′: FOOT FORMATION:
      Given syllabics a, b, where a ≤ b:
      (i) a → b iff b is weak, i.e. b is head of a rhyme of the
      form |b (→ {C})| ←/ #;
      (ii) otherwise, a = b, b → a

That is, weakness is constituted by a rhyme which contains (apart from the rhyme head) only a consonant either followed by a word boundary or dependent to the right. Otherwise, b is strong, is identical in precedence to a and forms a foot on its own.

The assignment of intralexical foot heads thus depends crucially on the ambisyllabic representations assigned as a result of the application of DA 1‴. This adds further support for their appropriateness additional to their role in simplifying the statement of the constraints on syllable structure and their compatibility with (failure to infringe) SPC.

9.

I assume once more that hypermetrical segments, in this case syllabics, are assigned by a modified SSC (33), which can be generalised and relativised to construction-types as in (64):

(64)   SSC′:
        Given segments a, b, c, where a ≤ b ≤ c and where c is unassigned by the current DA rule, a → c; with respect to DA 1‴, a < b < c, a → b.

The last provision allows for the fact that, whereas in the case of the coronals which are hypermetrical with respect to DA 1‴ another segment or construction (b) dependent on a must intervene, with the final syllables of nouns and derived adjectives which are hypermetrical with respect to DA 2′, there need be no intervening syllabic, as with (58b) vs. (c), so that a = b.

Application of DA 2′ and SSC′ gives the derivation in (65), starting from (62a):

(65)   (a)

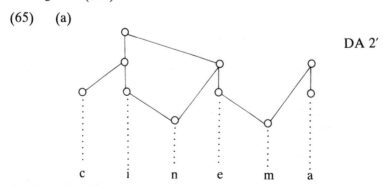

DA 2′

(b)

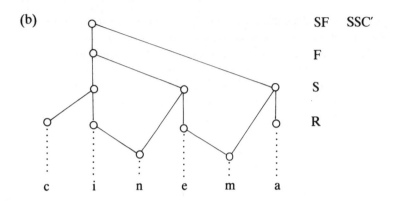

which creates a superfoot (SF).

Some suffixes render the preceding syllable hypermetrical as well as themselves, as illustrated in (66):[18]

(66)　(a)　álimony, ádvocacy, malígnancy
　　　　(b)　pálliative, génerative, delíberative, rebárbative

Notice, for instance, that the penult in *malignancy* is strong according to DA 2′; absence of stress is attributable to hypermetricality. If the prepenult is weak, then the result in such instances is a foot of four syllables, two of them hypermetrical. Again SSC′ must be iterative (cf. (34)).

It is possible to establish some independent evidence for configurations like that in (65b), containing a superfoot. But firstly we must examine the effects of foot formation on syllabification and, before that, conclude our discussion of foot formation itself.

10.

Some words show two or more sequences of syllables constituting feet. Consider examples like those in (67):

(67)　(a)　índicátion, réstitútion
　　　　(b)　próstitúte, pédigrée

In (67a) the penultimate syllable is strong and so forms a foot (of which it is the head) with the final syllable. The prepenult is weak; it forms the second syllable of a foot whose head is the first syllable of the word. The final syllable in (67b) is strong by DA 2′ (63) and so forms a foot on its own, whereas the penult is weak and forms a foot with the preceding (initial) syllable. Strong initial syllables followed by a foot head are also foot heads. Consider the bipedal forms in (69):

(68)   (a)   reáction, péntáthlon, ásbéstos
        (b)   rébáte, mándáte, áthléte

which contain a strong syllable followed by a complex foot (a) or which consist of only two strong syllables (b).

Forms like those in (69), however:

(69)   (a)   múlligatáwny, ábracadábra
        (b)   ánecdóte, stálagmíte

suggest that non-final non-monosyllabic feet in nouns may display hypermetricality. (69a) contain two feet the first of which is a superfoot, in that it contains a hypermetrical third syllable. The second syllable in each of (69b) is apparently strong by DA 2′ but does not take the headship of a foot; this is allowed for if it is a hypermetrical syllable with a simplex nucleus, as allowed with respect to DA 2′.

Hayes (1982) suggests that 'extrametricality' might be restricted to the right edges of words (though he notes some apparent counter-examples). Adoption of an account involving hypermetricality in the present instances (and see further section 14) means that it cannot be so restricted. I suggest that the restriction involves rather the SSC: it applies only to the right edge of right-modified constructions.

I return below (section 13) to the nature of the restriction on pre-final feet consisting of three syllables. Notice already, however, that the presence of many suffixes does not permit a medial hypermetrical ('weak retractors'); thus contrast (70a) and (b):

(70)   (a)   sólenoíd, páranóid
        (b)   mollúscóid, aráchnóid
        (c)   cýlindróid

Only if the penultimate is weak does it reject foot headship, as in (a). The strong penults in (b) are not treated as hypermetrical and assume the headship of a foot. Instances like (70c) I assume to be underlyingly disyllabic (cf. note 12), with eventual syllabification of the hypermetrical sonorant or insertion of a weak vowel. Cf. too *Hottentot, Jackendoff*, with initial stress: again I take the medial syllable to originate in a hypermetrical sonorant coronal. (Kiparsky (1979) and Hayes (1982) suggest instead a rule de-stressing the penultimate of a trisyllabic form which contains a sonorant.)

The first syllables in *pedigree* and *anecdote* are not strong, but they are nevertheless foot heads. However, in the case of the former foot head status is ensured by DA 2′(i), in that the initial syllable is followed by a weak syllable, provided that the medial is not counted as hypermetrical. But in *anecdote* the medial is clearly hypermetrical: it is strong by DA 2′. However, in that case the first syllable will be assigned headhood of a foot by SSC′ (64), specifically under the case where a = b.

As we have observed, some pre-foot head initials are not themselves foot heads (recall (56c) vs. (b)). This will be so if the rhyme of the initial syllable contains only, apart from the nucleus, a consonant which depends to its right, as required by DA 2′(i) (63). Compare (71a) and (b):

(71)   (a)   applause, degree
        (b)   Attlee, (68)

The first syllable in (71a) is weak by DA 2′; whereas that in (68) and (71b) either is complex or ends in a post-nuclear consonant, such as the /t/ in *Attlee*, which cannot open the final syllable and thus is not dependent to its right. In this case it constitutes a foot head. (Exceptional here are forms like *éssay, sátire, Híttite* — cf. e.g. Liberman & Prince 1977: 2.5, 2.8.) One problem with assuming the application of DA 2′ with respect to the initial syllables in (71a) is the apparent absence of an a element, if we take the initial syllables to be a weak b. I am assuming that the a position where the b element is an initial weak syllable, as in (71a), is occupied by a 'silent stress', i.e. an unrealised foot head: see further 14 below.

With monosyllabic words like *man* that are weak by DA 2′ it is obviously undesirable to suggest such an interpretation: i.e. that they form the modifier in a foot whose head is a 'silent stress'. Such monosyllables are themselves intralexical foot heads, and, if they belong to lexical categories, constitute utterance foot heads, as with *go* in (15) and (16) above. Rather, I suggest that monosyllables are hypermetrical; DA 2′ will fail to apply at all in their case, and they will achieve foot headship by virtue of SSC′ (64), under the option whereby a = b = c. Monosyllabic words are hypermetrical foot heads.

I conclude this section with some examples of three-footed words, wherein foot formation is again in accord with DA 2′:

(72)   (a)   /extra/metri/cality
       (b)   /io/ni/sation
       (c)   /monophthon/gi/sation

The final syllable in (a) and the third in (c) are hypermetrical.[19] As indicated, we return in 13 to a consideration of some of the constraints imposed on multipedal words, particularly those involving hypermetricality.

11.

Foot formation creates constructions within which ambi-dependencies (the ambisyllabicity resulting from DA 1‴) hold at that point. However, it would appear that these are not simplified in accordance, retroactively (!), with the modifier convention (53). A configuration like that in (73):

(73)

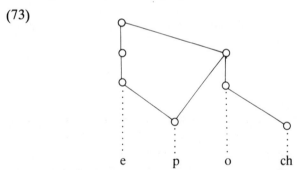

e   p   o   ch

is simplified not by elimination of the arc linking /p/ and the following vowel (the dependency relation introduced later, by DA 1‴(ii) rather than by DA 1‴(i)) but rather by removal of the dependency on the stressed vowel which precedes. Phonetically, intervocalic consonants following a stressed long vowel belong uniquely with the following syllable (Fallows 1981). This is in accordance with SPC (39), in that, once foot formation creates a double path from *e* to *p*, only the longer path (measured in adjunctions) is retained. We have further support for preferring SPC to the modifier convention.

There is, however, an interesting limitation on the applicability of SPC in this case. After short vowels ambisyllabicity is retained. Contrast (74a) and (b):

(74)   (a)   Petrie, epoch
         (b)   petrol, epic

The medial plosives in (74a) are aspirated and without glottal reinforcement, as befits a syllable initial; compare the glottalised forms in (1) above. However, the medial plosives in (b) are both aspirated and glottalised (cf. Higginbottom 1964; Anderson 1969); i.e. they display the characteristics of both syllable-initial and syllable-final position. Compare also Fallow's (1981) experimental observations, which accord with Jespersen's description of the distinction between such as (74a) and (b) as one of 'open contact' between the nucleus and the following consonant vs. 'close contact' (1969: 12.6). All of this strongly suggests the appropriateness of an interpretation attributing ambisyllabicity to (74b). Presumably, as Giegerich (1984) suggests, this is associated with the provision of weight for stressed syllables.

Further evidence for ambisyllabicity after short vowels is provided by the failure of /i/ to tense in the first syllable of a word like *pity*. In an open syllable /i/ is eligible for tensing: recall (3) above, and contrast the closed syllables in (4). Indeed, as we observed in section 1, /i/ does not occur at all finally in stressed syllables. This suggests that the first syllable in *pity*, unlike the second, is closed, here by the following plosive. Again this is provided for by the assumption that ambisyllabicity is retained after short vowels.

Ambisyllabicity is also abandoned quite generally, however, at the boundaries of feet; feet-final syllables are finally minimal: they end at the beginning of the following (stressed, initial maximalist) syllable. Thus, in a two-footed form like *pedigree* the *gr* sequence belongs uniquely to the second foot. And we can contrast the medial plosives in (75), which are foot-initial:

(75)   patrol, depict

with those in (74b) in lacking glottalisation; rather, like those in (74a), they show simply the aspiration associated with syllable-initial position. We return below to the principle governing foot-boundary syllabification; clearly, it doesn't follow from the SPC, which would in these favour final maximalism.

At this point, however, we can return to the kind of superfoot structure proposed at the beginning of 9: recall, e.g., (65b). We are now in a position to offer some independent support for such a structure — rather than, say, one in which the final two syllables are co-dependents of the same node.

Notice in the first place that in such a form as the first in (76):

(76)   pentecost, pederast

the /k/ is aspirated and unglottalised, suggesting that it is not ambisyllabic. This follows from the occurrence of a foot boundary between the second and third syllables, given that feet are finally minimalist. Observe further that the vowels in the final syllables in (76) also fail to be eligible for reduction. Now, one thing that inhibits vowel reduction is the presence in the same syllable of an onset that is not shared with the preceding syllable. (On the importance of syllable structure with respect to the possibility of vowel reduction, see e.g. Ross 1972; Anderson & Ewen, to appear: Ch. 2.) Compare (77), with ambisyllabic medials and vowel reduction in the following syllable:

(77)   hónest, módest, hárassed, búttock

with (78), where a medial consonant belongs entirely with the final syllable and the vowel of that syllable does not reduce;

(78)   íncest, prótest, gýmnast, époch

Again, the non-reducibility of the final syllables in (76) can be associated with the absence of ambisyllabicity conditioned by a foot boundary.[20]

12.

In the cases we have considered, the stray segment convention, as embodied in SSC′ (64), applies at the right edge of right-modified constructions, the rhyme and the foot. This seems to be rather typical, certainly for English. And it may be related to the preference for enclisis in foot-prominent languages (recall section 1 above): SSC′ provides a means of accommodating unintegrated segments and syllables without destroying the integrity of the constructions. This is not possible with, for instance, pre-foot-head stray syllables.

Are there other similarities between the right-modified constructions? Recall, for example, that ambidependency is retained, in certain circumstances, within the foot (cf. (74b)). It seems appropriate, in the light of this, to return to our discussion of ambidependency within the syllable, and, specifically, within the right-modified rhyme.

By the end of section 8/ we had concluded that ambidependencies within the syllable could be eliminated, if this is appropriate, by deployment of either the generalised modifier convention (53) or of SPC (39). These do not, however, always yield the same results. For instance, whereas (53) (or (45)) assures a rhyme of the form of (44c), if, on the other hand, we drop (53), thus creating ambidependency, as in (79):

(79)

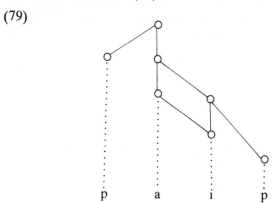

p   a   i   p

then application of SPC will give (80), given an obligatory status for the rhyme in English:

(80)

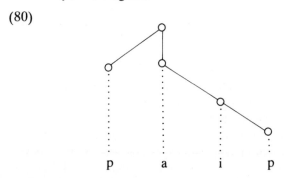

p   a   i   p

In other instances, (39) and (53) yield the same result, as in the case of (40).

The regularities holding within the foot suggest: (a) that the modifier convention (53) be dropped, given the preference shown for (39); (b) that ambidependencies in the syllable also may be (partially) retained. What I am going to suggest is that ambi-dependencies are retained within the other right-modified construction, the rhyme; whereas there is no evidence for ambi-dependency within the syllable as such (with the exception of the /i̯/ of /i̯u:/), i.e. involving the onset and the syllabic as well as nucleus and coda. Thus, I assume that ambidependencies among left-subordinates of the syllabic are eliminated by SPC (39); while within the rhyme, just as partially within the foot, ambi-dependencies are retained, compatible with other constraints. Let us now consider what kind of evidence there might be for this.

Crucial here is evidence that a sonorant in the position of the /n/ in /sprint/ continues to be dependent on the preceding vowel, as in (38), rather than simply on the following consonant, as in (40).

Much of the discussion of Anderson & Jones (1977; and cf. already Anderson & Jones 1974: 3) is devoted to trying to show that a large range of 'processes' (lengthenings, mutations) in the history of English is associated with two specific environments and that these environments are associated with very similar processes. These two environments are: syllables whose rhymes contain a sonorant and another consonant, and feet in which the two syllables are separated by a single consonant.

For instance, the process of BREAKING in Old English is associated with the sequences /l/ or /r/ + a consonant (*eald* 'old', *heorte* 'heart'), where /l/ and /r/ are 'back' (Lass & Anderson 1975: Ch. III, 4),[21] and we find the diphthong sequences [æa̯] ‹ea› and [eo̯] ‹eo› in place of simple [æ] and [e] (cf. *bæc* 'back', *bed(d)* 'bed'). The same modification is associated with another environment, that for BACK UMLAUT, whereby stressed front vowels diphthongise before a back vowel where no more than one consonant intervenes (*ealu* 'ale', *heofon* 'heaven'). Given the dependency of the sonorant associated with breaking on the preceding vowel, we can characterise what these two environments have in common in terms of (81):

(81) $\{\{|V|\} \{i\}\}_a \overset{\le}{\to} \{\{C \not\to\} \{\sim i\}\}_b, \{C\}_c;$
       where a is a foot head (stressed) and b $<$ c iff b $\equiv \{C\}$.

i.e. a front vowel governs a back sonorant and another consonant; and the two environments are differentiated with respect to the second condition, which relates the relative position of the b and c elements to the consonantality of b. If b is consonantal we get (82a); otherwise (b):

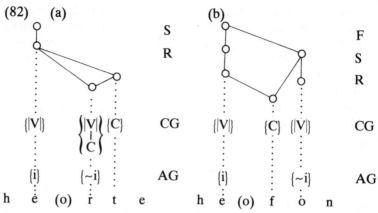

The outer braces in (81) enclose segments, the inner gestures; 'C ↛' is a segment in which |C| does not govern, i.e. either a vowel or a sonorant consonant; CG in (82) = categorial gesture, AG = articulatory gesture.

The skeleton of the characterisation in (81), viz. {|V|} $\overset{\leq}{\to}$ {C ↛}, {C}, recurs in a number of processes throughout the history of English, with and without the second condition of (81). The collapsibility of (82a) and (b) and the like depends on the retention of ambisyllabicity in rhymes, specifically the retention of the dependency of a pre-consonantal sonorant on the preceding nucleus.

A rather more compact illustration of the equivalence of the two manifestations of such a skeleton (in Anderson & Jones's (1977) terms, a 'vowel-strengthening schema') allowed for by the condition is provided by an attempt to formulate those aspects of the shape of the stem which determine selection of the appropriate Dutch diminutive suffix in the examples of (83):

(83) (a) ui 'onion' — uitje
      (b) maan 'moon' — maantje
      (c) urn 'urn' — urntje
      (d) deksel 'lid' — dekseltje
      (e) bal 'ball' — balletje
      (f) wandeling 'walk' — wandelingetje
      (g) jak 'jacket' — jakje; mand 'basket' — mandje

(Examples are from Ewen 1978, 1980a: Ch.11), which provide a detailed discussion of this phenomenon.) We find -*tje* rather than -*etje* or -*je*[22] after a long vowel (a), after a long vowel + a sonorant (b), after a short vowel + two sonorants (c), after a form consisting of a disyllabic foot which ends in a sonorant (d); -*etje* is associated with forms containing a short vowel followed by a single sonorant (e) and two-footed forms whose second foot is of the same character as the single foot in (e), i.e. as in (f). After obstruents we find -*je*.

As implied by the preceding description, the forms selecting -*etje* can be characterised as ending as in (84):

(84) $\{|V|\}_a \overset{\leq}{\to} \{|V| \to C\}_b|$, where a is a foot head.

(The foot head governs to its right only a sonorant consonant.) For the -*je* forms we have (85):

(85) $\{|V|\}_a \overset{\leq}{\to} \{ \nrightarrow C\}_b$, where a is a foot head.

What is of interest, however, in the present context is what unites the forms taking -*tje*. We can associate the configurations in (86) with the corresponding forms in (83):

(86)   (a)   (b)

What characterises these configurations is the requirement in (87):

(87) $\{|V|\}_a \overset{\leq}{\to} \{C \not\to \}_b \to \{C \not\to \}_c;$
        where a is a foot head and a = b iff c $\equiv$ $\{|V|\}$.

which includes both the monosyllables of (86a-c) and the
disyllable of (d). In the monosyllables a → c; in the open monosyllable (a), a = b, in conformity with the second condition. Again,
the characterisation of this class depends upon the retention of
ambidependency within the rhyme; only then do (86a-c) show a
configurational correspondence with the disyllabic (d).

Notice finally some further support for the retention of
ambidependency in configurations like that in (79), (86a) and
(86b). Unrestricted application of DA 0.1 and DA 1''' will assign
two dependency relations to the two vowels that make up the
diphthong in forms like *buy*, one nuclear (the first vowel is head of
the nucleus), the other as part of rhyme structure (the first vowel is
head of the rhyme): cf. (86a). Given that the second vowel is a
rhyme- as well as a nucleus-modifier we can formulate in the most
general way the requirement that stressed rhymes in English
always contain a modifier: /bat/, /bai/, */ba/. At the same time
the distinctiveness of the restrictions on complex nuclei requires
that the two vowels in e.g. (79) also belong to a construction which
does not include the following consonant: this is ensured by application of DA 0.1 prior to DA 1'''.

I conclude, then, that ambidependency is retained within right-
modified constructions, partially within the foot (after a foot head
with a simplex nucleus) and totally within the rhyme. I am not
aware of evidence for retention within non-right-modified
structures like the syllable. Where it is not retained, ambidependency is apparently resolved in accordance with SPC (39),
except in the case of ambidependencies holding across a foot
boundary. Now, the foot, which appears to be the maximal domain
for ambidependency, has ambidependencies at its boundaries
resolved in such a way as to maximise foot- and thus syllable-
initials at the expense of finals. This is also true of the
ambidependencies within the foot, whose resolution we have been
attributing to the application of SPC. And intrasyllabic resolution
also maximises the onset, though at its other margin, by the
elimination of superfluous dependencies on the syllabic (as with
the /r/ in (51e)). Perhaps then we can dispense with appeal to

SPC in these cases also in favour of a general requirement that in the resolution of ambidependencies onsets are maximised.

13.

We can now proceed to a consideration of the dependency relations holding between foot heads. In multi-footed forms, the first of two foot heads will normally govern the second only if the second is monosyllabic; together they form a F^2 (second-level) foot — recall the utterance-level representation in (17)). So (67/68/69b) develop a F^2 in which the first foot head governs the second, as in (88):

(88)

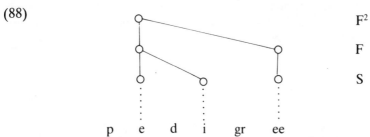

F^2

F

S

p   e   d   i   gr   ee

In (67/68/69a) the second foot is complex; so the first foot head does not govern.

We can thus formulate F^2 formation as in (89):

(89)   DA 3(i): F^2 FORMATION:
         Given foot heads a, b, where $a \leqslant b$, $a \longrightarrow b$ iff b is weak,
         i.e. $\sim \exists$ syllabic c, $b \longrightarrow c$

This gives (88) by subordination of the second foot head of the two foot heads produced by DA 2″ to the first, given that the second is not complex.

In the three-footed words in (72b/c) above, the second foot is subordinated to the first in accordance with (89): the second foot is not complex. The complex final feet are not affected by (89). However in (72a) also the second foot is governed by the first foot head even though the second foot is apparently complex. This suggests that medial foot head modifiers are hypermetrical with respect to (89):

(90)

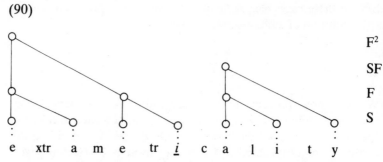

(The underlined syllabic is hypermetrical here.) Again, the complex final foot (a superfoot) is unaffected by (89).

After DA 3(i), or in its absence (if the condition is not met), groups are formed. The rightmost of two independent foot heads or the sole independent foot head in a word is assigned group headhood, as shown in (91):

(91)   (a)   i.

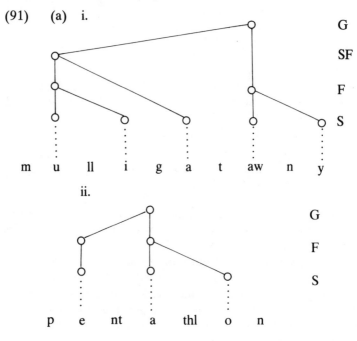

(b)   i.

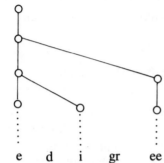

G

F²

F

S

p   e   d   i   gr   ee

ii.

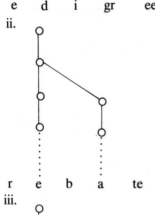

G

F²

F

S

r   e   b   a   te

iii.

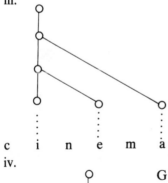

G

SF

F

S

c   i   n   e   m   a

iv.

G

F

S

m   a   n

In (91b) there is only one independent foot head in each case (after F^2 formation); so it becomes group head, head of the word-tree. In (91a) the second of two independent foot heads is head of the group.

Group formation might be formulated as in (92):

(92)   DA 3(ii): GROUP FORMATION:
        Given foot heads a, b, where a $\leqslant$ b and a $\not\rightarrow$ b, b $\rightarrow$ a.

which can obviously be collapsed with DA 3(i), with consequential elimination of the second condition (a $\not\rightarrow$ b) from (92).

DA 3(ii) will also apply to originally three-footed trees which have undergone DA 3(i), as in (90), to give (93a):

(93)   (a)

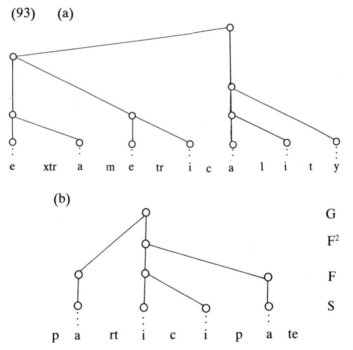

In (93b) the second foot progressively subordinates to itself the final weak one (by DA 3(i)) and the first (by DA 3(ii)).

Associated with F^2 and group formation are constraints on the feet whose heads may also be heads of such. For example, the head of a superfoot may constitute the head of a F^2 or a group but not both. Thus, the head of the superfoot in (91b.iii) is a group head but not a F^2 head, as is that in (90); while in (72c) the superfoot head is a F^2 head but not a group head; in (91a.i) it is neither. These assignments are made without recourse to the constraint. But appeal to it does account for some apparent asymmetries. Thus, in a form like that in (93b) or (94a):

(94)　(a)　Ass*i*nibóine
　　　(b)　Kálamaz*óo*
　　　(c)　ónomátop*óe*ia

where the last foot is weak and so not a group head, a superfoot cannot be formed on the basis of the preceding three syllables, in that the head of such a superfoot would be both a F^2 head and a group head. Rather, in such circumstances, hypermetricality is not available for the penultimate syllable, and the prepenult quite regularly becomes head of a foot (and F^2 and group). Contrast (91a.i); and observe that this also, of course, allows words with monosyllabic final feet which are idiosyncratically strong, as (94b), to show pre-final superfeet, in that again the superfoot is not a group head.

This seems to be a weight-reducing constraint, in limiting suprasyllabic structural depth. Similarly, four weak syllables to the left of a group head, as in (94c), are not permitted to support a superfoot: the first four syllables in (94c) constitute two binary feet, the first subordinate to the second, which is in turn subordinate to the group-head penult. See further 14 immediately below, where an attempt is made to generalise the condition just proposed, so that it will also accommodate examples like (94c), and others.

Group formation completes our account of the essentials of the formation of intralexical structure. Assignment of a lexical group head to every word is intended to characterise the fact that each word may bear an utterance tonic, though some, such as *it* in *It's a foggy day today* are extremely unlikely to do so, except for metalinguistic purposes (Werth 1983). Clearly, given the complexities associated with the structure of word-trees in English, many loose ends remain. Two of the most salient are the concern of the section which now follows.

14.

Prefixes on verbs act as hypermetrical with respect to foot

formation and, where relevant, F^2 formation. Thus, for example, the verbs in (95):

(95)   (a)   permit, submit
         (b)   underbid, reset

do not take initial stress even though the second syllable is weak by DA 2′ (63). The second syllable behaves as a monosyllable and thus achieves foot-head status (cf. 10 above). The prefixes behave as if word-final: so those in (95a) are weak by DA 2′; but those in (95b) are strong (they consist of a strong syllable or are disyllabic) and thus constitute a distinct foot. So, the prefix and stem are MUTUALLY HYPERMETRICAL.

This is true also of prefixed verb forms where the stress on the final syllable is 'regular', in that that syllable is strong, as in (96):

(96)   (a)   subsist, persist
         (b)   understand, remake

The prefixes in (a) are again weak by DA 2′, if considered word-final, whereas those in (b) are strong and thus constitute a separate foot on their own.

Given the final stress of such forms, it appears that the strong (with respect to DA 2′) prefixes in (95/96b) are also hypermetrical with respect to F^2 formation. Even though the following foot is non-complex, the heads of such prefixes do not constitute the head of a F^2. Instead group formation (DA 3(ii)) gives (97), for example:

(97)

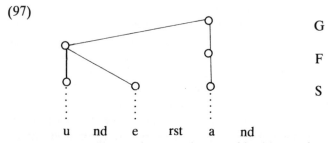

```
                                    G
                                    F
                                    S

u    nd    e    rst    a    nd
```

Contrast nouns like *underground, remould,* with two feet the first of which contains a F^2 head.

Hypermetricality with respect to F^2 formation is also character-istic of non-prefixal disyllabic two-footed verbs, such as those in (56b), and of a subset of non-derived adjectives. The first syllables of disyllabic non-derived adjectives are hypermetrical with respect to DA 3(i) if both syllables are strong: cf. *august, rotund, overt,* all with final stress, and derived forms like *nubile, schizoid,* with initial stress in conformity with DA 3(i). Adjectives with pre-final sequences which are strong by virtue of disyllabicity also show the expected (non-hypermetrical) pattern, as in *táciturn, difficult.* Verbs in which the sequence preceding the final foot contains a weak syllable which is not prefixal also do not show hyper-metricality: thus, the verb *implement* shows initial stress, with the final monosyllabic foot subordinate to the first, in accordance with DA 3(i).[23]

There remains notably the question of the initial syllables in forms like (95/96a), as well as those in *applause* and *degree* and the like, noted above (section 10): i.e. initials which are not footed. How are they to be accommodated structurally? Attachment to the following foot head would violate the status of foot as a right-mod-ified structure, and is quite unmotivated. Direct attachment to a following group head would violate the hierarchical principle, and is similarly unmotivated. The alternative of simply leaving such initials unattached is equally unpalatable, in that some word struc-tures would thereby cease to be trees. It seems preferable to associate stranded initial syllables with a preceding unrealised foot head, which will itself be attached to the following group head, ensuring a tree structure compatible with the structural properties we have so far observed. That is, *applause,* etc. will be associated with a configuration like that in (97), except that the first foot head will be unrealised; like that in (97) it will be hypermetrical.

In connected speech, at the utterance level, such a foot head will be realised as a 'silent stress' (Abercrombie 1965b,c), as in (98a):

(98)   (a) $//_\Delta$ a/ppl*au*se // greeted the per/formance //
        (b) //much a/ppl*au*se // greeted the per/formance //

where '$_\Delta$' indicates the silent stress, or is identified with a preceding foot head, as in (98b). In this way we can formulate the rhythmic expectations of such a form in terms of a lexically unrealised foot head, introduced in just these cases of stranded initials.

Given such a view of initial weak syllables, we could perhaps formulate the constraint that excludes the possibility of a superfoot in (94c) as one excluding the embedding of one group within another in (non-compound) intralexical structure. For, if syllables two, three and four in (94c) constituted a superfoot, the initial syllable would form the second part of a foot with unrealised head, and this unrealised head would be dependent on the head of the superfoot in its role as a group head, and this group head would in turn be dependent on the group head (G^2) penult. The same constraint (rather than appeal to the hypermetricality with respect to DA 3(i) of non-initial syllables in medial feet) would account for the fact that in (94c) the initial syllable as head of the first foot has the third syllable (head of the second foot) dependent on it (rather than vice versa, despite the strength of the medial syllable), forming a F^2; otherwise, a group structure would again be formed which was subordinate to the group head (G^2) penult.

The most notable exceptions to such a constraint arguably involve cyclicity. Consider the structures in (99):

(99)   (a)

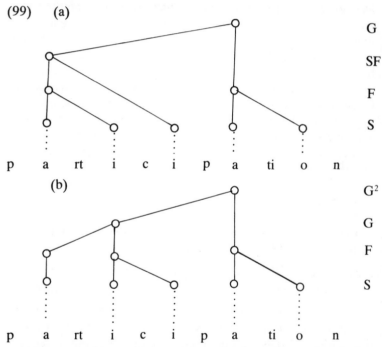

which characterise alternative pronunciations of the 'action' noun derived from (93b). (93b) is as predicted by the DA rules for a verb which contains a pre-final sequence that is not entirely pre-fixal, given the constraint on the construction of superfeet discussed in the immediately preceding section. (99a) is similarly in accord with the rules as they affect nouns, and if no account is taken of derivational structure. This is not the case with (99b).

However, (99b) can be allowed for if it involves an alternative
in whose derivation word-internal word boundaries are respected
and in which this makes a difference. That is, structure is assigned
initially in [$_N$ [$_V$ *participate*] *ion*] to the verbal constituent, as in
(93b). On the following cycle, the penultimate is made, quite
regularly, a group head, except that the node made dependent on
the final group head (the penultimate syllable) is itself a group
head rather than a foot head merely; but the rest of the structure
associated with the verb is left intact, in conformity with DPC.
Iconoclastic, for example, involves a similar alternation and similar
alternative derivations, except that there we have a denominal
adjective rather than a deverbal noun.

Formation of a G^2 structure is thus allowed if it is formed on a
distinct cycle to the G which it subordinates (cf. the discussion of
compounds in the immediately following section). Therefore,
given cyclicity, all of (99) do conform to the constraint that prevents the formation of a superfoot on syllables two-to-four of
(94c). This is distinct from the depth constraint proposed in the
preceding section. I include both of these as part of a generalised
STRUCTURAL DEPTH CONDITION, tentatively formulated in
(100):

(100)   STRUCTURAL DEPTH CONDITION:
    (a)   F, SF, F^2, G, G^2 exhaust the set of suprasyllabic con-
        structions;
    (b)   G and G^2 are assigned on different cycles;
    (c)   a superfoot head can support only one further head-
        ship.

I leave uninvestigated here the possibility of further depth
limitations. We should note, however, that (100) supplements the
syllable depth condition (31) and that, among other things, it
imposes a rather similar restriction, albeit at a higher level; viz. one
expressible as (100)′:

(100)′   GROUP DEPTH CONDITION:
    No foot head in English is more than two degrees of
    dependency from a group head.

Again, I leave aside here an investigation of the basis for this
parallelism between infra- and suprasyllabic structure.

(99), as observed, are compatible with (100), as is even, say, a
form such as *antidisestablishmentarianism*, which contains five

feet, two superfeet, a group and a G^2. Formation of a superfoot on
syllables two-to-four of (94c) is precluded by the second part of
(100), in that the second syllabic would thereby constitute a G
head dependent on the penult as G^2, both headships being
assigned on the same cycle. (100c) embodies the restriction
illustrated by (94a/b) proposed in 13 above which precluded the
formation of a superfoot in the former but not the latter case.

15.

The pattern established by DA 3 is replicated with compounds,
which are morphologically again words consisting of other words
but where the more inclusive word consists of more than one constituent word (rather than, say, one word + a suffix, as in (99)).
Group formation provides each word, including the constituents of
compounds, with a unique group head. Compounds thus present
us with competing group heads.

This is resolved in the first place — and in the regular instances!
— by application of an analogue of DA 3(i) (89), where for foot
heads in that formulation we substitute group heads:

(101)   DA 4(i): COMPOUND FOOT FORMATION:
        Given group heads a, b, where a $<$ b, a $\rightarrow$ b iff b is weak,
        i.e. $\sim \exists$ group head c, b $\rightarrow$ c.

Thus, the two component words of the compound in (102a) each
have group heads provided by DA 3(ii) (92):

(102)   (a)

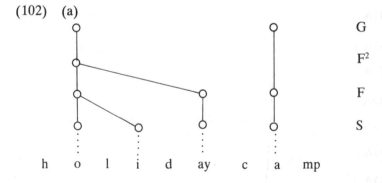

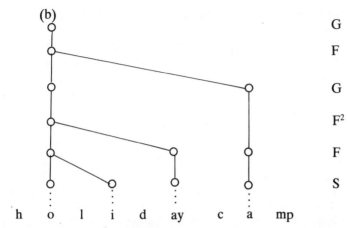

h   o   l   i   d   ay   c   a   mp

In terms of DA 4(i) the first head will govern the second by virtue of the weakness of the latter. And at this point DA 3(ii) can re-apply to assign group headship to the only eligible node in the representation for the word *holiday camp*.

DA 4(i) provides the normal pattern for two-word compounds, including formations like *monosyllable* and *television* whose initial elements behave like independent groups in assuming group head-ship with respect to the form as a whole. Notice, however, that just as the initial syllables of disyllabic non-derived adjectives like *augúst* are hypermetrical with respect to DA 3(i) (cf. 14), so the first group in compound adjectives is 'ignored' by DA 4(i): *clean-cút, skin-déep*. (So too such compound verbs as might be

(103)   [[[holiday]   [camp]]   [hostess]]

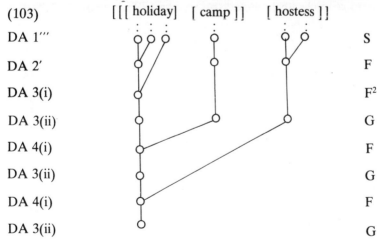

motivated.) Exceptional are some such compounds with a noun as first element: *cólour-blind.* (See further Liberman & Prince 1977: 308).

DA 4(i) applies cyclically with reference to the (morphological) constituency of the compound. So we get the derivation resulting in (103).

Each conferment of a group head coincides with the reading of a word boundary.

Cyclicity is associated with the creation of a group head for each word, which allows reapplication of DA 4(i) and, as a consequence, of DA 3(ii). It is not certain that we should associate intra-word structure with cyclicity, except that it may be appropriate within words which contain forms that are themselves words (cf. 14). However, as observed there, there seems to be no motivation for allowing cyclic application of intralexical rules to destroy previously erected structure, contrary to DPC (6), rather than simply carrying out the kind of promotion envisaged in 14.

If we assume that there are three-word compounds in English in which the latter two words form a constituent, then perhaps (104b) is an instance:

(104)   (a)   [[[winter][holiday]][camp]]
       (b)   [[winter][[holiday][camp]]]

(104a) ('camp for winter holidays') has the same morphological structure as (103), apparently — though, exceptionally, *winter* fails to constitute an F head with respect to *holiday*, which thus becomes overall group head. But (104b) is a compound (if this, rather than phrasal status, can indeed be motivated) whose second part is complex ('holiday camp for use in winter'). On the appropriate cycle DA 4(i) will thus be inapplicable.

This derivation is charted in (105):

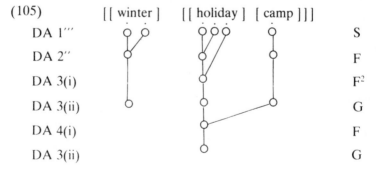

(105)   [[winter]   [[holiday] [camp]]]

DA 1'''   S

DA 2''   F

DA 3(i) F^2

DA 3(ii)   G

DA 4(i)   F

DA 3(ii)   G

At this point the derivation blocks: the configuration is eligible for neither DA 4(i), in that the second part, headed by *holiday*, is strong (it contains a dependent group head), nor DA 3(ii), which applies to foot heads not group heads.

So we need a group-head analogue to DA 3(ii), just as DA 4(i) is an analogue to DA 3(i). I give this in (106):

(106)   DA 4(ii): COMPOUND GROUP FORMATION:
Given group heads a, b, where a $<$ b, b $\rightarrow$ a.

This can be collapsed with DA 4(i) (101) as an 'otherwise' alternative.

In terms of DA 4(ii) the derivation of (104b) can be completed as in (107):

(107)

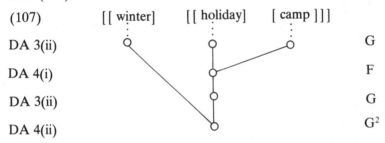

Holiday is the head of a second-level group.

Clearly, DA 3 and 4 can be collapsed. All that a unified formulation need specify is that in these cases dependency assignment applies with respect to foot *or* group heads. This will also allow for 'mixed' applications, such as that involved in the derivation of (99b) above, whereby a foot head comes to govern a node assigned group headship on the previous cycle.

16.

In all of the first parts of the dependency assignments I have formulated, the term 'weak' is used. In some instances this is clearly motivated by a parallelism in the conditions for 'weakness' that pertain. Specifically, in DA 0.1(i) (50a/46), DA 3(i) (89) and DA 4(i) (101), 'weakness' is defined as in (108):

(108) $\sim \exists$ vowel/syllabic/group head c, b $\rightarrow$ c.

'Weakness' has to do with the non-complexity of the construction headed by b, in particular the absence of a modifier.

Clearly, too, 'weakness' in DA 2' (63) is concerned with the non-complexity of the construction headed by b:

(109)   b is head of a rhyme of the form $|b(\rightarrow\{C\})|$ ←/#.

And a certain reinterpretation would make possible an even closer parallelism. What (63) says is that, in order for b to be weak it must have no modifier (cf. (108)) or it must have dependent on it only one consonant which is allowed not to be dependent on something other than b (to its right) only at word boundary. This last provision (involving word boundary) was to provide for foot formation in verbs and non-derived adjectives (and verbal prefixes — recall section 14), wherein a final rhyme of the shape $\{|V|\} \rightarrow \{C\}$ is weak, as in (56a). Say, rather, we regard a word- (or prefix-) final consonant in such forms as hypermetrical (cf. Hayes 1982: 2.2). Then we can reformulate 'weakness' with respect to foot formation as simply:

(110)   ~ ∃ segment, c, b → c, unless c ←

'Weakness' is ensured if b's rhyme does not contain a consonant or it contains a single consonant dependent to its right.

A further advantage of such an analysis is that we no longer have to allow for stress on monosyllables like *man* in terms of hypermetricality with respect to DA 2' (cf. 10). Rather, given that neither they nor their final consonant are hypermetrical, they will no longer be weak, by (110). Accordingly, SSC' (64) can be restricted to sequences of the form a ⩽ b < c: i.e. in all cases where SSC' applies, b is distinct from c. All stressed syllables are strong by DA 2'; and after stress assignment, all stressed syllables contain a complex rhyme, given the retention of ambisyllabicity after short vowels. I suggest, therefore, that we substitute the characterisation of weakness for DA 2' given in (110) for the original formulation.

Suppose now that the pre-stress ambisyllabicity created by DA 1''' is simplified, prior to application of DA 2', in terms of the initial maximalist assumption. In that case, the condition for 'weakness' with respect to foot formation could be further simplified, and further assimilated to (108), as in (111):

(111)   ~ ∃ segment c, b $\overset{\le}{\rightarrow}$ c.

(The precedence requirement here is needed to ensure that c is part of b's rhyme.) This characterisation is possible if all ambi-syllabics are reassigned to the following syllable.[24]

One problem with this, of course, concerns the /s/ + plosive clusters discussed in 8: although /s/ + plosive is a possible syllable-initial cluster, a syllabic immediately preceding them is not 'weak' with respect to foot formation: recall (60/61e). They repre-sent a major motivation for the interpretation of 'weakness' in this case as involving ambisyllabicity. One possibility — though I am unaware of much independent support of it — would be simply to exclude medial syllabifications which violate the sonority hierarchy. This would rule out /s/ + plosive as a medial syllable-initiator. Despite the possibility of word-initial /s/ + plosive sequences, medially the syllable boundary comes uniquely between the two segments. Assuming initial maximalist sylla-bification otherwise, we have (112), rather than (60/61):

(112)　(a)　ci-ne-ma
　　　　(b)　re-pen-tant
　　　　(c)　al-ge-bra
　　　　(d)　pen-tath-lon
　　　　(e)　as-bes-tos

Correctly, only (112a) and (c) conform to (111), and thus reject stress.

One slight support for this suggestion concerning medial sequences might come from the observation that medial /s/ + plosive sequences are uniquely ambiguous in being in their entirety possible finals or initials; this is not true of other clusters, but only of single medial consonants. The aberrant syllabification could be taken as a response to just this.

Our account of post-foot-formation ambisyllabicity after short vowels in forms such as those in (74b) will also have to be revised, if such a proposal is accepted. Given initial maximalist pre-stress-assignment syllabification, ambisyllabicity will have to be (re-) introduced after foot formation in just the circumstances exemplified by (74b). Further, some medial /s/ + plosive clusters will have to be resyllabified after foot formation, to allow for the weakness of the first syllables in (113a) compared with those in (b):

(113)　(a)　aspáragus, aspérsion, askánce
　　　　(b)　athléticism, Atlántic, antícipate, alpáca

The initial syllables in (b) are closed; they include the consonant following the syllabic; this is not true of (a). Foot-initial syllables override the pre-stress requirement formulated immediately above that medial /s/ + plosive sequences are heterosyllabic. Rather, foot-initial syllables are uniformly maximalist initially. So that the first syllables of the forms in (113a) are uniformly open, non-foot-forming and reducible.

It may be that a more adequate account of 'weakness' in foot formation lies in the direction I have indicated in this section. But it seems to me that while (110) is quite consonant with the formations otherwise offered here, the step from (110) to (111) rests at this point on too many unsupported and problematical assumptions.

Even more remote, apparently, from the characterisations of 'weakness' we have been considering so far are the specifications included in DA 0.2 (50b) and DA 1‴ (50c). DA 1‴, and to some extent DA 0.2, we might expect to be distinctive anyway, given that it is responsible for the formation of the heterogeneous constructions rhyme and syllable; essentially, it establishes the priority of the nucleus over co-constituents that are not more vocalic. DA 0.2 invokes consonantality; it makes more consonantal co-constituents dependent on the head of the cluster.

With both DA 0.2 and DA 1‴ 'weakness' has to do with the internal constitution of b rather than external dependency relations. As we have just observed, with DA 0.2 b is 'weak' if its preponderance of $|C|$ is less than that of a; in DA 1‴ b is 'weak' if a is a vowel, i.e. $\{|V|\}$. My use of the term 'weakness' here reflects a claim that lack of a dependent should be equated with lack of relative preponderance (of $|V|$ or $|C|$). This is in accord with the equation within dependency phonology of preponderance with governorhood. But it is unclear to me how this is to be embodied in the characterisations of 'weakness' themselves.

17.

The dependency assignments we have been looking at in the immediately preceding sections are all intralexical: they form word-trees. As such they do not vary with respect to information structure or considerations of rhythm and tempo within the utterance. Syllable, foot and group formation in utterances is sensitive not just to the lexical structures we have just been considering but also to these non-lexical factors. We can draw an analogous intra- vs. extra-lexical distinction with respect to tune assignment. Group formation in utterances provides the basic unit with respect to which tune-text associations may be formulated; and both utterance groups and utterance tunes, or INTONATION contours, are in part determined by information structure. In 'tone languages' certain tunes are lexicalised, as TONE contours, associated with word rather than utterance groups; and are thus idiosyncratic or morphologically determined (and subject to local phonological constraints). We can thus draw a similar distinction between the phonological structure of the word and that of the utterance, on the one hand, and tone and intonation, on the other.[25]

I am in no position to provide here (or, perhaps, anywhere) a theory of information structure. (Cf., however, Ladd (1978); Gussenhoven (1983), for some proposals concerning the phonological role of information structure.) But, to the extent that alternative information structures can be regarded as 'variations' associated with a particular syntactic structure, we can at least out-line potentential utterance patterns on the basis of lexical and syntactic information, without in most cases being able to specify motivations for choice between alternative potential patterns. I take it that in its phonologically determined aspects, utterance structure is a projection of sequences of word-trees, just as word-trees are projections of sequences of segments. Let us consider, then, potential projections deriving from sequences of word-trees and relevant syntactic information.

I offer some tentative suggestions concerning word-to-utterance associations in (114):

(114)   DEPENDENCY ASSIGNMENT IN UTTERANCES:
        (i) Each word syllabic is a potential utterance syllabic (with variation according to tempo).
        (ii) Each non-subordinated group head in a lexical word and each foot head and subordinated group head which is not adjacent to a group head is a potential utterance foot head (with again variation according to tempo and, as illustrated below, rhythmic requirements).
        (iii) The last utterance foot head of each disjoint syntactic phrase (i.e. one that is not immediately part of another) is

a potential utterance group head (with ultimate selection and variation from this pattern being based on information structure).

(iv)a.   A syllabic which is not an utterance foot head depends on the left-adjacent foot head; if there is no foot head to the left in the same group, it depends on an unrealised foot head ('silent stress').

b.   A foot head which is not an utterance group head depends on the right-adjacent group head; if there is no group head to the right in the same group ('de-accentuation'), it is F^2-subordinated to the left-adjacent group head.

c.   The last of several group heads in an utterance (defined by information structure) is a G^2 head; each non-final group head depends on such a G^2 head.

Consider the application of (114) in relation to (16) above, whose structure we can now provide with a more adequate character-isation than was given at that point.

We can associate with such a sequence the (abbreviated) word-trees and the phrasal bracketings assigned in (115):

(115)

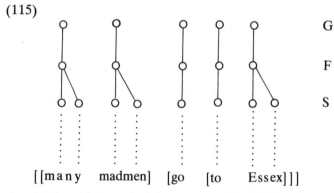

Application of the principles suggested in (114) will give us the associations represented in (116):

(116)

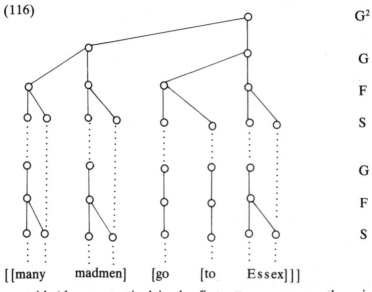

G²

G

F

S

G

F

S

[[many   madmen]   [go   [to   Essex]]]

or, with 'de-accentuation' in the first utterance group, those in (117):

(117)

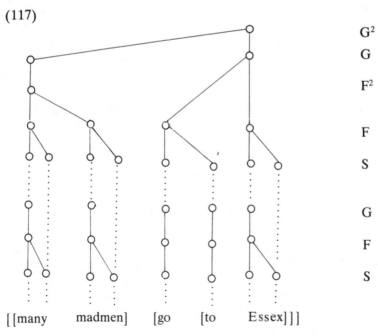

G²

G

F²

F

S

G

F

S

[[many   madmen]   [go   [to   Essex]]]

(114) associates each of the word syllables in (115) with an utterance syllable in (116) and (117), on the assumption that the tempo is not too fast. Each of the group heads in the lexical words corresponds to an utterance foot head. There are no word foot heads which are not group heads, nor any subordinate group heads, as in compounds: I am assuming that *madmen* is an 'obscured' compound — contrast *mad-women*, where, nevertheless, the second (subordinated) group head is adjacent to the first and so normally gets no utterance foot head. *To* as a non-lexical word also normally gets no utterance foot head; rather, it is adjoined to the preceding foot by (iv.a) in (114). However, it seems clear that even non-lexical words should be assigned word foot and group heads: we need, for instance, to distinguish between the two syllables in *about* and *over* — even though it is only in contrastive or rhythmically appropriate circumstances that the distinction shows up in utterances. There are only two disjoint phrases in (115) (cf. (114iii): the prepositional phrase is an immediate constituent of the verb phrase. We thus have two tone groups with heads *mad-* and *Ess-* in (116) and *man-* and *Ess-* in (117). In (117) the second utterance foot follows its group head, and so is subordinated to it by (iv.b) in (114); cf. too (17) and (18) above.

Foot heads in lexical words that are not the word group head may or may not be utterance foot heads depending on the rhythmic environment. A foot head adjacent to another which outranks it (as in 91a/bii)) is normally not an utterance foot head. Non-adjacent word foot heads depend for their utterance status on tempo and the rhythmic environment. Compare, for example, the utterances in (118):

(118)　(a)　// all the / indi/cations // Δ are / positive //

　　　　(b)　// Δ there's / no indi/cation of // bad / faith //

in which after an unstressed syllable the first word foot head in *indication* is associated with an utterance foot head (a), but not after a stressed syllable (b).

Non-lexical words are normally footed with a preceding stressed syllable (cf. (114iv.a)), as with *to* in (116/117), or with a preceding unrealised foot head (if no foot head precedes in the same group), as with *are* in (118a) and *there's* in (118b). Similar options are available (though provided lexically — cf. section 14) to the initial unstressed syllables of lexical words, as we observed with respect to the examples with *applause* given in (98a) and (b).[26]

But a non-lexical word may receive utterance footship to break up a sequence of unstressed syllables, or so that it can receive a (contrastive) group headship, as in (b) and (c) respectively in (119):

(119)   (a)   // J*o*hn's // Δ gotta / le*a*ve //
        (b)   // J*o*hn // Δ has / got to / l*ea*ve //
        (c)   // J*o*hn // Δ has / g*o*t to / leave //

Similarly, a sequence of two or more non-tonic-bearing mono-syllabic lexical words may have utterance foot headship denied to a non-initial instance (cf. Giegerich 1979: 3.2.2, 1981):

(120)   ... // Δ the / two old / m*e*n //

Characteristically, the last foot head is also a group head.

Now, this is reminiscent of the situation in which we find stress-reversal (illustrated in (20) above). In both cases we have 'de-footing', or rather failure to foot, of a word foot head preceding the utterance group head. But with stress-reversal the 'deposed' foot head, as well as being group head of a word, has its utterance foot headship 'usurped' by a preceding lexical foot head in the same word. Compare the pair in (121):

(121)   (a)

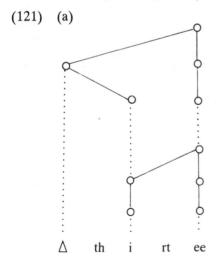

Δ   th   i   rt   ee   n   came to dinner

(b)

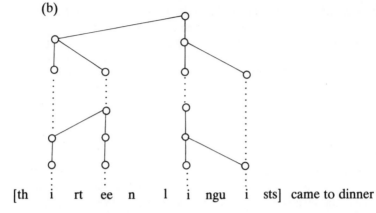

[th   i   rt   ee   n   l   i   ngu   i   sts]   came to dinner

In (121a) the word group head *-teen* quite regularly becomes the utterance group head associated with the phrase, whereas the adjacent word foot head *thir-* is footed with a preceding 'silent stress'. However, in (121b), where the word group head precedes another which is assigned the utterance group headship, the preceding foot head *thir-* is preferred as utterance foot head. Notice that the following group head need not be adjacent; consider e.g. (122):

(122)   (a)   thirteen wise virgins
         (b)   thirteen alert virgins

Even though in (b) *thirteen* is followed by a weak syllable, reversal still occurs. This suggests that what is crucial is that *thirteen* does not terminate a group.

We can thus define the condition for stress-reversal as in (123):

(123)

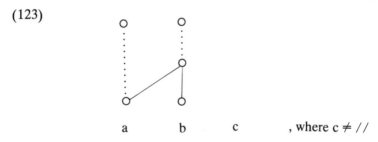

a   b   c   , where c ≠ //

a, b, c must be adjacent. But notice that this means construction-adjacent (recall the head convention of (27)). Thus, syllables dependent on a may intervene between the elements in (123): in (20b) this is indeed the case. And the presence of a syllable dependent on b does not in itself trigger reversal, as in (124a), as compared with (b), where reversal is in accord with (123) (Giegerich 1981):

(124) (a) well-fúnded
       (b) wéll-funded bánk

However, such instances are much more susceptible to individual variation.

Where condition (123) is met but utterance group headship is nevertheless assigned to *thirteen* — i.e. we have 'de-accentuation' of following feet — either syllable may bear the tonic. Consider the contrastive *THIRTEEN (not twelve) linguists came to dinner.*

I am assuming, then, that a configuration like that specified in (123) overrides normal application of the principles formulated in (114). (120) involves a similar condition, except that a and b are monosyllabic words. We have, however, in both these cases, not a 'transformation' (structural mutation) but an alternative mapping between the word and utterance representations. It may be that we can so limit all building of utterance structure, thereby imposing a significant constraint on utterance formation.

Utterance structures, as we have seen, are sensitive to extra-lexical factors. And whereas lexical units are among other things the domain for stating the distribution of phonemes (cf. above, particularly note 4), utterance units form the domains for low-level phonetic processes such as those exemplified in (6/7) and (10/11). Our initial discussion, in conflating word and utterance units, ignored this distinction.

Another difference, at least at foot level and above, may be that utterance construction, unlike lexical, may be non-binary. The lexical feet and groups we have been led to propose have all been binary;[27] they obey the SINGLE DAUGHTER CONDITION:

(125) SINGLE DAUGHTER CONDITION:
       Given segments a, b, where $a \neq b$, $a \rightarrow b \mapsto \sim \exists$ seg-
       ment c $(\neq a,b)$, $a \rightarrow c$.

There is no more than one segment adjoined to any other. However, it is not obvious that this is true of utterance feet and groups.

In an example like (126), for instance:

(126)

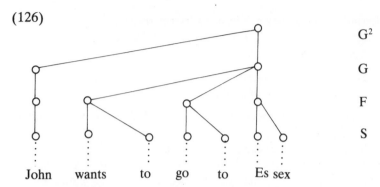

there seems to be no phonological motivation for grouping into a single constituent the two feet subordinate to the second group head. Consider too the examples in (118) and (119). Similarly, is there any motivation for imposing further structure on the ternary second foot in (127):

(127)

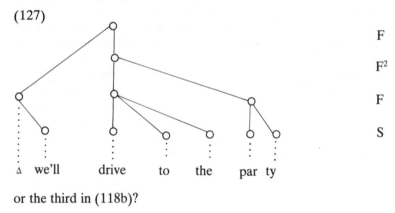

or the third in (118b)?

Notes

*Much (probably most) of whatever is of consequence in what follows grew out of conversation and collaboration with Colin Ewen and Heinz Giegerich, to whom much non-blame-imputing thanks. I am similarly grateful to Fran Colman and the hot German sun, who specifically helped me to get together the version, some of which managed to get presented at the Essex Conference on Dependency Phonology. A number of improvements (I think) resulted from discussions at the Conference and afterwards, for which I would like to thank, in particular, the aforementioned (minus the sun) and a cast of thousands, including Mike Davenport, Jacques Durand, Charles Jones, David Leslie, Ken Lodge, Cathair Ó Dochartaigh, Andy Spencer, Jørgen Staun and Nigel Vincent. This final version benefited from a meticulous scrutiny by Jacques Durand.

1. The /k/ in *acrid* and *Mecca* shows both syllable-final and syllable-initial characteristics and is thus ambisyllabic: see section 11.

2. /i/ does not occur finally in stressed syllables; once more, section 11 discusses the consequences of this for syllabification.

3. Of course, some dialects of English show a slightly different distribution: consider, e.g. Scots *howff* 'place of resort'. But some restrictions remain. I remain unconvinced by suggestions that English shows onset-syllabic constraints parallel to those evidenced between nucleus and coda. (See further on rhymes Vincent (this vol.).) Of course, in languages without codas we expect in terms of the neutralisation condition (30) that there will occur onset-syllabic restrictions. This seems to be evidenced in Mazatec (Pike & Pike 1947: 87). However, we cannot derive support from this (*pace* Davis 1982) for a conclusion that languages *with* codas also lack a rhyme. Moreover, onset-coda restrictions do not argue for some kind of discontinuous constituent including just those two, given that this constituent would violate the otherwise well-supported continuity assumption, that the character of the restrictions is distinctive (as requirements of non-identity of (sub-)segments), and that they can be construed as representing conditions on overall syllable shape (see again section 5 below).

4. Long vowels do occur in syllables which are typically (*miasma, biology*) or often (*alibi*) not the stressed syllable of a foot in utterances. I shall be arguing that these syllables are lexical foot heads, however: cf. section 13. Phonemic distribution is sensitive to lexical rather than utterance units; contrast the low-level phenomena of (6), (7), (10) and (11). See further section 17.

5. This is even true of languages like French, with low foot-prominence (see section 4 below), where it might be argued that the relevant unit for cliticisation is apparently the group, the pronoun clitics thus being proclitics. However, this may reflect rather a residue of SXV word order (cf. the Middle English negative proclitic of (8)). And, indeed, optional foot formation (Selkirk 1978; Durand, this vol.) makes enclitics of [ə]-syllable words.

6. I continue to ignore here for the moment the possibility of complex nuclei: we take this up in section 7.

7. This claim makes the rather interesting prediction that 'VP' will occur only in clauses in which the subject and object(s) appear on different sides of the verb. For discussion see Anderson & Ewen to appear; Anderson, to appear b.

The requirement that the head of any construction be unique underlies Matthews's (1981: 86-8) major criticism of the expressive power of dependency grammars. He notes specifically that whereas it seems reasonable to say that in a phrase like *up till Friday* both *up* and *Friday* modify *till*, the fact (on the assumption that it is one) that *up till* form a construction to which *Friday* does not belong is unexpressed in a dependency representation such as (i):

(i)

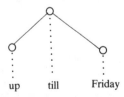

But this relationship cannot be expressed only if we maintain the requirement that the head of each construction-type must be unique to it. Otherwise the relationship can be expressed as in (ii):

(ii)

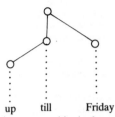

up   till   Friday

(utilising the notion of subjunction proposed in Anderson 1971), such that the construction-types remain determinate even though they share a head, in that they differ in the direction of modification. The crucial distinctness is in construction-type, which may not always be signalled purely by the identity of the head.

In fact, the relationship expressed in (ii) seems to me to be inappropriate; rather we have (iii):

(iii)

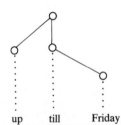

up   till   Friday

(discussed further in Anderson, to appear b). But, either way, the expressive power of dependency representations is limited in this respect only by the 'unique head' assumption, which in such instances is unwarranted.

A representation similar to (ii) is available in the case of Matthews's other type of example, illustrated by *has brought the book*, where he alleges a like problem. But since the 'problem' arises only on the assumption that 'auxiliaries' modify the non-finite verbs that accompany them, which, it seems to me, is unsupportable (cf. e.g. Anderson 1976: Ch. II), it need not even be pursued as such.

8. It need not be our concern here to explore the motivations for 'de-accentuation', which are associated with the character of the information structure associated with the utterance (see §3 (17)). It is perhaps worth noting, however, that 'de-accentuation' may be more or less 'marked' or contrastive with respect to information structure. For example, 'de-accenting' of a noun is more contrastive than removal of group headship from a (certain class of) verb, as in (17), which could be said to involve the informationally 'unmarked' configuration: *left* as group head would be contrastive. On 'degrees of accentability' see particularly Ladd 1978: IV.4 — and for an alternative account of such phenomena cf. Gussenhoven 1983.

9. Cf. here Robinson 1970. A convention such as (27) is a consequence of the claim, fundamental to dependency grammar, that no pre-lexical categories need be posited: a construction is defined by its head, and possibly also modifier position (cf. note 7); and, further, categorial reference in the formulation of syntactic regularities need only be to lexical categories, given the viability of the head convention. The status of a lexical category, as construction label or lexical label, is determined by (27). Thus, not even defined pre-lexical category labels need be involved. This imposes significant limitations on the character of both syntactic structures and the rules which relate them.

(27) encapsulates (and renders superfluous) the 'A-over-A constraint' (e.g. Chomsky 1964) and its descendants, in that, given a sequence ... a_i... [... a_j...], where a_j is subordinate to a_i and categorially identical to it, a_j will be ignored by any regularity invoking the category a unless another subordinate of a_i is also mentioned in the rule.

10. This formulation is generalised in section 12 to include rhymes which contain a complex nucleus but not necessarily a consonantal coda.

11. On the description of these various restrictions as 'neutralisation' see Anderson & Ewen 1981. The appropriateness of the label, however, is not important to the present discussion.

12. Strictly, the class of hypermetrical obstruents is that of the anterior coronals, given that /tʃ/ and /dʒ/ do not function as such. In dependency terms, these can be excluded by requiring that the b segment in the characterisation suggested in note 13 below be simplex.

It may indeed be that hypermetricality should be extended to non-obstruent coronals such as the final ones in e.g. *cylinder* and *rectangle*. The final syllable in these forms (whether containing a syllabic sonorant consonant or /ə/) is ignored by either or both of foot formation and F^2 formation (DA 2' and DA 3(i) — see sections 10, 13) in that the word head is the first syllable even though the second one is strong with respect to both DA 2' and DA 3(i). This is allowed for if final syllables are allowed a hypermetrical sonorant coronal, and such forms are thus disyllabic (cf. Chomsky and Halle (1968: 25-6) on the *cylinder* cases). However, the sonorants are eventually made dependent (at utterance level?) on the preceding foot head, with syllabification of the sonorant itself or via insertion of a vowel.

The distribution of such hypermetrical sonorants is also distinctive, it would appear, in that they are not limited to word-final position but rather must come to occupy final position in a foot: cf. section 10 on *Hottentot*, etc. Such a distribution also accounts for the observed difference between pairs like [$_N$[$_V$*condens*]*ation*] and [$_N$[$_V$*compensat*]*ion*] with respect to reducibility of the second syllable: in the latter it is typically reduced. I interpret this as a reflexion of the hypermetrical status of the nasal, which is in foot-final position in both noun and verb. It will eventually syllabify or gain a 'reduced' syllabic ahead of it. In pronunciations of the former lacking reduction, hypermetricality of the nasal is prevented with respect to the sequence enclosed by [$_V$] (and in the corresponding verb form) in that the nasal is not final therein. It is able to occupy foot-final position only after the noun termination is added. (On such cyclicity see section 14). The noun and the base verb must thus contain a full vowel in the second syllable.

13. We can formulate the condition for hypermetricality in this instance as selecting as such the b segment in a sequence of the form:

$$\{C\}_a\{\{C\}\{\sim u\}\}_b \{C\}_0 \#$$

where either (i)$\{C\}_a \supseteq \{C\}_b$ or (ii) a is hypermetrical. This selects all coronals ($\{\sim u\}$), including the sonorants of note 12, though for them the most appropriate final boundary is a foot rather than a word boundary. Indeed we can reformulate the hypermetricality condition to refer to foot boundary in that medial non-sonorants will never meet such a condition. (To exclude sonorants from hypermetricality the specification of b would have to be $\{C\!\rightarrow\}$.) Also selected by our formulation as hypermetrical are the /z/ of *adze*, the /s/ of *tax* and *text* and the final /t/ of *act*, which meet condition (i), as well as the final /t/ of *text* by condition (ii), given that the preceding /s/ is itself hypermetrical.

Not selected are the final coronals in *bind*, *wood*, *wild*, which are 'extrametrical' for Kiparsky (1981). However, these involve a rather different kind of restriction; they are not in conflict with the sonority slope but the absence of rhymes of this character ending in /b/ and /g/ instantiates (in Kiparsky's own terms) 'idiosyncratic restrictions' (and, in the case of *bind* and *wild*, we have violations of Kiparsky's 'length restriction' — though not of the syllable depth condition (31)). Moreover, only voiced obstruents show the restrictions on cluster formation (cf. *pimp, cunt, kink*) and occurrence after /u/ (*poop* 'shit', *root, cook*), though again only the coronal occurs after long vowel + nasal (*pint*), as an idiosyncratic restriction. If the final consonant in *bind*, etc. is included in the set of hypermetrical coronals, then this class cannot be given the unified specification suggested above. The class will also have to exclude the final coronal in e.g. *test*, in view of the acceptability of forms like *cusp* and *desk*. These are correctly excluded by the formulation given here in that the sonority condition is not infringed. So too are examples like *soft*, which again are in conformity with the sonority slope but, in this case, show 'idiosyncratic exceptions': /-fp/, */-fk/. None of the 'idiosyncratic restrictions' noted in this paragraph are to be accounted for in terms of hypermetricality.

Many instances of final-coronal hypermetricality are morphologically conditioned (*tacks, licked*, etc.). In these cases hypermetricality might be eliminated as an independent concept: it is a consequence, perhaps, of the interaction between morphological rules and the rules of syllabification. Giegerich (1985) proposes a treatment, involving initial maximalist syllabification and zero rhymes, which eliminates the remaining cases as such. In the context of the present discussion, the most that we can say is that each non-morphologically-motivated case of hypermetricality which meets condition (i) in the formulation given above is paralleled by a morphologically motivated one as *tax* by *tacks*).

14. If apparent absence of an initial onset in early Germanic in fact involves an onset realised by [ʔ] (Lass 1983), then the null provision may be omitted from these formulations: see further below.

On Germanic and other alliterations, in this respect, see Cairns & Feinstein (1982), who show that Kiparsky's sonority-based analysis of syllable structure complicates the formulation of such regularities.

15. On the DPC see section 7 (particularly the formulation in (52)) and Anderson & Durand, this vol. The historical development — and possibly the morphophonology — of e.g. pre-nasalised plosives is more complex, in that if these originate in sequences of syllabic nasal + plosive, desyllabification of the nasal creates a sequence which violates the sonority slope and is thus presumably reinterpreted as a configuration such as is associated with /sp-/ in (38). This configuration is then monosegmentalised in conformity with DPC. This is confirmed by the fact that in pre-nasalised plosives the plosive element is clearly the governor; such segments, like affricates, are primarily plosives: they show a similar distribution to, are frequently allophonically related to and are grouped in phonological processes with plosives (Anderson & Ewen forthcoming: 3.3.3). Such observations are incompatible with Ewen's (1982: particularly section 4) analysis, in which the dependency relations between these elements are in accordance with the sonority hierarchy.

Headship for the plosive element in pre-/post-nasalised and affricate complexes does not, of course, preclude reference by phonological regularities specifically to the dependant; e.g. with respect to nasalisation of adjacent vowels in the case of the nasalised plosive (S.R. Anderson 1976) or in the determination of English number and tense allomorphy (cf. *pits* vs. *pisses, pitches* and *pitted* vs. *pissed, pitched*). However, this influence is limited to the side on which such modifiers occur: hence e.g. the asymmetry of nasalisation spread from pre-/post-nasalised segments.

16. It is possible that other instances of [i]/[j] and [u̯]/[w] can also be represented lexically as /i/ and /u/. However, in their case, (48), without the

government requirement, would apply before nucleus formation DA 0.1, and they thus would participate in cluster formation instead. However, this also depends on an assumption that long vowels like /i:/ and /u:/ be represented lexically as monosegmental but 'tense' ({|V,V|}, whereas a sequence [wu] is differentiated as {|V|} {|V|}. Given that both long monophthongs and diphthongs are associated with a complex nucleus in the word-tree, the following associations would be required:

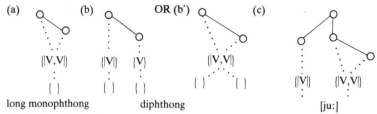

(a) long monophthong   (b) OR (b') diphthong   (c)   [ju:]

An interpretation such as given in (a), (b') and (c) requires that DA 0.1 (i) (50a = 46) be eliminated in favour of (or be supplemented by, if (b) is retained) a provision like:

$$a \overset{\le}{\to} b \text{ iff } a = b \text{ and } a,b \equiv \{|V,V|\}.$$

Vowels like the final one in *pity*, which are derivatively tense, gain a {|V,V|} specification but of course remain single-noded in the word-tree.

17. A segment made head by a dependency assignment rule cannot then be made a modifier by the same rule: thus DA 1‴cannot reapply to (55) etc. to make one or other syllabic dependent on the other.

18. Other suffixes, on the other hand, are 'meta-metrical', in conferring headhood irrespective of the structure of the syllable concerned. Thus, the adjective-forming -*ic* suffix in English imposes foot headship on the immediately preceding syllabic, whatever the character of the syllable: *ecléctic, anáemic, históric, echóic.*

19. In order for the second syllable in (72c) to be weak, [fθ] in English must be a permissible initial. This is attested by *phthisic(al)* and *phthongal.* However, such an initial sequence is apparently not in conformity with the sonority slope. This is resolved if [fθ] is a complex single segment, one (indeed) that is often reduced to [θ]. This reduction is resisted only when the [f] can be interpreted as part of the preceding syllable, as in *diphthong.*

20. It is also the case that some speakers realise /t/ or /d/ as a flap only when the segment is ambisyllabic; so that we have a flap in *phonetic* but not *emeritus*, in accordance with the analysis for trisyllabic feet suggested here.

Old English feminine *ō*-nouns retain the nominative -*u* inflexion only if the stem ends in a single ambisyllabic consonant. Contrast *faru* 'journey' with *lār* 'learning' and *wund* 'wound' (Campbell 1959: 585-8). In the latter the inflexional vowel has been dropped, given that the stem does not end in a single consonant which can be ambisyllabic with respect to the nuclei on either side. With disyllabic stems the -*u* is absent also, even though the preceding syllable is 'light', as in *duguð* 'band of warriors' or *efes* 'eaves' (Campbell 1959: 589(6)). Again, this is in accord with the assumption that ambisyllabicity is absent between the second and third syllables of trisyllabic feet: [*fa*[*r*]*u*] vs. *[*lā*][*rV*], *[*du*]*g*[*u*][*ðV*]. The *V* in the latter two examples is dropped in Old English.

21. I ignore here the additional complication that breaking also occurs before /x/, whether or not a consonant follows, as in *seah* 'saw', *feaht* 'fought'. One might suggest, following Lass & Anderson (1975: Ch. III), for example, that in this case the possible absence of a following consonant is compensated for by the more

consonantal character of /x/; or, rather, that the greater consonantality of /x/ does not require external support. That is, the environment for breaking is, more precisely (utilising again the notation of Anderson & Ewen 1980):

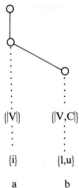

      a   b

where a is the affected (front vowel) segment, and with b, V ⟶ C iff l ⟶ u and ∃ segment c, c = {C}, c ⟶ b. That is, if the b element is a liquid ({|V|⟶|C|}), then the |u| is a secondary articulation and vice versa, and there is a third, consonantal segment c which follows b and governs it. Given the condition, this formulation collapses the two environments:

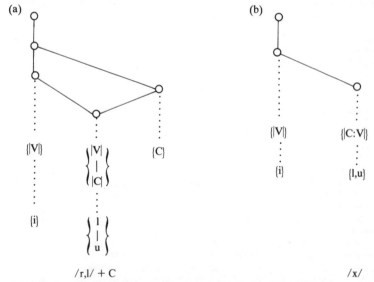

      /r,l/ + C   /x/

(No voiced velar plosive ({|C| ⟶ |V|}) occurs in this environment.) We are concerned here only with environment (a).

    22. The account given here is much simplified. Notice, for instance, that the initial consonant of the suffix assimilates to the articulatory position of the preceding sonorant, as in *zalmpje* 'salmon', *duimpje* 'thumb'. For this and other details see again Ewen 1978, 1980a: Ch. 11.

23. This is also exceptionally true of *circumcise* (cf. *circumvént*) and *súpervise* (cf. *supervéne*). Certain nouns are also exceptional with respect to DA 3(i): *expertíse, voluntéer, thirtéen, princéss*, etc. It is possible that in their case we should associate hypermetricality with the presence of certain suffixes (Liberman & Prince 1977: 2.8; Schane 1979). However, not all *-ess* formations, for example, show the same pattern as *princess*: *hóstess, wáitress, mistress* (the latter two with reduced second syllabics). Again, we don't seem to be able to reduce hypermetricality to an interaction with morphology (cf. note 13 above); indeed, here distribution of hypermetricality seems to be partially lexical.

And the set of nouns which show hypermetricality with respect to DA 2' (63) seem to be even more idiosyncratic: with such forms as *Alabáma, anténna* any pre-penultimate syllables are hypermetrical in this respect. There are some apparent restrictions, however. The pre-penultimate sequence must be capable of forming a foot (i.e. is polysyllabic or a strong monosyllable), as in the above examples or in, say, *Mississippi* and *bandana* (contrast *patina, cinema*). Again (cf. the prefixed verbs), the hypermetrical sequence is footed by itself. The result is a two-footed form in which the second foot is strong by DA 3; and so its head comes to be group head. Many such forms also end in a vowel, as in the preceding examples; but, clearly, neither condition is sufficient: witness e.g. *álgebra*.

24. A problem with assuming initial maximalist syllabification from the start is that final syllables would then display a quite different pattern of syllable and specifically rhyme structure from non-finals, which would show much more restricted codas (cf. section 8). This would be at least in part compensated for by the presence of final zero rhymes (Giegerich 1985): codas including parts which were apparently unique to final position in the word would constitute the onsets of the syllables terminated by zero rhymes. However, to be fully general, such a solution would require the positing of final zero rhymes with respect to a much wider range of forms than they have so far received motivation for (cf. on these motivations Giegerich 1981). Moreover, if we assume initial maximalist syllabification, the /dʒ/ in *lounge*, for example, would presumably constitute the onset to a syllable with zero rhyme. But this is difficult to reconcile with the constraints holding within such rhymes as a whole (which are even more restrictive than those illustrated in (5)): the existence of such restrictions in this and other instances suggests that such final consonants belong with the preceding rhyme rather than being a distinct onset.

25. Tone sequences are aligned with the word group head and assigned to the syllables of the word by tune-word association, just as intonation contours are oriented with respect to the utterance group head and then associated.

26. I have suggested two rather different treatments for (typically unstressed) lexical words and the unstressed initial syllables of lexical words: the latter are associated lexically with a preceding unrealised foot head, whereas with the former this arises as a possibility only at the utterance level. This discrepancy would be removed if rather than assigning lexical foot head (and thus group head) status to non-lexical words, we provided them too with an unrealised foot head to their left (cf. section 14). But this would then presumably require the positing of an unrealised group head (otherwise unmotivated); it would also not allow us to differentiate between e.g. *over* and *about* (if these are non-lexical); and it would obscure the greater (though admittedly restricted) potentiality of non-lexical words (compared with the unstressed initials of lexical) to be assigned utterance group headship.

27. On the assumption embodied in the preceding discussion, (lexical) infrasyllabic structures are also in certain circumstances non-binary: cf. e.g. (26) and (38). However, all the rules of lexical dependency assignment formulated above are binary in character.

3 SEQUENCE, SEGMENT AND CONFIGURATION: TWO PROBLEMS FOR DEPENDENCY PHONOLOGY

Mike Davenport & Jørgen Staun

1. Introduction

The problems we wish to consider in this paper are essentially 'demarcation disputes'.* The first concerns the distinction between the segmental representations of the categorial gesture and the configurations for segment sequences, specifically with regard to the dependency treatment of affricates. The second concerns the division between the categorial and initiatory gestures, particularly with regard to (a) the status of the glottalic opening component |O|; and (b) the dependency relations that have been claimed to hold between the two gestures. We hope to show that these areas are problematical for the model as it now stands because the 'lines of demarcation' are not drawn sharply enough, and we shall suggest that a certain amount of restructuring of the categorial and initiatory gestures is necessary.

2. The Representation of Affricates

Let us first consider the problem of the characterisation of the affricates. In Anderson & Jones (1977: 126), affricates are represented, without discussion, as in (1):

(1) (a)   (b)

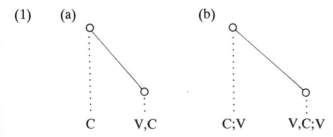

C   V,C   C;V   V,C;V

135

(In fact only the representation of the voiceless affricates (1a) is given, but it is clear that (1b) must represent the voiced congeners.) These structures are also adopted in Ewen (1980a), where they are justified on the grounds that the unexpected dependency relations indicate the difference between such sounds and 'normal' segment sequences. (We return to Ewen's arguments later.) Given the characterisations in (1), Engl. ⟨judge⟩ would appear as in (2):

(2)

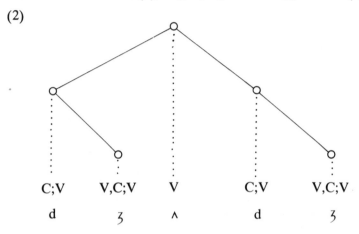

| C;V | V,C;V | V | C;V | V,C;V |
| d | ʒ | ʌ | d | ʒ |

As Ewen points out, this characterisation departs in two important respects from other representations within the framework. Firstly the syllabic governor |V| directly governs a segment (|C;V|) to which it is not immediately adjacent, whilst at the same time it does not directly govern the segment (|V,C;V|) which *is* immediately prior to it in linear sequence (i.e. there are adjacent segments between which there is no immediate dependency relation). Secondly, since the first segment governs the second (|C;V| → |V,C;V|), this involves a governing segment /d/ (|C;V|) which exhibits a degree of sonority *lower* than that of the segment it governs, /ʒ/. Thus the representations in (1) involve the relaxing of two of the basic principles on which the model is founded: (i) that the dependency relation progresses regularly from the syllabic governor outwards; and (ii) that the more sonorant a segment, the lower its degree of dependency, i.e. more sonorant segments govern less sonorant segments (though for a radically different approach to syllable structure, see Anderson's contribution to this volume). These two principles are illustrated schematically in (3):

(3)

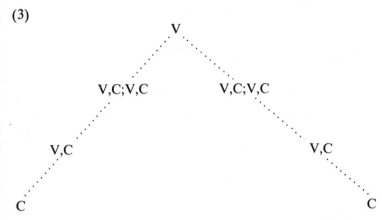

Can such departures be justified? Indeed, are they necessary in the first place? Obviously, part of the answer lies in the phonological status afforded to the affricates — i.e. whether they are regarded as an independent segment type or as a sequence of stop + fricative, without unit status. As is well known, this is an area of considerable disagreement among linguists, and we do not intend to argue for one position or the other here. Phonetically at least there is general agreement that there is no clear justification for the 'independent segment' approach — most observers agree that there is no regular distinction between what are traditionally referred to as affricates and sequences of stop + fricative at this level (cf. e.g. Catford 1977; Sommerstein 1977, etc.).

However, in his discussion of this area, Ewen (1980a) cites some evidence which appears to run counter to the general consensus; in both Greek and Polish, data are available which seem to suggest a contrast between a unit affricate on the one hand and a sequence of stop + fricative on the other. In Polish the putative minimal pairs are e.g.

(4)   trzy (three, nom)   ~   czy (whether)
       utrze (rub, 3 sg fut)   ~   uczę (teach, 1 sg pres)
       Ewen: [t₇ʃ₇]   ~   [č₇]
       Schenker: [tʃʃ]   ~   [tʃ]

i.e. words involving a spelling contrast ‹trz› ~ ‹cz›. It is not at all clear from Ewen's presentation exactly what the difference between the pairs is. The two sets are transcribed as shown in (4); ‹cz› by the usual American symbol ([č]), and the ‹trz› set by the

European double symbol ($[t\int]$) (cf. Ewen 1980a: 228). According to e.g. Schenker 1966: 44f, the difference between the pairs seems, as indicated in (4), to be one of length (or gemination), and only in allegro varieties — $[t\int]$ for ‹cz› versus $[t\int\int]$ (for ‹trz›). In non-allegro varieties, both sets would seem to have the same pronunciation, $[t\int]$, the initial /t/ of ‹trz› not being affricated. However this may be, these phonetic data shed no light at all on the phonological distinction (or lack of one) between unit and sequence, since the two sets are clearly distinguished underlyingly in Polish as /t∫/ (=‹cz›) vs. /tʒ/ (=‹trz›), where the voiced fricative devoices due to the preceding voiceless stop, which is then affricated in allegro varieties, giving surface $[t\int\int]$.[1]

Despite this lack of clear phonetic evidence Ewen assumes (1980a: 229) that 'at least phonologically our system of representation must enable us to make a distinction between the two categories' (i.e. unit vs. sequence), and he therefore adopts the representations given earlier in (1) as a means of achieving this. Indeed, Ewen claims that this representation avoids the necessity of producing phonologically-based arguments for one position or the other (these being often difficult to assess unless one is working within exactly the same conceptual framework, as they are commonly based on pattern congruity or economy or some such). Ewen claims that the dependency phonology characterisation 'removes the need for a decision on the question of a mono- or bi-segmental analysis' (1980a: 215) since it is in a sense neutral between them, or at least compatible with both: there are two elements in the characterisation — |C| and |V,C| (for the voiceless set) — but, parallel to the treatment of e.g. prenasalised consonants and /s/ + voiceless stop clusters, they show a 'more intimate' relation to one another (via the reverse dependency structure) than do other two-segment sequences.

However, as we outlined above, this characterisation is only possible at considerable cost to the general principles of the model, in that it involves not only sequence reversal (which as we have noted is also present in the representation of e.g. /sC/ clusters (cf. Ewen 1980a, etc.)) but, more drastically, dependency reversal (since the stop governs the fricative and not vice versa). It is this latter aspect of the characterisation that is particularly problematical, since, unlike sequence reversal, which is necessary elsewhere, dependency reversal is only found for the representation of affricates. This in itself ought to arouse one's suspicions, but there is a much more serious drawback for the model as a whole if the structures in (1) are adopted. As they stand, they are in direct opposition to one of the more interesting insights encapsulated by dependency representations: that the internal structure of the syllable is not random, but rather governed by the principle of increasing sonority. As has been pointed out on a great many occasions in work on dependency phonology, the notation directly reflects this principle, whereas a feature-based model is unable to do so in any non *ad hoc* way (cf. e.g. Basbøll 1974; Hooper 1972, etc.). In representing affricates in terms of 'dependency reversal', much of the basis for the model is thereby weakened. The consequences of this, not considered by the proponents of the characterisations, are not happy ones. If less sonorant segments are allowed to govern more sonorant ones, then the insight concerning syllable structure is lost; the model becomes as *ad hoc* as the feature-based systems it attempts to replace. There can no longer be any generalisation expressed through the representation of sequences of segments with regard to syllable structure, since there can be no principled restraints on combinatorial and dependency possibilities for such segment strings. Structures like those in (1) must be allowed, but only in the case of affricates — all other similar representations must be prevented by some entirely unmotivated constraint (but see Anderson's contribution to this volume for a suggestion that such structures are needed elsewhere in the categorial gesture). This seems to us to be an unacceptable weakening of the model, and one which, it could be argued, reduces its interest in this area to near zero. And this on the basis of a sound type about which there is no general agreement.

Recall that Ewen claims the representation of the affricates to be neutral with regard to this unit vs. sequence controversy, in that whilst two segments are involved, they exhibit reversed dependency, and as such are typologically distinct from other two segment sequences. It seems to us that this misses an important point: the representations in (1) are *not* neutral. They claim quite overtly (if not necessarily intentionally) that the affricates are indeed bisegmental and not unary, in that the characterisation of the affricates is made in the representation of segment sequences. That is, the configurations occur at the point at which the dependency relationships between the phonic segments of a lexical item are determined: on the 'output' of the categorial gesture.

Thus, in the lexicon, Engl. ‹chuckle› might include the following categorial information (shown in (5)) if the figurations in (1) are correct:

(5) |C| |V,C| |V| |C| |V;V,C|
       / t   ∫   ʌ   k   l   /

which would be realised by the appropriate dependency rules (including whatever mechanism is necessary to ensure sequence and dependency reversal for the first two segments) as (6):

(6)

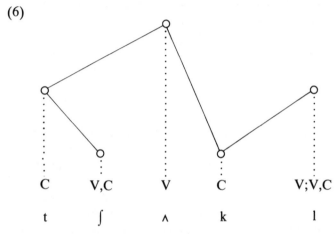

This means that the relationship between the /t/ and the /∫/ here is of exactly the same order, if not the same type, as that between say /ʌ/ and /k/ or /k/ and /l/. By using the configuration in (1) for the affricates, Ewen is characterising what is claimed to be a phonological category in terms of the representations appropriate for sequences of segments. In doing so, Ewen is presumably following Anderson & Jones (1977), where the configuration is first proposed. Anderson & Jones in fact present the structure without any explanation or motivation whatsoever, and make no attempt to incorporate it within the system as a whole. It is not at all clear what status the configuration has in relation to the categorial gesture, or indeed, to the sequential representations. But if we retain their characterisation, then the affricates are not a speech sound type at all, any more than say /kl/ or even /st/; they are simply the result of the juxtaposition of two independent (categorially defined) sound types whose dependency relationship is doubly aberrant. The representation in (1) cannot be used to represent an independent speech segment since it necessarily entails sequence. For affricates to have any categorial (as opposed to sequential) status in dependency phonology they must, like any other unit, be characterised within the categorial gesture, and not as a by-product of the sequence dependency rules.

Note that this confusion between categorial and sequential representations leads Ewen to propose at least one spurious argument in favour of the configurations in (1). He states (1980a: 232) that affricates are more likely to pattern with stops than with fricatives in phonological processes, and that this, in addition to the fact that affricates in general develop historically from stops rather than fricatives (cf. e.g. PGmc */k/ $\rightarrow$ OE [tʃ]), suggests that they are to be considered as a subclass of stops. The dependency configurations directly represent this in that the |C| governs the |V,C|. But, one could use the same reasoning to claim that |V|+|V;V,C| sequences in structures like (7):

(7)

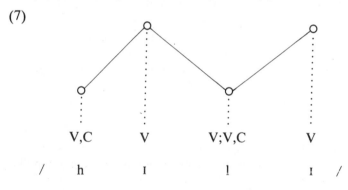

| V,C | V | V;V,C | V |

/   h   ɪ   !   ɪ   /

are a subclass of vowels, presumably something one would not need to do too frequently.

How then are the initial elements in words like ‹chuckle› and ‹juggle› to be represented within the framework? As we have seen, the representations in (1) do not sidestep the unit/sequence problem; rather, they entail a sequence interpretation, and this moreover at what we feel to be an unacceptable cost to the model as a whole. There are, of course, two directions possible here, and the notation does not obviate the necessity of making a choice. Either affricates are an independent segment type, in which case they must be characterised in the categorial gesture, or they are not, and some characterisation along the lines of that proposed previously (i.e. involving sequential representation) must be adopted, but without concomitantly weakening the theoretical basis of the model.

If the first option is preferred, that affricates are monosegmental, then it is not at all clear to us just how they might be represented in the categorial gesture. One possibility might simply be to adopt the structures in (1) as the categorial representation. To do so would, however, introduce adjunction (i.e. precedence relations) into the categorial gesture for this one segment type only, and we would again be faced with the problem outlined earlier of preventing other such structures (or of justifying them!). (See Anderson's paper in this volume, and Anderson & Ewen (to appear) for the (tentative) claim that such structures might indeed be found elsewhere within the categorial gesture, for instance in the representation of phonologically short diphthongs.) Or it may be that the exceptional character of the affricates is to be captured in terms of some sort of 'secondary articulation' structure representing the fricativisation of the stop, though it is not immediately apparent to us how this might be achieved. If the sequence approach is adopted, then the picture is perhaps less complex. One possibility would be to use a representation similar to that proposed for /sC/ clusters; the 'greater governs lesser' sonorancy principle remains intact, and thus results in sequence reversal. Thus Engl. ‹ditch› would be represented categorially as (8):

(8) |C;V| |V| |C| |V,C|
         /   d   ɪ   t   ʃ   /

which would result in (9) via the sonorance dependency rules:

(9)

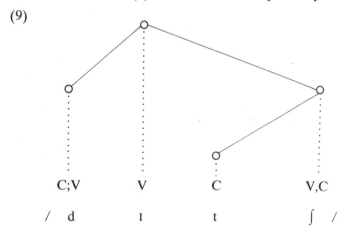

C;V   V   C   V,C

/   d   ɪ   t   ʃ   /

This would, it seems to us, still allow the unusual nature of the affricates to be expressed (in terms of sequence reversal), and at the same time preserve the insight given by the notation concerning syllable structure. Furthermore, no *ad hoc* constraints are required to avoid undesirable configurations.

Note that if this is correct, then affricate sequences become in some sense mirror images of the /sC/ clusters (or indeed other sibilant + stop clusters like Md. Germ. /ʃt/, etc.). These clusters only exhibit sequence reversal in initial position — compare ⟨spill⟩ with ⟨lisp⟩ in (10):

(10)   (a)

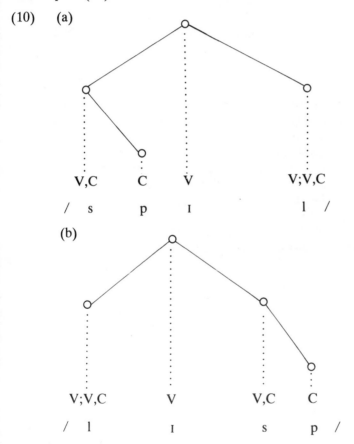

V,C   C   V   V;V,C

/   s   p   ɪ   l   /

(b)

V;V,C   V   V,C   C

/   l   ɪ   s   p   /

whereas the affricate configurations exhibit this reversal in final position — compare the initial and final sequences in ⟨church⟩ in (11):

(11)

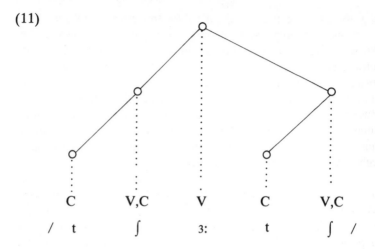

	C	V,C	V	C	V,C
/	t	ʃ	3:	t	ʃ /

Such a characterisation seems to have at least one drawback, however. If indeed it is the case that in initial position there is nothing unusual about the structure of the affricates, then this would miss the common intuition speakers have that words like ‹judge› consist of only three segments rather than five. It might be possible to circumvent this by having a representation involving more layers of dependency than in (11), such that both /t/ and /ʃ/ are directly governed by |V| at the same time as /ʃ/ governs /t/, as in (12), but to do so might well be to lay oneself open to the charge of simply playing with the formalism, rather than capturing any genuine insight:

(12)

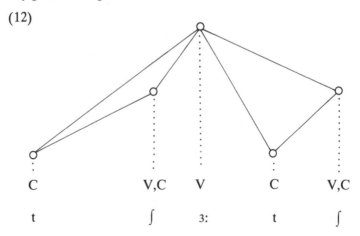

C		V,C	V	C	V,C
t		ʃ	3:	t	ʃ

3. Glottalic Opening and the Gestures

We suggested above that part of the problem with regard to the characterisation of the affricates was to do with the confusion between what is or should be represented by the segmental configurations on the one hand, and the sequential structures on the other. A similar confusion arises in Ewen's most recent treatment of another sound type open to both a mono- or biseg-mental analysis, the pre-aspirated stops (such as occur in Md. Icelandic or Sc. Gaelic (for details, cf. Ewen 1982). Here, how-ever, the confusion centres on the component |O|, glottalic opening. This component is one of three initiatory gesture com-ponents (the other two being |G| and |K|, representing glottalic and velaric initiation mechanisms respectively). In the representations of preaspirated stops, however, |O|'s initiatory status is far from clear. Thus, |O| appears independently as an element in a sequential representation in (13) (from Ewen 1982: 64):

(13)

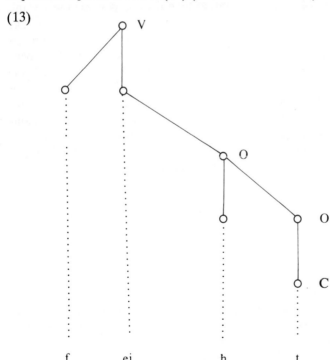

Similarly, |O| combines freely with the categorial components |C| and |V|, as in (14), the representations for the Icelandic stop system:

(14)

O   C

| |

| |

C   O

/p t k/ ~ [pʰ tʰ kʰ]   /b d g/ ~ [p t k]

(Ewen 1982: 64)

In earlier treatments of this material (Ewen 1980a,b), it is quite clear that |O| does indeed belong in the initiatory gesture, and that it is the two *gestures* (categorial and initiatory) that are involved in the dependency relations, rather than the components themselves. In the latest version this is not at all obvious; nowhere is the initiatory gesture mentioned in connection with |O|, and configurations like (13) and (14) appear without any indication of a possible difference in status between the various components.

This (uncharacteristic) lack of clarity is, we feel, symptomatic of a more general problem, that of the nature of the relationship between the categorial and initiatory gestures, and it is to this that we now turn. There is little doubt that segmental representations involve the notion of gestures, and that this should involve a separation of locational information (i.e. that pertaining to the articulatory gesture) from manner and phonation/airstream information. What seems to us to be less certain is that the current treatment of phonation and airstream types is appropriate. Within the categorial gesture, as we have seen, there is interaction between the components |C| and |V|, which combine to represent a wide range of manner of articulation types. However, the only phonation type allowed for in the categorial gesture is that equivalent to the Jakobsonian [+/− voice]. No other glottal states are allowed for: if aspiration, creaky voice, breathy voice, etc. are to be described, then the initiatory gesture, and in particular the component |O|, is called upon. Unlike the other two gestures, the initiatory gesture does not function as an independent unit; rather, as we outlined earlier, it and the categorial gesture enter into dependency relations in much the same way as the gestural components. Thus, the three way contrast between voiceless, voiced and creaky voice segments found in Hausa (Ladefoged 1971: 17) is represented as

(15)
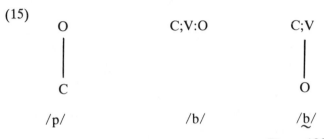

(Ewen 1980a: 316)

where the greater the degree of glottal opening, then the greater the degree of initiation: for voiceless segments the initiatory governs the categorial gesture, for voiced segments the gestures are co-dependent, and for creaky voice, the initiatory gesture is subordinate, since these sounds show least glottal opening. It is the implications of this proposed 'special relationship' that we wish to examine, particularly that (i) dependency relations may hold between gestures and not just components, and (ii) that different phonation types should be accounted for cross-gesturally (since |O| and |V| appear in different gestures). Connected with these questions is the status of the other initiatory components |G| and |K|, and whether these also should be involved in the proposed initiatory/categorial dependencies.

Let us begin a consideration of these problems by examining the motivation behind the separation of phonation types, i.e. for having |O| in the initiatory gesture and |V| in the categorial.[2] The basic argument for this is to be found in Chapter 5 of Ewen 1980a (pp. 131ff). Using Ladefoged (1971) as his starting point, Ewen argues that the feature [+/− voice] is insufficient to characterise all the possible phonation-type contrasts found in various languages, and that Ladefoged's 'n-ary' feature [glottal stricture] would be more appropriate. He then argues that the two features are not mutually exclusive, but rather are both necessary. He claims that

[voice] is, phonologically, a feature like [continuant] and [sonorant], in that categories like voiced stop ... appear to

behave in the same way with respect to various kinds of hier-archies. However, the important distinction in this respect appears to be between the presence and absence of voice, rather than between various *degrees* of voicing (Ewen 1980a: 132 (his italics)).

Thus, the᠂ two features are representative of two independent parameters and Ewen suggests (p. 132) that they should be assigned to different gestures, [voice] to the categorial and [glottal stricture] to the initiatory. Now the motivation or separating the phonation types seems to us to be well-founded enough; glottal stricture does seem, as Ewen claims, only to be phonologically relevant in languages which have an opposition between three, rather than two, glottal states. However, an argument for such a separation is not automatically an argument for assigning the two parameters to different gestures as well. Ewen argues (1980a: 310) that 'it is the nature of the interaction between glottal opening and the representation of the categorial gesture ... which makes it appropriate to claim that the component of glottal opening belongs to a separate gesture', i.e. it is the fact that the two gestures interact in dependency terms that determines that |O| is an initiatory com-ponent: |O| is initiatory because it interacts with |C| and |V|, which are categorial components. In other words, |O| is initiatory because it is not the same as |V|, i.e. is not categorial. If it is not categorial, then it must be initiatory, and the proposed relationship between the two gestures will inevitably support this. But, the argument is clearly fallacious; there is no necessary step from arguing that |O| and |V| are different to claiming that |O| must therefore be in a different gesture; it could equally well be assigned to the same ges-ture as |V|.

Another argument put forward in support of an analysis whereby |O| belongs in the initiatory gesture, based on the notion of phonological complexity, looks at first to be rather more com-pelling. If |O| is initiatory in nature, then it is possible to represent languages which involve other glottal states than [+/− voice] as more complex, since they will require an extra gesture for their representation (cf. Ewen 1980a: 133f). Thus, a language like Danish, for example, which has no voiced stops, but which makes a contrast between voiceless aspirated and voiceless unaspirated stops as in (16)

(16)   aspirated   unaspirated
       pil   (arrow)   bil   (car)
       tale (speak)   dale (valleys)
       kasser (boxes)   gasser (gases)

(cf e.g. Heger 1975; Thorsen & Thorsen 1978), will require configurations identical to those already given for Icelandic in (14) to
capture this contrast. This means that Danish will be represented
as being more complex than, say, English (to take a random
example), by virtue of the fact that it requires three, rather than
two, gestures. But it does not appear to us to be particularly
natural that the Danish contrast should be represented as being so
much more complex as to involve an extra gesture when it seems
to serve exactly the same function as [+/− voice] in English. It is,
for example, susceptible to neutralisation after /s/ and finally in
the same way as the voicing contrast, but this parallelism cannot be
allowed for if |O| forms part of the initiatory gesture.

For Danish, the postulate that |O| is initiatory raises the further
problem that |O| is required in the description of the stops, but not
for the description of the fricatives, which make only a [+/−
voice] contrast (as in 'fin' (fine) ~ 'vin' (wine)). That is, it will be
difficult to assess the 'degree of complexity' of Danish if the
initiatory status of |O| is maintained: one subset within the system
will require only two gestures (the fricatives) whilst for another
(i.e. the stops) three gestures are needed. So, within the consonant
system, two clearly related subsets have to be treated in completely
different ways. If, on the other hand, |O| is a categorial component
(as we shall claim), the difference between English and Danish will
be much less marked (though still present, of course). Danish will
belong to a middle group which involve only two gestures but
include |O| in the categorial representations, as opposed to
languages like English, with only two gestures and no |O|, on the
one hand, and e.g. Sindhi, with categorial |O| and glottalic
initiation, i.e. all three gestures, on the other. Thus it would be possible to allow for more than two grades of typological complexity
in this area, a capability not available to the current version of the
model.

Thus there seems to be sufficient evidence to merit a change in
the model with regard to the status of |O|. We believe that the
problems outlined above can be minimised by assigning categorial
status to |O|. That is, we propose that |O| forms part of the

categorial gesture along with |C| and |V| and that it enters into dependency relations with these. It is quite possible that |O| should be considered in some sense subsidiary to |C| and |V|, in that it probably does not alone constitute a gesture. That is, the presence of |O| in a representation will presuppose the presence of |C| and |V|, whereas the reverse implication will not hold (i.e. the presence of either |C| or |V| does not imply the presence of |O|). But this is a point that will require further investigation, in particular a consideration of the preaspiration evidence mentioned above discussed in Ewen 1982, where it is argued that |O| alone adequately characterises this phenomenon (cf. the tree in (13) above in this regard). This is, however, beyond the scope of the present paper.

Irrespective of how this may be resolved, our proposal does not infringe the original motivation for decomposing segments into articulatory and categorial gestures: the features [voice] and [continuant] can still be shown to act together with the major class features, one of the main reasons for operating with a categorial gesture (cf. Lass & Anderson 1975: app. II, Ewen 1980a: Ch. 5). Indeed we believe our proposal to be intuitively more natural, in that, for example, neutralisation rules can be shown to operate along a single hierarchy cross-linguistically (cf. Danish and English stop neutralisation after /s/, etc.). Similarly, the proposal allows for a richer expression of phonological complexity, in that at least three, possibly four, 'levels of typological complexity' are available, as was illustrated by the brief discussion of Danish, English and Sindhi in this regard.

If the proposal concerning the categorial status of |O| is well-founded, then the motivation for operating with inter-gestural dependencies (between the initiatory and categorial gestures) is considerably weakened. But there are other reasons for considering such dependencies to be unnecessary. Firstly, it seems counter-intuitive — or better, inconsistent — to argue at great length for the propriety of decomposing segments into gestures, and then, once having established these, to operate with representations which obscure the boundaries between the gestures by allowing inter-gestural interaction. If one is going to operate with discrete subdivisions within segments, surely it is appropriate to maintain their discreteness. Secondly, it is not clear why, if inter-gestural dependency relations are possible, no such relations are proposed between e.g. the articulatory and categorial gestures.

Strictly speaking this is formally equally plausible, but no explanation is offered as to why such relations are found to obtain only between the categorial and initiatory gestures. If it is argued that no such relations are found elsewhere because the dividing line between, say, the articulatory and categorial gestures is clear-cut, then we may use this as an argument against the proposed categorial/initiatory interaction by asking why, if there are indeed two gestures here, the dividing line is not equally clear-cut, so that no inter-gestural relationship need be resorted to. Finally, we find the inter-gestural relation hypothesis spurious because no motivation is adduced to support it other than that it captures the gradual nature of the relation between different glottal states: but, as we have seen, this can be allowed for equally well if |O| is a component in the categorial gesture.

Thus there seems to be some quite compelling evidence favouring an approach whereby |O| is categorial and inter-gestural dependencies are unnecessary. However, before we can say that the latter claim in particular is fully justified, we must consider the evidence concerning glottalic and velaric initiation. Ewen's discussion of this (1980a: Ch. 9) seems to lead to a situation where it is necessary for the initiatory and categorial gestures to interact after all. In characterising glottalic initiation Ewen sets up the component |G|, which represents both glottalic initiation and the relative height of the glottis. When |G| is present the initiatory gesture again enters into dependency relations with the categorial gesture. And in this case it looks as though an inter-gestural solution is necessary to account for a system such as (17) [= Ewen 1980a: 342, fig. 9.57].

(17)

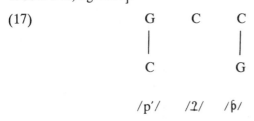

which involves a glottal ejective, a glottal stop and a voiceless glottal implosive. In (17), the relative preponderance of the initiatory gesture (i.e. |G|) is determined by the relative height of the glottis, which is raised for /p'/, lowered for /ɓ/. However, this seems to be the only system in which |G| alone enters into a gradual relation with the categorial gesture. In all the other systematic representations proposed by Ewen, |G| does not enter into such relations except in combination with |O| (cf. as an example (18) below). That is, in these representations |G| cannot be said to motivate inter-gestural relations; these are rather a result of the fact that it is necessary in Ewen's version to allow initiatory gesture representations involving |O| to interact with the categorial gesture. Thus in (18) the presence of |G| is not a motivation for the dependencies, since it has no dependency relation to |O| (cf. the representation {|O.G|}), and, since all the segments are implosives, it clearly does not indicate an ejective/implosive distinction (as is the case in (17) above).

(18)
$$
\begin{array}{ccc}
\text{C;V} & \text{C;V:O.G} & \text{O.G} \\
| & & | \\
\text{O.G} & & \text{C;V} \\
\end{array}
$$

$$
/ɓ/ \qquad /ɓ/ \qquad /ɓ̈/
$$

(Ewen 1980a: 343, fig. 9.59)

Now if it is only in (17) that the presence of |G| determines the nature of the dependency relation between the categorial and initiatory gestures, then it is worth considering whether this constitutes sufficient motivation for maintaining the inter-gestural relation analysis. But before we consider this, let us envisage what a description of glottal phenomena might look like if (17) were to be disregarded. A first approximation is given in (19), which illustrates the characterisation of /ɓ/ (cp. the representation in (18) above):

(19)

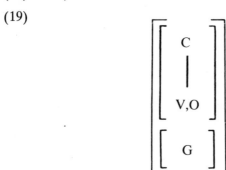

Here, the presence of glottalic initiation and a lowered glottis is allowed for by the presence of an uncombined |G| in a discrete initiatory gesture. The difference in glottal stricture between /ɓ/, /ɓ/ and /ɓ̰/ is then taken care of in terms of the relative prominence of |O| in the categorial representations. We return to this below, where we shall see that there is reason to change this preliminary account of the internal structure of the initiatory gesture.

We must now consider the system in (17), which, as we have mentioned, seems to argue for an analysis which does indeed involve inter-gestural dependency relations. In (17), |G| functions independently within the initiatory gesture; its relative prominence is not a result of the presence of |O|, as it is in (18). Though (17) would seem to be appropriate for the (hypothetical) system it describes, there are nonetheless some problems associated with it. Firstly, it is not at all clear that the voiceless glottal implosive /ƥ/ is systematically used in human language: Catford (1977) reports Pike as having noted them in Tojolabal (Guatemala), but Ladefoged (1975) states that 'in the production of implosives, the glottis is not usually completely closed' (1975: 116) and has only voiced examples of this initiation type. It is at any rate clear that such sounds are very very rare, but as the evidence (and our competence to assess it) is limited, we will not push the point here. A second difficulty with (17) is that, as Ewen acknowledges, no gradual relation exists beetween /p'/ and /ƛ/ on the one hand, and /ƛ/ and /ƥ/ on the other. This constitutes a more serious problem, as the main reason for introducing inter-gestural relations was that they allow for the expression of just such gradual relations; in (17) there is no explanation for the fact that this is not fully exploited, i.e. that /ƛ/ is not represented as {|C.G|}. Finally there is a problem which concerns not just the representations in (17), but has a more general impact. In (17) a dominating |G| represents glottalic pressure, as in the configuration for /p'/, while a subordinate |G| represents glottalic suction. But in (18) no such implications hold for the relative position of |G|; in the representations for e.g. /ɓ/ and /ɓ̰/ |G| is respectively dependent and governing, but both configurations represent ingressive sounds. (This is, of course, due to the fact that in (18) |G| is simply 'tagged onto' the (initiatory) component |O|.) This difference between (17) and (18) is clearly unsatisfactory, and is yet further evidence for claiming that the system in (17) does not constitute a substantial counter-example to our 'no-interaction' proposal.

An analysis whereby the initiatory gesture is discrete is also supported by evidence from the velaric initiation sound types. Ewen characterises velaric initiation by means of the initiatory component |K|, which is present when velaric initiation is employed and absent otherwise. Now this in itself points to a characterisation of the kind shown in (19), such that |K| is present in the initiatory representation when needed and otherwise is not. The appropriateness of this is further emphasised by the fact that |K| alone cannot constitute the initiatory representation: it always occurs in combination with other initiatory components, and hence does not in itself determine the dependency relationship with the categorial gesture. The behaviour of |K| then does not motivate the use of inter-gestural relations; again, these follow from the necessity of allowing initiatory representations involving |O| to combine with categorial representations. But, as we have argued, |O| is better accommodated in the categorial gesture anyway, so no justification remains for inter-gestural relations involving either |K| or |G|.

4. The Initiatory Gesture

Let us return to the representation in (19) and sketch out our proposal for a discrete initiatory gesture in a little more detail. As we suggested earlier, the representation in (19) is still inadequate as a full characterisation for the segment. The initiatory gesture must involve rather more than simply the presence or absence of the components |G| and |K| (if |O| is reassigned to the categorial gesture). Particularly, there is in representations such as (19) no way of distinguishing the two sound types involving glottalic initiation; those produced with pressure (e.g./p'/, etc) and those produced with suction (/ɓ/,/ɓ/, etc). The mere presence of |G| is not enough, since it does not in itself characterise either egressive or ingressive airstream movement. Nor can this be indicated elsewhere, since if the initiatory gesture is to have any function, then it must be to characterise the airstream mechanism involved in the production of a particular sound type. According to e.g. Catford (1977), there are two important aspects to initiation (cf. Catford 1977; Ch. 5): the direction of the air flow (ingressive vs. egressive), and the location of the initiating pulse — the lungs, the larynx and the velum being the phonologically relevant possibilities (1977: 64).[3]

In the current version of dependency phonology, however, only one of Catford's two aspects is directly represented; the three initiatory components represent the various locational possibilities (though not particularly appropriately in the case of |O|, which is used for pulmonic initiation as well as glottalic opening). To the extent that it is represented at all, pressure vs. suction is dealt with in terms of the dependency relations between the categorial and initiatory gestures. Thus, as we stated earlier, in (17) above, a dominant initiatory gesture involving |G| alone represents pressure, whilst in subordinate position it represents suction. If, however, |G| is combined with |O| in the initiatory configuration, suction is always involved, irrespective of the relative positions of the two gestures. Further, the presence of |O| alone represents (pulmonic) pressure, and |K| (alone or in combination) represents (velaric) suction (cf. Ewen 1980a: Ch. 9).

However, if, as we have claimed, the gestures cannot enter into dependency relations with one another, and if |O| is in fact a categorial component, then not even this extremely unrevealing way of representing the distinction in airstream direction is available. Some other means must thus be found. What we tentatively suggest here is that *both* aspects of initiation be represented directly in terms of components within the initiatory gesture; not only location as at present, but also air flow direction. This latter we propose be represented by the component |I|, which implies something like Catford's 'initiator velocity'. In his discussion of airstreams, Catford claims that:

Pressure and suction types of initiation refer in fact to opposite ends of a parameter, or scale, of *initiator velocity* on which pressure implies positive rates of [vocal tract — MD/JS] volume *decrease* (generating positive pressure) and suction implies negative rates of volume decrease (generating negative pressure) that is rates of volume *increase* (1977: 64, his italics).

This characterisation would fit nicely within a dependency system: alone or in dominant position, |I| would thus involve pressure (i.e. positive values for volume decrease) and in subordinate position would involve suction (i.e. negative pressure). This distribution is of course essentially arbitrary, but it seems at least intuitively appropriate to let a preponderance of initiator velocity represent outward movement of the initiator, this being the most common type of initiation.

What then of Catford's second parameter, location? Here, we suggest, the components |G| and |K| should be retained, representing glottalic and velaric initiation respectively, and that it is with these that |I| enters into the dependency relations outlined above. Thus, the distinction between the glottalic ejective /p'/ and the implosive /ɓ/ would be characterised within the initiatory gesture alone as in (20)

(20)

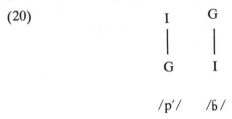

where the distinction is made in terms of the relative positions of |I| and |G|; when |I| governs, we have an ejective, when it is governed, an implosive.

Given this characterisation of sounds with glottalic initiation, we might expect that sounds involving velaric initiation (the 'clicks') will be represented as (21)

(21)   K
                             |
                             I
                            /ʇ/

where the subordinate |I| indicates that suction is present. However, this is probably unnecessary, since no languages regularly exhibit the other possibility, velaric egressives. Thus the simple combination of the components |I| and |K| will be sufficient here, as in (22):

(22) |I.K|

There remains the characterisation of sounds with pulmonic initiation, the most basic (and the only universal) initiation type. One possibility would be to propose a further component |P| to represent such types, and have it combine with |I| much as |G| and |K| do. But to do this would, it seems to us, fail to capture the fact that pulmonic sounds are indeed universal, and as such should have a representation which is simpler than that for the non-universal initiation types, just as elsewhere in the model there is a general correlation between the degree of universality of a segment and the configurational complexity of its characterisation. This is achieved in the current version of the model in terms of the simple presence of |O| or the absence of any initiatory gesture representation (at least phonologically) for such segments, but, as we have shown, such a solution is no longer tenable. What we suggest is rather that the presence of an uncombined |I| is sufficient, since this represents (unspecified) pressure, i.e. the most basic, and is also less complex than the configurations in (20) and (22), in that only one component is present. If this is appropriate, then as in the categorial gesture, there may be a difference in status between the various initiatory components, such that the presence of |G| or |K| in a representation implies that |I| also occurs in the initiatory specifications, whereas |I| does not necessarily involve the concomitant presence of either |G| or |K|. (We are indebted to John Anderson for pointing this out to us.)

Note that this proposal means that if it should prove desirable to allow for the system in (17) discussed above, involving voiceless glottalic implosives, this can be done without resorting to any form of inter-gestural dependencies. This is shown in (23), where the ejective/implosive distinction is accounted for within the initiatory gesture alone:

(23) | Cat. | C | C | C |
| --- | --- | --- | --- |
| Init. | I;G | I | G;I |
| | /p'/ | /ʔ/ | /ɓ/ |

5. Summary

We thus suggest that the discreteness of the various elements of the model be preserved, not only with regard to the distinction between segmental and sequential representations, but also with regard to the distinctions between gestures within the segment. We have further suggested that the component |O| be reassigned to the categorial gesture. (24) gives a summary of some of the possible representations such a restructuring of the initiatory and categorial gestures might involve:

(24)　　Cat.　　C　　　C　　　C　　　C;V　　C
　　　　Init.　　I　　　I;G　　G;I　　G;I　　I,K
　　　　　　　/p/　/p'/　/ɸ/　/ɓ/　/ʔ/

　　　　Cat.　　O;C　　C;V,O　C,O;V　V,O;C
　　　　Init.　　I　　　I　　　I　　　I
　　　　　　　/pʰ/　/b̰/　/b̤/　/n̥/

　　　　Cat.　　C;V,O　C,O;V
　　　　Init.　　G;I　　G;I
　　　　　　　/ɓ̰/　/ɓ̤/

Note finally that these representations are in each case the simplest possible, i.e. assuming |O| to be absent wherever it is not necessary. It may well be that in specific languages |O| will also be relevant in the configurations for say voiced stops; thus the five-way contrast in Uduk (Ladefoged 1971: 27) might be characterised as in (25):

(25)　　Cat.　　O;C　　C,O　　C,O　　C;V,O　C;V,O
　　　　Init.　　I　　　I　　　I;G　　I　　　G;I
　　　　　　　/pʰ/　/p/　/p'/　/b/　/ɓ/

where the full range of combinatorial possibilities is exploited.

Notes

*This paper is a somewhat longer version of that presented at the Dependency Phonology Conference, Essex University, Sept. 1983. Our thanks to all who have commented on it, both at the conference and subsequently, especially John Anderson, Jacques Durand, Colin Ewen, Inger Henriksen, Ken Lodge and Cathair Ó Dochartaigh.

1. It is interesting to note, though, that the voiced congeners, represented by ‹drz› and ‹dż›, which are not discussed by Ewen, do perhaps show some evidence for a genuine phonological contrast —. cf. ‹drzemie› (nap, 3 sg pres) vs. ‹dżemie› (jam, loc). Here, there is a similar surface distinction in allegro speech, with the ‹drz› set being [dʒʒ] and the ‹dż› set [dʒ]. Phonologically, however, both sets will be /dʒ/ — thus it affricates are not a separate category the surface distinction is difficult to account for.

2. The arguments presented in the following section would also apply to the 'reorganised' account of gestures within dependency phonology sketched out in

Ewen's contribution to this volume, and discussed in detail in Anderson & Ewen, to appear. Rather than referring to independent categorial and initiatory gestures, our arguments simply apply to the phonatory and initiatory subgestures of the categorial (supra-) gesture.

3. This outline of initiation provides a further (though negative) argument for the inclusion of |O| in the categorial gesture, as proposed above, since glottalic opening (i.e. |O|) is not *per se* relevant to initiation: it is the movement of the larynx itself, rather than the degree to which the glottis is open, that is important. Thus, unlike the other initiatory components (|G| and |K|), |O| does not represent the location or movement of an initiatory organ, and thus does not belong in the initiatory gesture.

4 FRENCH LIAISON, FLOATING SEGMENTS AND OTHER MATTERS IN A DEPENDENCY FRAMEWORK

Jacques Durand

Introduction

This article is devoted to French liaison and the way it interacts with other rules of the phonology of French. The treatment offered, in the wake of Clements and Keyser (1981, 1983), assumes that the notion of 'floating' or 'extrametrical' segment allows for a better description than competing alternatives based on truncation or insertion. I have, however, considered a different and arguably broader set of processes than they could deal with in a book devoted to phonological theory, using French for exemplification only. In addition, I have tried to be as explicit as possible about the consequences of positing floating segments for the structure of lexical entries and underlying phonological representations. One of the claims I shall in fact be making is that much of the debate between 'abstract' and 'concrete' approaches to French phonology associated with the deletion-insertion analysis evaporates once floating segments find a status within the description. For this reason, sections 1 and 2 restate some of the main dividing lines between abstract and concrete approaches, while giving the necessary background for the rest of the discussion. Last, but not least, I have attempted here to describe a sizable portion of the phonology of French within a dependency phonology framework and shown that insights normally associated with metrical and autosegmental accounts could naturally be integrated within the model.[1]

1. Liaison and Other Rules in Classical Generative Phonology

1.1 *The Phonology of Liaison*

The phenomenon of French liaison — a type of phonological adjustment between words — is traditionally interpreted as the pronunciation of the final consonant of a word when it is followed by a word beginning with a vowel which is closely connected to it. The consonant which appears in liaison is said to be mute otherwise. Examples of liaison and non-liaison involving the words *les*, *petit*, *vous* and *dans* are given in (1) and (2) below:

(1) les enfants [lɛzɑ̃fɑ̃]; petit écrou [p(ə)titekru]; vous avez [vuzave]; dans un jour [dɑ̃zɛ̃ʒur]

(2) les chats [lɛʃa]; petit mot [p(ə)timo]; c'est petit [sɛp(ə)ti]; vous voyez [vuvwaje]; dans Paris [dɑ̃pari].

In classical generative phonology, the traditional description of liaison (cf. Grevisse 1964: 56; Fouché 1956: 434) is assumed to be essentially correct and reinterpreted as implying that

> the underlying form of those words which can undergo liaison must in all cases terminate in a consonant, and that this consonant is dropped whenever there is absence of liaison, i.e., in utterance final position or before a word beginning with a consonant sound (Schane 1968: 1-2).

In other words, liaison rather than being an active process linking two words is merely the result of not applying a rule of deletion (TRUNCATION, (3) below) of final consonants under certain conditions. A standard formulation of TRUNCATION, which I intend to be neutral between various alternatives, is as follows:

(3)   TRUNCATION
$$[+ \text{obstruent}] \Longrightarrow \emptyset / - \quad \begin{Bmatrix} \begin{Bmatrix} + \\ \# \end{Bmatrix} C \\ \# \quad \# \end{Bmatrix} \quad \begin{matrix} \text{(a)} \\ \\ \text{(b)} \end{matrix}$$

The idea that French phonology incorporates a general rule of TRUNCATION is defended in S.R. Anderson (1982), Dell (1970, 1973a/1980), Milner (1973), Noske (1982), Schane (1968, 1974), Selkirk (1972/81) to name but a few and the reader is referred to Love (1981) and Tranel (1981) for comprehensive surveys of competing analyses within the *Sound Pattern of English* (SPE) mould. The original formulation by Schane (1968) — who set the phonology of French on a new course — attempted to link liaison with elision on the grounds that the two processes were mirror-images of each other. Subsequent research, however, has failed to endorse this. In particular, as pointed out by Schane himself in his 1974 recantation, 'There is no French truncation rule', if we leave aside a few words like *si*, *la* and *tu*, elision does not involve the deletion of the class of vowels before a vowel but in fact only applies to schwa (cf. *l*̷*ami*). The merging of these two processes turns out to be less than convincing and has a number of unhappy consequences that we need not explore here once again.

One corollary of the idea that the 'long form' of the alternating words considered so far is the underlying form is the postulation in synchrony of a process of nasalisation and nasal consonant deletion to explain variations such as the following:

(4) bon élève   [bɔnelɛv]   vs.   c'est bon   [sɛbɔ̃]
     divin ami   [divinami]   c'est divin [sɛdivɛ̃]
     plein hiver [plɛnivɛr]   c'est plein [sɛplɛ̃]

Two competing versions are to be found in the literature: a two-rule statement as in (5) or a transformational treatment (Selkirk, 1972/81) as in (6).[2]

(5)   (i) NASALISATION

$$V \Longrightarrow [+\text{nasal}]/- \begin{bmatrix} C \\ +\text{nasal} \end{bmatrix} \begin{Bmatrix} \# \ \# \\ \# \ C \end{Bmatrix} \quad \begin{matrix} \text{(a)} \\ \text{(b)} \end{matrix}$$

      (ii) NASAL DELETION

$$\begin{bmatrix} C \\ +\text{nasal} \end{bmatrix} \Longrightarrow \emptyset/- \begin{bmatrix} V \\ +\text{nasal} \end{bmatrix}$$

(6)   NASALISATION (one-step version)

$$V \quad \begin{bmatrix} C \\ +\text{nasal} \end{bmatrix} \begin{Bmatrix} \# \ C \\ \# \ \# \end{Bmatrix}$$

$$1 \qquad 2 \qquad 3 \ \Longrightarrow \ 1 \ \emptyset \ 3$$
$$[+\text{nasal}]$$

The underlying forms of the above alternants will therefore be /bɔn/ *bon*, /divin/ *divin*, /plen/ *plein* (assuming this word is related to *plénitude*, etc.) and the claim will be entertained that the nasal vowels are merely surface entities in French.

Unfortunately for the analyst, the data of (4) are not the only pattern attested in French. In what is considered the standard accent, a number of words exhibit a nasal vowel in liaison as in (7).[3]

(7)   mon élève   [mɔ̃nelɛv]   j'ai dit 'mon'   [ʒɛdimɔ̃]
       un ami   [ɛ̃nami]   j'en veux un   [ʒɑ̃vøɛ̃]
       en hiver   [ɑ̃nivɛr]   en décembre   [ɑ̃desɑ̃br]

The difference between (4) and (7) has given rise to a lot of debate in the literature as to what the most appropriate treatment should be. Various powerful devices such as the notion of exception features to exceptions features (Schane 1973) or local rule ordering (Dell 1970, 1973b) have been put forward to account for this difference. Selkirk (1972/81: 243ff) suggests that all items like those in (7) should be represented with underlying nasal vowels (i.e. /mɔ̃n/, /ɛ̃/, /ɑ̃n/). This seems the best solution within the envisaged framework.

The description given so far has been purely mechanical. Quite a lot of care, however, has gone into the need to justify this type of analysis for French. The main argument for assuming the existence of underlying final consonants deleted in certain contexts has been the need to capture the similarities between liaison, inflection and derivation. We shall refer to this as the 'parallelism hypothesis'. Consider:

(8)   PARALLELISM HYPOTHESIS

	PHRASE FINAL	LIAISON	INFLECTION	DERIVATION
PETIT	[pti]	[ptitekru]	[ptit]	[ptitɛs]
	petit	*petit écrou*	*petite*	*petitesse*
METTRE	[ilmɛ]	[mɛtil]	[mɛtɔ̃]	[mɛtabl]
	il met	*met-il?*	*mettons*	*mettable*
DIVIN	[divɛ̃]	[divinami]	[divin]	[divinite]
	divin	*divin ami*	*divine*	*divinité*

The rules we have formulated so far cannot work without making a number of auxiliary assumptions about French. Some of the main ones are:

(a) Feminine words of the *petite* type although regularly pronounced without a final vowel in standard French (i.e. [p(ə)tit]) are assumed to have an underlying final schwa which is the uniform marker of the feminine. Evidence for it is sometimes said to be given by a surfacing before *h-aspiré* words (e.g. *petite house* [p(ə)titəus] — see (c) below. Morphological schwas are also argued to occur in verbal forms. In addition 'protective' schwas are postulated medially in words like *omelette* [ɔmlɛt], and finally in words like *lune* [lyn] to block NASALISATION.

(b) A number of words (*cap* [kap], *lac* [lak], *sec* [sɛk]) have to be marked as exceptions to TRUNCATION.

(c) *h-aspiré* words which begin with a vowel phonetically but appear to behave as if they were consonantal (e.g. *la honte* [laᶾt] not **l'honte*) are assumed to have an underlying consonantal segment initially which we shall write /H/ to avoid controversy as to its precise nature. All the studies done within this set of assumptions have been said to be 'abstract' in the sense that starting from familiar alternations we are led further and further away from the surface and end up with underlying forms which require complex rule ordering, absolute neutralisations, Duke of York gambits and the like, to be actualised.

1.2 *The Syntax and Stylistics and Liaison*

Pre-generative descriptions of French assume that if the phonological conditions for liaison are fulfilled we can distinguish three grammatical types of context: (a) obligatory; (b) optional; (c) forbidden. Examples of these are given below:

(9)
(a)	DET + N	*les amis*	[lɛzami]	*[lɛami]
(b)	AUX + COMP	*est ici*	[ɛtisi] or	[ɛisi]
(c)	NP + VP	*les amis arrivent*		[lɛzami ariv]
				*[lɛzamizariv]

Where liaison is optional, its frequency will be relative to a variety of 'stylistic' factors. To quote a well-known maxim: 'The more elevated the style the more liaison occurs.' A common way of handling the relative frequency of liaison has consisted in setting up a number of registers or scales of formality: e.g. colloquial, careful and formal.

In major work on this topic, Selkirk (1972/81, 1974) has tried to show how some of the traditional assumptions could be integrated within a generative approach. She takes as correct a version of the TRUNCATION rule given above (see (3)). Hence liaison will only occur when at most *one* word boundary separates two units which is a way of expressing the classical notion that liaison depends on the syntactic cohesion between words. She argues that the facts of liaison follow directly from SPE universal conventions on the distribution of boundaries coupled with language-specific readjustment rules. Thus an adjective and a noun strung together should be separated by two word boundaries but, since liaison does occur in *petit acte* /p(ə)titakt/, a convention will be proposed which — informally stated — transforms ADJ # # N into ADJ # N. In addition to this, Selkirk contends that the re-adjustment rules are maximally stated in terms of $\overline{X}$ syntax and in turn provide evidence for the layering of syntactic categories this model makes possible. She also develops an account in which the idea that French has three levels of formality — an idea which finds its roots in Grammont's and Fouchés's work — is accepted and elegantly integrated within the description (see too Milner 1973). She departs, however, from tradition in lumping together cases of obligatory and optional liaison in her basic style.

A number of difficulties raised by Selkirk's boundary approach have already been noted in the literature. For instance, Basbøll (1978:8) has pointed out that

> According to several investigations of 'word-reduction'-phenomena ... it appears to be generally the case that the more casual or 'reduced' the style level becomes the more grammatical boundaries lose effect. But in Selkirk's framework, exactly the opposite is the case: the higher and more distant the level of style becomes the more instances of # # are reduced to #.

(See too Tranel's section (1981: 170-5) on Selkirk (1972/81) which summarises a number of objections to the analysis in question.) Recently, however, Selkirk's analysis has been subjected to a devastating critique by Morin and Kaye (1982) who show that her approach in terms of boundaries makes a number of false predictions and that, while there is an undeniable link between the facts of liaison and syntactic structure, these facts do not provide crucial evidence for (or against, for that matter) the $\overline{X}$ model. Rather,

> the traditional approach, according to which the syntactic environment in which a liaison occurs is defined category by category, and sometimes even word by word, appears to be essentially correct (1982: 326).

In a test which partially duplicates Morin and Kaye's experiment and explores a few areas they left untouched, I found over-whelming evidence for the correctness of their conclusions. The test involves the reading of two sets of sentences graded stylistically like theirs and a passage designed to evince an even higher degree of formality than the sentences. Ten subjects were involved. Contrary to what Selkirk (1972/81) predicts, for instance, an inflected adjective followed by a complement does NOT behave like an inflected noun followed by its complement, and the latter in turn does NOT behave like an inflected verb followed by its complement despite the fact that they all instantiate the X category. Thus, even in the reading of a literary passage, I found no occurrence of liaison in ADJ-COMP phrases like *prêts/à tout faire* or *insolents/envers tous,* whereas liaison does occur in N-COMP and V-COMP phrases such as *soldats⌢à moustache grise, marmots⌢en bas-age,* on the one hand, and *réussit⌢à obtenir de lui, se mit⌢à le tenailler,* on the other. But statistically, whereas liaisons in N-COMP structures never exceeded 50%, they were (across subjects, that is) close to the 100% mark for some of the V-COMP examples. An examination of whether liaison could be blocked by traces left by Wh-movement or Clitic-movement, as claimed by Selkirk, also disproved this claim. The majority of the subjects made a liaison in e.g. *Le courage que sa présence donnait⌢à ces gens* and *Adolphe les ménerait⌢au pouvoir*; but, more interestingly, *all* the subjects made at least one liaison in one of the crucial contexts.

It is also doubtful that the notion of three (or four) scales of formality makes very much sense. It is not so much that the choice of three is arbitrary. After all, if some empirical consequences could be shown to derive from it, that would be ample justification. But, the empirical consequences of the assumption of discrete registers are rather hard to find. Thus consider a sentence of our reading passage: *quelques audacieux officiers sérieux et appliqués.* The passage was read twice by two of my ten subjects (with interesting discrepancies!) so that the figures below refer to twelve realisations. The number of observed liaisons (L) and non-liaisons (NL) were as follows:

(10)

	L	NL
quelques_audacieux	12	0
audacieux_officiers	7	5
sérieux_et appliqués	4	8

These results cast serious doubts on Selkirk's tripartite division since she assumes that liaison in *quelques audacieux* and *audacieux officiers* both belong to her Style I ('conversation familière') whereas liaison in *sérieux et appliqués* ('lecture/discours') belongs to Style III. But, liaison in *quelques audacieux* appears to be CATE-GORICAL and is traditionally classified as such, whereas it is VARI-ABLE in the other two cases. Of course, we could readjust our notion of what belongs to these styles but none of the studies based on corpora (see Ågren 1973; Malécot 1975; Encrevé 1983) reveal the sharp discontinuities one would expect if three or four discrete styles were posited. Suppose then that we fall back on a different position: a number of discrete registers can be set up via scales of implication. Obligatory liaison will be our base line since by definition it is presupposed by variable liaisons. But, within variable liaison we can for instance assert that *et ceteris paribus* liaison in $ADJ_{p1} + et + ADJ_{p1}$ presupposes liaison in $ADJ_{p1} + N$. Our test does not give us much cause for optimism since, in what one would assume is an identical situation, one subject made the liaison in *sérieux et appliqués* but not in *audacieux officiers*, and there is no reason to believe that other scales of implication would not lead to the same results. This can always be explained away as a lapse or the result of a different principle of euphony interacting with other grammatical and situational factors. The difficulty is that in setting up these scales all we have — since intuitions in this domain are extremely misleading — is sets of figures from the various corpus studies. But when it is realised, for instance, that the likelihood of liaison varies even for the forms of a single verb (see e.g. Ågren's study where *est* liaised 97% of the time, *sont* 86%, *étaient* 63%, *sommes* 58%, *était* 21%, etc), it is hard to see how to weigh the various figures across phrases to establish our putative scales of implication. As I do not believe either that the figures so far obtained, or their mathematical transformations, should be written into the competence grammar (see Encrevé 1983, for a justification of this position within a detailed socio-linguistic study of French liaison), I shall assume hereafter that we should return to the traditional position that liaison is either obligatory (categorical), optional (variable) or forbidden. Variable liaison will be simply coded by making rules optional. In addition, I shall suppose that the phonological rules can make reference to surface syntactic structure rather than operate simply in terms of boundaries. I shall, however, occasionally avail myself of the possibility of using boundaries as a mere abbreviation for morphological or syntactic divisions. I leave open the question as to whether a universal theory of boundaries makes predictive claims not expressible otherwise.[4]

2. Concrete Alternatives

2.1 *Liaison as Epenthesis*

In 1.1 I have outlined what I take to be central assumptions made in classical generative phonology. Despite the fact that it is possible to offer an elegant account of French along these lines, a number of objections have been raised within a more 'concrete' perspective. (See Klausenburger 1977, 1978a, b; and Tranel 1981). I shall limit myself to a few selected topics which play a role in the rest of the discussion.

If it is assumed that TRUNCATION is a major phonological rule of French and that doomed segments are metrically identical with fixed final consonants (as in *cap* and *sec*), one needs to mark a very large number of words belonging to this latter category as exceptions to TRUNCATION. The problem is not solely of statistical implausibility but rather the fact that this goes against trends in French expanding this 'exceptional' class while the 'normal' class is being reduced: compare the creation of abbreviations (*faculté* [fakylte] ⟹ *fac* [fak]), acronyms (FNAC [fnak]), borrowings (e.g. *basket* [baskɛt]), or the restoration of final consonants (*août* [ut]), with the well-known erosion of liaison consonants.

Questions also arise as to the postulation of 'protective' schwas which are central to the abstract account of French. Thus a medial /ə/ is necessary in words like *omelette* to block NASALISATION: if the underlying form was /ɔmlɛt/, the wrong surface from *[ɔ̃lɛt] would be derived. Yet, Tranel (1981: 29-32) reports that in an experiment he devised a number of subjects never realised this schwa even in *slow speech* and he argues that for those who do there is a possible correlation between speech and knowledge of the spelling system. In addition, the idea presented in Selkirk (1972/81; 329-30) that a schwa which is 'otherwise dormant, will rise to the surface' before *h-aspiré* words (so that *étrange hasard* would always be [etrãʒəazar]) does not correspond to an invariable realisation (other realisations are [etrãʒ/azar] and [etrãʒ?azar]) and creates a learnability problem. As pointed out by Love (1981: 84-5) and Tranel (1981: 286-8 *et passim*) such collocations are rare, indeed exceptional; one hears quite commonly schwas which can only be interpreted as epenthetic in such contexts (*avoir honte* (avwarə̃t])); and therefore the notion that this test could allow native speakers to reconstruct an implicit schwa or would guarantee its existence is dubious at best.

Finally, the PARALLELISM HYPOTHESIS (cf. 1.1) has been subjected to a great deal of criticism. Inconsistencies across liaison, derivation and inflection have not been difficult to find. Thus beside *petit—petite—petitesse*, we notice *hardi—hardie—hardiesse*, on the one hand, and *poli—polie—politesse*, on the other. Within derivation itself, there are enough inconsistencies to make the analyst uncomfortable: compare *tabac—tabatière—tabagique*; *sirop—sirupeux—siroter*; *clou—clouer—clouter*, etc. We also have to account for the fact that whereas liaison consonants are dwindling away, gender consonants based on Ø-C alternations are stable. Tranel (1981: 271-2) mentions as indirect evidence of this the existence of dialects of French, such as the Wallon dialect of Roux, where liaison consonants have totally disappeared but gender consonants are as stable as in the standard accent: thus one would observe petit [pti], *petit homme* [ptiɔm] vs. *petite* [ptit].

To avoid such difficulties, advocates of a concrete approach have argued that the historical process of truncation has undergone rule inversion. Although this is sometimes written as:

(1) $\emptyset \implies C/V - V$
       (where syntactic and stylistic conditions are left out)

this cannot be correct since it does not tell us which consonant to insert.[5] Thus to account for ADJECTIVE liaison, to limit oneself to this instance only, we in fact need the following rules:

(2)   (a) $\emptyset \implies n/\tilde{V} - V$ (*certain ami*)
       (b) $\emptyset \implies t/V - V$ (*petit ami*)
       (c) $\emptyset \implies z/V - V$ (*joyeux élève*)
       (d) $\emptyset \implies g/V - V$ (*long été*)
       (e) $\emptyset \implies r/V - V$ (*premier été*)

Moreover individual items have to be marked as to what epenthesis rule they undergo. The presence of a number of rules as in (2a-e) has been seen as an advantage by e.g. Morin & Kaye (1982: 316-17) since: 'These rules are complex and violate certain conditions on recoverability (cf. Kaye 1978), and one would expect the rules of (62) to be reduced in number or even eliminated altogether.' And this is exactly what is happening. As more and more items lose their diacritics (e.g. *long* l5/ [+(2d)]), the rule loses its vigour and is finally bound to be wiped out.

Ultimately, as in the Wallon dialect of Roux, all the rules in (2) can be expected to disappear.

2.2 *Drawbacks of the Concrete Approach*

While it is generally agreed that an account of French in concrete terms (cf. Tranel 1981) is possible, doubts remain as to the various aspects of this type of approach. First of all, what arguably is a *unitary generalisation* — i.e. the presence of a consonant in liaison contexts — is obscured by (2a-d) which could just as well be a set of unrelated insertion rules. Secondly, if we consider the behaviour of *h-aspiré* words, while there is much sociolinguistic variation, we do not want to say that each *h-aspiré* word must be marked [— (2a)], [— (2b)], [— (2c)], etc, to account for *grand hameau, petit hameau, joyeux hameau,* etc. If this were to be the case, we would expect some speakers to have lost one of these exception features and not the others (e.g. say systematically *grand hameau* vs. *petit hameau*). I do not know of any evidence showing this type of systematicity to be present in the speech of given speakers[6]. Thirdly, while there are exceptions in the correspondence of liaison, derivational and inflectional consonants, it is perhaps misguided to expect a treatment applying to all cases since we are not dealing with unsuppressible phonetic rules. At the same time, if feminine and liaison consonants are introduced epenthetically as in Tranel (1981), the relationship that does usually exist between them is not expressed. Thus *heureux* takes a /z/ in liaison and a /z/ in the feminine (and in derivation) but since these consonants are the product of two distinct mechanisms, they might as well be unrelated (e.g. /z/ in one case and /k/ in the other). While a *via rule* can always be written (e.g. z ⟸⟹ k), it seems to be an extraneous device for recording regularities that have not been captured. It is not clear that they are superior to minor rules which adjust the underlying consonant whenever there are deviations from the pattern of identity (e.g. *doux* with /z/ in liaison and /s/ in feminine and derivation). Finally, the dying out of liaison in various contexts needs not prove that it is individual rules of insertion which are being lost. For instance, the ADJ-N contexts may have already moved in modern French towards being an optional rather than an obligatory liaison context (e.g. one hears *petit Italien* or *grand Italien* beside *petit Italien* and *grand Italien*). In addition, the prenominal position for adjectives is heavily restricted. It is therefore not surprising that unusual sequences such as, say, *blond Italien* (given by Tranel 1981: 271) should be pronounced — perhaps always on the rare occasions they would be uttered — as (blɔ̃italjɛ̃], rather than the theoretical ?[blɔ̃ditaljɛ̃] or [blɔ̃titaljɛ̃]. Liaison depends on the syntactic proximity of the relevant items and by putting a word in an unusual, marked position we are, so to speak, surrounding it with quotes increasing its distance from its neighbours. In Selkirk's (1972/81) approach, the language-specific readjustment rule reducing ADJ###N to ADJ#N in French, might not apply to adjectives not marked in the lexicon for the specified position.

The above remarks cannot of themselves deal a death-blow to the concrete approach and are not intended to do so. Much in theoretical research depends on the type of data and regularities one is willing to consider and many of the criticisms directed at the abstract approach are to the point. There is no doubt, in particular, that the uniformity in lexical entries taken for granted in the standard model (the 'one underlying form per morpheme outside suppletion') was over-optimistic. On the other hand, it is questionable that the reduction of all morphophonological problems to an annotation of lexical entries and the formulation of surface rules is the most insightful way of dealing with the phenomena under consideration. In the remainder of this article, I shall argue that by having recourse to a richer conception of suprasegmental structure we can solve many of the difficulties inherent in both approaches considered so far.

3. A Dependency Treatment of French Phonology

3.1 *French Liaison*

Is it possible to devise a treatment of French liaison which combines the virtues of the deletion and the insertion approaches but also avoids their most blatant shortcomings? A very important step in the right direction has been taken by Clements & Keyser (1981, 1983) and the analysis sketched here — while framed in a dependency framework — retains the main insights of their work but explores areas they left untouched.

We shall assume that an initial dependency structure has already been determined in the lexicon such that for each word the base line is the segmental tier and built upon it is the dependency hierarchisation giving information about (a) the sonority hierarchy;

(b) the prosodic hierarchy (rhyme, syllable, foot). To anticipate on later developments the word *prudence*, in its surface form, would have the following partial dependency characterisation:

(1)   *prudence*

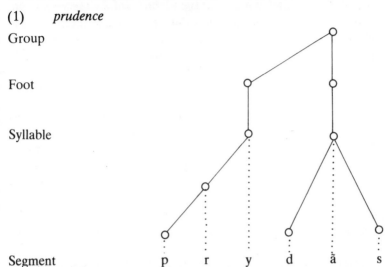

Group

Foot

Syllable

Segment   p   r   y   d   ã   s

I shall have little to say here about the sonority hierarchy and the internal structure of segments. My main concern will be with prosodic structure and, unless the discussion requires further elaboration, I shall operate with standard phonemic symbols.

Since 'word' stress does not play any role within the discussion, I shall leave it out of my account. Within the logic of Anderson & Durand (this vol.), word stress would be a case of lexical group stress. The resultant dependency structure for *prudence* is given in (1). Arguments for feet are given later so that, for the moment, we shall simply suppose that the lexical entries for *ami, deux* and *turc* are as in (2):

(2)

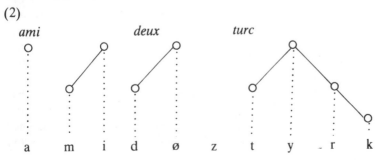

ami   deux   turc

a   m   i   d   ø   z   t   y   r   k

For *ami* we have a multirooted tree. If word stress was indicated as in (1), the last vowel would be the unique governor of the whole word. Notice that for *deux* the last consonant is 'floating' (or 'stray' or 'extrametrical'), whereas the final consonants of *turc* are attached to the syllable governor /y/.[7] A standard liaison example would be provided by a phrase like *deux amis turcs* [døzamityrk]. Let us posit a structure like (3) as our initial structure.

(3)   *deux amis turcs*

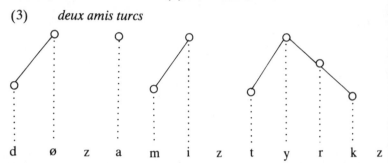

d   ø   z   a   m   i   z   t   y   r   k   z

The final /z/ in *amis* and *turcs* is also stray but, this time, results from morphosyntactic rules of agreement. It is there to account for possible liaisons in cases like *deux amis allemands* [døzamizalmã]. We shall consider that floating segments are to be attached to the right by a rule we shall simply call LIAISON.

(4)   LIAISON
       Attack a floating non-syllabic segment rightward if there is an immediately adjacent syllabic governor. (Stylistic and syntactic conditions are left out.)

In dependency terms, this can be diagrammatically represented as follows:

(5)   LIAISON (dependency formulation)

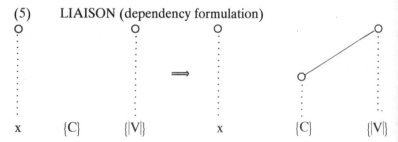

x   {C}   {|V|}   x   {C}   {|V|}

The rule of LIAISON is an early linking which should not be confused with ENCHAINEMENT studied later. If we apply

LIAISON to (3), the result is:

(6)

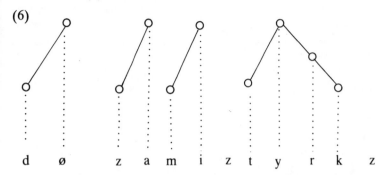

| d | ø | z | a | m | i | z | t | y | r | k | z |

The two occurrences of the plural marker /z/ remain unattached since the immediately adjacent rightward segment is not a {|V|} in the first case, and is altogether lacking in the second case. If a segment is not picked up by LIAISON, it is deleted by the following rule ordered after LIAISON.

(7)   FLOATING CONSONANT DELETION
       A floating {C} without syllabic governor is deleted.

It is tempting to think that perhaps LIAISON does not need to be stated at all since, on the assumption that resyllabification is an everywhere rule, the floating consonant would be correctly attached in (6), i.e. [zami] is a possible morpheme not *[ztyrk]. This temptation ought to be resisted since *petit rameau* is pronounced [p(ə)tiramo] with deletion of the floating /t/. But since /tr/ is acceptable syllable-initially, it is hard to comprehend — if LIAISON is automatic resyllabification — why the floating /t/ is not purely and simply attached to the /r/ in *rameau.* Our formulation of LIAISON is designed to avoid such problems.

3.2 *Some Concrete Objections Answered*

While this may not be apparent at first sight, an approach formulated in terms of floating segments allows us to circumvent well-known objections raised by 'concrete' phonology against the classical generative analysis. For a start, as in most dependency treatments, I take it that prosodic structure is not given but constructed. Lexical items, so to speak, start life as chains of segments upon which we build the dependency hierarchisation. This means that floating consonants are marked as exceptions to the rules of syllable formation within the lexicon (but not elsewhere, obviously, since they go on to acquire syllable status in the course of derivations). In a sense, this solution is quite close to the 'concrete' account which claims that TRUNCATION — were it to be acceptable — is not an across-the-board phenomenon but applies to marked items only. We do not need here to mark *turc* as [-TRUNCATION] or to posit — as Dell (1970) advocates — a protective schwa. The final /k/ is not floating and therefore is not affected by LIAISON. Given this analysis, we can easily account for examples which were problematic for the standard analysis. Thus consider Tranel's remarks (1981: 210-12) concerning exceptional alternations such as *oeuf—oeufs* [œf] — [ø], *boeuf—boeufs* [bœf] — [bø], *os*, (sg) — *os* (pl) [ɔs] — [o]. Speakers of French, in unguarded speech, tend to level these alternations and use a form identical to the singular one for both singular and plural: *un oeuf* [ɛ̃nœf] — *des oeufs* [dɛzœf]. In the standard paradigm *oeuf* has to be marked as [-TRUNCATION] in the singular, whereas the plural is regular (/œf+z/ will yield [ø] via TRUNCATION and œ-RAISING in word-final position). It is therefore odd that speakers instead of removing the exception feature on the singular go on to making the plural irregular as well *vis-à-vis* TRUNCATION. Taking this in conjunction with the observation that the class of exceptions to TRUNCATION is for ever expanding (cf. 2.1 above), one is justified in having serious doubts about TRUNCATION. But, within our analysis *oeuf* would be treated as regular in the singular, with the final consonant marked as floating when the plural feature is assigned to this word. For clarity's sake, let us say that the input to the phonological rules would be:

(8)

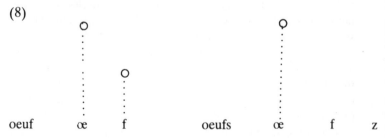

| oeuf | œ | f | | oeufs | œ | f | z |

The elimination of [ø] as a plural form is explicable since it involves an exception feature whose removal simplifies the lexical entry and gives a uniform realisation to the morpheme in question. By the same token, since floating consonants also involve an exception feature preventing their attachment as part of the coda of syllables, their gradual dwindling away is not so mysterious after all. For clarity's sake we shall hereafter refer to this exception feature as [-CODA ATTACHMENT].

The reader will notice that despite objections by Tranel (1981) and also Morin & Kaye (1982: 319-23) I adopt here the systematic plural hypothesis. Morin & Kaye, in fact, go as far as to claim that 'it seems plausible to suppose that the *z* has been reanalysed as an optional stylistically elevated mark of the plural for post-nominal adjectives. This is the conclusion reached by Gougenheim (1938: 59-60) who observes that in the pair *un nez aquilin/des nez-z-aquilins* "an aquiline nose/aquiline noses" the *z* liaison appears only in the plural and behaves phonetically and morphologically as a plural prefix of the adjective' (p. 320). Evidence for this thesis is taken from examples like *des selles de compétition-z-anglaises, des voitures de compétition-z-anglaises, des casques de compétition-z-anglais* where a /z/ that prescriptive grammarians would banish appears in spontaneous speech. Since the expressions preceding the adjective are not lexicalised and the second noun is singular — two theses they defend by careful analysis — how can we interpret this /z/ which should not be there? Could it be, they ask rhetorically, that the /z/ is an original plural on the Head noun which has been moved to a pre-adjectival position. Their reply is:

First, words that show a phonetic singular/plural distinction, e.g. *cheval* (sg)/(*chevaux* (pl) 'horse/horses' retain the plural marker, which shows that no transfer has taken place, cf. (73)(a); note also that the complement remains unmarked before a *z* liaison as in (73)(b) which shows that it must be considered morphologically singular, and hence not the source of the /z/ liaison. Second when a word is followed by two adjectives the *z* marker may appear before both adjectives (although this kind of liaison tends to be avoided in general) as in (74).

(73) (a) des chevaux de course-z-arabes
           'Arabian race horses'
      (b) des selles de cheval z-anglaises
           'English (horse-)saddles'
(74)   des armes z-automatiques z-américaines
           'American automatic weapons'

(p. 322).

Let us leave aside Gougenheim's phonetic argument as to the eventual attachment of the /z/ marker since this is taken care of by our formulation of LIAISON. What the above arguments show is that the standard morphosyntactic distribution of the plural marker /z/, as given by Selkirk (1972/81), is at the very least incomplete and wrong in places. The presence of a plural before the second adjective of (74a) is only a problem for Selkirk's theory. Since the universal conventions she adopts for the distribution of boundaries predict [#automatiques#] [#américaines#] and she does not have a language-specific readjustment rule for ADJ-ADJ sequences, TRUNCATION in her analysis should always delete the final /z/ in *automatiques*. What is at stake here is lack of observational adequacy. Liaison is possible and, in our account (as in Selkirk's), all adjectives inherit +*pl*, spelled as /z/, from their nominal governor. To reflect the facts accurately LIAISON must optionally be allowed to apply in ADJ-ADJ sequences in elevated style. There is no gain in simplicity in Morin & Kaye's treatment since they too have to specify this context for possible plural insertion. Let us now turn to (73a-b).

(9)

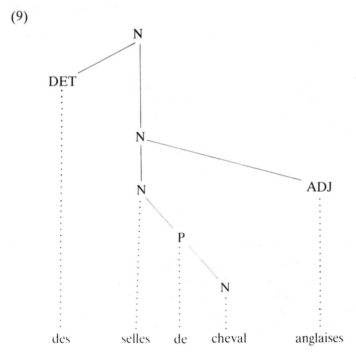

The plural form of *chevaux* in (73a) shows that the plural feature is indeed a property of the Head noun. These sentences as such do not disprove that the Head noun can be followed by a plural /z/ marker which would be deleted after *selles* in (73b) by FCD. The fact that the second /z/ does not appear to be attached to *course* in (73a) and *cheval* in (73b) seems quite appropriate syntactically. The syntactic representations of (73a) and (b), and of (74a) on one interpretation, would run along the lines of (9) in dependency terms (cf. Anderson & Ewen, to appear) and (9') in corresponding $\overline{\overline{X}}$ terms:

(9')

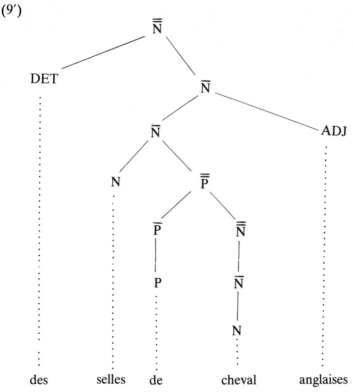

Limiting ourselves to the $\overline{X}$ model, which may be more familiar to the reader, we can give two accounts of the distribution of $+pl.$[8] Either the feature in question percolates up from N to $\overline{N}$ (and $\overline{\overline{N}}$) and becomes attached to the whole phrase dominated by $\overline{N}$ (and $\overline{\overline{N}}$) or it percolates down from the top node with similar effects. Either way, there is no reason why it should be attached directly to *course* and *cheval* in (73a) and (b) since it would affect the whole phrase dominated by $\overline{\overline{N}}$. The /z/ marker is simply adjacent to the last item of the PHRASE that it affects.[9] Such a treatment entails a proliferation of /z/ markers that would not be picked up on independent grounds (e.g. $\overline{\overline{X}}$ boundaries strongly inhibit liaison). Another explanation may also be possible. Morin & Kaye claim that their examples of [N *de* N] groups are not lexicalised. But while they may not be fossilised and stored as whole units, they may well be generated in the lexicon as a type of compound. Notice in favour of this possibility that the [*de* N] complement of the Head noun does not behave like a syntactically generated PP (cf. e.g. the lack of DET usually obligatory in French). In that case, we expect a plural marker for the whole compound noun [N *de* N] with percolation of the feature +*pl* down to the Head.[10]

3.3 *Nasalisation*

Since we have argued that liaison consonants are floating underlyingly, there is strong *prima facie* evidence in favour of representing a word like *bon* as in (10):

(10)

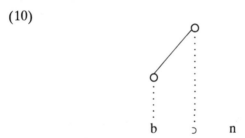

The underlying oral vowel is postulated to account for the liaison form *bon accord* [bɔnakɔr] (cf. 1.1) where the floating /n/ has been picked up by LINKING. How can we account for *bon cadeau* [bɔ̃kado] then? In the standard analysis, there is a rule of NASALISATION which nasalises an oral vowel followed by a nasal consonant when the next morpheme or word begins with a consonant or at the end of a phrase. But, if we suppose that NASALISATION applies only if the nasal consonant involved is floating, then we can cash in on the existence of the rules of LIAISON and FCD to explain VN-V alternation. Let us formulate NASALISATION as follows:

(11) NASALISATION

$$V \rightarrow [+\text{nasal}]/ - \begin{bmatrix} C^* \\ +\text{nasal} \end{bmatrix}$$

(where the asterisk designates a floating segment — a convention we shall continue using below)

and adopt the following order: LIAISON, NASALISATION, FCD. If the underlying representation of *bon cadeau* is:

(12)

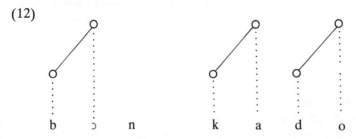

LIAISON will fail to reallocate the /n/ to the beginning of *cadeau* since the onset is already filled. The vowel /ɔ/ will therefore undergo NASALISATION and then the /n/ will be deleted by FCD. This solution is rejected by Clements & Keyser for the following reasons: 'nasal truncation is a more general rule than obstruent truncation, applying not only word finally but also word internally, as in *bon* [bɔ̃], *bonté* [bɔ̃te] (compare *saint* [sɛ̃], *sainteté* [sɛtte]). Moreover, word final nasal truncation is almost entirely restricted to /n/ ...' (1983: 100). I find these arguments less than convincing. For a start, words like *sainteté* belong to a set of words which end in *-eté* in the spelling: *fausseté, hâtiveté, naïveté, gracieuseté, tardiveté*, etc. While there might be disagreement about the best morphophonological analysis of these forms, the obvious alternatives consist in either deriving them from the feminine or, preferably, within the framework of this paper, from the stem +/ə/+/te/ (which would involve voicing adjustments in some cases) (cf. 3.4). The fact that there is no truncation in *sainteté* is therefore to be expected and we also notice that words such as *souveraineté* or *mitoyenneté* do not exhibit nasal truncation. Secondly, an examination of inverse dictionaries fails to reveal any productive process on the pattern of *bonté* (compare *-ité* and *-eté*). This is to be expected since a case can be made for a general insertion of schwa before consonant-initial suffixes (cf. Dell 1978). Let us now turn to Clements & Keyser's second point: nasal truncation is restricted to /n/ (if we leave aside a few alternations like *parfum—parfumer, nom—nommer*). This is true but not decisive. It is by no means the case that ALL the obstruents occur in liaison. Thus Encrevé (1983), in a sizable corpus, found only the following liaison consonants in descending order of frequency: /t,z,r,n,p/ (cf. too Malécot (1975)). While this is a problem if truncation is envisaged as a major rule of French, it fits in very well with our analysis. The fact that /n/ is the only nasal consonant left in liaison does not affect the argument since singular nouns do not constitute possible inputs to liaison. Even if *nom* is /ɔm*/ underlyingly, the nasal consonant would not be allowed to surface, except in derivational forms.

It is often said that the right environment for NASALISATION in French is the presence of a tautosyllabic nasal consonant after the vowel undergoing the rule in question (although most accounts within the generative paradigm have not been able to bring this out). Since we describe this process as triggered by a nasal consonant which does not metrically belong to the preceding syllable, we may appear to be failing to capture an important generalisation. It is, however, debatable, as argued at length in Tranel (1974, 1981), that nasalisation still operates in this manner synchronically in French. A number of words exhibit tautosyllabic sequences word-internally and word-finally contrary to what is predicted by an across-the-board rule of NASALISATION. We list a few examples in (13) and refer the reader to Tranel's demonstration that recourse to protective schwas raises more problems that it solves:

(13)   (a)   clamser [klamse], stencil [stɛnsil]
        (b)   binse [bins], suspense [syspɛns]
        (c)   omelette [ɔmlɛt], samedi [samdi]
        (d)   amnésie [amnezi], omnisport [ɔmnispɔr]

Notice too that French speakers have no difficulties with syllable-final nasals in prefixes like *circum-*, in acronyms (SAVIEM [saviɛm], SAMDA [samda]) and in truncated forms like *mathélem,* [matelɛm], short for *mathématiques élémentaires.* Within our framework only forms that involve floating consonants would be subject to NASALISATION. Words like *sens* [sãs] or *fonds* [fɔ̃] which never alternate would be entered surface-phonemically. We also assume that the contrast between *bon ami* [bɔnami] and *mon ami* [mɔ̃nami] (cf. 1.1) is to be accounted for as in Selkirk (1972/81) by treating words of the *mon* type (*ton, son, on, en, rien, un, chacun*) as having a nasal vowel followed by a floating consonant underlyingly. When our suggestions are compared with e.g. S.R. Anderson (1982), where a syllable-sensitive rule is advocated and no nasal vowels are underlying, it should be borne in mind that (a) nasalised and non-nasalised variants of liaison can only be explained by either 'assum(ing) that the same rules apply to these forms but in different orders' or by 'saying that *mon* words undergo a less constrained nasalization rule — one with only the segmental, and not the syllabic, conditions of rule 21' (1982: 570); (b) provision has to be made for the above 'exceptions' (see (13)) and this would involve the postulation of internal 'protective' schwas which are weakly motivated (compare our argument in 3.4 for morphological schwas); (c) non-alternating words, if not represented surface-phonemically, create indeterminacy problems (cf. Tranel 1981: 37-40); (d) Anderson's statement of NASAL-ISATION has to make reference to the deletion of the nasal consonant which is taken care of by the independently justified rule FCD in this article.[11]

3.4 *Morphological and 'Protective' Schwas*

We have left aside until now the question of how to represent feminine adjectives. It is clear that within the framework adopted here final schwas are not necessary to save final consonants from deletion. Since final schwas are always deleted by a rule of absolute neutralisation, it might seem preferable to represent feminine adjectives with fixed final consonants. Thus, *petite* and *bonne* would have the dependency structures in (14):

(14)   petite   bonne

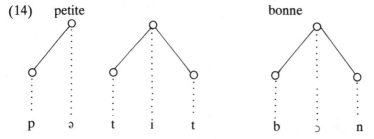

In that case, the liaison form will be obtained either by taking the structure in (14) as the dictionary representations of the lexemes PETIT and BON (*à la* Bloomfield) and by making the consonant floating if [-fem] is chosen or, as in natural generative phonology, by listing all the possible consonants in the lexicon. The second solution, while plausible for cases of suppletion (e.g. *mon—ma—mes*), once generalised to all lexical items reduces the lexicon to a collection of disparate facts. The first one does not tie in optimally with derivational facts mentioned below. If, on the other hand, we assume that lexemes PETIT and BON are entered in the lexicon with floating consonants and, as in the classical analysis, a schwa is introduced as the result of a morphological rule of agreement, it will pick up the floating consonant assuming, as we are doing throughout, that syllable structure rules apply after morphological material has been added. Since a foot structure (with ambisyllabicity within the foot) is defended in 3.5, the input to the phonological rules for *petite* and *bonne* will be:

(15)   *petite*   *bonne*

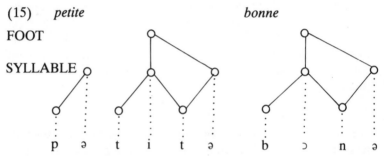

Can these final schwas be at all justified? It seems to me that the strong case made against 'protective' schwas by e.g. Tranel (1981) and Love (1981) loses much of its force given the analysis adopted here. Final schwas in Schane-type accounts are postulated in two classes of contexts: (a) in morphological contexts (feminine adjectives, some feminine nouns, verbal forms); (b) at the end of words like *porte* and *disque*, whatever their gender, by contrast with other words like *sac*, *sept*, or *lest* which are marked as [-TRUNCATION]. Given that the difference between the two subsets of words in (b) seems in practice to be based on spelling, that the crucial *h-aspiré* test allowing us to differentiate them is of doubtful validity and that all final schwas are neutralised, critics have been right to point out that 'protective' schwas pose a serious learnability problem (see Tranel 1981: 201-2, 293-4). But notice that for us words like *poste* and *disque*, since they never alternate and always behave like *sac*, *sept*, or *lest*, can simply be entered in the lexicon with fixed final consonants. What we need to establish is whether some defence can be made of morphological schwas.

What we observe here is the possible convergence of inflectional and derivational facts. Thus, within the verbal system a great number of verbs (see class 2 in de Félice 1950) have the same final consonant pronounced in all the tenses before a vowel (cf. PAR-TIR: *partons, partez, partait, partirons, partis*, etc) except that (a) the first three persons of the present indicative show no final consonant (*je pars* [ʒəpar], *tu pars* [typar], *il part* [ilpar]); (b) the final consonant is pronounced in first, second and third singular/plural present subjunctive forms (*parte* [part], etc.) and in the third person indicative present (*partent* [part]). All these forms are easily explicable on the assumption that in (b) there is an implicit morphological schwa as the uniform marker of the categories in question; in (a) extrametrical endings such as /z/, /z/ and /t/ mark singular forms in the first three persons of the present indicative. No doubt an alternative account in terms of lexical storage or insertion can always be entertained. But it does seem to me that if we deny that children learning a language can reconstruct an abstract vowel (which is unspecified, as is argued later) in contexts such as these, then we are severely limiting their linguistic abilities on *a priori* grounds.

Let us now turn briefly to derivational matters. Consider, for instance, forms in *-ité* and *-eté*, two suffixes which appear to be in supplementary distribution. Taking a sample from Warnant's (1973) rhyming dictionary:

(16)   (a)[12]   religiosité   [rəliʒjozite]   (religieux)
                 onctuosité   [ɔ̃ktyozite]   (onctueux)
                 immortalité   [imɔrtalite]   (immortel)
                 virtualité   [virtyalite]   (virtuel)
                 objectivité   [ɔbʒɛktivite]   (objectif)
                 passivité   [pasivite]   (passif)

       (b)   souveraineté   [suvrɛnte]   (souverain)
                 joyeuseté   [ʒwajøzte]   (joyeux)
                 sainteté   [sɛ̃tte]   (saint)
                 gracieuseté   [grasjøzte]   (gracieux)
                 oisiveté   [wazivte]   (oisif)
                 tardiveté   [tardivte]   (tardif)

If we assume that /ite/ and /əte/ are respectively added to bases with floating consonants, we can explain the similarity between the consonants used in derivation and feminine consonants. Thus, if the feminine of *souverain*, i.e. *souveraine*, is /suvrɛn*ə/ and *souveraineté* is /suvrɛn*əte/, the floating consonant, which is always doomed after causing NASALISATION in nouns, would be saved from deletion by the following vowel. For adjectives like *passivité* [pasivite], from /pasif+ite/, there is a voicing shift. This shift occurs whenever adjectives ending in *-if* precede a vowel-initial suffix (cf. *actif—activisme*, *relatif—relativisme*; *actif—activer*, *relatif—relativiser*). If feminine words are analysed as taking a systematic schwa marker, we can easily explain alternations such as:

(17)   *oisif—oisive* [wazif]—[waziv]; *passif—passive* [pasif]— [pasiv]; *tardif—tardive* [tardif]—[tardiv]; etc.

The alternative would consist in arguing, for instance, that in (16b) we have a derivation from the feminine form and this would support the Bloomfieldian underlying representations given in (14). While this type of analysis has occasionally been defended (see Moody 1978), there is no evidence that the femininity of the base plays any role in the semantics of such word-formation rules (see Aronoff 1979). In fact, semantically it is the unmarked masculine which is required in the interpretation of e.g. *oisiveté* 'l'état/fait d'être oisif'. The presence of a graphical -e- in -eté and the surface phonetics makes the case for derivation from the feminine look much more plausible than it really is. When we look at the forms in (16a), it is far less obvious why we should want to start from the feminine.

The line of reasoning we have rehearsed above consists in arguing that morphological schwas are not required in a 'protective' capacity since other mechanisms are available to prevent the deletion of a final consonant. On the other hand, by positing the existence of an abstract vowel, /ə/, a set of apparently unrelated facts in verbal morphology, feminine and derivational formations find a unitary explanation. One standard objection is that this schwa must be systematically deleted in final position (see 2.1 on the *h-aspiré* test) by a rule which has roughly the following form:

(18)   E — FIN (OBL)
        ə ⟹ Ø / —— #

and therefore that we are dealing with a purely 'fictitious' segment. However, we shall formulate E-FIN in 3.2 in such a way that it also covers the optional deletion of the schwa of monosyllables (e.g. *tu le veux*/ tyləvøz* / $>$ [tylvø] or [tyləvø]). This latter schwa is not controversial underlyingly since it can surface and, by having a single rule in both cases, we do not set up a special process deleting morphological schwas once their 'protective' job has been carried out.

One of the remaining problems that we have to face is the phonological nature of the abstract vowel that we are positing. /ə/ on the surface alternates between Ø and [œ] (and [ɛ] as well, see 3.5) and neither of these alternants can be taken as the source segment, as is carefully argued by Dell (1973a, b). Dell, himself, simply uses the symbol /ə/, without specifying its feature composition. Sure enough, some hole in the vowel system could be found to accommodate /ə/, but it could legitimately be objected that in so doing we are proving once again that we are dealing with a type of 'fictitious' segment that should be ruled out of phonology. S.R. Anderson (1982: 550ff) has actually presented persuasive arguments, given the surface alternants of /ə/, for treating this vowel underlyingly as 'a structurally-present syllabic nucleus WITH NO ASSOCIATED PHONOLOGICAL FEATURES'. This solution, which he introduces as a theoretical innovation within the standard paradigm, finds a natural integration within dependency phonology where, following Lass & Anderson (1975), it is proposed to analyse the feature composition of segments into submatrices: within our framework (cf. Anderson & Durand, this vol.: ϕ3) /ə/ is categorically a {|V|} with no associated articulatory content, in other words:

$$\begin{bmatrix} \{|V|\} \\ \emptyset \end{bmatrix} \quad \begin{matrix} \text{CATEGORIAL GESTURE} \\ \text{ARTICULATORY GESTURE} \end{matrix}$$

For convenience sake, we shall go on using the symbol /ə/ both at the phonological and the phonetic level, leaving the reader to operate the necessary readjustments.

3.5 *E-variations, Schwa Deletion and the Foot*

In this section, I shall attempt to relate some central aspects of the phonology of French (in particular E-ADJUSTMENT and some aspects of schwa deletion) to the rules described so far. My contention will be that, here as well, richer suprasegmental structure, involving in particular the foot, yields a more insightful treatment.

All standard generative accounts of French phonology agree that French should incorporate a process of E-ADJUSTMENT to deal with alternations such as the following:

(19) (a) protéger   — protégeons   — protégera   [e—e—ɛ]
          céder   — cédions   — céderons   [e—e—ɛ]
          lécher   — léchait   — léche   [e—e—ɛ]
          premier   —   première   [e—ɛ]
          dernier   —   dernière   [e—ɛ]

      (b) mener   — menons   — mène   [ə— ə—ɛ]
          jeter   — jetons   — jettera   [ə— ə—ɛ]
          appeler   — appeliez   — appel   [ə— ə—ɛ]
          hotelier   —   hotellerie   [ə—ɛ]

Apart from functioning as a redundancy rule excluding surface morphemes like *[sek] (cp. *sec* [sɛk]), E-ADJUSTMENT functions dynamically in that new items such as truncated forms (*bénéfice* ⟹ [benɛfj]) or acronyms (UNEF [ynɛf]) conform to it. On the face of it, given that the morphological schwas which would be postulated in the forms of (19) are deleted during derivations, it is tempting to wait for /ə/-deletion to take place and to state this process as a simple closed syllable adjustment. Thus Lowenstamm (1981: 598) writes:

(20)   CLOSED SYLLABLE ADJUSTMENT (CSA):
        /e/ ⟹ [ɛ]/ — C₁]ₛYLL

Unfortunately, there are difficulties in following such a course. As argued in Dell (1973: 199ff), there is strong evidence that, at the stage when E-ADJUSTMENT operates, schwas have not yet been deleted. For a start, there are a number of forms such as *célébrera* ([selɛbrəra] < /selebrəra/) or *céderiez* ([sɛdərje] < /sedərie/) where the schwa is never deleted. Secondly, if E-ADJ had to wait for schwa deletion to operate, a form like *achèvement* [aʃɛvmã] which is underlyingly /aʃəvəmã/, given the rules of schwa deletion that are adopted here (and by Dell and others), should yield *[aʃvəmã] as one possible variant, whereas E-ADJUSTMENT followed by /ə/-loss always gives the right pronunciation. Thirdly, after schwa deletion a form like *cédera* /sedəra/, pronounced [sɛdra], would become [sedra] which should be syllabified as seŞdra and thus not constitute an input to E-ADJUSTMENT.[13] Now, if it is the case that schwas are still present when E-ADJUSTMENT operates, a form such as *protégera* (/prɔteʒəra/ɔ > [prɔtɛzra]), will have to be syllabified as prɔŞteŞzəŞra, unless in order to save CSA we syllabify the /ʒ/ leftward. But, adopting this latter course is somewhat perverse since we would then be invoking exceptions to otherwise perfectly general rules of syllabification merely to avoid puzzling counter-examples. Dell (1973: 202ff) therefore ends up by formulating E-ADJ in the following manner:

(21)   E-ADJUSTMENT (Dell's version)

$$e \implies [\varepsilon]/ - {}^{\frown}C_1 \begin{Bmatrix} \# \\ C \\ [-\text{seg}] \end{Bmatrix} \begin{matrix} \text{(a)} \\ \text{(b)} \\ \text{(c)} \end{matrix}$$

(where ${}^{\frown}C_1$ indicates that the consonant *must* belong to the same morpheme as the input vowel)

In addition, he has to stipulate that C_1C is not an obstruent-liquid sequence in order to account for the difference between words like *secteur* [sɛktœr] with [ɛ], and words like *régler* [regle] with [e].

We are now on the horns of a dilemma: CSA is inadequate and yet (21) appears to miss obvious generalisations connected with syllable structure. Thus, the condition on C_1C we have just con-sidered is necessary if we can no longer appeal to syllable structure: notice that *secteur* with [ɛ] would be syllabified as *sec\$teur*, where *régler* with [e] is *ré\$gler*, and this is exactly what CSA could account for. The problem is how to take into account the fact that /ə/ has a distorting effect on syllable structure. The ploy used by S.R. Anderson (1982) consists in positing a rule of resyllabification whereby the relevant consonant in, say, *protégera* is moved leftward, allowing for a formulation in terms of closed syllable adjustment (and a very elegant rule of stranded schwa deletion) with subsequent release of the consonant when a vowel follows. As was said above, this is a purely formal way round the problem. What motivation is there for assuming that the vowel preceding schwa captures the crucial consonant? Why is /ə/ the only vowel causing such strange happenings?

I wish to argue here, along similar lines to the ones sketched in Durand (1976, 1980), that a better analysis is possible if we posit richer suprasegmental structures than just syllables. Following Selkirk (1978), let us assume that there is a unit called the foot which has the formative as its domain at the lexical level, which can reapply optionally at sentence level, and whose composition is defined as follows: operating from right to left, make every schwa a dependent of the immediately adjacent leftward syllable governor, if there is one, otherwise give foot status to every syllable governor. More details and a defence of the foot are given below but this should suffice for the moment. The words *mène*, *sec* and *protégera* will have the following abstract representations:

(22)   *mène*   *sec*

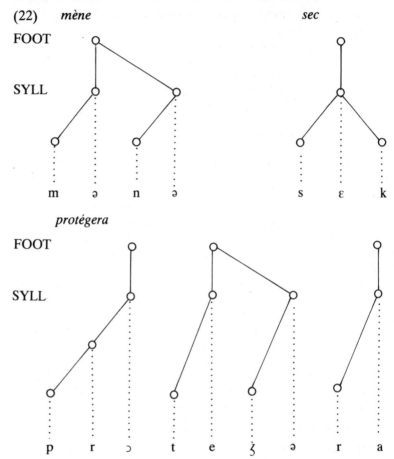

If we can avail ourselves of the concept of the foot, the formulation of E-ADJ can be much simpler and much more enlightening than the linear statement given in (21). E-ADJUSTMENT occurs whenever {e,ə} govern (directly or indirectly) the immediately adjacent right-hand side segment. In the case of *sec* (where the vowel [ɛ] is lexical but where E-ADJUSTMENT functions as a redundancy rule inducing restrictions on hypothetical underlying forms /sek/ or /sək/), the vowel /ɛ/ governs /k/ at the level of the syllable. In the case of *protégera*, /e/ governs /ʒ/ indirectly via /ə/: there is a path in the dependency graph leading from /e/ to

/ʒ/. The same reasoning would hold for *mène*. The rule of E-ADJUSTMENT can simply be written as:

(23)   E-ADJUSTMENT (first dependency version)
{e,ə} ⟹ [ɛ]/ — C
(where C is a dependent or subordinate of {e,ə}).

A more technical formulation of E-ADJUSTMENT (cf. Anderson & Durand, this vol.) would be as follows:

(23′)   E-ADJUSTMENT (second dependency version)

$$\begin{bmatrix} \{|V|\} \\ (\{|i,a|\}) \end{bmatrix} \Longrightarrow \{|a;i|\} \ / - C$$

where V —» C

In (23′) the parentheses have the standard SPE interpretation: when the enclosed components are absent, the vowel has zero articulatory content (i.e. is a schwa). When the enclosed vowel components are present, they characterise a mid front unrounded vowel and thus apply to both /e/ and /ɛ/ since we have under-specified the mode of combination of the two components |i| and |a|. Finally, the C is represented as a subordinate of V since every dependent is also a subordinate (cf. Anderson & Durand, this vol.: 2.2). We thus avoid the collapsing within braces of unrelated elements while making optimal use of the relations holding between co-constitutes of a dependency graph.

It is, however, argued by Anderson & Ewen (to appear) and Anderson (this volume) that the foot is universally a domain for ambisyllabicity. If we take advantage of this the prosodic structure of *protégera*, which we can take as representative of the whole relevant class, will become:

(24)   *protégera*

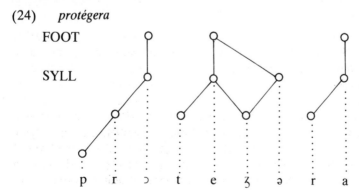

In that case, we can purely and simply return to CLOSED SYLLABLE ADJUSTMENT as stated in (20). There is a sense, however, in which both elements so far identified — the foot structure and ambisyllabicity — can be argued to play a role in E-ADJUSTMENT. The process in question can be envisaged as a process of *strengthening* whereby schwa in a strong position is given articulatory content and /e/ (|i;a|) by being converted to [ɛ] (|a;i|) moves in the direction of |a| — the strongest vowel in Romance and arguably universally (see Foley 1977).

Let us now turn to a definition of the foot in French. We need to separate sharply the LEXICAL FOOT, which applies to lexical entries, from the SENTENCE FOOT, which operates rather late within derivations. By making this distinction, we circumvent one of Noske's criticisms (1982: 295ff): i.e. that Selkirk's approach wrongly predicts *[tymɛl(ə)dɔn] for *tu me le donnes* which has three possible realisations [tyməldɔn], [tymlədɔn], [tymələdɔn]. The lexical foot will be defined as follows (cp. Selkirk 1978):

(25)   THE LEXICAL FOOT (obligatory)
Given a (b), where a < b, and a and b stand for syllabics, a → b iff b is weak (i.e. schwa), otherwise b → b iff b is strong (i.e. a fully specified vowel)
Domain: # ... #   *Application*: Right to Left

One of the problems with Selkirk's definition of the foot, in the absence of crucial examples, is that its domain — although specified as here — appeared to be the *word* in its more or less ordinary sense. If this were the case, Noske (1982) would be right in objecting that words like *revenir* /rəvənir/—[rəvnir], *devenir* /dəvənir/—[dəvnir], *démesure* /deməzyr/—[demzyr] are straight counter-examples to a foot-based approach since E-ADJ should yield *[rɛvnir], *[dɛvnir], *[dɛmzyr]. But, if we suppose that the lexical foot is limited to categories bounded by # ... #, these words will no longer prove problematic. Now, there are good reasons to believe that this decision is not *ad hoc* since (a) it fits in with the general picture concerning foot formation in other languages (cf. Anderson & Ewen, to appear); (b) it has independently been argued by Basbøll (1978) that prefixes in French are separated by # from the base. In consequence, *revenir* would be ##rə#vən+ir##, *devenir* ##də#vən+ir##, and *démesure* ##de#məzyr##. Notice that even if one were to disagree about the precise choice of # in some cases, the principle we are simply appealing to is that every time a strong boundary is encountered it inhibits foot linking and the domain of foot formation is reset. Given our definition of the foot, a word like *revenir* will inherit the following suprasegmental structure lexically:

(26)   *revenir*

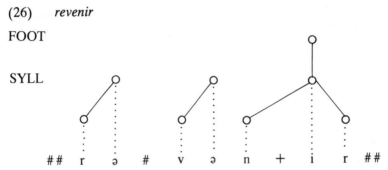

and it will remain unaffected by E-ADJ. Finally, we will note that the third class of counter-examples cited by Noske (i.e. words like *derechef* [dər(ə)ʃɛf], not *[dɛr(ə)ʃɛf]) raises a different problem. First of all, although *derechef* appears to be monomorphemic in contemporary French, it may well have retained its original morphemic structure (de#re#chef) for the purposes of phonology — if only rather exceptionally. Secondly, words with a graphical *e* in the first two syllables — even if they are monomorphemic — must always be treated with caution. As Morin (1978, 1983) has pointed out, many graphical schwas are in fact stabilised — that is they have become œ-type vowels which are not deletable. My own judgement is that in a deletion context — e.g. *il attira derechef mon attention* — we would observe [ilatiradər(ə)ʃɛfmɔ̃natãsjɔ̃] not *[ilatiradrəʃɛf ...]. While the judgement in question can be disputed, it is worth remembering that Dell (1973a: 230) notes that it is common for rare or literary words (like *derechef*) to be exceptions to schwa deletion; thus in *cheminer* the first vowel *e* is stable, whereas in the much more common word *ch(e)min* it is deletable and hence a *bona fide* schwa. As far as I can judge, all of Noske's counter-examples fall within one of the categories so far examined.

The sentence foot is defined identically to the lexical foot but its domain is the sentence and it is *optional*. All the schwas which have not been picked up by the rules of lexical foot formation are now reconsidered. If we take as an example *il faut revenir*/il fot* rəvənir/, once the floating /t*/ has been deleted, the input to sentence foot formation will be:

(27)[14]

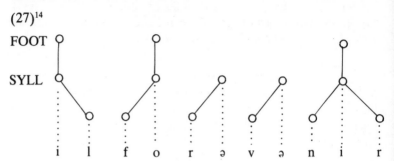

Three possible parsings in terms of foot (with foot-internal ambi-syllabicity) will be possible:

(28)   (a)

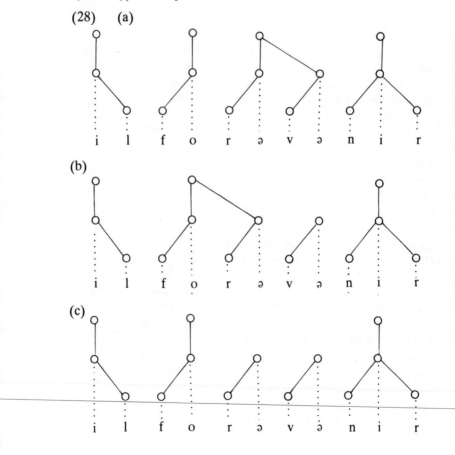

If we now reformulate E-FIN as in (29):

(29)   E-FIN (obligatory)
        /ə/ ⟹ Ø / VC —
        where V ⟶ ə (i.e. /ə/ is the weak member of the foot)

the three correct surface pronunciations corresponding to (28a-c) will be generated — viz. (28a) [ilforəvnir], (28b) [ilforvənir], (28c) [ilforəvənir].[15] The reader can verify that the conventions and rules examined so far would not produce the impossible realisation *[ilforvnir] (see Selkirk 1978 for more details). Notice that E-FIN also applies to all the forms which have a word-final morphological schwa (e.g. *petite*), where e.g. Dell (1973) had to have near-identical separate statements. We can also explain easily the otherwise puzzling fact that *ils partent demain* /ilpartədəmɛ̃/ can only give rise to [ilpartdəmɛ̃] or [ilpartədəmɛ̃] not *[ilpartədmɛ̃] (cf. Dell 1973: 232-3). The reason is that the final schwa in *partent* is governed by the preceding vowel as the result of the *lexical foot*, and that it is therefore not available as a potential governor of the schwa in *demain* when, at a later stage, the *sentence foot* is formed. Facts which required complex conventions in a linear framework find a simple and natural explanation here.

The points examined so far allow us to establish the following order of rule or convention application: LEXICAL FOOT FORMATION, E-ADJ, LIAISON, NASALISATION, FCD, SENTENCE FOOT FORMATION, E-FIN.

The arguments deployed in this section favour the use of the foot to explain the ambisyllabic nature of the consonant conditioning E-ADJ and the deletion of a weak vowel in a weak position (E-FIN) over S.R. Anderson's purely formal solution (1982). But what assures us that using the foot in French is not another formal trick? Notice that since there is ample evidence for the foot in a variety of languages (see Anderson & Ewen, to appear), this constraint is — in one way of putting it — part and parcel of 'universal grammar' and does not add to our theoretical machinery. Since French has usually group-final stress it can, by definition, only be weakly footed. The fact remains that those schwas which are realised in weak governed positions (as exceptions to deletion or as a result of epenthesis) are unstressed in relation to other vowels. Thus in words like *jetterions* or *entrelacs*, the first and last syllables are more salient than the middle one. Each of them could bear an empathatic stress under various

conditions, whereas we cannot have *[ʒɛ″tərjɔ̃] or *[ɑ̃″trəlak]. By
contrast, with vowels other than /ə/, emphatic stresses on the
second syllable of trisyllabic words are often reported in the literature (cf. *il est affreusement laid* given as [ilɛta″frøzmɑ̃lɛ] by
Armstrong 1955: 156). The prominence relation that we need to
represent the surface stress contour of *jetterions/entrelacs* is no
more than a surface reflex of an underlying difference between
/ə/ and the other full vowels of French. Rather than assign /ə/ a
[-stress] feature as is usually done in standard linear accounts, we
mark the potential prominence of every full vowel in relation to
schwa through the construction of the foot.

3.6 *Elision, Enchaînement and Canadian Laxing*

Before closing this article, we need to make a brief reference to
elision and *enchaînement*. Elision involves the obligatory deletion
of schwa in e.g. *l'ami* /lə#ami/ > [lami]. *Enchaînement* refers to
the forward linking of word-final consonants before vowel-initial
words leading to the homophony of e.g. *petit ami* [pəʃtiʃtaʃmi]
and *petite amie* [pəʃtiʃtaʃmi]. In our account, the floating /t/ in
petit ami is resyllabified forward by LIAISON, which is an early
rule, whereas the second *t* in *petite* /pətit+ə/ is ambisyllabic
underlyingly and simply closes the second syllable of the word
after the deletion of the morphological schwa by E-FIN. We therefore need to move it forward in *petite amie* if our account is to be
complete. S.R. Anderson (1982: 562-3) accomplishes this by a
transformational rule which telescopes the two processes as in
(30):[16]

(30)   ELISION-ENCHAINEMENT

$$[_{\text{SYLL}} \quad \text{X} \quad \text{(C)} \quad \text{ə} \quad] \quad (\#) \; [_{\text{SYLL}} \quad \text{V} \quad \text{X} \;]$$
$$\qquad\qquad 1 \quad\;\; 2 \quad\;\; 3 \qquad\quad 4 \qquad\qquad 5 \quad\; 6$$

$$\Longrightarrow [_{\text{SYLL}} \; 1] \quad [_{\text{SYLL}} \; 2 \quad \emptyset \quad 4 \quad 5 \quad 6]$$

The apparent advantage of S.R. Anderson's solution is that *h-
aspiré* words can be treated as vowel-initial and characterised by a
unitary exception feature. I would argue that the behaviour of *h-
aspiré* words is too complex to provide a crucial argument in
favour of this collapsing.[17] Within the framework adopted here, I
do not see any substantive reason for amalgamating elision and
enchaînement. Elision, I interpret as in (31):

(31)   ELISION

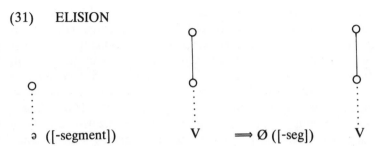

ə ([-segment])   V   ⟹ Ø ([-seg])   V

that is to say, as the deletion of a weak vowel before a stronger
vowel — a parochial manifestation of the general principle 'vocalis
ante vocale corripitur' much explored by Foley (1977). On the
other hand, *enchaînement* — ordered after ELISION — is a
resyllabification process, which it will be noticed does not apply
to the last consonant as Anderson formalises it, but rather to the
last consonantal node and its potential lefthand dependent since
l'eau traverse /lo#travɛrs/ and *l'autre averse* /lotr#avɛrs/ are
homophonous. At the stage *enchaînement* applies, *l'autre averse*
has the following representation:

(32)   *l'autre averse*

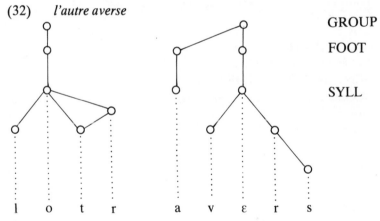

GROUP

FOOT

SYLL

l   o   t   r   a   v   ɛ   r   s

where the dependency hierarchisation in terms of sonority gives us
the kind of structure we require (although, as throughout this
article, I have only given a 'flat' internal structure to the syllable).
If is not clear that this would be handled so elegantly in a metrical
or indeed in a three-tiered framework.[18]

In lieu of conclusion, let us consider one aspect of Montréal
French which fits in neatly with the various assumptions we have
made so far. In this accent, a high vowel becomes lax in closed

syllables: compare *lu* [ly] and *lutte* [lʏt], *doux* [du] and *douce* [dœs]. 'Interestingly', as Tranel (1981: 269) points out, 'whereas *petit ami* 'boyfriend' can only be pronounced [ptitami], *petite amie* 'girl friend' may be pronounced either [ptitami] or [ptʊtami], showing that, whereas the linking consonant [t] in *petit ami* automatically belongs to the next syllable, the gender consonant [t] in *petite amie* may close the preceding consonant'. These facts — while puzzling within a TRUNCATION treatment — are easy to explain for us. The [t] of *petit ami* is a floating consonant and therefore cannot condition laxing. On the other hand, in the feminine *petite*, the relevant [t] closes the syllable containing /i/ at all stages until *enchaînement* resyllabifies it. The two pronunciations Tranel is referring to result from a different ordering with respect to *enchaînement*: if LAXING precedes *enchaînement* we obtain [ptʊtami], if, on the contrary, LAXING follows *enchaînement* the result will be [ptitami].

The main rules and conventions considered in this article are ordered as follows:
LEXICAL SYLLABLE FORMATION
LEXICAL FOOT FORMATION
E-ADJ(USTMENT)
LIAISON
NASALISATION
FLOATING CONSONANT DELETION (FCD)
SENTENCE FOOT FORMATION
E-FIN
ELISION
CANADIAN LAXING — ENCHAINEMENT OR
ENCHAINEMENT — CANADIAN LAXING
SCHWA SPELLING

Notes

1. I wish to thank all the participants at the Dependency Phonology Conference held at Essex (September 1983) for their comments on a preliminary version of this paper. I owe John Anderson a special debt of gratitude for forcing me to re-examine my (parsimonious) assumptions about suprasegmental structure and live dangerously. Wyn Johnson must also be thanked for suffering my long monologues about French liaison and helping me with her comments and criticisms. I have received useful feedback from Ken Lodge and Roger Hawkins.
2. Once again the formulations are intended to remain neutral between competing solutions: see Tranel 1981, for a thorough presentation. In addition a

rule of vowel lowering (cf. *divin ami* vs. *c'est divin*) would have to adjust the output. An interesting problem in the 'two rules' approach is the relation between TRUNCATION and NASAL DELETION. This question will preoccupy us later. See Love (1981: 113-14) for some remarks on this. S.R. Anderson (1982) analyses nasalisation as syllabically conditioned (see 3.3).

3. There is a large degree of dialectal variation in this area: see the synchronic and diachronic survey in Tranel (1981: Ch. 4) who gives us the 'standard' dialect: *bon, plein, certain, prochain, ancien, divin,* vs. *mon, ton, son, un, chacun, commun, aucun, en, bien.*

4. See Nespor & Vogel (1982), for recent discussions of the intermeshing of syntax and phonology with reference to external sandhi rules.

5. Rules like (1) more carefully formulated are to be found in Tranel (1981). For this to work, we need to assume that the inserted consonant is unspecified and that its variable feature content corresponding e.g. to /n,t,z,g,r/ is the result of further mechanisms filling in the phonetic details as (2) does. It is therefore not clear that even then we are dealing with a single insertion rule.

6. This point does not commit us to claiming that there is uniformity of behaviour of *h-aspiré* words *vis-à-vis* elision and *enchaînement* as well: see note 17. Cf. too Clements & Keyser on the use of 'umbrella' features in concrete descriptions and the formal difficulties this entails (1983: 113).

7. To be more precise, a distinction should be made between 'extrametrical' and 'floating' elements. The analysis defended here is in terms of extrametricality by contrast with Encrevé (1983) whose approach is in terms of floating segments. The use of the term 'floating' in this article should not, however, lead to any ambiguity, all the more so as the analysis of such phenomena as tones or vowel harmony in dependency phonology would not follow the autosegmental route. For some problems with Encrevé's 1983 analysis, see Durand (1985).

8. At the time of sending this article to the press, I have very kindly been sent four recent articles by Bernard Tranel (Tranel 1984, to appear a, b, c). Tranel (to appear a) clarifies some of the implications of the type of analysis adopted here with respect to the status of the plural suffix and that of the extrametrical consonant. In particular, it has to be assumed here that the extrametrical consonant does not obey the Peripherality Condition (Hayes 1982) according to which the addition of a suffix automatically cancels the extrametricality of the preceding segment which should reintegrate the base (e.g. *petits* /pətit*#z*/ $\implies$ /pətit#z/). If the /t*/ here was reintegrated to the coda of the second syllable of *petit*, it would obviously not delete. Another solution, which I find quite appealing, is to consider, along the lines of Tranel (1981), that plural affixation in French is post-lexical.

9. Notice that there is no strong reason to suppose that the change /al/ to /o/ in words like *cheval* is tied to the presence of a /z/ marker to the right. It seems best to have a morphological rule changing /al/ to /o/ in the presence of a feature [+pl] on the noun itself for the small set of words behaving like *cheval*. This need not preclude plural spelling as /z/ to the right of *chevaux* to account for elevated liaison as in *chevaux arabes* [ʃəvozarab]. All we need to do is order the /al/ > /o/ rule before the general rule spelling out the feature [+pl].

10. In case it is felt that a contradiction is involved here in explaining these facts in $\overline{\text{X}}$ terms after criticising Selkirk's $\overline{\text{X}}$ approach to liaison in 1.2, remember that the arguments there were against using $\overline{\text{X}}$-theory as a *strong predictor* of liaison contexts. It was stressed, however, that as such the facts of liaison do not disprove either the $\overline{\text{X}}$-theory. The line of reasoning adduced here supports any theory which allows for layering involving Heads and phrases (be it dependency grammar, $\overline{\text{X}}$-theory or a mixed PS-dependency system).

11. As pointed out in Tranel (to appear a), the analysis of nasal vowels

adopted here and the use of floating segments in general raise a number of problems with respect to the rule of o-raising which neutralises the /ɔ/-/o/ distinction in the direction of [o] in word-final position. This rule has somehow to be complicated to prevent the raising of the /ɔ/ in *bon ami*, so as to avoid *[bonami]. One solution, formulated in linear terms, would be to postulate a rule such as (i): (i) {|u,a|} ⟹ {|u;a|} / — S ([-nas])* #. (See Anderson & Durand, this vol., for an explanation of the symbolism.) The reader is referred to Tranel (to appear a) for a critique of the point of view defended here within an insertion framework.

12. Some of the forms of (16a) also involve ε~a, ø~o alternations best treated as Learned Backing. See Dell & Selkirk (1978).

13. An additional reason given by Dell for ordering E-ADJUSTMENT before schwa deletion rules is the need to account for alternations like *cachet*(n)—*cacheter*(v). In our framework, *cachet* would at best have a final floating consonant which could not cause E-ADJUSTMENT. We prefer to think that since the consonant in the word in question is never realised and only surfaces in learned derivations, it is better to postulate that reanalysis has taken place: *cachet* = /kaʃɛ/. Notice that there are speakers who pronounce this word [kaʃe], whereas the surface ε's in (19) are obligatory. On E-ADJ, see too Tranel (1984, to appear b, c).

14. Like S.R. Anderson (1982), we need to posit a late rule of SCHWA SPELLING which gives articulatory content to non-deleted and epenthetic schwas (e.g. *ours blanc* /urs#blã/ > [ursəblã]). The precise realisation will vary from context to context: compare the quality of schwa in the example just given which may be a phonetic [ə] with the stressed schwa in *bois-le* which often approximates [ø] or is identical with it. Like Dell and Anderson, let us assume that in (28a-c) non-deleted schwas are realised as the full vowel [œ]. As there is no reason to suppose that foot formation once applied is not pervasive, the schwas which are realised as [œ] and are not in a weak position within a foot will be given foot status at the surface level. In e.g. (28c) once the two /ə/'s are spelled as [œ], they will therefore be footed.

15. Following Selkirk (1978) and S.R. Anderson (1982), I limit myself to cases where only *one* consonant separates the governing vowel from schwa. Where more than one consonant occurs in this intervocalic position, deletion is either optional or forbidden according to the type of cluster: e.g. /ə/ is not deleted in the context O—C. It is also possible that /ə/ is reinserted in certain contexts (see Dell 1973a), b, 1977). Noske (1982) adopts a radically different approach where schwa deletion is a context-free rule guided by independent constraints on syllable structure. A detailed discussion of his paper would take us too far afield but it should be noted that: (a) the algorithm he uses, as he admits himself, does not yield the correct result for VCəC sequences (e.g. *pudiquement*): it predicts *optional* deletion where it is *obligatory* in the accent he is describing; (b) he needs a special rule to account for the deletion of final morphological schwas (e.g. *petite*); (c) he has to make rather debatable assumptions about the cost of various sequences (e.g. treat an obstruent-liquid sequence as monosegmental); (d) he does not account for E-LOW. If these and various other difficulties can be surmounted, his treatment will pose a challenge to a foot-based approach.

16. To be more precise, Anderson's rule also caters for non-truncated final consonants (as in *petit ami*) since he postulates a process of TRUNCATION.

17. In fairly normative accounts of French phonology, *h-aspiré* words are said to behave as if they were consonant-initial (except with respect to schwa deletion — see below). In that case, I do not see any strong reason not to posit an abstract consonant (/H/) in onset position not specified for articulation (like schwa). This has the advantage of offering a locus for the glottal stop that many speakers use in

enchaînement contexts with these words (e.g. *petite housse* [pətitəus] or [pətit2us] or [pətitə?us]. The usual objection to this is that, whereas we have # Oə sequences word initially, /H/ cannot precede /ə/. This is hardly surprising since in that case we would have potential zero syllables, given our analysis of /ə/. In terms of exception features, *h-aspiré* words would have to be specified here as [-LIAISON], [-ELISION], [-ENCHAINEMENT]. I believe this is correct for many speakers who are differentially inconsistent with respect to these three rules. For instance, my parents (Midi-French) always say *le Hollandais* without eliding the /ə/, but variably *leś Hollandais* or *leśˆHollandais* and always (?) *petite Hollandaise* [pətitolãdɛz]. In the reading test referred to in 1.2, four out of ten readers said [ãn5grwa] for *en hongrois*. Yet, when prodded about the language in question, they all spoke of [lə5grwa], *le hongrois*. The high variability offered by these words is stressed by de Cornulier (1978) and Tranel (1981: 295ff); see Clements & Keyser (1983: 111-13) for a critique of the 'concrete' approach in this area. With regards to the possible pronunciation of schwas before *h-aspiré* words in sequence such as *petite housse*, I favour an insertion analysis rather than imposing restrictions on E-FIN (see Iverson 1983).

18. My colleague I. Roca has pointed out to me that if we retain formulation (30), we could be argued to be resyllabifying the onset node in a three-tiered approach. But, outside morphological schwas, I do not see any overriding reason to posit a final /ə/ underlyingly at the end of words terminating in an OL cluster (e.g. *table*). This is the position of Schane (1968: 31) but see Noske (1982) for a contrary view. In any case, at the stage *enchaînement* occurs /ə/ would arguably have been deleted even if underlying.

5 SEGMENTAL AND SUPRASEGMENTAL STRUCTURE*

Colin Ewen

1. Gestures and the Segment

The degree of componentiality assigned to phonological representations has been the subject of some debate within recent years, and various proposals have been made for subdividing the segment into clearly defined subgroupings, or GESTURES. Such proposals date back to Lass & Anderson (1975) and Lass (1976), and in recent works on dependency phonology (Anderson & Ewen 1980a; Ewen 1980a) involve a subdivision of the segment into three gestures: the ARTICULATORY, the CATEGORIAL, and the INITIATORY. Broadly speaking, the articulatory gesture in such models involves all purely locational parameters — i.e. properties such as backness, labiality, and retroflexion — while the categorial gesture is concerned with the characterisation of roughly the same set of parameters as Chomsky & Halle's (1968) major class features, i.e. degree of stricture of approximation and sonorancy, but with the addition of Chomsky & Halle's [continuant] (a 'manner of articulation' feature) and [voice] (a 'source' feature). The distinction between the two gestures, then, is more akin to that between the Jakobsonian 'source' and 'resonance' features. Phonological processes making reference to various kinds of sonority hierarchy — e.g. syllable structure and lenition — are characterised by the primes within this gesture. The initiatory gesture, finally, involves not only initiation proper — i.e. features characterising airstream mechanisms — but also degree of glottal stricture, where this is relevant to phonological description.

Notice, then, that two phonetic parameters, vocal cord vibration and degree of glottal stricture, which are subsumed by some phonologists (e.g. Chomsky & Halle 1968; Ladefoged 1971) under a single phonological feature [voice], are not only kept separate in the system of phonological parameters, but are also assigned to distinct gestures. This, it is claimed, appropriately captures the fact that sonority hierarchies of the type mentioned above typically make reference only to the presence or absence of voicing (together with other properties not concerned with the state of the larynx), while the *degree* of opening of the glottis (involved in the distinction between, say, breathy and creaky voice) does not play such a role. The assignment of this feature to a separate gesture, then, allows all and only the phonological primes within the categorial gesture to be involved in 'major class' and sonority characterisation.

It is clear that such gestures within the segment have much in common with the notion of TIER in autosegmental phonology. However, there are two important areas of difference. In autosegmental phonology, features occupy different autosegmental tiers according to the nature of the particular process in question. Thus, in a process of nasal spreading, the feature [nasal] might occupy an autosegmental tier whose boundaries do not coincide with those of segments on the other tier(s), while in other processes a different feature may be extracted from the whole, and the utterance autosegmentalised in a different way. In proposals for gestures, however, subdivision in the way outlined above is basic to the universally valid characterisation of the segment, and forms part of its lexical specification. That is, it is not utilised only in the characterisation of clearly 'autosegmental' phenomena, but, rather, characterises a claim that phonological rules will be expected to make reference to the features of one gesture only: each gesture forms a domain within the segment. In the extreme case, languages may not utilise the features of a particular gesture phonologically; thus, languages which neither have contrastive airstream mechanisms nor make phonological use of phonatory contrasts other than simply presence vs. absence of vocal cord vibration will require no reference to representations within the initiatory gesture in their phonologies.

The second apparent area of difference involves the fact that gestures, in the treatment outlined above, are concerned primarily with the structure of the segment, while autosegmental tiers were originally set up in an attempt to characterise the claim that the boundaries of various phonological properties did not necessarily coincide. As I shall show below in section 3, however, these two points of view are not necessarily incompatible: gestures can be interpreted autosegmentally. Indeed, Anderson & Ewen (to appear: 7.6) propose that language-particular gestures are appropriate within particular (sub-)gestures for the characterisation of 'autosegmental' processes such as vowel harmony. These QUASI-GESTURES (or 'autosegments' or 'prosodies') are associated with the appropriate node in the suprasegmental structure, depending on the scope or domain of the quasi-gesture in question.

2. An Alternative Gesture-system

It seems, however, that the tripartite division of the segment into gestures is somewhat understructured. In particular, there are grounds for proposing that, as might be expected, the categorial and initiatory gestures are more closely related to each other than to the articulatory gesture. Arguments of this sort rest on the behaviour of stop systems in languages which do not utilise a voicing opposition to distinguish between stop series, but an opposition involving aspiration, i.e. degree of glottal opening. Thus, as is familiar, many languages have two sets of voiceless stops: one aspirated and one unaspirated. In dependency terms, this opposition may be represented as in (1), which shows the series found in Icelandic:

(1)   O   C
            | |
            C   O
       $[p^h \ t^h \ k^h]$ $[p \ t \ k]$

                              (cf. Ewen, 1980a: 9.4).

Here, clearly, degree of glottal stricture plays an important categorial role in the language — and notice too that languages which have |O| in the stop series often utilise it categorially in other ways, e.g. in having voiceless sonorants, either in their phonological systems, or as a result of phonological processes, as in Icelandic (cf. Thráinsson 1978; Ewen 1982).

In the light of this type of evidence, then, it seems appropriate to treat the two sets of segmental primes involved not as belonging to separate gestures, but to distinct subgestures within the categorial gesture. These two subgestures are the PHONATORY SUBGESTURE (cf. the term 'phonatory gesture' used in earlier work on dependency phonology — Anderson & Jones 1977; Ewen 1977), and the INITIATORY SUBGESTURE, as in (2):

(2)

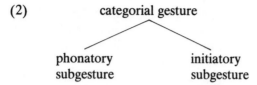

Such a categorisation seems more appropriate for the character-isation of the relation between the various sets of features than the earlier tripartite structure.

The notion of subgesture is also appropriate to the structure of the articulatory gesture. Here, as well as purely locational properties, we find the distinction between orality and nasality. Ladefoged (1971) suggests that four phonetic processes can be distinguished in speech production, one of which is the 'oro-nasal process'. This can be incorporated within the model proposed here as a distinction between a LOCATIONAL and an ORO-NASAL SUBGESTURE:

(3)

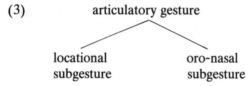

The modification to the gestures proposed here involves the following allocation of the various dependency components to the subgestures (for discussion of the particular components, see Anderson & Ewen 1980a, to appear; Ewen 1980a):

(4)

	categorial gesture		
phonatory subgesture	|V|,|C|	|O|,|G|,|K|	initiatory subgesture
locational subgesture	|i|,|u|,|a|,|ə|, |l|,|t|,|d|,|r|,|λ|	|n|	oro-nasal subgesture

articulatory gesture

As well as the two gestures proposed above, we also require a TONOLOGICAL gesture (cf. the tonological tier in auto-segmental phonology — Goldsmith 1976). It is not my concern here to discuss the internal structure of this gesture (but see Anderson & Ewen, to appear: 7.5); it is clear, however, that it will be required in phonological representation. Its incorporation gives the following structure for the segment:

(5)

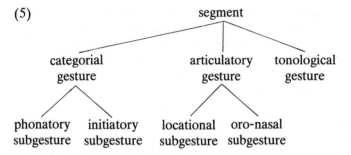

3. The Segment in Phonology

The notion of gesture has so far been presented as forming part of the structure of individual segments. However, it is clear that things are not as straightforward as this presentation might suggest, given the claims that each gesture represents a distinct domain for phonological processes and that the boundaries of these processes do not necessarily coincide (cf. the discussion in section 1). While the domain of each (sub-)gesture will often share the same boundaries, this will frequently not be the case. It is therefore necessary to establish whether the representations of some particular gesture characterise the notion of SEGMENT as such, or whether this notion has to be established by some external means.

It seems appropriate to suggest that the concept of segment can be determined from the representations of the phonatory sub-gesture. That is, each occurrence of (some combination of) |V| and |C| can be interpreted as constituting a segment. An analogous claim is made within various versions of autosegmental phonology. Thus, in the CV phonology of Clements & Keyser (1983), we find three-tiered representations, such as that for *Jennifer* in (6):

(6)

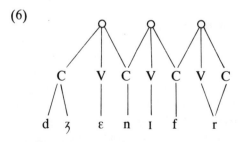

I shall not be concerned here with the SYLLABIC TIER, whose elements are represented by σ. Rather, I want to consider the relationship between the other two tiers — the CV-TIER and the SEGMENTAL TIER. The segmental tier has a vocabulary consisting of 'single-column phonetic matrices characterizing consonants and vowels in the usual manner' (Clements & Keyser 1983: 25); i.e. standard feature matrices. The CV-tier, on the other hand, has various functions. Firstly, the elements of this tier represent functional positions in the syllable, any segment being dominated by V being interpreted as a syllabic peak, any dominated by C as a non-peak. In addition, they can be interpreted as 'sub-syllabic units of timing'. Perhaps most relevant for the discussion here, however, is that the 'useful but ill-defined notion of "phonological segment" can best be reconstructed at this level' (1983: 11). Thus, in cases where there is not a one-to-one correspondence between the CV-tier and the segmental tier (as in the first C and in the syllabic consonant in (6)), the number of elements on the CV-tier determines the number of phonological segments, rather than the number of elements on the segmental tier. The affricate in (6), then, is interpreted as a single segment, associated with two feature matrices, while the rhyme of the final syllable consists of two segments, phonetically realised as a syllabic consonant.

More generally, the CV-tier is seen as the SKELETON of a phonological representation, in that it is associated not only with the syllabic and segmental tiers, but also, where appropriate, with other autosegmental tiers, such as language-specific tiers required for particular processes.

How is the notion of segment to be defined in dependency phonology? Do we need to incorporate a tier — or perhaps gesture — corresponding to the CV skeleton proposed by Clements & Keyser, or are the elements of dependency phonology sufficient to characterise the phonological segment?

It seems that there is no need to propose a structural tier whose *sole* status is functional, for example in serving to define the phonological segment. A CV-tier is only required in the model discussed above because of the failure to assign sufficient internal structure to the 'segmental' tier: i.e. to the tier with phonetic content. Specifically, it is the fact that Clements & Keyser do not separate the categorial features of the segmental tier from the articulatory features which forces them to introduce an extra structural entity. In a model in which appeal is made to a division of the segment into gestures, this problem is overcome. Notice that the need to postulate a separate CV-tier arises essentially from possible mismatches between categorial and articulatory specifications; i.e. situations in which, for example, one categorial specification corresponds to two articulatory specifications (often giving rise to complex segments — cf. Ewen 1980b, 1982; Anderson & Ewen, to appear: 7.3). But the representations of the categorial gesture (specifically the phonatory subgesture) correspond to the elements of the CV-tier in the sense that they too define the distinction between syllabic peak and syllabic non-peak (in terms of the relative prominence of |V|). Moreover, they are available for interpretation as units of timing in exactly the same way, and thus convey the same information about segment status. Due to the independently motivated decision to assign greater structure to the feature matrix (or its dependency equivalent), there is no need to introduce a purely structural tier.

In this interpretation, then, the CV-tier is abandoned, and the information present on the tier can be derived from the representations of the categorial gesture, while the remaining phonological information is to be found in the articulatory gesture. These two gestures can be associated in exactly the same way as the two relevant tiers in the autosegmental model. Thus, a syllable such as *mad* will have the following representations in the two models:

(7)   C   V   C
         ⋮   ⋮   ⋮
         m   a   d

(8)   {|V;C|}   {|V|}   {|C;V|}
         {|u|}   {|a;i|}   {|i|}

(where the elements on the segmental tier in (7) are, of course, merely abbreviations for the appropriate feature matrices, whereas the dependency representations of the articulatory gesture in (8) are in themselves fully specified).

In dependency phonology, the relationship between the phonatory subgesture and the sonority hierarchy is direct — syllabic structures are a projection of the segmental representations of the phonatory subgesture in terms of the relative prominence of |V| and |C| (see further section 4 below). In the normal case, the hierarchical structure is directly determined by the linear order of the segments and their phonatory representations. This holds too for at least some phenomena for which 'complex segment' analyses have been proposed. Prenasalised consonants such as [m͡b], for example, involve violation of the sonority hierarchy, but have a suprasegmental structure which is 'regular' in the sense that the more sonorant element [m] governs the less sonorant element [b] (cf. Ewen 1982; and for an alternative view Anderson & Ewen, to appear: 3.6.3). However, affricates such as [t∫], in which no violation of the sonority hierarchy is apparent (at least in syllable-initial position), must be treated as single segments, with a complex internal structure, involving intrasegmental adjunction of one categorial representation to another, as in (9):

(9)

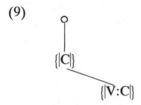

(For further discussion of this and other approaches to the structure of complex segments, see Anderson & Ewen, to appear: 6.3.4, 7.3.)

The nature of the relationship between the various gestures is quite straightforward: the representations of the articulatory and categorial gestures are linked simply by association lines, without the dependency relationship being of any relevance. This appears to hold universally: there are no circumstances under which segment-types are distinguished by a difference in the dependency relation holding between the components of the two gestures.

Within the individual gestures, however, this is not the case. As well as dependency relations holding between components, there are situations in which the representations of subgestures also display such relations. Thus, for languages in which the glottal opening component |O| functions distinctively (e.g. in the stop system of Icelandic and the nasal system of Burmese), it has been proposed (cf. Ewen 1980a: 9.2, 9.4; Anderson & Ewen, to appear: 5.1.1) that the various categories are distinguished by the relative prominence of |O| and the phonatory representation, as in (10):

(10) (a)

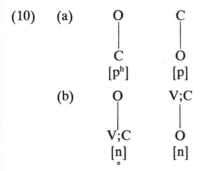

The representations of the individual subgestures, then, show greater interaction than those of different gestures, thus lending support to the particular subdivision of the segmental matrix adopted in section 2.

4. Metrical and Dependency Structure

The notational systems of metrical phonology and dependency phonology start out from the same fundamental belief with respect to suprasegmental structure — that we need to set up a non-linear system of representation to capture relative prominence holding both between segments and between suprasegmental units. However, the two systems differ in certain interesting respects, which I shall explore in this section.

Metrical trees contain three types of information. The first is simply linear order, and the second a hierarchical grouping in terms of constituency, giving the familiar constituency tree in (11):

(11)

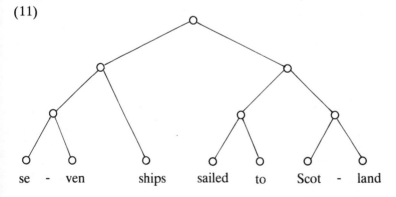

The third type of information, relative prominence, cannot, however, be represented directly in the geometry of the tree, as the
prominence relation must be defined as holding between the two
sisters of a constitute, i.e. between two elements on the same hierarchical level. Thus, the two sisters are marked for relative
prominence by means of the two diacritic labels *s* and *w*, as in
(12):

(12)

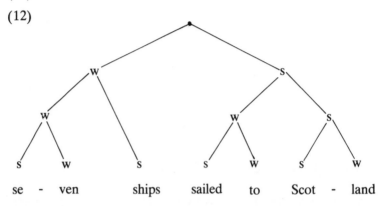

se - ven   ships   sailed   to   Scot - land

Here we have a structure in which the interpretation of the
grouping of two elements in terms of constituency prevents the
direct expression of the strength or prominence relation in the
structure of the tree. Contrast this with the corresponding
dependency tree in (13), where the dependency relation is represented on the vertical dimension:

(13)

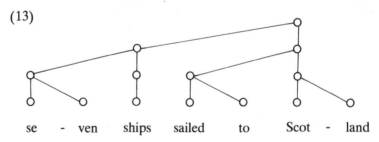

se - ven   ships   sailed   to   Scot - land

This tree gives exactly the same information about grouping and
strength relations as does the constituency tree, but it does so more
economically, in that the dependency relation — specifically the
adjunction of one element to another — defines grouping and
relative strength simultaneously in the geometry of the tree. We do
not require the diacritic labels *s* and *w* superimposed on the nodes

defining the two sisters of a constitute.

Notice that, contrary to what has sometimes been claimed, neither notation is inherently binary (cf. the discussion in Giegerich this vol.: 1). Thus, as well as the binary metrical structures in (14a), those in (14b-d) are also formally possible:

(14)   (a)

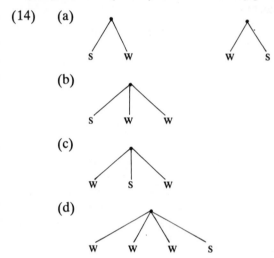

(b)

(c)

(d)

Similarly, there is no formal reason why a governor in a dependency diagram may not have more than one adjoined element. This allows the structures in (15b-d), in addition to the binary structures in (15a):

(15)   (a)

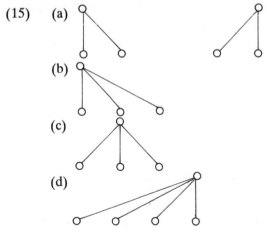

(b)

(c)

(d)

It may or may not be the case that such non-binary structures should be excluded on empirical grounds — however, neither notation excludes them *a priori.*

The structures in (14) and (15) have multiple *w* elements. But there is again no formal reason within metrical notation for disallowing multiple *s*, as in (16):

(16)   (a)   (b)

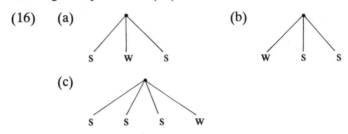

(c)

This seems less desirable: although it is perfectly possible to envisage analyses with, for example, ternary feet (as allowed by (14b) and (15b)), it is difficult to see what structures such as those in (16) would be used for. But this problem does not arise within the dependency framework. Consider (17), the dependency equivalents of (16):

(17)   (a)   (b)

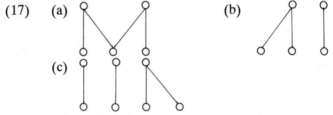

(c)

In terms of the dependency notation, none of these structures can be interpreted as a single unit. (17a) has two governors, which are heads of two different constructions, although they share an ambidependent element, while (17b) and (17c) show elements which, at this hierarchical level, are simply unrelated, although (as in (17a)) they may, of course, be subordinated to a common governor on a higher level. Indeed, if we assume that any well-formed construction must have a single governing element, this must be the case.

So, while neither notation is inherently binary, the only objectionable possibility — a single structure with two heads — is excluded by the dependency notation, while appearing to be formally permissible in metrical phonology.

A further area in which the notational system of dependency phonology appears to be superior to that of metrical phonology is in its treatment of the clearly intimate relation between segmental and suprasegmental structure. In metrical phonology, *s/w* relations within the syllable are established on the basis of a sonority hierarchy, given by Kiparsky (1979) as (18):

(18)   stops, fricatives, nasals, l, r, w, j, u, i, o, e, a

(Notice that other hierarchies, differing in various details, have also been proposed.) Syllabic structures within dependency phonology, however, are built up by dependency assignment rules, again on the basis of relative sonority. However, as noted in 3 above, relative prominence can be determined from the phonatory representations, established on independent phonetic and phonological grounds, and not by means of an apparently arbitrarily assigned sonority hierarchy such as (18).

5. Dependency Trees

The projection of the phonatory representations onto a dependency tree involves first a non-hierarchical representation of segments, as in (19):

(19)

```
 •   •   •   •   •   •   •   •   •   •   •   •   •   •   •   •   •   •   •   •   •   •   •
 |   |   |   |   |   |   |   |   |   |   |   |   |   |   |   |   |   |   |   |   |   |   |
V,C  V V,C  V   V V,C V   C V,C V,C V   V   V   C   C   V V,C C   V   C   V   V   V   C
 |       |
 V       C                          V,C V                        V,C       C   V
 s   ε   v   ə   n   ʃ   ɪ   p   s   s   e   ɪ   l   d   t   ə   s   k   ɔ   t   l   ə   n   d
```

(However, even (19) may be over-structured as a lexical representation of the string. In particular, it can be argued that lexical representations are not only non-hierarchical, but also non-linear, in the sense that, within the onset and the rhyme, the linear ordering of segments is also predictable from the phonatory representations. For discussion of this viewpoint, see Anderson, to appear d.)

(19), then, is the dependency equivalent of the autosegmental CV-tier (or 'basic' tier; cf. van der Hulst & Smith 1982c: 24). As noted above, the representations of the articulatory gesture will be associated with the phonatory representations in (19). The tree-building rules of dependency phonology operate on (19) to give a structure such as (20), in which the number of nodes above the segmental node dominating any particular configuration represents the number of headships held by that segment: thus, /ɪ/ of *ships* is head of, successively, its rhyme, its syllable, its foot, and its tone group:

(20)

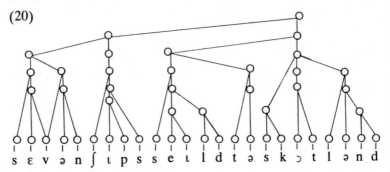

As has been pointed out (Anderson, this vol.; Anderson & Ewen, to appear), the various subjunction paths in a structure like (20), although they are unlabelled, nevertheless determine the prosodic categories involved, by virtue of the alternating patterns of the adjunction paths of the obligatory categories. There is no need within dependency phonology for explicit labels defining prosodic categories, as is found in some versions of metrical phonology.

6. Trees and Grids

I want finally to consider the relationship between dependency trees and metrical grids. The metrical grid is utilised by Liberman & Prince (1977) to characterise various rhythmic properties which, they suggest, can only be defined 'derivatively' in metrical trees.

(21)

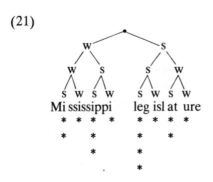

Grids are interpretive devices: in particular, they represent the extent to which sequences are 'eurhythmic' (cf. Hayes 1984); and they also define the notion of rhythmic 'clash', which can trigger various rhythmic adjustment rules. Thus van der Hulst (1984: 140) gives the example in (21).

As van der Hulst notes, the grid in (21) is derived from the corresponding tree with the aid of Liberman & Prince's RELATIVE PROMINENCE PROJECTION RULE, which states that 'in any constituent on which the strong-weak relation is defined, the designated terminal element of its strong subconstituent is metrically stronger than the designated terminal element of its weak subconstituent', so that the number of marks above each syllable in the grid indicates its prominence relative to the other syllables. Thus, while no information is given about grouping, relative prominence can be read off the grid. In (21), there is a rhythmic clash (in that there are adjacent marks on two successive levels), and a rhythmic adjustment rule applies to the grid, to give (22), and the corresponding tree in (23):

(22)

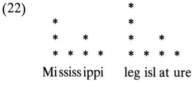

(23)

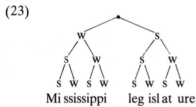

The relationship between metrical trees and grids is, however, not uncontroversial, as noted by Giegerich (this vol.: 3-5). Various metricists (e.g. Liberman & Prince 1977; Hayes 1984) maintain that both trees and grids are necessary in metrical representation. In such proposals, a clash in the grid brings about a change in the tree, as in (21)-(23). Others, such as Giegerich (1983b, this vol.) argue that the grid is merely an interpretive device, which is totally superfluous in that the configuration in (24) is adequate to define the notion of rhythmic clash in forms such as (21):

(24)

Prince (1983), on the other hand, claims that only grids are required in metrical representation (cf. Selkirk 1984b). Notice that Prince claims that in a grid representation — in which grouping is not defined — prosodic categories can be represented in the form of grid levels, as in (25):

(25)   P: *
        Wd: *
        Σ: * *   *
        σ: * *   *
                antique chair

(where P is 'phrase', Wd 'word', Σ 'foot', and σ 'syllable'. For discussion of this approach, see Giegerich, this vol.: 5).

For a general discussion of the tree vs. grid controversy, see van der Hulst (1984). The controversy is, however, simply not relevant within dependency notation, since the types of information found in metrical trees *and* in metrical grids are already present in dependency trees. Consider (26), the dependency equivalent of (21):

(26)

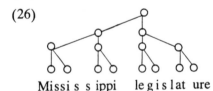

Missi s s ippi   le g i s l at ure

(where I ignore the subsyllabic structure). Here we find the usual information about grouping, as in the metrical tree in (21). But, in addition, the dependency relation — in particular the presence of the subjunction paths denoting the various headships of the particular segments — gives us the same information as is present in the grid in (25). Thus, the clash is defined not by the interaction of marks on the grid, but by the nodes defining the fact that the third syllable of *Mississippi* and the first of *legislature* are two successive group heads without an intervening node dominating an immediately lower category, thus triggering the change of stress such that *Miss* becomes head of the first group.

Two observations are in order here. Firstly, I am not claiming that (26) is necessarily the appropriate dependency representation of the string *Mississippi legislature*; rather, (26) merely illustrates that any metrical tree/grid representation can be assigned a dependency equivalent which contains the same sort of information. In the case of (26), the status of the nodes above the level of the foot needs further discussion (see, for example, Anderson & Ewen, to appear: 3.4.3-4).

Secondly, the distinction involved in stress shift or iambic reversal processes such as these should perhaps be interpreted not as involving a transformational or structural *change*, but rather as illustrating a difference between lexical and utterance structure, as in (27) (where, for the sake of illustration, I continue to assume the validity of the suprasegmental structure in (26)):

(27)

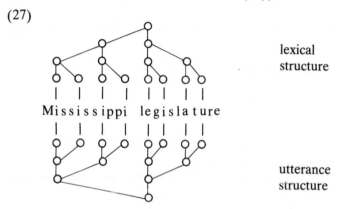

lexical structure

utterance structure

where the lexical structure is linked by association lines with the utterance structure. (For discussion of the relationship between lexical and utterance structure, see Anderson, this vol.; Anderson & Ewen, to appear: 7.7; Anderson & Durand, this vol.)

There is still a further aspect of the relationship between metrical and dependency structures which should be noted, however. A dependency interpretation of the sort outlined above removes the ambiguity inherent in metrical tree structures such as (28) and (29), discussed by Giegerich (this vol.):

(28)

(29)

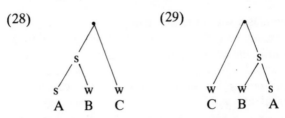

(29) is compatible with either of the grid interpretations in (30):

(30)   (a)   *   (b)   *
                  *   *   *   *
                *   *   *   *   *   *
                C B A   C B A

and this leads Giegerich to propose the following supplementary convention, in an attempt to provide a one-to-one relationship between trees and grids:

(31)   In a metrical tree structure [such as (28)] or [(29)], there is a strength relation B = C.

thus allowing only (32) as an interpretation of (29):

(32)   *
              *
          *   *   *

where (32) is what Prince (1983) calls the 'minimal interpretation' of the corresponding tree structure.

As well as the structures in (28) and (29) being ambiguous with respect to grid interpretation, a particular grid structure may itself be an interpretation of more than one metrical tree. Thus, (30a), as well as corresponding to (29), is also an interpretation of (33):

(33)

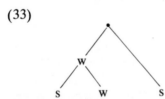

We have a situation, then, in which one tree may have more than one grid interpretation (if the convention in (31) is not utilised), and a single grid may be the result of interpreting more than one tree.

Such ambiguities do not arise in dependency structures. The tree associated with (32) is:

(34)

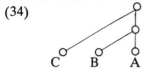

while the dependency equivalents of the grids in (30) would be:

(35)   (a)   (b)

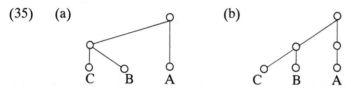

in which, crucially, one of the elements B and C is head/governor of some construction. As such, then, the fact that a metrical tree can be given more than one grid interpretation is attributable to a failure in metrical notation to distinguish various possible structures, all of which apparently occur in language:

(36)   (a)   (b)

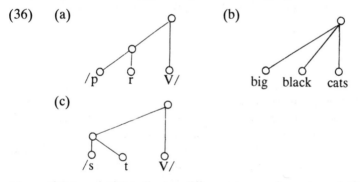

    (c)

where (36a) and (36c) display different types of onset, and (36b) is a dependency interpretation of (29) (assuming Giegerich's convention (31)).

Thus the ambiguities inherent in both metrical grid and metrical tree notation are resolved by the adoption of a notation which simultaneously defines constituency and relative prominence, and whose suprasegmental structures are directly determined by segmental representations. In general, it is the intimate relation between segmental and suprasegmental structure within the dependency model which leads to a more satisfactory account of the issues discussed here.

Acknowledgement

My thanks are due to John Anderson and Martina Noteboom for comments on earlier versions of this article. Remaining imperfections are not their fault.

6 RELATING TO METRICAL STRUCTURE[1]

Heinz Giegerich

1. On Theory and Notation

Few phonologists would disagree these days with the claim that suprasegmental phonological representations are structured and that these structures are by and large autonomous of morpho-syntactic bracketing. Thus, current phonological theory recognises a hierarchy of larger-than-segment phonological constituents comprising the syllable, the foot, the phonological phrase, and arguably more. While the pre-theoretical reality of such units has never been under serious dispute — phoneticians have accepted their existence long since[2] — it has been one of the major advances of post-SPE generative phonology to make them part of phonological theory: they are recurrent and predictable, and they serve to express a large number of phonological generalisations more elegantly and, often, more adequately (Anderson & Jones 1974; Hooper 1976; Kahn 1976).

A phonological theory containing such a hierarchy of immediate constituents has to make explicit statements in answer to the following two, partially independent, questions: (a) How are the boundaries of syllables, feet, and phonological phrases determined? And (b) What is the internal structure of each constituent? Moreover, and again independently of the former two questions, a third issue arises: the choice of a notation, or explication-language (in the sense of Wunderlich, 1979: Ch. 7) for the expression of generalisations that come under this particular aspect of the theory.

One and the same notation can be used for different theories: Chomsky & Halle (1968), for example, adopt a notation for the representation of stress which had previously been employed in the phonemicist framework of Trager & Smith (1951). Conversely, more than one notation may be proposed for one and the same theory. These may be equally suited to their task; one may be generally superior; one may be superior in particular aspects while in other aspects the other one may be better. The mutual independence of theoretical and notational issues has been discussed by McCawley (1973) and by Anderson & Ewen (1980a/b). In what I have to say in this essay it is of particular importance in that I shall be almost exclusively concerned with one of the several notational systems currently under debate, leaving aside the others and making a number of (possibly objectionable) theoretical assumptions which I spell out in 2 below. But before doing that, let me say a few words about the notational system under discussion here — that of metrical phonology. (More detailed introductions are found in van der Hulst & Smith (1982c) and in Giegerich (1985): Chs 1, 5).

Metrical phonology is a notation for phonological constituency which permits binary branching only and in which sister nodes are labelled [S W] or [W S] (where S stands for 'stronger than W' and W for 'weaker than S'). No other labelling or branching is permissible: (1a) below is an example of a structure permitted in the notation; the ones in (1b) are ruled out:

(1)   (a)

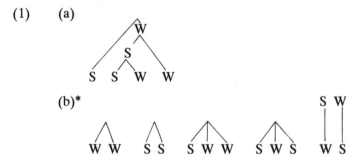

The labels S and W are not in fact labels in the sense current in other constituency notations: they have no local interpretation. The only possible interpretation of a node is one in relation to its sister: a node is stronger or weaker than its sister and no other possibility of interpretation exists.

It has been assumed in the literature on metrical phonology, following a claim to that effect by Liberman & Prince (1977, hereafter LP), that the binarity of structure is a necessary logical consequence of the relationality of the properties expressed in the metrical tree. Strictly speaking, this is not true: there is nothing inherent in the notation that rules out, for example, ternary structures such as the ones given in (1b) above. Structures like [S W W] or [S W S] simply fail to define a relation among the two nodes with identical labels, the two Ws in the former and the two Ss in the latter. (Note that the latter would then have the problem of being a constituent with two heads.) A metrical tree containing ternary branching is therefore not maximally structured but it is — while in some respects problematical — by no means ill-formed — unless, of course, the list of notational conventions contains a statement to just that. effect. I shall here assume the presence of such a statement although the theoretical claim that all phonological constituents are binary, implied by this notational convention, is really far from uncontroversial. But I shall in what follows at least go a little way towards substantiating such a claim, by showing that the internal structures of both the syllable and the foot are *minimally* binary-branching. Whether any such constituency structures are also *maximally* binary is a question that I have to leave unanswered (but see Leben (1982) for a discussion of some evidence to this effect). Since the problem of binarity is a theoretical one, and not primarily a notational one, it naturally arises within other notational systems also — notably for dependency phonology. The crucial difference between the two notational systems is that metrical phonology is, owing to the relational character of the S/W labels, inherently minimally binary — each constituent must have a sister — while dependency phonology imposes no such constraint. I shall return to this problem below; meanwhile, the reader is referred to a dependency phonologist's view in this debate (Ewen, this vol.: 4).

A metrical tree thus contains two hierarchies: the hierarchy of phonological constituents mentioned above (although the stipulation of binarity results in a number of nodes greater than that motivated by the hierarchy), and a hierarchy of relative prominence. That the two hierarchies can be collapsed into one has been recognised by the proponents of other notational systems also, again, notably by dependency phonologists (Anderson & Jones 1974, 1977; Ewen 1980a, this vol.; Anderson, this vol.). The reasons for doing so will become apparent in 2 below. But in order to link up the second hierarchy — that of relative prominence — with pre-theoretical facts, another statement has to be added to the notational conventions of metrical phonology. What has to be stated is an interpretive convention that converts the non-linear representation of relative prominence into the linear prominence contour of speech, comprising the sonority contours among segments within syllables, the stress contours among syllable nuclei within words, and the 'sentence stress' contours among the stressed syllables of words within higher-level constituents. The fact that more than one phonetic parameter is involved here is one of the reasons why individual nodes in metrical phonology are not subject to local phonetic interpretation: S^W describes a sonority pattern within syllables and a stress pattern above that level where 'stress' in turn corresponds to a number of parameters: pitch, duration, loudness and so forth. A convention has to be found, then, that interprets the hierarchy of relative prominence so that it reflects the multi-parametered prominence contours in speech.

Above the level of the syllable, there is a precedent for a linear representation of such properties: the numerical stress values of SPE. But note that SPE's numbers by no means have the status of pre-theoretical 'facts' that could serve as a yardstick for the observational adequacy of any linearisation of metrical structure. They are nothing but the expression of theoretical reasoning about phonology — to be more precise, they are the representations of a particular phonological theory in terms of a notation which is essentially unilinear and has no way of isolating the parameters mentioned above. Both the theory and the notation are called into question by metrical phonology (among other notations) and its theoretical background. I shall adress myself to the question of linearising hierarchic structures of metrical phonology in section 3 of this essay — after spelling out what the theoretical assumptions are that the metrical notation has to do justice to, and how it does that.

2. Phonological Constituency Structure and Metrical Phonology

Syllables, to start with the least inclusive one of the phonological constituents listed in 1 above, are associated with sonority peaks in strings of segments (Hooper 1976): if we assume that segments can be hierarchised universally in terms of their sonority[3], then the syllabic nucleus will always be the most sonorous segment of the syllable, and the non-syllabic segments of the syllable will generally be grouped in such a way that sonority decreases from the nucleus towards both margins. Thus, *lilt* constitutes one syllable and *little* constitutes two, simply because the sequence /lt/ decreases in sonority while /tl/ does not. This characteristic of syllable structure seems to be violated systematically in Germanic languages, for example, by the behaviour of sibilants in onsets (such as English *stick*, German *Stock*) and more generally by the behaviour of coronal segments in syllable-final position (as in English *fix*, *act*, etc.). Despite this and other language-specific peculiarities, the principle seems to stand (Kiparsky 1979).

Ample evidence has been given that a unit thus defined is useful in the statements of the domains of a number of segmental processes (Vennemann 1972; Anderson & Jones 1974; Kahn 1976 and others). Whether it is necessary to make a reference to syllables in the description of each such process is a difficult question; in a number of cases, it unsurprisingly isn't, simply because a large number of the criteria responsible for syllabification are directly derivative from properties of the string itself and reference may therefore be made to those properties directly rather than to the syllable boundaries derived from them.

But consider the well-known problem of stress placement in English words like *'algebra* vs. *de'tergent*. In order to account for this difference, SPE are forced to treat the V̆CC cluster in the former as light and that in the latter as heavy, despite the presence of /r/ and a voiced stop in both. SPE's solution, while it is entirely *ad hoc*, seems to work but it misses the generalisation that stress placement in these two cases (as in all others) can be viewed as directly related to syllabic boundary placement (Anderson & Jones 1977: 95 ff.) in such a way that *detergent* has a heavy penultimate syllable, attracting stress, while *algebra* has a light penult and the stress falls on the antepenult. I shall return to this issue shortly; let us discuss syllable structure and the principles that govern syllable boundary placement separately.

Assume that syllables have the following internal structure (Pike & Pike 1947):

(2)

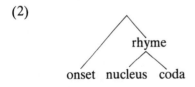

Assume further that in a variety of stress languages, such as English (Anderson & Jones 1974) and German (Giegerich 1985), heavy syllables of the form (C)VV or (C)VC attract stress while light syllables of the form (C)V in comparable positions fail to do so. A heavy syllable is then a syllable with a branching rhyme.

Kiparsky (1979) has proposed a universal syllable template which expresses the characteristics of syllable structure given above in terms of the metrical notation. I quote this template in (3):

(3)

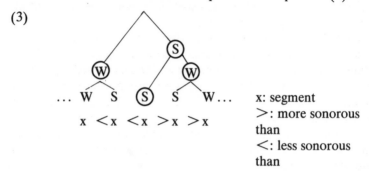

x: segment
>: more sonorous than
<: less sonorous than

The template gets mapped onto strings in such a way that its relative prominence relations reflect the sonority relations among neighbouring segments: the nucleus is the most sonorous element. This implies the presence of a convention that interprets the prominence relations that hold within the metrical tree in such a way as is indicated underneath (3). I return to this question in section 3 below.[4] In (4), two monosyllabic mappings are given, the former well-formed, the latter ill-formed:

(4)

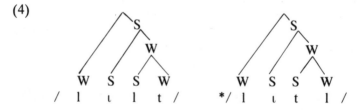

little cannot have a monosyllabic mapping because an S^W structure cannot be mapped onto a string of increasing sonority like /tl/.

The circled nodes in (3) above reflect the constituents of syllables given in (2): the root branches into onset and rhyme, the rhyme into nucleus and coda. The minimal expansion of the template is W^S; that is, the stipulation of binarity in the notation requires every syllable to have an onset as well as a (possibly non-branching) rhyme.[5] There is some evidence in favour of such compulsory onsets — evidence, it seems to me, that can be interpreted as evidence in favour of the minimal binarity that distinguishes this notational system from others. Firstly, of any consonants to the left of the syllabic, at least the one next to the syllabic will be the onset of this syllable rather than (part of) the coda of the preceding syllable. This observation is also borne out generally by the principles that govern syllabification, which I shall briefly discuss below. Secondly, in instances where no such consonant is available (as in (5) below) the resulting empty onsets are frequently filled by glottal stops (*fester Vokaleinsatz*: Krech 1968; cf. Anderson, this vol.: 6). Empty onsets are in fact necessary conditions for pre-vocalic glottal stops to occur. The prosodic account of this phenomenon made possible by the metrical notation (Giegerich 1984) compares rather favourably with segmental accounts. (Cf. again Anderson, this vol.: 6; and Lass 1983 for alternative proposals.)

Given the template of metrical phonology, or any other device of other notational systems, principles of syllable boundary placement are provided independently by phonological theory. It is widely held that syllabification is initial-maximal: sequences of the form CVCVCV ... are (almost) universally syllabified as CV.CV.CV. ... (Kiparsky 1979). In the metrical notation, this means that the template is extended over as many segments as possible towards the left. (Recall my earlier observation that this notation entails compulsory onsets.) If syllabification is also final non-maximal, effectively ruling out overlapping syllables for this stage of the derivation[6], then the following picture emerges for words such as *algebra* and *agenda*:

(5)

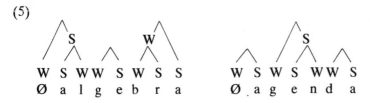

Note that the syllable weight required for the operation of the English Main Stress Rule is brought about rather elegantly by the model that I have been outlining: a light syllable is a structure whose right-hand branch does not branch further. In a heavy syllable, the right-hand branch is complex. The appropriate configurations are given in (6):[7]

(6)   light syllable: heavy syllable:

Let us move upwards a step in the hierarchy of phonological constituents: the roots of the syllables in (5) have to get connected up in such a way that feet are formed. Feet have the recurrent pre-theoretical characteristic of being the unit of timing in English and other stress-timed languages (but see note 2). Moreover, they have fixed prominence contours: foot boundaries coincide with the left-hand boundaries of stressed syllables. In the metrical notation, the foot may be represented by the following template, which is mapped onto the roots of previously erected syllable structures.

(7)   foot:

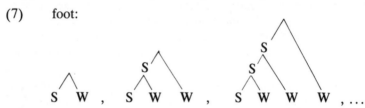

Like the syllable, the foot justifies its existence as a phonological constituent by figuring in the structural descriptions of certain phonological processes. Thus, the flapping of intervocalic /t/ in certain accents of English can (in part) be attributed to the absence of a foot boundary (Selkirk 1980b; Leben 1982). Aspiration of voiceless stops in English is restricted to non-foot-final positions (Anderson & Ewen, to appear) and is strongest in the foot-initial position. Similarly, foot-initial empty syllable onsets are favoured over other such onsets by the prevocalic glottal stop in German (Krech 1968; Giegerich 1983a, 1984).

The placement of foot boundaries (or 'pedification', to coin another hideous term) is governed by rules that are traditionally called rules of word stress. For this is what these rules do: they place the initial S of the foot template (7) on a syllable which is eligible for 'receiving stress', that is, for becoming the prominent syllable of a foot. As this syllable is the leftmost in the template, each stress placement is the placement of a left-hand foot boundary. As for the right-hand boundary, note that the template

(7) is unbounded on the right. We may assume that the template is extended to the right over all the syllables in a given utterance that do not qualify for 'word stress', i.e. that are not foot-initial. As a result, the syllables of an utterance will be completely organised into feet, and feet do not overlap.

In English, the selection of foot-initial syllables is governed by a variety of factors, including syllable weight (Anderson & Jones 1977) and distance from the end of the word (Chomsky & Halle 1968). For *algebra* and *agenda*, the pedification process results in the following structures (omitting intrasyllabic structure):

(8)

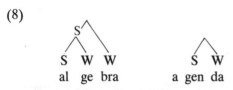

In current phonological theory, it is assumed that all lexical items contain at least one foot-initial ('stressed') syllable (Chomsky & Halle 1968). This raises at least two questions: 1. What happens to the initial syllable in *agenda*? And 2. How do feet get formed in monosyllabic lexical items, like *long*?

In the earlier literature on metrical phonology (LP; Kiparsky 1979; Selkirk 1980b[8]), *agenda* is given the metrical tree in (9):

(9)

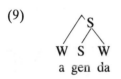

Structures like that were prompted by a desire to give an equivalent of SPE-type stress numbers, into which a metrical tree could ultimately be converted, rather by an interest in phonological constituency structure. There is no evidence to support the claim, implicit in (9) and defended, for example, by Booij (1983), that the binary tree linking *a-* with the material on its right dominates a phonological constituent that has a place in the hierarchy of suprasegmental constituents given in section 1. Any phonological process involving word-size units or their boundaries makes reference to the morphosyntactic bracketing (in which the word does figure) rather than to prosodic structure. The word simply does not have the same prosodic integrity as, say, the foot. For that reason it may not form a metrical tree — indeed, in the case of *agenda* there is no prosodic word node: the initial syllable is part of the preceding foot.

This leads me to the second question raised above: how do we represent the fact that lexical monosyllables 'bear stress' in English or, better, that they are foot-initial? Given that the minimal expansion of the foot template (7) has two syllable-dominating constituents, *long* would be assigned the structure given in (10) below — recall that the notation is minimally binary.

(10)

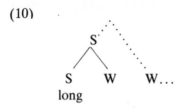

In isolation, the notational system produces an empty syllable slot for the right branch of the structure. However, it will be recalled that we stipulated a mechanism which spreads the foot template to the right up to the next foot boundary. Such a process, which works across at least certain ones of the boundaries provided by the morphosyntax, results in the filling of empty slots and yields, for example, structures like (11):

(11)

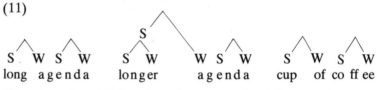

The empty slot of (10) only surfaces empty in such cases where no material is available on the right of the S to fill the sister node of that S. Thus, our model produces surface-empty nodes in cases like the following:

(12)

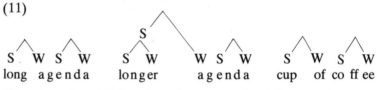

S   W S   W   S   W S   W
long Ø meeting   po lice Ø escort

(Note that the initial syllable of *police* will in turn be taken up by a W node provided by the preceding foot.[9])

As I have argued elsewhere (Giegerich 1981, 1985: Ch. 4), the theoretical claim that feet are minimally binary is rather well supported by a variety of independent phenomena. Firstly, the durational behaviour of monosyllabic feet is strikingly similar to that of bisyllabic feet in English. Secondly, English characteristically has enclitics (such as *cuppa tea*, etc.), where phonological structure produces units that override morphosyntactic brackets, while the mirror-images of such units (proclitics) appear to be systematically absent (Abercrombie 1965c). Moreover, zero syllables figure crucially in a variety of metrical transformations (Giegerich 1985: Ch. 4). Positing zero syllables in cases like those in (12) above is therefore not so much a problem caused by the binarity of the notation; rather, it expresses an aspect of phonological theory which any notational system that does not insist on the minimal binarity of the foot would find rather harder to express.

Obviously, a lot remains to be said about the details of foot boundary placement — especially in polysyllabic English words — and the organisation of feet into higher-order structures within words. Rather than discussing such problems, let us take another step upwards in the phonological hierarchy and look at phonological phrases.

Consider the following example:

(13)

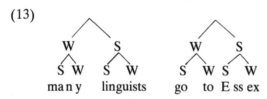

What are the 'observables' in terms of phonological phrasing? There are two units, corresponding to the syntactic phrases NP and VP and (optionally) separated by a pause. Within each constituent, the final foot(-initial syllable) is more prominent than the first in terms of some phonetic parameter, presumably pitch.

In (13) above, a metrical structure is given that reflects these observations. In this case, the metrical structure is an almost exact copy of the syntactic surface structure — the only deviation being that *go* forms a foot that spreads across a syntactic boundary. We have already accounted for this phenomenon: *go* is a lexical monosyllable and *to* is non-lexical, therefore not eligible for the foot-initial position.[10]

Not a lot is known about the placement of phonological phrase boundaries. They do not seem to coincide necessarily with the syntactic boundaries (see Selkirk 1980a; Nespor & Vogel 1982) even if they do in the case discussed above. But let us assume that in the cases where they do not coincide with the syntax, they are derived from the syntax (see Giegerich 1983b for some such derivations).

I shall not go further into the details of the demarcation and internal structure of the phonological phrase. The general properties of this unit seem comparable to those of the constituents discussed earlier: the placement of its boundaries is predictable from the syntax, its internal prominence pattern is fixed (it is right-strong in English, as shown in (13) above). These observations allow us to complete the structures of (11) and (12). Adjective plus noun combinations constitute phonological phrases, and nouns, as heads, are prominent. This yields the following structures:

(14)

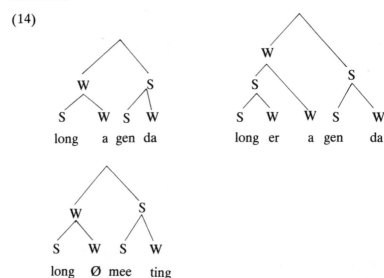

As is the case with syllables and feet, it may be expected that the phonological phrase is helpful — if not necessary — in the description of phonological processes. Some such processes have been cited in the literature: *raddoppiamento sintattico* in Italian (Nespor & Vogel 1982), Iambic Reversal in English (Selkirk 1980a), and undoubtedly more. It would, on the other hand, be surprising if phonological processes could be found that *require* reference to phonological phrasing, given that this phrasing is directly derived from syntactic structure. This would imply that the processes in question may equally well make reference to the syntax directly (cf., for example, Giegerich 1983b on Iambic Reversal).

More could be said about the properties of this particular phonological constituent. The discussion could be continued, moreover, with similar descriptions of higher-level constituents such as the intonational phrase and the utterance (cf. for these, again, Nespor & Vogel 1982). Both these constituents appear to be right-strong in English. Whether they have clearly distinct phonological identities is an unanswered question. In the absence of compelling evidence on this matter, one may well take the view that *all* metrical structure above the foot is a copy of the syntactic structure with right-strong prominence relations (and with certain adjustments, cf. Giegerich 1983b), so that a separation of constituents above the foot level may not be necessary in a formal way. In any case, we can now complete the metrical structure of *many linguists go to Essex* by linking up the two phonological phrases given in (13) above:

(15)

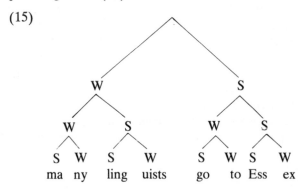

Rather than pursuing the question of high-level phonological constituents, let us turn to the second aspect of hierarchisation in phonological constituent structure: the claim that all phonological constituents have heads (in terms of prominence) and that headness is additive. As the hierarchy of constituents has been worked out so far, the following picture emerges: in a string of segments, the most sonorous one constitutes the nucleus of a syllable. Certain nuclei 'receive stress': those of foot-initial syllables. Among foot-initial syllables, a further contouring takes place according to their position in higher-level phonological constituents. Let us assume, then, that the entirety of the prominence contour of a given utterance can be determined in terms of the way segments are placed in the hierarchy of phonological constituents.

To demonstrate this, let us go back to (15) above. Syllable structure is not given in this analysis (since not enough details of this issue were given earlier), the bottom-level nodes in (15) represent syllables. The rules of foot boundary placement determine which of those are S. Among these, the heads of phonological phrases (*ling-* and *Ess-*) are more prominent than their sisters. Of these two, in turn, *Ess-* is the more prominent. This syllable, then (or, to be more precise, the nucleus of this syllable) is the head of the entire phonological construction; unlike any other terminal node in this structure, it has Ss all the way up the tree.

As has been mentioned before, the prominence characteristics of the different levels of structure add up in speech to some kind of prominence contour which is part of the linear sequence of the phonetic representation. In order to achieve this rather complex mapping of a non-linear structure onto a linear sequence, an interpretive convention has to be formulated as part of the notational system. This convention will determine each segment's behaviour within the contour according to the way it is dominated by Ss and Ws in the metrical tree. One example of the working of this convention has already been given: recall (3) above. How does the internal structure of the syllable template express the claim that each syllable has a single sonority peak? And if the peak can be identified as the element dominated by S nodes all the way up, how does the tree express the sonority behaviour of those segments that are not the peak? I shall address this question in the following section.

3. The Interpretation of Metrical Structure

LP discuss two conventions for the interpretation of metrical structure but only one of them is eventually recommended. The first one consists of an algorithm, which I shall give in (16) below. This algorithm converts the hierarchic representation into one of the numerical type used by Chomsky & Halle (1968). Rather strikingly, it produces exactly the same numerical stress contour for (almost) any given string as Chomsky & Halle do with their model. As I pointed out before, the mere fact that it is possible to invent such an algorithm doesn't make LP's model of English word stress more recommendable than it would be without the algorithm: there is nothing in the SPE numbers that is *per se* factual, or 'true' in a pre-theoretical sense — in fact, the SPE model has on occasions been criticised for being too highly articulated and therefore unrealistic. For that reason it would be misguided to construct a metrical model in such a way that it — with the help of an auxiliary algorithm — lives up to SPE standards of detailedness.

I have noted before one instance where LP's model sacrifices one of the principles of the theory of phonological structure for the sake of stress numerology: the case of unstressed initial syllables ((9) above). It is only because LP want to calculate stress numbers for all the syllables of isolated lexical items that they construct unique word-trees for these isolated items. In terms of phonological structure, there is no justification for doing so since the word is not a phonological constituent. Note that leaving the initial syllable unattached in a word like *detergent* could bear out the same information about this syllable's lack of 'stress' — except that this information would not be accessible to LP's algorithm. Here is the algorithm:

(16)   If a terminal node *t* is labelled *W*, its stress number is equal to the number of nodes that dominate it, plus one. If a terminal node *t* is labelled *S*, its stress number is equal to the number of nodes that dominate the lowest *W* dominating *t*, plus one.

Leaving aside the problems of the tree structures on which this algorithm crucially depends, let us now look at the information that it extracts from a given metrical structure, for example the one in (17):

(17)

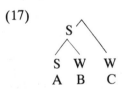

The following prominence relations are expressed in the tree itself: A > B, [AB] > C. Moreover, it seems reasonable to infer A > C — more on that below. No relation is defined in this structure between B and C. LP's algorithm, on the other hand, gives for (17) a strength contour 1-3-2, thus interpreting B < C. If such an interpretation is to be proposed, it can only be done on the basis of empirical evidence; there is nothing in the structure (17) itself to warrant it. I am not aware of any such evidence. On these grounds, the algorithm has to be rejected.

LP do not seem to like it much either, for they use, in a disguised form, a different convention, made explicit in a paper by Paul Kiparsky (1981: 245). I quote it in (18):

(18)   The beat of a subtree labelled *S* is stronger than the beat of its sister subtree labelled *W*,

where the beat is the strongest element in a subtree. Applied to the structure in (17), this yields the interpretation that I suggested above: A > B and A > C. No interpretation is made with respect to B and C. Characteristically, any metrical configuration of the form W̯ W̯ is uninterpreted.

I mentioned above that LP in fact use this convention, rather than the algorithm in (16), for the interpretation of their tree structures but disguise it. It comes in the disguise of metrical grids. Metrical grids are formal structures of some complexity, for which the reader is referred to LP (pp. 311-15). I shall here just give a few visual demonstrations.

A metrical grid consists of rows and columns. The bottom row (level 1) has one element per syllable. Each grid element may have another one immediately above it, which may in turn have another one immediately above it, and so forth. Column height measures metrical strength, so that the grid is a linear representation of strength values. A sample grid is given in (19a) below; the one in (19b) is ill-formed as the column over syllable B contains a gap.

(19)   (a)   (b)

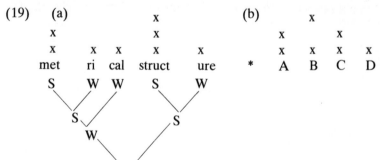

Grids are aligned with metrical trees by a projection rule that is in fact identical with Kiparsky's convention. Thus, in (19a) above, the first syllable of *metrical* is stronger than the second and the third; the first syllable of *structure* is stronger than the second and also stronger than the first syllable of *metrical.* The problem inherent in this interpretation is that no prominence relation is defined among the second and the third syllable of *metrical.* They may be, under Kiparsky's convention (and LP's tree-grid projection rule) equally strong or either may be interpreted as stronger than the other. Thus, the two grids in (20) below are also well-formed for *metrical*:

(20)   x   x
          x x   x   x
          x x x   x x x
          metrical   metrical

LP's model of stress in English requires this permissiveness crucially for two independent reasons. I shall give one now and the second one in 4 below. Both, I shall argue, stem from some fundamental problems with LP's tree structures and result in excessive power on the part of the grid.

In LP's model, rhythmic alternation in phrases like *five black cats, pretty little girls*, etc. is produced by adding grid elements in certain columns. In (21a), I give these phrases with minimal grids and no rhythmic alternation. In (21b), the grids have alternating contours — compatible, it will be remembered, with the interpretive convention for trees.[11]

(21)   (a)

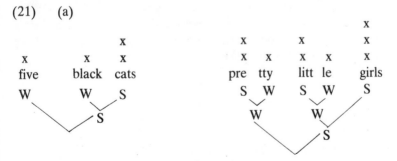

(b)

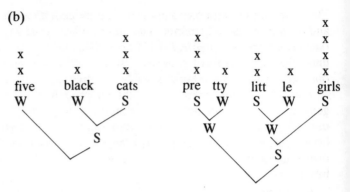

So far so good. The prominence contour over the two adjectives will in speech either be flat, as in (21a), or it will alternate as in (21b). The problem is that LP's notation also permits tree-grid alignments such as the ones in (22):

(22)

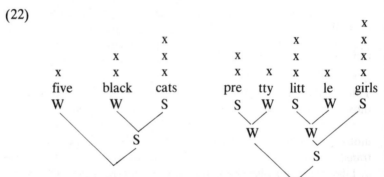

The former contour does not occur at all (arguably with the exception of emphatic stress on *black*), and when the latter does it means girls that are pretty little. And for that reading the metrical tree structure will be that in (23):

(23)

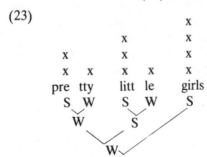

There are two possible solutions to this problem, one rather *ad hoc*
and one on principled grounds. The *ad hoc* solution would rule out
rising contours like the one in (22) except where the tree structure
unavoidably requires them, as in (23). This solution would seem
observationally correct.

The second solution rules out variable tree interpretation altogether, producing one and only one grid per tree. I shall pursue
this option here, although it may appear more costly at first sight,
because it will enable me to dispense with the grid as a formal
device altogether. This consequence will be demonstrated in 4
below.

In pursuit of the second option, then, let us ensure that the
interpretation of metrical trees is invariable. This implies that in a
tree like the one in (17) above, we interpret invariably B = C.
Here is an appropriate convention, supplementary to (18) above:

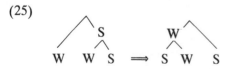

(24)   In a metrical tree structure   A   B   C   or   C   B   A,
        there is a strength relation B = C.

This interpretation rules out the grids in (22) above as well as
those in (21b), allowing only those in (21a).

Consequently, contours like the ones in (21b) will have to be
motivated in the metrical tree. This is done through a metrical
transformation.

I have argued elsewhere (Giegerich 1983b; 1985: Ch. 4) in
favour of a metrical component of the grammar, sited between the
syntax and the phonology. In this component, metrical structures,
roughly isomorphous with the syntactic surface structure, get
adjusted by operations of phonological phrasing, stress shifts and
other transformations, all motivated by the requirements of timing
and phrasing in speech. These operations perform, among other
things, the tasks of Langendoen's (1975) readjustment rules. As
for the alternating contour that we have to produce for *five black
cats*, etc., the metrical transformation will look like this:

(25)
```
      /\                  /\
    /  \'S             W'/  \
  /   /\            /\    \
 W   W  S   ⟹     S  W    S
```

The output structure of (25) has a grid of the form (21b).

The first one of the two distinct tasks that the grid performs in LP's model is thus taken care of: by introducing a new metrical transformation — and note that LP's model cannot do entirely without such transformations anyway — the number of possible interpretations for each tree can be restricted to one. In other words, the grid is no longer needed for this task.

4. On 'Grid Phonology'

The function of a notational device may be either illustrative or formal. In a formal device, formally defined operations are possible, or certain configurations, again defined in formal terms, can be interpreted in such a way that they predict some 'real life' situation in the empirical domain that the notation serves to describe. Metrical tree structure clearly is such a formal notation. Illustrative devices, on the other hand, are matters of (usually visual) convenience only. They have no operations defined on them, nor do they express anything in terms of their representations that could not (if with greater effort) be interpreted in the absence of the device. They are purely interpretive and therefore, strictly speaking, unnecessary.

A well-known analogy from syntax will serve to clarify this distinction. In an *Aspects*-type transformational syntax, the functional notion of 'subject' is expressed in terms of syntactic categories, so that subjecthood is an illustrative term applied to the NP immediately dominated by S (Chomsky 1965: 68 f). Subjecthood is thus not part of the formal notation but part of an optional additional notation whose purpose it is to illustrate the properties of certain configurations in the formal notation.

The same can be said about notions like the onset, rhyme, nucleus, and coda of syllables. I argued in 2 above that these intrasyllabic constituents are relationally defined in the metrical structure of the syllable: labelling the nodes in the tree according to this hierarchy of constituents would thus be purely illustrative since the constituents are present in the structure anyway and their labels can be read off the structure.

An illustrative notation is not part of a theory, then, since it does not serve crucially in the representations of the theory.

The question arises now what kind of device the metrical grid is.

I shall in this section look at some more of the uses that the grid has been put to by LP and by Prince (1983). In both these papers, the grid is a formal device (hence my *ad hoc* term 'grid phonology') dealing with the properties relating to the prominence behaviour of phonological units, in the former along with tree structure and in the latter on its own. I shall argue in this section that the grid is unfit for the expression of such phonological properties, simply because it fails to define phonological units, and that it can therefore only have the status of an illustrative device. I shall thus pursue a line of reasoning already started in the preceding section, where I argued that the grid should only be allowed to illustrate properties already present in the metrical tree.

In LP's model, the metrical grid has a formal function in the statement of the Iambic Reversal Rule: a metrical structure of the form W^S reverses into S^W in a context which LP characterise in terms of a specific grid configuration. Here is an example:

(26)
```
              x                        x
       x  —  x              x          x
   x   x  —  x              x    x     x
   fourteen men    ⟹       fourteen men
   W    S    S              S    W     S
        \  /                \   /
         W                   W  /
          \  /                \/
           \/
```

The grid configuration that triggers reversal is, in LP's terms, the clash indicated by the horizontal lines in (26): Isambic Reversal serves to resolve grid clashes (adjacency of grid elements on two contiguous levels). The same configuration shows up in the following cases, all candidates for reversal — note that this notation quite elegantly captures the fact that the syllable from which prominence

(27)

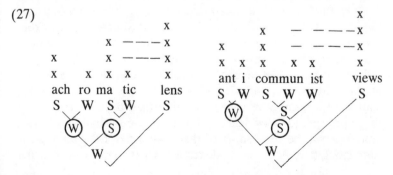

gets shifted need not be adjacent to the stronger syllable on its right that causes the shift, so long as their respective grid columns clash.

The nodes subject to reversal are circles. It is quite clear that not all structures that share these characteristics are equally likely to actually undergo reversal. The width of the clash seems to play a major part in the factors governing likelihood — *fourteen men* seems more likely to reverse than *anticommunist views* or even *anticommunist opinion.* This criterion might correlate in some way with differences in speech tempo. Another criterion is the familiarity of the words that are candidates for reversal: familiar ones will be more likely to undergo the rule than rare ones. And finally, the reluctance or willingness to apply the rule may in many instances be speaker-specific. For those reasons, I suspect that an attempt to provide formal criteria for an item's likelihood to undergo reversal might be doomed to failure, and conversely, that formalising the niceties of the reversal rule may prove impossible simply because no two linguists seem to agree on their data.

But let us return to LP's model. Two arguments of different strength can be raised against their solution. The first one was put forward by Kiparsky (1979), who demonstrates that whatever is expressed in the grid clash is also present in the tree so that the entire structural description of Iambic Reversal can equally be read off the tree alone. Here is Kiparsky's version of the rule:

(28)

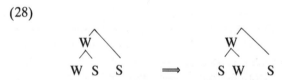

What Kiparsky demonstrates here is in effect the reduction of the grid's status to that of an illustrative device. In its second function, too, the grid is not as essential as LP claim it is; note that the likelihood criterion of distance between the shifting stress and the head is also stateable in terms of tree structure.[12]

It might be argued here, of course, that the evidence in favour of the grid as a formal device is cumulative, that it simplifies matters in a number of instances rather than being essential in a single process. (The evidence in favour of the syllable as a formal notion, it will be recalled, is of that nature.) Not so, for what is cumulating here is in fact evidence against the grid. Consider the next argument against the use of the grid as a formal trigger of Iambic Reversal, based on cases like the following:

(29)

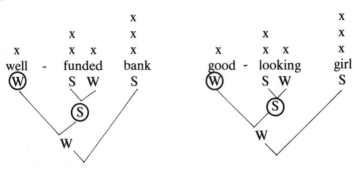

The circled nodes in this kind of structure are candidates for reversal but no grid clashes show up in the grids. The problem, as LP point out, rests with the representation of lexical monosyllables like *well* and *good*.

I argued in 2 above that the rules assigning 'word stress' should be viewed as rules that place foot boundaries within lexical words. Given that the initial syllable of a foot has high relative prominence (cf. the foot structure templates given in (7) above), this operation determines both the prominence of the initial syllable and the structure of this particular phonological constituent, whose role in the description of various phonological processes was mentioned before. One of the regularities concerning foot boundary placement is the fact that lexical monosyllables are foot-initial. Clearly, a model that only predicts the placement of stressed syllables, and neither foot structure nor the placement of foot boundaries, fails to meet the well-attested claims of the phonological theory that I sketched in section 2.

And this is what LP do, rather reminiscent of the SPE approach to stress. They observe the stressedness of lexical monosyllables and decide to reflect this property locally in the metrical grid by adding another grid element to the respective columns. Thus, they represent the phrases of (29) above like this:

(30)

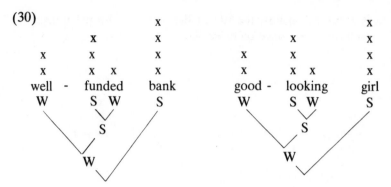

The grids in (30) are compatible with the conventions given by LP for the alignment of grids and trees. Under LP's additional convention of extra strength for lexical monosyllables, they automatically show the desired clash, which is required as a trigger for Iambic Reversal. The problem is that the representations in (30) state nothing about the foot structures of which *well* and *good* are the initial syllables.

To give another example, recall (15) above, here given in terms of LP's model and complete with grid:

(31)

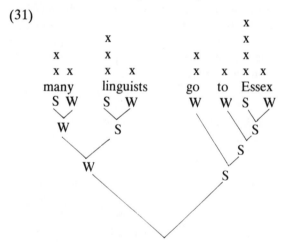

The difference between my model and LP's shows up in the representation of *go to*. In (15) these two syllables constitute a foot, in (31) they don't. (31) misses a generalisation despite the fact that it shows the 'stressed' syllable in the grid, thanks to LP's provision of extra strength for lexical items. Note, incidentally, that (15) would have exactly the same grid representation as (31), the difference being that the grid for (15) would be illustrative of the metrical tree and the one in (31) illustrates morphosyntactic information not encoded in the tree.

If the theoretical claims concerning foot structure are to be realised in phrases like *well-funded bank*, etc., we get structures like the one in (32):

(32)

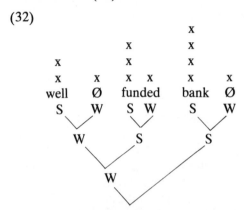

Unsurprisingly, the grid in (32) contains the desired clash.

Let us now reconsider *fourteen men*: this structure, too, has to be enriched with the representations of foot structure for which I have been arguing. Here is the version that the present model produces, in line with what I claimed earlier about foot boundary placement:

(33)

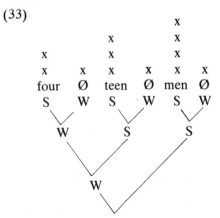

All three syllables of this structure are foot-initial. The foot-initial position of the first syllable is a condition for Iambic Reversal — consider, in contrast, a case where the first syllable is 'unstressed' and therefore unattached to the material on its right:

(34)

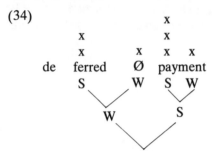

In previous models (LP, Kiparsky 1979), cases like this were barred from reversal by a condition that required syllables onto which the S could be shifted to be segmentally specified as [+ stress]. Properties relating to this segmental feature are, although they are clearly prosodic in nature, only indirectly reflected in the metrical tree and not at all in the grid. In those models, both the metrical tree and the grid fail to make the prosodic distinction between *fourteen* and *deferred* that is responsible for their different attitudes towards Iambic Reversal: an LP-type representation of *deferred* would be identical with that of *fourteen* given in (26) above, except for its segmental [stress] specifications.

Under the present theory of phonological structure, the metrical tree structure of *deferred payment* fails to meet the structural description of Iambic Reversal. Under this theory, the metrical notation bears out the difference between the two phrases in the clearest possible way. Note that in this case the grid, although it also bears out this difference, is completely uninteresting in that it is entirely redundant.

Let me try to summarise my arguments against models that employ both the tree and the grid as formal notational devices. I have shown in two separate instances — which happened to be the only two purposes for which LP proposed the grid — that the grid is inadequate as a formal device and that it can only be an illustrative device, by definition redundant, which interprets metrical trees. The two test cases were the representation of rhythmic alternation and the formal statement of Iambic Reversal. In the former case, the grid has excessive power. I proposed to curtail this power by making rhythmic alternation an issue of phonological structure, reflected in the tree, rather than one of alternating heights in the prominence peaks that are structurally parallel. As a consequence, the grid bears out rhythmic alternation but it only illustrates what is present in the tree.

In the latter case, the picture is rather similar. The grid can function as a formal device in the statement of Iambic Reversal only if, again, it states things not present in the tree. In this case, I have shown that the things that LP's grids state *must* also be stated in the tree (in terms of foot structure), for independent reasons relating directly to phonological theory. Again, the status of the grid is reduced to that of an illustrative device which interprets one aspect of metrical tree structure.[13]

5. 'Grid-only Phonology'

In a recent study, Prince (1983) takes the idea of grid phonology one step further. Looking at a limited number of rhythm-related problems in phonological prominence, he proposes to do away with metrical trees and to express all properties relating to phonological prominence by means of the metrical grid.

Prince's paper is tentative in many ways but it sketches a number of interesting arguments. One of these sketches deals with the grid-phonological equivalent of Iambic Reversal. I shall here briefly summarise the way in which Prince handles this process, partly because the bulk of what he has to say about the grid phonology of English is also devoted to this issue, partly because it will enable me to show that all the problems of grids as formal devices that I pointed out in the LP model unsurprisingly persist in this one, and more emerge.

Here are two examples:

(35)	(a)	phrase			x					x	
		word		⊗	x				⊗	x	
		foot	x	x	x	x		x	x	x	x
		syll	x	x	x	x x		x	x	x	x x

Dundee marmalade ⟹ Dundee marmalade

(b)	phrase				x				x
	word			Ⓧ	x		Ⓧ		x
	foot	x		x	x		x	x	x
	syll	x	x	x x	x		x	x x x	x

achromatic lens $\implies$ achromatic lens

Prince incorporates in his notation Selkirk's prosodic categories: they appear here as names for either single grid levels, as in the cases above, or as contiguous bands. It is not clear how many levels are occupied by each of the prosodic strata. Note also that the prosodic categories in this notation do not define the boundaries of phonological constituents but only their prominence peaks. Moreover, note that the notion 'word' figures in this hierarchy: illegitimately, as I have argued earlier, but crucially for this notation, as we shall see.

The operation that we have been calling Iambic Reversal is now rather simple: Prince's rule simply says Move x. The circled x in both examples is moved leftward onto the nearest grid column where it can be sited without having an empty space underneath it.

Move x always implies a leftward movement in English, just as our reversal was always iambic. No Move x is possible in the following case:

(36)

```
   x                    x
   x    x               x    x
 x x    x             x x    x
 x x    x x           x x    x x
```

antique dealer $\not\Longrightarrow$ antique dealer

Only one x may be moved. And since moving x would in this case inevitably create a gap in the grid, no movement is possible.

Prince's account of this particular rule is strikingly elegant. However, it runs into problems (as he himself observes) in cases like the following:

(37)

```
            x                      x
     x      x      x               x
 x   x  x   x      x   x   x   x
 x x x  x   x      x x x   x   x
```

Japanese bamboo $\implies$ Japanese bamboo

A phrase like this is likely to undergo Move *x* and the way the rule operates presents no problem: *x* moves onto the nearest landing site on its left. The problem is that through this operation no grid clash gets resolved.[14] Once again, then, the grid clash as a trigger of the rule turns out to be rather problematic.

The reader will recall from my earlier discussion of Iambic Reversal that metrical tree structure provides an accurate description of the contexts in which this rule applies. Metrical tree structure is partially determined by syntactic structure, and this aspect of metrical tree structure is in fact crucial in this case: in the absence of metrical trees, the syntax has to be referred to directly. Consider the following phrases:

```
(38)  (a) ph                    x                         x
          wd    x         (x)  x              x    (x)   x
          ft    x      x  x    x              x    x x   x
          sy    x      x  x  x  x             x    x x  x  x
```
          Jim's thirteen lectures ⟹ Jim's thirteen lectures

```
      (b) ph                x                           x
          wd⎰          (x)  x               (x)         x
             ⎱ x        x   x        x    x    [X]  x          x
          ft    x    x x    x        x    x    x x   x          x
          sy  x x    x x    x        x    x    x x   x          x
```
          one-thirteen George Street ⟹ one-thirteen George Street

Movement of the circled *x* is quite straightforward in both cases. But having moved this *x* in (38b), we still have a grid clash involving the boxed *x* which Move *x* would be able to resolve. The problem is that Move *x* must be prevented from doing this as *thirteen*, in this phrase, fails to shift its stress in most people's speech.

Prince discusses two alternative ways out of this problem, one invoking a syntactic bounding condition on Move *x* ('In a structure [[AB]C], shift motivated by C is ordinary between B and A but it is unnatural if it takes place entirely within B'), the other as a subjacency condition: Move *x* may only apply one level down from the peak of the motivating stress. Height is defined by syntactic constituency. Either way, syntactic structure has to be appealed to, in the absence of sufficient metrical structure, to formulate the conditions under which Move *x* operates.

In comparison, note how clearly metrical tree structure specifies the reversal contexts in these two phrases:

(39)

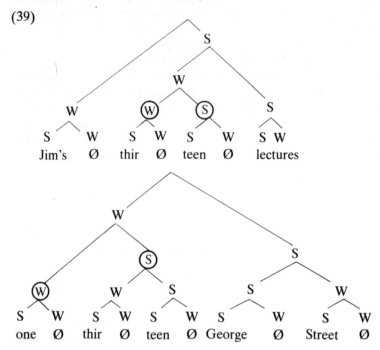

In each case, the circled nodes undergo Iambic Reversal, and the structural description of this rule in terms of tree structure correctly rules out reversal of *thirteen* in the latter phrase. There is no more straightforward way of expressing the environment in which this rule applies than through the metrical tree. Having to resort to syntactic conditions like the ones stated above implies a considerable loss of elegance.

Arguments like this are familiar: if reference is made to phonological structure, the contexts in which a number of phonological regularities occur can be stated more elegantly than without such reference. This is in itself a strong argument in favour of phonological structure.

It is quite clear that all the problems of 'grid phonology' that I discussed in 4 above are also present in Prince's 'grid-only phonology'. In 'grid phonology', a metrical tree that adequately represents phonological structure renders the grid redundant. 'Grid-only phonology' has no way of representing phonological structure, just as the grids in LP's model fail to do this job. Giving up the metrical tree therefore means stepping back into the SPE era of phonological theory, a position that has been shown to be unsatisfactory long since.

It might be objected here that phonological structure is in fact present in Prince's grids — I mentioned above that the rows in the grid carry the names of Selkirk's (1980b) prosodic categories. But I also mentioned that stating the fact that a certain phonological unit has its prominence peak on, say, foot level does not mean that the boundaries or the internal structure of that foot have thus been defined. And the definition of the boundaries of phonological constituents is a crucial operation in phonological theory, one that 'grid-only phonology' cannot perform in a non-arbitrary way.

Notice also that the category 'word' figures crucially in the hierarchy of Prince's grid levels although I pointed out earlier that the word is not among the phonological constituents. Let us see what happens if the level 'word' is deleted from the hierarchy of levels, in a phrase like *one-thirteen George Street*:

$$
(40) \quad
\begin{array}{lccccc}
\text{phrase} \Big\{ & & & & \text{x} & \\
 & & & \text{\textcircled{x}} & \text{x} & \\
\text{foot} & \text{x} & \text{x} \ \text{x} & \text{x} & & \text{x} \\
\text{syll} & \text{x} & \text{x} \ \text{x} & \text{x} & & \text{x} \\
\end{array}
$$

one-thirteen George Street

The crucial change in representation involves *one*, which is now only two levels high. Consequently, *-teen* is only three levels high and the structure in (40) wrongly predicts the circled *x* to shift onto *thir-*. Once more, we have a case where morphosyntactic information finds its way into a grid representation of a prosodic structure, inextricably linked with phonological constituent structure.

The categories that name the levels in Prince's model are thus suspect in two respects: they fail to demarcate the constituents whose peaks they represent, and they include at least one category that is non-phonological in nature. As a direct consequence of the lack of phonological constituency in his model, Prince has to appeal to morphosyntactic structure in his account of prosodic phenomena; that this in itself is a problem was noted earlier.

As a matter of principle, these problems of Prince's model are shared by the other models employing metrical grids, discussed in 4 above. They are also present in a recent alternative account of the 'grid-only' phonology of English (Selkirk 1984b), where, moreover, the phonological constituent 'foot' is given up. All these are issues on which any form of 'grid phonology' does not see eye to eye with the theory of phonological constituency structure — regardless of whether the notational system employed within the latter theory is that of metrical or of dependency trees. Research on 'grid phonology' is likely to make considerable advances in accounting for the prominence contours of speech as well as the operations that change those. Any other phenomena relating to phonological structure, it won't come to grips with.

Notes

1. This essay grew out of my fringe contribution to the Dependency Phonology Conference, University of Essex, September 1983. An earlier written version was circulated by the Indiana University Linguistics Club (1984) under the same title. I have retained the title because the essay still is what it has been since the Essex conference: a reaction to Prince (1983) and an attempt to show that metrical grids are as redundant in a metrical phonology as they are in a dependency phonology. I am indebted to the participants of the conference for their critical comments, in particular to John Anderson, Jacques Durand and Colin Ewen. They will not accept responsibility for my views or for the faults in my arguments.

2. This is not strictly speaking true of the foot: despite Lehiste (1977) and Allen (1975), the controversy about stress-timing is still unresolved — cf. such recent contributions as Roach (1982) and Dauer (1983). If it turns out that the foot has no pre-theoretical reality as a timing unit in the so-called stress-timed languages, then its status in phonological theory becomes that of a theoretical construct, whose usefulness is not necessarily affected by the absence of timing evidence, especially since none of the other properties attributed to the foot in phonological theory seem to depend crucially on its durational behaviour.

3. A version of the sonority hierachy sufficiently detailed for our purposes is cited by Ewen (this vol.: 4).

4. Note that in this template the nucleus is non-branching. It has been suggested (Booij 1983; Clements & Keyser 1983) that such an analysis is unacceptable because it groups the second elements of English diphthongs with following consonants rather than with the syllabic. However, if it is assumed that the syllable template is mapped onto morphophonemic representations, rather than phonetic ones (as Booij, Clements & Keyser seem to imply), then diphthongs would at the point where the mapping takes place still be represented as non-complex segments and the problem would simply and systematically not arise. Thus, for *find* the initial syllable structure assignment would yield:

(Cf. note 7 below on excluding the final consonant from this structure.) During the course of the derivation the structure would then acquire a branching nucleus (since only what is mapped initially needs to conform with the template) and yield:

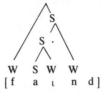

The observation that the derived structure fails to define a prominence relation among the two parallel W nodes is irrelevant to the argument: all necessary prominence relations are expressed at the point of the initial mapping and the subsequent derivation does not actually produce *wrong* prominence relations — it merely ceases to express certain ones of these relations. That the second element of the diphthong is more sonorous than the following consonant is independently ensured by the fact that the inserted segments are always non-consonantal.

5. Note that the constituents given in (3) are relationally defined in the template in such a way that the onset is always the left-hand daughter of the root; the rhyme is the right-hand daughter; if the latter branches then its left daughter is the nucleus and its right daughter the coda. The labels of (3) are therefore not part of the metrical notation.

6. This is not to say that ambisyllabicity does not 'exist' — on the contrary: Fallows (1981) has given evidence that single consonants after short stressed vowels are typically ambiguously syllabified. However, what I do claim is that ambisyllabicity should be treated as a low-level phenomenon, produced by a late rule which spreads the structure of light stressed syllables to the right, thus rendering such syllables heavy and the consonants in question ambisyllabic. (See Giegerich 1985: Ch. 2 for details; and Anderson, this vol.; Kahn 1976 for alternative models.)

7. For the heavy/light distinction to be produced appropriately in final syllables, some additional mechanism has to be invoked that deals with word-final consonants. In words like *fraternal*, for example, the final syllable has to be analysed as light, despite being CVC, in order not to violate the Main Stress Rule. Along the lines of Hayes (1982), I assume that such consonants are not syllabified with what precedes them; but rather than simply calling them 'extrametrical' I suggest that they should be treated as onsets of (otherwise empty) syllables (Giegerich 1985: Ch. 2). Such an analysis is compatible with the rather radical initial maximal syllabification that characterises this model.

8. In Selkirk's model (1980a,b), the nodes of metrical trees carry prosodic category labels such as syllable, foot, word (!), phonological phrase, etc. I assume (and, to some extent, argue) here that all such notions are relationally defined in this model and need not therefore be stated in the tree.

9. The present model may fruitfully be extended so as to allow for 'silent stresses' (Abercrombie 1971), which in our notation would be represented as feet with a zero syllable in S position. Thus, in sentence-initial or phrase-initial positions we might get

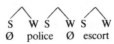

10. The optional pause between the two phrases may be represented as an optional 'silent stress' (recall note 9 above), initial to the second phrase:

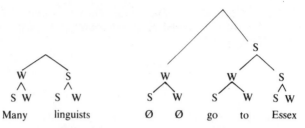

(Note that once we have posited the empty S node, our model of the foot automatically produces the empty W.) Abercrombie (1971) notes that 'silent stresses' serve to disambiguate expressions like *old men and women*. The two possible metrical structures would then be these:

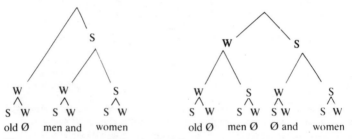

The two structures are distinct in the following ways. The former has enclisis of *men and* while in the latter the presence of an $_{XP}][_{XP}$ syntactic boundary blocks such enclisis. (This type of syntactic boundary probably blocks the expansion of the foot template to the right in a general way.) Moreover, syntactic phrasing is reflected by phonological phrasing in that the former structure contains one phrase and the latter two.

11. The structures numbered 21, 22, 23, 26, 27, 29, 30, 31 are given, for the sake of the argument, in terms of LP's model. In particular, they do not contain such foot structures as I proposed in section 2.

12. See Giegerich (1985: Ch. 4) for a fuller discussion of Iambic Reversal which, while subscribing to Kiparsky's solution, goes into a number of details not relevant to the present issue.

13. The same is true, in my impression, for the model of grid-tree interaction proposed by Hayes (1984). In his proposal, the grid has a teleological role in Iambic Reversal rather than the causal one it has in LP: Iambic Reversal is not caused by grid clashes but happens, independently of such clashes, in order to achieve 'eurythmic' grid patterns. Note that Hayes, like LP, gives a degree of grid strength to lexical monosyllables that is not reflected in the metrical tree.

14. Prince's tentative answer to this question resembles that of Hayes (1984) — cf. note 13 above: Move *x* operates in order to produce eurythmic patterns. Throughout the rest of Prince's paper, however, Move *x* is assumed to be triggered by grid clashes.

7 A DEPENDENCY APPROACH TO SOME WELL-KNOWN FEATURES OF HISTORICAL ENGLISH PHONOLOGY

Charles Jones

1. Opening Remarks

Since its earliest beginnings the model of dependency phonology has been concerned with the problems that arise from historical change. Indeed, part of the motivation for the model's development stemmed from the feeling that there was a need to provide more convincing descriptions as well as explanations than those which were available through standard handbooks for even the best-known historical phonological phenomena. This writer was concerned by the fact that standard accounts of phonological change left the impression that a great many, often unrelated processes were involved even in the history of one particular language, none of which, it seemed, was particularly connected to any other even where there appeared to be rather obvious similarities either in structural description, structural change, or both. The reasons for such a state of affairs are many, but they can be set down in no small part to the history of the subject itself. Historical description of the English language (and to a large extent of German as well) has been 'period orientated'; scholars have tended to confine their attentions to individual 'periods' such as Old or Middle English — temporal spans often as not selected for sociological or historical reasons rather than on any purely linguistic criteria. Only very rarely are attempts at more extensive coverage to be found. One of the consequences of this state of affairs has been the development of separate nomenclatures for changes within particular periods, often giving rise to the impression that 'different name means different change'. The range of descriptive labels in the history of English phonology is quite extensive — we find references to Breakings, Smoothings, Umlauts, Mutations, Palatal Diphthongisations, Metatheses, Consonantal Epentheses, Open Syllable Lengthenings and Vowel Shifts, to name but a few. While one does not necessarily wish to argue here that temporal phonological change is confined to a very limited number of operations (although there seems to be some evidence that the number of types is not large (Anderson & Jones 1974: 160ff)), we shall try to demonstrate nevertheless that, by utilising a model with greater componentiality than any hitherto available, we are able to make quite general statements about certain historical processes normally treated as disparate, while this in its turn will lead us to raise the question concerning the predictability of (historical) phonological alternation itself.

We shall limit our discussion to a consideration of two conditioning phonetic environments as they affect phonological change in a fairly extensive chunk of English historical data. The changes they affect are well-known and have been discussed a great many times in the literature. However, we shall attempt here to provide something more in the way of a general formulation both for the affecting environments themselves and for the alternations they produce in the phonology of the period. We shall encompass an historical range which embraces the eleventh to the fifteenth centuries — middle Old English to late Middle English — examining the behaviour of stressed vowels (principally in monosyllables) in two phonetic environments: (a) before fricative continuants (especially [x]); and (b) before non-nasal sonorant consonants (principally [r] and [l]) in isolation as well as in clusters. We use the term 'before' in a metaphorical sense, of course, since we shall be making continual reference to the tenets of dependency phonology with its inter- and intrasegment compositional claims as outlined in Anderson & Durand (this vol.).

2. Stressed Vowels before Fricatives

In this section we shall take a detailed look at the processes which are traditionally labelled as Breakings and Smoothings within our period as they occur before fricative continuants, and especially before [x]. Let us commence by considering a set of alternations generally known as Middle English breaking (Jordan 1968: 178ff; Lass & Anderson 1975: 198-9):

eME	lME	
ehte	eight	'eight'
streht	streight	'stretched'
faht	faught	'he fought'
draht	draught	'draught'
broht	broughte	'he brought'
þohte	thoughte	'he thought'

Vowels of either backness specification can act as input to this diphthongisation process just so long as they are NON-HIGH; items like [nixt] and ['prux] at this date remaining unaffected. The innovation involved in the above is obviously a diphthongisation whereby [e] $\Longrightarrow$ [ei], [o] $\Longrightarrow$ [ou] and [a] $\Longrightarrow$ [au] — that is, some kind of pitch transition from a non-high to a high pitch configuration. A Chomsky & Halle-type formulation for Middle English Breaking might be:

$$\emptyset \Longrightarrow \begin{bmatrix} +\text{voc} \\ -\text{cons} \\ +\text{high} \\ \alpha\text{back} \\ : \end{bmatrix} \bigg/ \begin{bmatrix} +\text{voc} \\ \alpha\text{back} \\ . \\ . \\ . \end{bmatrix} - \begin{bmatrix} +\text{cons} \\ +\text{cont} \\ +\text{high} \\ +\text{back} \\ . \end{bmatrix}$$

although such does little more than describe a context for the vowel epenthesis and highlight the low-level assimilation processes connected with the 'new' vowel so produced; the frontness coefficient of the epenthesised segment being a function of that of the vowel input, while its highness is determined by the value for that feature in the [x] segment. As such, the formulation tells us nothing, for example, about the exclusion of [+high] vowels from the change at this historical period, nor does it offer any suggestion as to why additional periodicity should be associated at the postvocalic peak in such a context. At the moment looking only at the mid vowels, we might characterise Middle English Breaking in dependency phonology terms as it relates to the structural change as follows:

the configurations [ei] and [ou] resulting from the input of [e] (|i| → |a|) and [o] (|u| → |a|). It is interesting to notice that the pitch transition takes place in the direction of the governing element in each of the complex input constructions: i.e. towards palatality and labiality (away from sonority and towards non-compactness). In such a context (however it is ultimately to be characterised) the vowel space is clearly increasing its non-sonority componentiality, a feature which will explain why high vowels like [i] and [u], being already purely palatal and labial, do not act as input to the process which is essentially one of non-sonorant vowel-space 'contamination'. At a later period in Middle English the high vowels in fact undergo lengthening before velar fricatives (themselves subsequently deleted) showing an increase in pure palatality and labiality registered superficially by durational increase, thus [nixt] ⟹ [niixt]/[niit], and [θrux] ⟹ [θruux]/[θruu].

Let us consider other processes in our period triggered by the [x] environment, but traditionally accorded descriptive labels other than Breaking. In the south-Midlands dialect of the late thirteenth century the diphthongs produced via Middle English Breaking before [x] were subject to a change called Smoothing such that, for example:

heigh	→ high	[hiix]	'high'
neigh	→ nigh	[niix]	'near'
fleih	→ fligh	[fliix]	'flight'
plough	→ plough	[pluux]	'plough'
inough	⟹ inough	[inuux]	'enough'

A DP characterisation of such an alternation might be:

wherein a segment which is |a|-containing has its |a|-ness diluted, such that the whole stressed vowel space is reinforced in the direction of the |~a| parameter of the governing |V| element: the result being a (relatively) long pure palatal or labial segment. Looking at these two changes, therefore, it would seem clear that the velar fricative context is one favouring |~a|-ness. Indeed, the Smoothing can be seen as a further working out of the chronologically earlier Breaking by achieving a pure palatal/labial vowel space before [x].

It should come as no great surprise, therefore, to find under the change known as Palatal Umlaut (Kentish, ninth century) such data as:

seox	$\Longrightarrow$	siex	'six'
reoht	$\Longrightarrow$	ri(o)ht	'right'
leoht	$\Longrightarrow$	liht	'light'

nor under Anglian and late West Saxon Smoothings:

seah	$\Longrightarrow$	sēh	'he saw'
eahta	$\Longrightarrow$	ēhta	'eight'
heah	$\Longrightarrow$	hēh	'high'

where the orthographic ‹ea› represents the diphthongal [æa], whose first element has — in this non-compact context — its governance sequence reversed to favour a dominant palatal element and its non-syllabic governed |a| element suppressed altogether, such that

Space forbids a more detailed treatment of several of the interesting idiosyncrasies of the above changes (see Jones & Nakao, to appear: Ch. 7) but it would seem clear that before a following velar fricative (although in the thirteenth century we find similar alternants before other fricative types, cf. ‹asche›/‹aische› and ‹fresche›/‹freische›) the vowel space is perceived as non-sonorous or achromatic.

It has been shown in much of the DP literature (especially Anderson & Jones 1974, 1977; Jones 1976) that when stressed vowels govern immediately to their right in a construction another segment which is |V|-prominent, then the overall periodicity of the vowel space in the item concerned will be augmented. This increase in periodicity normally occurs in a position immediately dominated by the stressed vowel and to its right (although stressed vowel segment internal |V| adding is also recorded) while, as we shall see below, the |V| adding to the item can occur in the shape of a new syllable peak, usually to be unstressed. One suggestion we might propose for such behaviour is that items taking the form of, for instance,

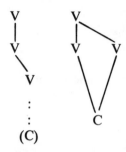

(C)

are perceived as somehow lacking in overall periodic 'weight'
across the entire item, the addition of the new vocalic element
rectifying this shortcoming. It would seem, however, that what
constitutes an 'ideal' weighting for items is subject to temporal
variation. Recall the instances of stressed vowel periodicity
increase before velar fricatives that we mentioned above, whereby
[nixt] ⟹ [niixt] and [θrux] ⟹ [θruux]. That the heavily
periodic rhyme produced by such a vocalic epenthesis:

$$
\begin{array}{l}
|V| \\
\quad \searrow \\
\quad |V| \\
\qquad \searrow \\
\qquad |V{:}C|
\end{array}
$$

was perceived by some speakers as 'too vowelly' can perhaps be
inferred from the subsequent deletion of the 'weakest' vowel-
containing construction in the item, such that [niixt] ⟹ [niit].

Perhaps analagous to such behaviour is that of stressed vowels
in Middle English when they occur in contexts like:

$$
\begin{array}{c}
|V| \\
|V| \quad |V| \\
\quad |C|
\end{array}
$$

here, stressed vowel lowering and lengthening is very likely to
occur (Malsch & Fulcher 1975). It would seem that to speakers
of this period a configuration such as the above would be perceived as 'insufficiently vowelly'; additional periodicity was added
to achieve what was felt to be a more 'canonical' vowel weighting
across the item such that we find:

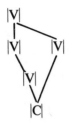

It has often been noted, however, that in TRISYLLABIC items (say inflected forms of disyllables which had already undergone this lengthening): ‹fādores› — vowel SHORTENING (or negative vowel lengthening) of the stressed element took place, since configurations such as

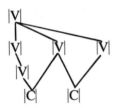

were perceived as 'too heavily periodic'. It is worth noting too that in many trisyllabic items involved in stressed-vowel shortening, this shortening was accompanied by raising: ‹sōmeres› ⟹ ‹sumeres› and ‹ēveles› ⟹ ‹iveles›. Given the relative inherent durational brevity of high, front vowels (Klatt 1976) we might view such raising as an alternative/additional stratagem for stressed-vowel shortening. Of course, notions such as preferred vowel 'weighting' for lexical items await experimental testing and vertification.

To return briefly to our instances of stressed-vowel behaviour before the voiceless velar fricative in Middle English, we can with some confidence suggest that the internal composition of the latter can be characterised as |~a:C| given the propensity for epenthetic vocalic elements in its vicinity to manifest non-compact characteristics.

3. Stressed Vowels before Non-nasal Sonorants

Stressed vowel behaviour is much less simple to characterise in our period before the non-nasal sonorants [r] and [l]. It is impossible to discuss in detail the full range of alternations which manifest themselves in such contexts here (see Jones & Nakao, to appear: Chs 6 and 7) but let us consider enough of them to give us the, at least superficial, sense of their type differentiation.

(a) Old English Breaking. Here the front vowels [i], [e] and [æ] have what is probably a labial [u] segment epenthesised between them and a following [r]/[l] (Lass & Anderson 1975: Ch. 3), such that the following alternants occur:

hirde/hiorde	'shepherd'
self/seolf	'self'
ærm/earm	'arm'

(b) In Middle English, a whole set of lowerings occurred in such contexts as we can see from the following:

shilling/shelling
third/therd
wild/weld
hilt/helt

(c) In Middle English, the high, front rounded vowel [y] was retracted (backed) to [u] in pre-[r] contexts, such that

wyrm	$\Longrightarrow$	wurm	
wyrcan	$\Longrightarrow$	wurcan	'to work'

Diphthongisations, lowerings and backings can hardly be said to constitute a natural class set of changes in such or any other types of environment. However, on a little closer inspection, we may be able to account for such phenomena under some kind of general tendency. The retractions of [y] $\Longrightarrow$ [u] witness a segment internal highlighting of a |u| element and a concomitant loss of palatality: (|u|, |i|) $\Longrightarrow$ |u|. The lowering of the pure palatal [i] to a construction contaminated by sonority, and the segment-external epenthesis of a labial segment (in Old English Breaking) to a stressed vowel which is mandatorily devoid of such a vocalic prime would also suggest that the non-nasal sonorant context is one which might be characterised as non-palatal — (|~i| $\Longrightarrow$ |~i,C|). On the other hand, we can see from the above data that mixed vowels behave rather differently in our environment. For instance, constructions involving (|u| $\rightarrow$ |a|) lose their sonority component (raise) in this context, as, apparently, do those (especially when they are long) involving (|i| $\rightarrow$ |a|) ([ee]) as we can see from such alternations as

⟨frere⟩/⟨freere⟩ and ⟨friir⟩/⟨freir⟩; ⟨breer⟩ and ⟨breir⟩/⟨briir⟩ 'briar' (although a like raising of high, mid front vowels also appears before other 'high' consonantal continuants — see ⟨dees⟩/⟨diys⟩ 'dice' and ⟨contrēven⟩/⟨contreiven⟩/⟨contriiven⟩). Such raisings clearly involve a loss of sonority in favour of the palatality or labiality of the governing element in the complex construction.

Stressed vowel behaviour before [r] and [l] is thus rather difficult to explain away in terms of a single tendency. There appear to be two directionalities: (a) there is a movement away from palatality towards either labiality or achromaticity — indeed, this may be the major of the two; (b) there is a tendency for 'mixed' vowels to have any sonority in their construction removed to leave a pure palatal or labial. (Such 'contradictory' behaviour appears to be characteristic of stressed vowels in pre-nasal contexts as well — see Beddor (1983).) The raising instance of ⟨freere⟩ is perhaps worthy of a tentative comment. This 'borrowing' from French enters the English language just at the time when the powerful rule (referred to above) lengthening stressed vowels in -CV(C)# contexts was operative. It has been observed (see Jones & Nakao, to appear) that while stressed vowels before obstruent initiating and terminating second syllables provided the optimal context for the lengthening rule to operate, the presence of a sonorant consonant in such positions (e.g. ⟨baril⟩, ⟨common⟩) generally blocked the functioning of the rule. This failure, we might suggest, was owing to the fact that items like:

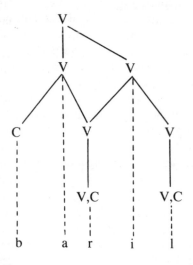

were already sufficiently 'vowelly' in their post-stressed vowel composition to make any further vocalic increase in that area 'non-canonical'. In the case of the ‹freere› (and, presumably ‹contrēven›) case, the lexically long stressed vowel preceding a highly vowel-prominent sonorant construction might too seem 'over-vowelly'; raising — to an inherently shorter high front (albeit relatively long) segment — might have been an alternative stratagem to stressed-vowel shortening.

Nevertheless, as we strongly argued for the velar fricative context — stressed vowels before segments like [r] and [l] should manifest additional periodicity in the lexical item; indeed, this is the case with the diphthongisations we have outlined above for Old English Breaking. However, this 'Breaking' is not a common feature of the phonology of Middle English before, say, [r]+C clusters; consider the following:

erl	eril	'earl'
erth	erith	'earth'
worhte	worohte	'he made'
wird	wirid	'fate'
fyrhto	fyrihto	'fear'

In all these instances, extra periodicity is indeed manifested in the items in question; their overall vocalic weighting is increased. However, the increase is not achieved by the epenthesis of a non-syllabic vowel immediately following the stressed element, but by an additional vocalic peak. The ‹erl/eril› alternation is particularly enlightening in view of what we have said above concerning the failure of stressed-vowel lengthening before heavily periodic materials at the end of its own syllable and the next (cf. ‹baril›). The ‹eril› form clearly manifests an alternative stratagem for achieving overall increased vocalic weighting throughout the item to that manifested in Old English where stressed diphthongal outputs are regularly to be found — ‹eorl›. While it seems that items with overall periodic content like the following are acceptable (and perhaps 'equivalent'):

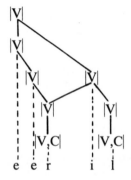

those with two vocalic elements with DD2 are interpreted as 'over-vowelly':

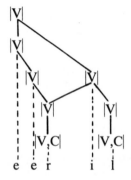

The idea that syllabicity is essentially a 'combinatorial' notion — i.e. linear lexical entries are subject to a considerable degree of predictability — was outlined in Anderson & Jones (1977: Ch. 3). Lying behind some of the notions in this paper too is the suggestion that historical (and other) phonological alternation is not simply a matter of the addition or subtraction of random processes to phonological rule systems. Rather, alternation is 'context predictable' — changes to stressed vowels will be a function of their contiguity with dependent elements which are themselves highly vocalic, while restrictions upon such changes will be dependent upon (as yet inadequately defined) notions such as the overall degree of periodic 'weighting' regarded as canonical for sequences of phonological segments.

8 THE ENGLISH VELAR FRICATIVE, DIALECT VARIATION AND DEPENDENCY PHONOLOGY

Ken Lodge

In this paper I want to consider the proposal put forward by Chomsky & Halle (1968), that English has an underlying velar fricative, in the light of a number of British English dialects and their historical development, and to see how dependency phonology can help us to elucidate that development.

First of all let us consider the reason for Chomsky & Halle's suggestion. The velar fricative is meant to account for the alternation *right — righteous* in contradistinction to *delight — delicious* (where the spelling of *delight* is misleading); in other words, to prevent the rule of trisyllabic laxing set up to account for the alternations in the Latinate vocabulary, exemplified by *divine — divinity, verbose — verbosity* and so on, from applying to *right* and producing the wrong form * [rɪʃəs]. With a velar fricative before the /t/, *right* does not satisfy the SD of trisyllabic laxing. (It also prevents the consonantal alternation [t] ~ [ʃ], but I am not concerned with that here.) Other words which contain underlying /x/ would be *nightingale* and *mightily* (cf. Chomsky & Halle 1968: 234). Once established in this way, it is also used to explain the occurrence of [ŋ] in *dinghy, hangar, gingham* and *Birmingham*, and surface [h] is also derived from it (ibid.). That it should be a voiceless velar fricative is obviously a historical consideration, since even within the SPE framework it could just as well have been /h/, which is [-voice], [+continuant] like all the voiceless fricatives and these are the crucial features in establishing this class in English.

Since such an element never appears on the surface in modern English (though it depends on the kind of English!), critics of abstract underlying elements of this type, in particular those who promote a more concrete (= 'natural') model of phonology (e.g. Hooper 1976), would wish to rule out such historically motivated segments. Underlying /x/ has either been rejected in the moves towards a more concrete phonology, or it has been left untouched.[1]

Leaving aside the question of morphological alternations and
their inclusion or otherwise in the phonological component for the
moment, I now want to look at some dialect material in relation to
the historical velar fricative. One problem with American accounts
of English phonology, especially those that claim to be panlectal
(e.g. Trager & Smith 1951; Chomsky & Halle 1968; Halle 1977),
is that American phonologists for the most part, do not take
account of some basic dialectal differences in British English. Since
American dialects stem from the Southern British dialects, from
the seventeenth century onwards, it is hardly surprising that
dialects representing earlier and divergent phonological systems do
not fit in easily, if a later stage is taken as basic (cf. Lass's
comments on this point; 1976: 26). The difference pertinent to the
topic in hand is that many Northern English dialects (i.e. not
Scots) have a number of distinctions not found in the South. These
are as represented in (1).

(1)   *wait*   /e:/   *weight*   /ɛɪ/
      bite   /aɪ/   *night*   /i:/,/ɛɪ/
      autumn /ɔ:/   *ought*   /ɔɷ/
      now   /aɷ/   *plough*   /u:/

The transcriptions are not intended to be phonetically accurate,
but represent in each case a number of variant pronunciations.
(See Orton & Halliday 1962-3; Orton & Barry 1967-71, for
details; Lodge 1973, for a brief discussion). As can be seen from
the forms in the right-hand column, the former velar fricative has
had a different effect in the North from in the South (and RP). It is
usually said to have been retained longer in the North, so that
sound changes affecting the Southern dialects and those in the
North were blocked where the /x/ was retained. It would appear
from written dialect material, such as the stories and poems of Tim
Bobbin written towards the end of the eighteenth century, that loss
of /x/ first occurred in the context: _C, and then in the context
_#, as demonstrated by the spellings in (2).

(2)   *saigh*   (*saw*)   *reet*   (*right*)
      leawgh   (*laugh*)   *thowt*   (*thought*)

In Orton & Halliday (1962-3: 280, 1099) the form [ənɣ:xf] is
recorded for *enough* at locality 5.12 (Harwood, Lancashire),
which must be considered a last remnant of the surface realisation
of /x/.

It would seem then that in the Northern dialects the velar fricative has left its mark more widely than in the Southern dialects and RP. In the former these 'extra' distinctions are clearly part of the phonological systems, but how are we to interpret them? Lass (1976: 3-39) has argued strongly against the use of *glide* as a class of sounds in English, and in favour of classifying long monophthongs and diphthongs in the same phonological class, namely vowel cluster: /VV/.[2] The only difference between the two phonetic types is whether or not the two Vs have the same set of feature specifications. If we follow Lass in this, the *gh*-forms, as I shall refer to them collectively, would seem to add more members to the /VV/ set (Lass's group B). Lass himself does not mention any *gh*-forms, but let us see if they fit into his schema.

First of all, we should note that his two sets are not differentiated by the SPE feature of tenseness. He rejects this feature as no more than a convenient abstraction designed to account for the Latinate morphological alternations of English so central to the SPE system. I will not reiterate Lass's arguments here, but refer the reader to (1976: 39-50), where he extends his arguments to other languages as well. I shall accept his arguments against tenseness and his proposals for a dichotomous vowel system in English as a basis for my own discussion of the *gh*-forms.

Some of the /VV/ set have certainly come from /VC/ configurations, as can be seen in the development outlined in (3).

(3)   OE [dæj], alternating morphologically with [daɣas],
         [j] represents a fricative articulation,
         > ME [dæi], with a non-fricative high-tongue vocoid,
         > ModE [deɪ] with /VV/.

In the North such forms have monophthongised, e.g. [de:], so the vowel cluster analysis is quite appropriate in this case. On this basis we can say that the same thing has happened to the *gh*-forms, but at a much later stage in the North than in the South. The first stage in the development of the *gh*-forms in the North and the South is that the /VC/ structure of words like late OE *ehta* and *dohtor* was subject to diphthongisation of the /V/ during the thirteenth century, as evidenced by spellings such as *eighte* and *doughter* respectively.[3] Presumably at this stage such diphthongal forms were allophonic before /x/. The subsequent deletion of /x/ involved a change in status of the preceding vowel phase.

Within a dependency framework we can represent the change

as in (4). I have ignored the dependencies between each segment for the time being.

(4)   Categorial gesture: |V| |C:V| ⟹ |V| |V||C:V| ⟹
        Articulatory
        gesture:
          front vowels: |(a→)i| |l.i| ⟹ |(a→)i| |i| |l.i| ⟹
          back vowels: |(a→)u| |l.u| ⟹ |(a→)u| |u| |l.u| ⟹

        Categorial gesture: |V| |V| |V|
        Articulatory
        gesture:
          front vowels: |(a→)i| |i| |i|
          back vowels: |(a→)u| |u| |u|

I have omitted the /t/ from the above formulation since it makes no difference to this part of the development. Note that even if we take the end-points of the diphthongal movement to be [ɪ] and [ʊ], |i| and |u| respectively will still appear in their representations. It would appear that the structure of the rhyme becomes overlong, forcing a reduction to /VV(C)/. To explain why such a reduction occurs, we might wish to propose that English has certain preferred syllable structures, which reassert themselves whenever some other phonological change puts pressure on them (cf. Lass & Anderson's recurring trimoric nucleus simplification rule; 1975: esp. 198-9; see also Anderson & Jones 1977: 159-79).

Let us now consider some of these other 'pressures' that helped to bring about and 'encourage' this particular change. They are as follows:

(a) English at this stage had five fricative phonemes /f s θ ʃ x/, plus two or three newly acquired ones from Old French: /v z/, possibly /ʒ/. (The status of [ð] is not clear, but is not important to my argument.) Old French did not reinforce the /x/ phoneme, since it did not have this sound, nor did it introduce a voiced partner */ɣ/.

(b) During the period when this change took place final unstressed vowels were being lost. This process converted disyllabic *eighte*, for example, into monosyllabic *eight*.

(c) Trimoric nucleus simplification was already a feature of the English phonological system.

(d) Since of all the fricatives /x/ has the elements |i| and |u| in its make-up, depending on the preceding vowel, which it shares with the preceding vowel, it is most likely to be susceptible to any changes in those particular prosodic features. (/f/ also contains |u|, but it does not alternate with |i| according to the vowel phase.)

A word should now be said about the nature of the changes brought about in /x/. Although in some instances deletion may be seen as a single step from segment to non-segment, there is plenty of evidence to suggest that, in historical terms at least, a whole series of gradual changes are involved before deletion takes place. Lenition and 'weakening by gesture change' are instances of such deletion paths (cf. Ewen's discussion, 1980a: 169-76; and Anderson & Durand, this vol.). A typical intervocalic deletion path in English would be: $x \rightarrow \gamma \rightarrow w \rightarrow \emptyset$. In the cases under consideration, where the position is final or before a final consonant, I would posit the following development: $x \rightarrow h \rightarrow \emptyset$. In terms of the specifications in the articulatory and categorial gestures given in (4), we have a loss of the |C| element and its associated |l| element. This leaves a voiceless vowel ([h]), which then disappears under trimoric nucleus simplification.

(5)   [ɛçt] $>$ [ɛɩçt] $>$ [ɛɩht] $>$ [ɛɩt], where [h] = [ɩ̥],
        [dɔxtər] $>$ [dɔɯxtər] $>$ [dɔɯhtər] $>$ [dɔɯtər], where
        [h] = [ɯ̥].

This interpretation of the changes does not fit in with what Ewen calls weaking by gesture change (1980a: 175-6), where [h] is treated as the 'minimal fricative' rather than a voiceless vowel. Consequently, I would like to suggest a somewhat different treatment of the categorial gesture in the light of evidence from the deletion paths.

In English there seem to be three deletion paths: lenition (as described by Ewen, ibid.), de-articulation of fricatives and de-articulation of stops.[4] These are all related to vocal cord activity: lenition involves vibrating vocal cords, de-articulation of fricatives open vocal cords, and de-articulation of stops closed vocal cords. If these are isolated as these separate types of categorial gesture: |V|, |O| and |ʔ|, respectively, then we can explain the deletion paths in each case as loss of all the other feature specifications before final deletion.[5] The changes given in the categorial gesture in (4) above must then be altered, as in (6).

(6) |V| |C:V:O| $\Longrightarrow$ |V| |V| |C:V:O| $\Longrightarrow$ |V| |V| |V:O|

In the last stage we have the specification for voiceless vowel. The de-articulation of stops follows a similar path, as in (7).

(7) |C:?| $\Longrightarrow$ |?|

All three deletion paths can be seen as a loss of |C|.

We must now consider the dependencies within the rhyme. If we wish to maintain that the phonetic changes in *gh*-forms preserve the dependency structure, we can represent them as in (8). (See Anderson, this vol., for arguments relating to dependencies within the rhyme.)

(8)

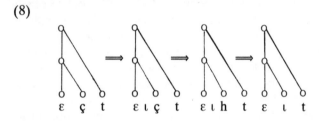

$$\varepsilon \quad \varsigma \quad t \qquad \varepsilon \iota \varsigma \quad t \qquad \varepsilon \iota h \quad t \qquad \varepsilon \quad \iota \quad t$$

In such cases /t/ is extrametrical until the final stage. There is a tendency in English to reduce the number of extrametrical segments, as can be seen from the way in which, for example, consonantal deletion operates in most forms of colloquial English, as exemplified in (9). (For a detailed discussion of consonant deletion, see Lodge 1981, 1984).

(9)

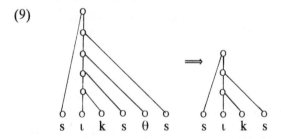

$$s \quad \iota \quad k \quad s \quad \theta \quad s \qquad s \quad \iota \quad k \quad s$$

With a move from /VCC/ to /VVC/ the /t/ is no longer extrametrical, because the nucleus has been extended to /VV/.[6] The [h] is deleted and the [ɪ] or [ʊ] takes its place. In the transitional structure I have not assigned any dependency to the [ɪ]. This is because it represents an allophonic change to begin with. If, however, we take the bottom level of the trees in (8) to represent the lexical phonological level, we can add an 'allophonic' level to account for the phonetic detail, as in (10).

(10)

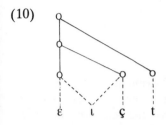

I have used dotted lines to show the dependencies at this sublevel. We can see from this that the [ι] is dependent on both the nucleus and the contiguous coda item, indicating its allophonic status.

This explanation of the development of the *gh*-forms applies to both Northern and Southern dialects. Why the Northern ones retained /x/ longer than in the South, I am not in a position to say, but clearly it meant that subsequent sound changes which affected the /x/-less forms along with other forms which never had /x/ anyway, e.g. the falling together of the vowel phrases in *gate, way* and *weigh*, were blocked in those dialects that retained it. In (11) I have given the development in schematic form of ME ā, ǽi and ēx, using Lass & Anderson's (1975) symbolisation. (11a) represents the Southern development, (11b) the North; (11c) represents those Northern dialects where ME ɛ̄ has fallen together with ēx, e.g. [pɛιz] *peas*, [ɛιt] *eight*.

(11) (a) ... (b) ...

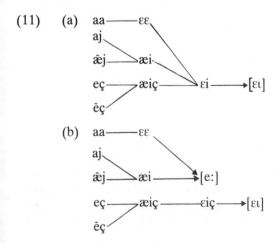

(c)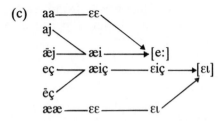

There may also be dialects where all the distinctions shown on the left in (11c) have fallen together. Note that in (11c) I have written εε for the transitional reflexes of both aa and æ æ. I do not wish thereby to imply that they fall together because of their apparent phonetic identity. (For a discussion of apparent phonetic identity without a coalescence of underlying forms, see Trudgill & Foxcroft's (1978) discussion of various East Anglian forms.) The details of the variation in the Northern dialects are fairly complicated, especially with regard to the back vowels, and I do not intend to go further into the individual developments. The accents in question, however, are homogeneous enough to fit into the general pattern proposed in this paper.

The following is a summary of the discussion so far. In both Northern and Southern dialects of English a diphthongisation process in the vowel preceding original /x/ in the *gh*-forms has rearranged earlier distinctions, but their subsequent development has been different in each case, producing a number of distinctions in the North not found in the South (as in (1)). In the Southern dialects, represented by the descendant described in SPE, the effect of this former velar fricative is found still in the morphological alternation *right — righteous.*

We can now move on to two further problems of a more general nature. Firstly, what is the status of morphological alternations with respect to the Northern *gh*-forms and the *right — righteous* alternation in all dialects; secondly, can we accept a panlectal treatment of the *gh*-forms in English?

With reference to the first question, we can see that several of the *gh*-forms are not involved in any alternations and others are involved in irregular tense formation, e.g. *weigh* and *buy — bought* respectively. Certainly we are not dealing with forms which undergo trisyllabic laxing in the SPE system. In fact, we are still only dealing with the forms used to justify the SPE analysis. At this point I think the three words involved: *righteous, nightingale* and *mightily*, should be looked at more closely. The last two are hardly supporting evidence for Chomsky & Halle's claim regarding /x/. *Nightingale* is surely a single lexical item without morphological alternations and without the need to undergo trisyllabic laxing. The free ride principle in this case gains us nothing, since an underlying (SPE) /ī/ in the stressed syllable produces the same result on the surface. *Mightily* appears to be another example where we need to block trisyllabic laxing, but the series *might — mighty — mightily* is exactly like *(sp)ice — (sp)icy — (sp)icily, spike — spiky — spikily*, which have never had any underlying velar fricative before the final stem consonant. We are, therefore, left with *right(eous)* as the only word series that needs /x/, whether we are dealing with the North or the South; in other words we are concerned with exceptions not generalisable relationships.[7]

The second question relates to how we interpret the obvious differences in the *gh*-words between North and South in terms of native speaker competence. It raises the problem of panlectal (and polylectal) grammars. Trudgill (1983: 8-30) presents some important evidence which throws panlectal grammars into serious doubt. He tests native speakers' ability to predict forms of English they have never heard before, and shows how, for the most part, even linguistically sophisticated people are bad at judging the acceptability of forms with which they are unacquainted. 'The more, the merrier' view of panlectal studies seems to be an unjustified starting-point. Of course, if we can account for a number of dialects with virtually the same system, so much the better, provided we do not overlook important differences in the process. We should be able to reflect grades of difference by locating the variation in different parts of the grammar, e.g. at the lexical entry level, at the distributional level, at the realisational level, and so on (cf. Trudgill 1983: 30; also Lodge 1984, for some discussion). The *gh*-forms furnish a good example of difference at the lexical entry level, not just in terms of distribution or lexical incidence, but of underlying contrasting units: *wait* and *weight* have the same underlying vowel phase in the South, but different vowels in the North, as represented in (1). The Northern dialects under discussion have two more diphthongs in the /VV/ set: /ɛɩ/ and /ɔɷ/. The /i:/ and /u:/ forms, which are also sometimes diphthongal (cf. Lodge 1973, 1984), have fallen together with the reflexes of ME ē and ō respectively. In this case the difference between North and South is in terms of lexical incidence.

To sum up, an SPE-type underlying velar fricative in Modern English is unjustified in the *gh*-forms, because the alternation *right — righteous* is exceptional rather than regular. The historical /x/ has produced a dialectal split between the North and South of England at the level of underlying units. How this came about can be explained with the help of a dependency model of phonology. However, the historical explanation is not necessarily an appropriate account of the present system of the Northern dialects with their 'extra' distinctions, any more than the SPE account is. Although from a historical perspective it may seem intuitively satisfying to account for dialect differences in terms of adding certain rules to reflect diachronic changes in some dialects and not others, as suggested by Lass (1976: 26), if we are to take the idea of native speaker knowledge seriously, then such a historical account may well be inappropriate, given the sort of evidence adduced by Trudgill (1983).

Notes

1. See also Pope (1972), where a more detailed discussion of the *gh*-forms is given. This contains some far-fetched morphological analyses, such as a 'sibling morpheme': *-ter ~ -ther*, as in *daughter* and *mother*, respectively. What the other parts of these words might be in Modern English is unclear to me.

2. It has been pointed out to me by Jacques Durand that the difference between SPE and Lass's suggestion may not be all that great, in that in Chapter 8, Chomsky & Halle propose an analysis of their /y/ and /w/ as [+son -syll -cons], which is another way of saying that there are non-syllabic vowels.

3. I am not concerned with *ax* in this paper, because no modern English dialects have retained a diphthongal form in words containing this sequence in Middle English. Note, however, the exceptional form [lëœxf] *laugh* at locality 5.12, Orton & Halliday (1962-3: 1000).

4. For a fuller discussion of lenition and de-articulation, see Lodge (1984: Ch. 7).

5. On the suggestion that |2| should be included as part of the categorial gesture, see also Lodge (1981); and for a discussion of alterations to the initiatory and categorial gestures, see Davenport & Staun (this vol.).

6. We must note that English is not entirely consistent in its avoidance of /V V Ct/ structures. If the two consonants are /st/, we find such structures in the lexical entry forms, e.g. *haste, waste*. With other consonant combinations a morpheme boundary must intervene, e.g. *chafed*.

7. There are compelling theoretical arguments in favour of abstract underlying phonological units based on morphological alternations (see in particular Dresher 1981, where he answers criticism of abstraction and demonstrates the weaknesses of alternative analyses made by natural phonologists), but there is also some interesting evidence from native speaker choices of opaque versus transparent morphologically related forms e.g. *opacity* versus *opaqueness* (see Aronoff &

Schvaneveldt 1978; Cutler 1980). This is not an appropriate place to attempt an answer to this particular problem, but we should perhaps question a system based on the Latinate alternations of educated English, as the SPE analysis is, when it is extended to systems used by linguistically unsophisticated speakers who rarely use such learned forms.

9 ON TRIDIRECTIONAL FEATURE SYSTEMS FOR VOWELS*

John Rennison

1. Aims and Setting

The main aim of this paper is to explore and further develop a feature system for vowels proposed by Jean-Roger Vergnaud at the GLOW meeting (March 1982) in Paris. This feature system will be compared at various points with competing approaches (SPE, natural phonology and dependency phonology). One major aspect of the proposed feature system which is not dealt with here in sufficient depth is that it should be compatible with supra-segmental phonological structures and processes such as vowel harmony, tonal phenomena, etc. which are receiving increased attention in current work on non-linear phonology. To my know-ledge, other researchers (e.g. Clements 1981; Hirst 1983) have tended to adapt the suprasegmental structures and formal devices to existing feature systems, rather than to consider a major reassessment of the features (although there are a few tacit changes in Halle & Clements 1983).

2. The Theoretical Background

There is little doubt that existing systems of distinctive features are able to formalise the vowel systems of natural languages to a sufficient level of observational adequacy, and that they can all claim a certain degree of descriptive adequacy, although usually from different areas or aspects of phonology. The problem is rather that feature systems such as those of SPE (Chomsky & Halle 1968) or of dependency phonology over-generate — the former quite considerably. This over-generation is not restricted to the vowel system, but extends to the features for consonants, and is probably most rampant at the interface between 'vowel features' and 'consonant features'. What happens if we apply a vowel-oriented feature to a consonant or vice versa? Could any language have a /b/ that is [+low, −back] or an /i/ that is [+coronal] (in contrast with their [−low] and [−coronal] counterparts, respectively)? More seriously, the SPE system permits the feature combination [+high, +low] which does not ('cannot') occur in any natural language. Appeal to the obvious physiological explanation for this non-occurrence does nothing to repair the formal system; the generalisation that [+high, +low] does not occur is either lost or must be stated by fiat somewhere within UG. The latter move would seem preferable to abandoning the binarity of distinctive features (which seemed, at one point, to be the alternative − cf. the contributions in Goyvaerts & Pullum 1975). However, 'dynamic' interpretation of features avoids this problem (see the next paragraph), when coupled with a tridirectional approach to vowel features. From the earliest days of generative phonology, natural phonology (D. Stampe, P. Donegan) opposed the bi-directional treatment of vowels (up-down; forward-back) and instead proposed a tridirectional system (perhaps most clearly characterised by Dressler 1975: 36) involving the three colours 'palatal', 'velar' and 'neutral' (i.e. low, when centrifugal). Later treatments (dependency phonology and the one outlined here) also use such a tripartite division of the vowel space, although the precise characterisation of the three extreme vowels varies somewhat (see section 5 on labiality/rounding).

A common characteristic of previous binary feature systems for vowels (though not of dependency phonology) is the 'static' interpretation of the phonetic content of any given feature. A given combination of features was assumed to produce (very nearly) the same phonetic result every time. A [+high] vowel *had* to be phonetically high, etc. Dependency phonology is less static in that it 'calculates' the position of the tongue-body and lips by adding together components. Thus an |i| and an |a| component can combine to give a mid front unrounded vowel. The system I would like to propose here is 'dynamic' in a more far-reaching way: the '+' values of the features I, U and A may be considered as vectors. Their directions are 'high front', 'high back' and 'low' respectively, but their forces may differ from language to language. Thus a vowel system such as that of Twana (Drachman 1969) with [e,o,a,ə] can be viewed as underlying /i,u,a,ə/ − i.e. a perfectly natural four-vowel system − with the phonetic oddity that the vectors I and U are unusually weak. Similarly, languages with a five-vowel system /i,e,a,o,u/ may have higher or lower phonetic variants of the high and mid vowels — but this fact need not be expressed in the phonological feature specifications. This kind of dynamic phonetic interpretation of features therefore combines the advantages of an SPE-type interpretation with those of dependency phonology-type 'components' to allow a higher degree of abstractness for the phonological representation where purely allophonic variations are concerned, without opening the door for greater abstractness across the board.

A different kind of naturalness is often appealed to in the justification of feature systems — though usually *a posteriori* — namely the typological naturalness of (a) individual segments; and (b) vowel systems/inventories. In SPE this kind of naturalness is taken most seriously in the discussion of markedness and linking conventions. In dependency phonology the first published discussion of (non-language-specific) typology seems to be Anderson & Ewen (1980a), and its role in the original formulation of that formal system therefore seems to have been small. If typological naturalness is taken seriously, the consequences are quite far-reaching, since previous systems have (understandably) been based on the better-known languages. Moreover, it seems that there is a large area of agreement between the naturalness of segments/ inventories and the suprasegmental phonological processes investigated so far within non-linear phonology. In what follows I will therefore pay more attention than is usual to typological evidence.

The following sections deal primarily with features for vowels, since I view these as the optimal starting-point for a feature system relating to higher-level phonological structures. This derives from the obligatory status of the syllabic element (usually vowel) within the syllable — or to put it metrically: the strong element of a syllable is usually a vowel and vice versa. The treatment of consonants is nevertheless of paramount importance to a feature system, and they will be touched upon briefly in section 7 below. As for the so-called major class features, it would seem that these become less important as work in non-linear phonology progresses. It is already clear that the true glides (/j,w/, etc.) are non-syllabic variants of the corresponding vowels. Perhaps the SPE feature [sonorant] will also turn out to be (at least partially) structurally definable.

3. What do we Demand of a Feature System for Vowels?

The first, most obvious demand on a system of phonological features for vowels is that it distinguish all vowel phonemes of any single natural language (existent or potential). This provides for observational adequacy. The content of the features will then give the system its descriptive and, hopefully, explanatory adequacy. I have found no cases where acoustic features are demonstrably superior to articulatory features for synchronic phonological analyses. Since I weight historical evidence as relatively unimportant for synchronic grammars, and since diachronic evidence is rarely anything like as unequivocal as synchronic evidence, I see no reason to incorporate acoustic phonetic features in a mentalistic theory of (synchronic) UG. This does not mean that perception or historical linguistics do not use acoustic cues or even *phonetic* features; rather, it seems that acoustic information is always actively (and sometimes wrongly) linked to phonological features. In other words, perception and historical linguistics cannot get by without the use of articulatory features alongside acoustic ones. The higher levels of phonology, on the other hand (i.e. up to phonetic interpretation) may well need only articulatory features (— as was tacitly assumed in SPE). In any case, I find this an interesting speculation which on the one hand calls for an explanation and on the other suggests quite fascinating further hypotheses, such as: Can historical phonology dispense with articulatory features for all changes that do not derive from synchronic phonological processes?

A second property which we demand of a feature system for vowels is that the characterisation of more natural (a) vowels; and (b) vowel systems/inventories, should be formally more elegant than that of less natural systems. There is a danger of circularity if a particular feature system is used to judge the naturalness of the languages, then the scale of naturalness is used to justify the feature system. This danger can be minimised if we use language descriptions that were based on different feature systems. Since much of the data on 'exotic' languages is either structuralist oriented or just simply mediocre linguistics (with a growing number of exceptions, thank goodness!), we avoid total circularity in the sources used for the present paper.

As mentioned above, the feature system outlined below is intended to fit in with current work in non-linear phonology (cf.

e.g. Rennison 1985). This involves a third requirement of feature systems: that (in conjunction with the other formal devices of the theory in which they are embedded) they should permit an elegant formalisation of phonological processes. This demand was first made by SPE, at a time when relatively few phonological processes (in particular, suprasegmental processes such as vowel harmony) had been systematically investigated. Since then we have learned much more about both segmental and suprasegmental phonological processes, and a new feature system should therefore be more adequate for the formalisation of natural processes. Again, it is difficult to avoid circularity in judging naturalness, except (as done below) in a very rough way when using quantitative rather than qualitative data. However, we do not expect a descriptively adequate theory to give an elegant formalisation of a process that is extremely rare or even unique.

Related to the demands for formal elegance is a less common criterion that I would like to look into here: a feature system should not over-generate too much, and when it does, it should at least raise interesting questions. An example of an uninteresting question is: What could [+high, +low] mean in the SPE system? An interesting question, on the other hand, might be: What is the difference between a /b/ that is [+round] and one that is [−round]? Clearly, this criterion is only a minor one, but it is nonetheless worthwhile to keep an eye on the implications of the formal entities that the theory over-generates. For they may be precisely the ones we need for problems that have not yet arisen!

As noted above, I do not consider the appropriateness of a feature system for describing historical changes as a reasonable demand on a phonological feature system (except in so far as the change reflects a synchronic process). If one accepts some form of modularity of language competence, then an obvious candidate for a separate module is the phonetic interpretation (which every system of phonological features needs). It is the phonetic interpretation which must allow for historical changes that do not derive from existing synchronic processes. For this reason it is at times difficult to compare the non-linear features proposed here with the features of dependency phonology (e.g. the interpretation of the |u| component as 'gravity'), since the latter formalism has had a strong historical bias since its beginnings (cf. e.g. Anderson & Jones 1977).

4. The Weighting of Criteria in Constructing a Feature System

The previous section discussed some of the criteria which will be used below (in section 5) in justifying the feature system for vowels proposed by Vergnaud and extended in this paper. Although each criterion was discussed in relation to the various feature systems under consideration here, it might be useful to compare the major weightings of each system, since these will obviously influence the choices of feature content in the respective system.

Natural phonology is based primarily on a wide range of external evidence, especially child language (e.g. Stampe's classic (1969) 'The Acquisition of Phonetic Representation'), but also aphasia (e.g. Dressler 1977), and other areas of psycholinguistics. With a little exaggeration, one might say that for natural phonology 'any process goes', and in a similar way, phonological features are introduced as needed to characterise these processes (although some considerable weight of evidence is always adduced).

Dependency phonology, as mentioned above, has been primarily concerned with the history of English (at least as a starting-point and ever-central area of data), and has spread from there into a variety of related languages. From a theoretical point of view, the major weight has been on dependency relations at various levels of phonology. Considerations of vowel inventories and African languages are relatively recent (Anderson & Ewen 1980).

In the present non-linear-based approach I would say that suprasegmental requirements dominate, followed by the naturalness of segmental inventories and processes.

5. A Non-linear-based Phonological Feature System for Vowels

In the course of what Clements (1981: 108) calls 'the "supra-segmentalization" (in a sense to be defined) of properties which are normally segmental in scope', Jean-Roger Vergnaud has proposed (in an oral presentation at the GLOW meeting in Paris, March 1982, which is still unpublished) factoring out the feature ATR (formerly 'tenseness' in vowels) so that it can be used in vowel harmony processes.

A typical West African language in this respect, which makes full use of ATR harmony, is Koromfe (a minor language spoken in the north of Burkina Faso). Here each phonological word (stem only or stem + suffix) contains either +ATR vowels only, or −ATR vowels only, with schwa belonging to both sets. (For a fuller description of Koromfe vowel harmonies, see Rennison 1985).

(1)　　KOROMFE (Burkina Faso, West Africa)

+ATR	[i]	[u]	−ATR	[ɪ]	[ɷ]	±ATR	[ə]
	[e]	[o]		[ɛ]	[ɔ]		
	[ʌ]			[a]			

All vowels in Koromfe also occur long, nasal and long nasal, thus giving 40 full vowel phonemes, plus schwa (which is always short, nasalises only allophonically, and usually takes on the 'colour' of its environment). There are also some diphthongs; but the treatment of length and diphthongs is irrelevant to the present discussion. The difference in vowel quality between the corresponding vowels in (1) is very small for the high and low vowels, but quite noticeable in the mid vowels (− which may explain the seven-vowel system postulated by Prost 1980). However, the +ATR low vowel, [ʌ], tends to vary between a central and back articulation whereas [a] is usually quite front. In some words the final (class suffix) /-ʌ/ may optionally become [o].

It is now widely accepted among phonologists that the specification of the feature ATR in such languages as Koromfe spreads from the word stem (whose ATR value is constant) to the affixes (whose ATR value varies depending on the word to which they are attached, but always agrees with that of the stem). The feature ATR must therefore be *available* in the segmental make-up of the vowels. Quite apart from the experimental evidence for tongue-root movement (cf. Ladefoged 1968), a scale of tongue height would be inadequate to capture the generalisations involved in ATR harmony, since the low vowel is not *raised* in Koromfe (and many other ATR harmony languages), but is *tensed* and slightly *backed* for the +ATR variant. Other ATR harmony languages have various phonetic realisations of the low +ATR vowel; pure raising seems to be one of the rarest. The actual ATR harmony processes can also be more complex than in Koromfe (cf. Clements 1981), but they make the same use of the segmental feature ATR.

Many languages, however, do not make such full use of the

vowel space or of the feature ATR. According to Clements (1981) the low vowel of Akan is neutral *vis-à-vis* ATR harmony, although the mid and high vowels harmonise. In such a language it is necessary to restrict the availability of the feature ATR to non-low vowels in some way. In languages such as Igbo there are only four vowels per ATR harmony set, hence the vowels have more room for phonetic variation. It would seem that underlyingly there is no low vowel, although (in agreement with the phonetic universal) the −ATR non-high vowel is phonetically [a]. The ATR harmony sets of Igbo are shown in (2):

(2)   IGBO (dialect of Onitsha, Nigeria)

   (a)   phonetically:

   +ATR [i] [u]   −ATR [ɪ] ([e]) [ʊ]
         [o]   [ɔ]
   [ɛ]   [a]

   (b)   phonologically:

   +ATR /i/ /u/   −ATR /ɪ/ /ʊ/
        /e/ /o/   /ɛ/ /ɔ/

In a language such as Igbo it is therefore necessary to restrict the availability of the feature A (see below), i.e. the 'lowness component' in dependency phonology terms, to vowels which are already either +I or +U. Such restrictions on the availability of features are nothing other than the phonological redundancies that have been known for years (cf. Stanley 1967). One interesting aspect of the present feature system is that it suggests that context-free redundancies such as 'there is no underlying /a/ in Igbo' are in fact context-sensitive within the feature make-up of segments. In other words, the absence of the specification +A depends directly upon the absence of both +I and +U. This may parallel the pre-lexical rules of natural phonology (cf. e.g. Dressler 1979).

From the discussion above it is clear that the feature ATR is well motivated and must be included in the feature make-up of vowels. Since we wish to make maximum use of features, the next step must be to consider what other uses the feature ATR could have within the vowel systems of natural languages. One immediate use which springs to mind is to distinguish the mid vowels of many seven-vowel systems of the type shown in (3):

(3)   a seven-vowel system: /i/   /u/
                                  /e/   /o/
                                  /ε/   /ɔ/
                                        /a/

Here, instead of postulating a three-value scale of vowel height, we can restrict the availability of the feature ATR to those vowels that are already +A and either +I or +U. This parallels the restriction of ATR to high and mid vowels in Akan (see above), but with a tighter restriction on the availability of ATR, and the further difference that ATR is not normally used for vowel harmony processes in languages with vowel systems as in (3).

As a side remark let me mention that there exist descriptions of West African languages that postulate seven-vowel systems as in (3) — with or without vowel harmony — that seem to be phonologically inaccurate. In my own work on Koromfe it took a considerable time to hear the tenseness distinction in high and low vowels even though I was looking for it (!). Of course, there is no reason why such seven-vowel systems should not exist — but caution is in order when dealing with older descriptions made before the discovery of ATR harmony.

The next feature I would like to single out for use in suprasegmental processes is ROUND. Here again, the evidence for the existence of vowel harmony processes using ROUND is overwhelming, particularly in the Altaic languages, but also in others distributed all over the world (cf. the contributions in Vago 1980c; Clements & Sezer 1982, on Turkish). I therefore take the motivation for the feature ROUND for granted and would just like to mention two consequences in connection with the maximal use of that feature: Firstly, in languages with natural vowel rounding we may have either backness or roundness harmony (although there may be typological reasons to prefer one over the other?); and secondly, there is a major difference here between the predictions of the present feature system and the system of dependency phonology, since the latter combines roundness and 'high backness' in a single component |u|.

Both these consequences are bound up with the fact that the natural state of affairs is for front vowels to be unrounded and (in most languages) for back vowels — especially the non-low ones — to be rounded. We might formulate this naturalness hypothesis in the form of an implication, as shown in (4):

(4)   (a)   If a language has front rounded vowels, then it also
              has the corresponding front unrounded vowels.
       (b)   If a language has back unrounded vowels, then it
              also has the corresponding back rounded vowels.

From an examination of a considerable number of languages
(including those in Ruhlen 1975 and UPSID) it would seem that
(4a) is an absolute universal of natural languages, while (4b) is at
best a widespread tendency. There are several languages with no
rounded vowels whatsoever, for example those shown in (5):

(5)   Languages with no rounded vowels:
       HIGI (Afro-Asiatic, Nigeria — data from Ruhlen 1975)

       i   ɨ   j   w
       e
       ɛ
              a

       IATMUL (Indo-Pacific, Sepik, Papua New Guinea —
       data from Ruhlen 1975)

            ɨ   j   w
            ə
            a

       IXIL (Mayan, NW. Guatemala — data from Ruhlen
       1975)

       i   ɯ   j
       ɛ   ʌ
              a

       MANAMBU (Indo-Pacific, Sepik, PNG — data from
       Ruhlen 1975)

       i
              a   ā

       UBYX (Caucasian, SW. USSR — data from Ruhlen
       1975)

            ə   j   w   w̰
            a

       NIMBORAN (Indo-Pacific, NW. New Guinea — data
       from UPSID)

       i   ɨ   ɯ
       "e"   "γ"
              a
       Note: ["e"] and ["γ"] are 'mid' mid vowels.

To the right of the vowel inventory, (5) also shows the inventory of glides/approximants for each language. Clearly, we cannot take this evidence at face value: we must first ask whether the lack of rounded vowels is phonemic or phonetic or both. Since Higi, Iatmul and Ubyx have the rounded labio-velar glide /w/, they are likely to have back rounded allophones of vowels, too. This goes particularly for Ubyx, since Caucasian languages often have widely diverging vowel allophones (cf. e.g. Job 1981 on Circassian; or Dressler 1975). In any case, these three languages do not violate the implication (4b), since they have no back vowels at all phonologically. The same goes for Manambu, although here too one would like to know what the allophones look like, since there is no labio-velar glide. Ixil and Nimboran, on the other hand, are direct contradictions of (4b). Moreover, there are also several languages that partially violate (4b), e.g. Amahuaca (Ge-Pano-Carib, E. Peru — data from Ruhlen 1975), which has /o/, but /ɯ/ rather than /u/, or some Upper Saxon dialects of German (W.U. Wurzel, p.c.), which have unrounded not only the front (umlaut) vowels, but also /u/ and /o/ to /ɯ/ and /ɣ/ respectively.

For these reasons it would seem inadvisable to give the implications (4a) and (4b) equal status, regardless of where (within the phonological formalism) they are to be captured. And once again we see that ROUND is a feature which *can* operate independently of vowel height and backness, even though in most languages roundness is (at least partially) redundant.

A further reason for wanting an independent feature ROUND is the phonological process of vowel rounding which can be conditioned by labial consonants. Indeed, one may even be tempted to subsume both the roundness of vowels and the labial place of articulation of consonants under a single phonological feature (e.g. LABIAL). However, the languages reviewed above provide a strong argument for keeping labiality and roundness distinct, since even languages with no rounded vowels have *some* (though few) labial consonants. Rather, it would seem that the natural state of affairs is for labial consonants also to be +ROUND — a redundancy which in turn accounts for the many rounding processes triggered by labial consonants.

In Koromfe we find both a vowel harmony process involving ROUND (not backness!) and a rounding process conditioned by labial consonants. (Again, for a more detailed treatment, see Rennison 1985.) Some relevant data are given in (6):

(6)   KOROMFE. Roundness harmony of final epenthetic
        vowels. (All forms given are the 'unmarked' verb form,
        which is also the imperative singular.)

  (a)   *The normal pattern*:

bakı	make
ganatı	undo
gʌri	rotate
fɛrı	cultivate
bɛllı	fan
keri	close partially
fegeti	revive
bırı	mature
dıŋgı	have an erection
digi	sow
bireŋgi	blacken
kɔkω	remove leaves
fɔ̃ŋɔtω	rest
dɔgsω	cross
foru	pound millet
boŋsu	love
dogtu	cut
fωsω	move
dωgω	abandon
tullu	bow
dũŋgu	carry on one's back
fusu	leave

  (b)   *With intervening labial consonant*:

babtω	lie down
gʌbu	bang, bump
gɛbω	scrape
hɛ̃msω	meet
bɛbω	travel
dɛbω	follow
jebu	chat
kıbtω	pinch
hibsu	fill
hibtu	fill
dubsu	respect etc.

(NB: For back vowels this is the normal pattern as
in (6a).)

Forms such as [gʌri] 'rotate', with a phonetically low central or back stem vowel, take the harmonised vowel [i], which seems to indicate that roundness rather than backness is primary (although such a minor phonetic drift of one low vowel does not present an insurmountable obstacle to a backness analysis with underlyingly non-back low vowels in both ATR harmony sets). Indeed, in a formalism which does not distinguish backness among low vowels (a characteristic both of the system proposed here and of dependency phonology), it would be impossible to formulate a backness analysis — nor would one wish to, since backness harmony typically, perhaps exclusively, relates to non-low vowels. Roundness harmony, on the other hand, as we have seen, can also relate to low vowels.

In Koromfe, roundness and backness for the most part go hand in hand, i.e. there are no vowels with 'unnatural' roundness. The phonetically natural link between velarity and roundness has thus been phonologised as 'roundness implies velarity', but not vice versa, and not 'non-roundness implies non-velarity'. In this way, only a round consonant (i.e. any labial) can in principle affect the colour of a vowel by rounding (and hence automatically backing) it, but non-labial consonants cannot affect vowels, and vowels cannot affect consonants.

The forms given in (6b) above are reminiscent of an anomaly of Turkish roundness harmony. There too, a labial consonant colours a following high vowel (changing expected [ɨ] to [u], at least historically — cf. Crothers & Shibatani 1980). Two differences *vis-à-vis* the Koromfe process are that in Turkish the labial consonant must be preceded by the low vowel [a], and that more than one vowel may ultimately be affected (i.e. the labial colouring can spread onto other vowels to the right). Typologically, such colourings by labial consonants affect only roundness harmony, never backness harmony — a further argument for the analysis of Koromfe given above. However, the forms in (6b) also present an interesting theoretical problem: How is the progressive roundness assimilation to be captured formally? Forms such as [babtɷ] 'lie down' show us that the assimilation is not local (indeed, another inflectional form of the same verb allows two intervening consonants before its rounded epenthetic vowel, namely [babtrɷ]). Nor is it structure-dependent in any obvious way, since the conditioning /b/ is in the coda of the syllable preceding the (syllable of the) affected vowel in forms like [babtɷ], but in the onset of the

syllable of the affected vowel in forms like [gʌbu]. I would therefore suggest that what is happening here is a linear process (and
hence something quite different from the non-linear process of
vowel harmony) which assimilates *all* segments between the labial
consonant and the end of the phonological phrase, provided that
the next vowel to the right is (a) phrase-final and (b) epenthetic,
in origin (i.e. not specified '+' for I,U,A or ROUND, and not
present at the most abstract level of Koromfe phonology). Two
classes of word forms in Koromfe support this analysis of roundness assimilation:

(7)   (a)   [sebe] 'swear', inf. sebelʌm from /sebl+ʌm/
      (b)   [kɪmɛtɪ] 'turn one's head'

Although the second vowel of forms as in (7a) is of epenthetic
origin, it does not undergo labial assimilation because it was
'coloured' at the most abstract level of Koromfe phonology (— and
hence is non-high). This indicates that the phrase-final vowels
affected by roundness assimilation must be 'weak' in some way
that the second /e/ in (7a) is not. Forms as in (7b) show that the
roundness of a labial consonant cannot colour a weak epenthetic
final vowel if it is further to the right than the next syllable. Clearly,
the intervening non-round vowel /ɛ/ stops the further per-
severation of roundness.

   To conclude this brief discussion of Koromfe roundness
harmony, let us consider some of the (relatively rare) words whose
stem contains a diphthong:

(8)   KOROMFE. 'Unmarked' verb forms (as in (6) above)
      containing diphthongs.

dɛɪsɪ	conquer
dɔɪsɪ	lengthen
dɔĩsɪ	be good
kʌusu	shout
bɔɷsɷ	recover
fɔ̃ĩsɷ	be afraid

Here the diphthongs with conflicting values for roundness show
both round and non-round final epenthetic vowels. Moreover, the
otherwise quite clear judgements of my informants on which final
vowel is correct were quite vague for the 'conflicting roundness'
diphthongs (i.e. they were not so quick to reject an alternative

form I offered with the other final vowel) — the forms given in (8) are the 'best', whereas those in (6) and (7) are the *only* possible forms.

The informants' uncertainty about some of the forms in (8) can be directly expressed in a non-linear analysis by choosing either the round or the non-round vowel as the syllable peak (see (9) below); a linear analysis, on the other hand, must formulate two distinct rules of roundness harmony, depending on whether the first or second vowel of the diphthong controls it.

(9)   A non-linear analysis of roundness harmony in 'conflicting roundness' diphthongs.

(a)   −ROUND   (b)   +ROUND
              /\   /\
     d ɔ̃ ĩ s ɪ   f ɔ̃ ĩ s ɷ
     −S +S   +S −S
     (S = SYLLABIC)

After this rather lengthy justification of the feature ROUND, the remaining features can be dealt with quite briefly. The three features reflecting the 'tridirectionality' of the tongue-body movements for vowels are I, U and A. Their similarity to the three components of dependency phonology is obvious, but probably not very far-reaching — after all, the vowel space is very much a tripartite object (especially when viewed phonologically rather than phonetically). In contrast with dependency phonology and with some non-linear proposals, I suggest that the traditional binary features (with values '+' and '−') should suffice (provided that the features are appropriate). Indeed, it would seem worthwhile investigating the possibility that the unspecified feature value 'O' (cf. e.g. Vergnaud 1980) could be replaced by '−' within a revised feature system (a topic too vast to go into here). This move would in effect make the value '+' the marked value and '−' the unmarked, and would only allow exceptions that are marked '+' for some feature. Similarly, only the value '+' could percolate down through phonological tree structures. However, even if such a reorientation of binarism should prove to be impossible, there is still a large body of evidence for tridirectional vowel features such as I,U,A. Remember, however, that these three features in the present framework refer to the tongue-body movements only: in particular, +U does not imply +ROUND (even though they most often co-occur) unless there is some language-specific rule ('naturalness condition', or

Table 9.1: Some Possible Interpretations of Feature Combinations

feature																
I	+	+	+	+	+	+	+	+	+	+	+	+	+	+	+	+
A	+	+	+	+	+	+	+	+	−	−	−	−	−	−	−	−
U	+	+	+	+	−	−	−	−	+	+	+	+	−	−	−	−
ATR	+	+	−	−	+	+	−	−	+	+	−	−	+	+	−	−
ROUND	+	−	+	−	+	−	+	−	+	−	+	−	+	−	+	−

interpretation: [ə] [ə] [ɘ] [ə] [ø] [e] [œ] [ɛ] [ʉ] [i] [ᴓ] [ɨ] [y] [i] [ʏ] [ɪ]

feature																
I	−	−	−	−	−	−	−	−	−	−	−	−	−	−	−	−
A	+	+	+	+	+	+	+	+	−	−	−	−	−	−	−	−
U	+	+	+	+	−	−	−	−	+	+	+	+	−	−	−	−
ATR	+	+	−	−	+	+	−	−	+	+	−	−	+	+	−	−
ROUND	+	−	+	−	+	−	+	−	+	−	+	−	+	−	+	−

interpretation: [o] [ɤ] [ɔ] [ʌ] [ɐ] [a] [ɐ] [a] [u] [ɯ] [ɵ] [ɯ̽] [ɵ] [ə] [ɵ] [ə]

whatever) to that effect. Hence the feature I refers to the high front tongue position, U to the high back and A to the low position.

The phonetic interpretation of the features discussed in this section can vary in the ways mentioned above in section 2, since I assume a 'dynamic' phonetic interpretation of at least the features I,U,A, and perhaps of (all?) others. Table 9.1 is therefore more a user's guide than a definition of the phonetic segments involved — for, crucially, the phonological features can be overridden by the phonetic interpretation in the far-reaching ways mentioned above. Thus, for example, the 'neutral vowel' or 'schwa' of a language will typically be [−I,−U,−A] in the phonological representation, although phonetically it may be something quite different from [ə] — and may vary in colour within a single language.

6. Non-linear vs. Dependency Phonology

Now that some of the basic characteristics of a non-linear-based system of segmental features for vowels have been sketched, let us briefly review the major areas of agreement and disagreement between that approach and dependency phonology, before considering two traditional ('segmental') phonological processes.

The non-linear features would seem to be more appropriate for the description of vowel harmony, since they more naturally capture the classes of vowels involved. Consider, for example, the three vowel harmony classes of Turkish given in (10):

(10)　　The vowels of TURKISH (from Crothers & Shibatani 1980)

	+palatal		−palatal	
+high	i	ü	ɨ	u
−high	e	ö	a	o
	−labial	+labial	−labial	+labial

If we consider [ɨ] and [a] to be underlying /ɯ/ and /ɤ/ respectively (a common assumption in previous treatments of Turkish vowel harmony), then the '+palatal' set is defined by +I in the present system, the '−palatal' set by +U, the '−high' set by +A and the '+labial' set by +ROUND. Moreover, if we assume that the underlying vowels of harmonising suffixes are specified all-minus for the features I,U,A and ROUND, we avoid the indeterminacy of 'archiphoneme' analyses. In addition, the unmarked vowel for the harmony features in Turkish turns out to be /i/ (which is −ROUND and −A, and has 'natural lip position') in the present system, which happens to be the initial epenthetic vowel in loan words with 'unpronounceable' initial clusters (H. Seifert, p.c.).

As regards the tridirectionality of the two feature systems under comparison, for many areas of data there is little or no difference in their predictions, except where labiality/roundness is involved. Alongside the cases mentioned above, there is the problem (for dependency phonology) of the roundness of central vowels. In dependency phonology |i| and |u| together give high front rounded /y/, and all three components together give mid front rounded /ø/ when the components are of equal strength. In the non-linear-based system, however, the corresponding vowels are unrounded /ɨ/ and /ə/ (the 'marked' schwa, whose phonetic interpretation is not so free as that of the all-minus 'unmarked' schwa). In order to deal more adequately with central vowels, Anderson & Ewen (1980a) introduce a fourth component, |ə|, which has the effect of centralising the articulation of a vowel. Note, however, that this theoretical 'afterthought' was introduced to patch up the obser-vational adequacy of the formalism for the kinds of vowel inventories discussed above, and is therefore descriptively problematic. In the non-linear-based system, centrality is readily interpretable as either 'weakness' (i.e. the absence of any I,U or A colouring) or as the 'neutralisation' of all three colours (i.e. when I,U and A are all '+').

A major difference between the two formalisms is the tilde notation of dependency phonology, which in my opinion opens the door for excessive over-generation — especially now that a centrality component has been introduced. In effect, the tilde allows a third feature value alongside the presence or absence of a component. But the issues are complex and their repercussions too far-reaching for discussion here — we will therefore simply note that the tilde notation is an area of differences, and pass on.

The major data base of dependency phonology has been the history of English. It would therefore be particularly appropriate if the superiority of a non-linear-based feature system could be demonstrated using such data. However, since the system put forward here has been developed primarily for synchronic phonology, I shall restrict the following discussion of i-umlaut to the (morpho) phonological process as it still exists today in German, a not-too-distant relative of English. A discussion of the analysis in Anderson & Jones (1977) would hardly be fruitful, since they themselves cast considerable doubt on the precise synchronic interpretation of various spellings, and are primarily concerned with the overall historical development.

In Modern German we can distinguish two types of i-umlaut process: one involving the raising of front (or at least non-back) vowels, and one involving the fronting of back vowels without concomitant unrounding (although such unrounding does take place in many dialects, cf. Rennison 1979, 1981). In (11) I give one form each for the alternations involved:

(11)   i-umlaut in MODERN STANDARD GERMAN
        (a)   non-umlauted
               [fɛlt]   'field'
               [gast]   'guest (sg.)'
               [brɒst]   'breast (sg.)'
               [ɔst]   'east'
        (b)   umlauted
               [gəfɪldə]   'fields (rare collective)'
               [gɛstə]   'guest (pl.)'

[brʏstə]   'breast (pl.)'
[œstlɪç]   'eastern'
(NB: Long vowels and diphthongs omitted)

The first alternation (e — i) is quite rare, although still morphologically transparent in many cases (e.g. *Erde* 'earth' — *irdisch*
'earthly'; *Berg* 'mountain' — *Gebirge* 'mountains (collective)'. We
might therefore wish to treat such forms by a separate umlaut rule
solely on the grounds of their relative infrequency (e.g. as a minor
vs. major rule). Moreover, many morphological rules which trigger
umlaut in the other three alternations in (11) never trigger umlaut
of the e — i type (e.g. suffixation with -*lich*, -*ig*; plural formation,
subjunctive, etc.). In a layer-ordered morphology-cum-phonology
of the lexical type (cf. Kiparsky 1982) the e — i umlaut rule would
therefore be on level 1 and not on later levels, while the other
umlaut rule(s) would be present on level 1 and at least one later
level.

In the non-linear-based feature system of this paper, the e — i
umlaut rule would have to be formulated as follows:

(12)   e — i umlaut in MODERN STANDARD GERMAN.
        $V \Longrightarrow [-A] / [\overline{+e-i \text{ uml.}}]$
        [+A]

Note that it would be possible to dispense with the rule feature 'e—i
uml.' in a grammar that allows phonological rules to be ordered
among morphological rules, even for the cases involving /o/
discussed below.

The other alternations in (11) can be formalised by the rule
given in (13). It is interesting that here the feature +I must be
used, rather than —A in the e — i umlaut rule (reflecting the fact
that a partial rather than total assimilation is involved); for this
parallels exactly the morphological split in the umlaut rule mentioned above.

(13)   Umlaut in MODERN STANDARD GERMAN
        $V \Longrightarrow \begin{bmatrix} +I \\ -U \end{bmatrix} / \underline{\quad} \begin{bmatrix} +\text{umlaut} \\ +\text{accent} \end{bmatrix}$

Note again that the specification '+umlaut' would be superfluous
in a layer-ordered morphology-cum-phonology, and '+accent'
would be replaced by the equivalent structural information in a

non-linear formalism. Moreover, since [+I,+U] is not a permissible feature combination for Modern German vowels, the
non-linear formalism which I am currently developing will automatically supply the equivalent of −U when a rule specifies a
change to +I. The −U in rule (13) can then be omitted.

As they stand, rules (12) and (13) make some interesting predictions about the phonology of Modern German which seem to
be borne out by the facts. Rule (13) suggests that the marking
'+umlaut' (or equivalent) will have no effect on vowels that are
already specified +I — and this is true for both the *e* and *i* of
Modern German: they do not change in any way when a morphological process that (otherwise) triggers rule (13) affects the word
in which they appear. Rule (12), on the other hand, suggests that
all mid vowels (i.e. also /o/) could be affected by this raising; in
Standard German this is not the case, but in some Austrian dialects we find such forms as in (14):

(14)   Some Austrian dialects of Modern German.
        [lox] 'hole', [Iɶkɐd̥] 'holey', [lɪkɐrl] 'small hole'

In the second and third forms, the underlying mid back vowel has
been raised, and in the third form it has also been i-umlauted (and
unrounded) to [ɪ]. We therefore see here that in such dialects rule
(12) also affects back vowels; and the independent status of rules
(12) and (13) is strikingly underlined by the fact that in forms such
as [lɪkɐrl] *both* rules have applied (− NB: The application of both
rules to *front* vowels is excluded by the SC of rule (13)).

Much more could be said about further details of i-umlaut,
especially in Austrian dialects; but these in no way detract from
the analysis presented here. I hope at least to have shown that the
feature system outlined here is potentially *at least* as appropriate as
dependency phonology on (or very close to) the latter formalism's
home ground.

The second type of segmental process to which I would like to
refer is the colouring of consonants in languages such as Gaelic
and most Caucasian languages. The facts seem to be quite straightforward: in such languages consonants have three 'colours',
palatal, velar and neutral. These 'colours' of consonants can cause
assimilations of neighbouring vowels. Sometimes labiality is linked
to velarity, sometimes it is not (cf. Dressler 1975). In the present
non-linear-based feature system the colouring of consonants will
be expressed primarily by the features +I (for palatal), +U (for

velar) and [+I,+U] or [−I,−U], depending on language, for neutral. The naturalness of the link between velarity and lip rounding will be expressed by some language-specific version of the universal markedness convention involved, and thus be independent of the colouring phenomena. In a dependency phonology analysis, on the other hand, colourings involving velarity would have to be expressed using different components in the articulatory gesture, since labiality/rounding cannot be expressed independently of the three basic 'directions' I, U and A.

7. Extension to Tongue-body Consonants

In this section I would like to speculate on a possible extension of the proposed system of vowel features to the consonants articulated with the tongue body. The general approach of what follows is similar to that of dependency phonology, although the details differ. Since I have not had access to a full, recent dependency phonology account of consonants, I will not attempt a comparison of the two formalisms.

Let us first introduce a feature which we will tentatively call OBST (for 'obstruent'), which produces an exaggerated movement of the tongue body towards the 'other articulator' (as defined by the other feature values for the segment involved). This obstruent will be a stop in conjunction with −A and a fricative with +A; we thus interpret the feature A with respect to obstruents as a vector which lowers or centralises (whichever is applicable) the tongue body in the direction of /a/ –– but only enough to produce a fricative, since the 'force' of the feature +OBST is much greater.

Table 9.2: Some Possible Interpretations of Feature Combinations. (For the interpretation of feature combinations with −OBST, see Table 1 above.)

feature								
I	+	+	+	+	−	−	−	−
U	+	+	−	−	+	+	−	−
A	+	−	+	−	+	−	+	−
OBST	+	+	+	+	+	+	+	+
interpretation:	[x]	[k]	[ç]	[c]	[χ]	[q]	[ħ]	[ʔ]

Leaving aside for a moment the effects of the feature ATR for consonants, we can draw up the chart shown in Table 9.2 for the feature specifications of (certain) obstruents.

Note that the true tongue-body consonants all involve either +I or +U, whereas the pharyngeal fricative /ħ/ has only the feature +A (for fricativeness *and* place of articulation simultaneously). Thus the formalism predicts that there are no pharyngeal stops — a fact which may, however, not hold water, since I recently heard that pharyngeal stops have been reported for some Amerindian languages (Eva Higgins, p.c.). In any case, they seem to be extremely rare compared with their fricative counterparts. The 'placeless' stop (−I,−U,−A) is the glottal stop. For the consonant /h/ we might use the specification for a voiceless vowel (following, e.g. Ladefoged 1982) — perhaps with [−I,−U,−A] underlyingly in the unmarked case, so that the actual tongue-body position of [h] is computed by the phonetic interpretation, depending on the neighbouring vowels. In table 9.2 I have given the voiceless phonetic interpretations: I assume that some feature will be necessary to regulate consonant voicing (as with /h/), although the matter still needs some thought, since voicing is 'natural' in vowels and sonorants, but 'unnatural' (context-free) in obstruents.

An immediate objection to Table 9.2 would seem to be the unnaturalness of the specification for /k/, in comparison, say, with /q/, which is typologically rarer, but has one less '+' specification. However, the specifications in Table 9.2 are only necessary in languages which need to distinguish a large number of consonants. If a language has no /q/, on the other hand, it can quite happily specify /k/ as −I rather than +I (the value given in Table 9.2), since the feature I is no longer distinctive for consonants that are +U. The phonological pattern of a given language, and in particular the processes in which vowels and consonants interact, will hopefully make a clear decision possible on the underlying feature specification of tongue-body consonants in that language.

Table 9.2 shows the exhaustive use of the available features in specifying tongue-body consonants. Similarly, Table 9.1 also shows *all* possible combinations of features. The present feature system therefore does not over-generate in the areas considered so far (with the possible exception of ATR for consonants, to which I will return below). It would therefore seem that evidence against this feature system will come from languages which make fuller use of the vowel space than the formalism can handle (e.g. a language with distinctive underlying low front and back vowels that cannot be specified using ATR or ROUND). This situation is parallel in some ways to dependency phonology before the 'centrality' component was introduced by Anderson & Ewen (1980a). Let us hope that a similar fate does not await the present formalism.

As mentioned above, there is no need for the feature ATR as far as the consonants in Table 9.2 are concerned. The question therefore arises what the effect of a change in ATR would be for a consonant. It may be that ATR is simply irrelevant for consonants, i.e. they can be specified for it, but that has no phonetic effect (just like empty categories in syntax). On the other hand, since ATR affects the tongue root, we might look for languages with pharyngeal consonants and ATR vowel harmony (if such a language exists). Anderson (1980, citing Puech, unpublished) suggests that Maltese ATR harmony originated in the loss of pharyngeal consonants; in that case we might expect never to find an ATR harmony language that had pharyngeal consonants. In any case, ATR certainly raises 'interesting questions' about phonologies of natural languages — and is the only feature still available for consonants within the present system, in case any holes have to be patched up.

8. Conclusion

It would be illusory to think that this feature system could be longer-lived than its predecessors. I nevertheless hope that it will stimulate some debate and perhaps encourage others to develop better feature systems for the segmental part of non-linear phonology.

Note

*This paper has benefited from discussions, etc. with fellow phonologists too numerous to name individually here, in Vienna, Paris, Sheffield, York, Colchester, Eisenstadt, and at M.I.T., Harvard and UConn. I thank them all for their contributions to my idea-formation processes, and absolve them one and all from any responsibility for the output.
An article exploring the applicability of the tridirectional features to the autosegmental treatment of vowel harmony in a variety of languages is in preparation.

10 CONSTITUENCY AND SYLLABLE STRUCTURE[1]

Nigel Vincent

The syllable has had a rather chequered career in twentieth-century phonology. As a legacy of traditional ways of talking about language, it was on a par with the concept of word, and had to fight, often unsuccessfully, for survival in a theoretically more parsimonious world. Normal practice amongst American descriptivists, for example, was to pass directly from the phoneme to the morpheme without seeking to set up or exploit any larger intermediate unit of phonological organisation. Elsewhere, too, attempts were made to define the syllable in terms of distributional patterns (cf. O'Connor & Trim 1953) so that it need not figure in the list of phonological primitives. Similarly, in classical generative phonology of the SPE type, the syllable is accorded no theoretical status, and generalisations are stated in terms of features and formatives via rules and the revealingly named morpheme-structure conditions. Voices of dissent were, of course, raised, notably those of Pike (see Pike & Pike 1947), the later Hockett (1955), and more recently Anderson (1969) and Brown (1970). Meanwhile European theorists such as Trubetzkoy, Hjelmslev and Firth had always recognised the independent status and structural importance of the syllable. It is only in the last decade, however, that there has come to be virtual consensus amongst phonologists of all persuasions that the syllable is an undeniable unit in the phonological structure of most, if not all (though see now Hyman 1985 for a different view), languages, and that phonological theory must accordingly be constructed in such a way as to accommodate this fact. Where there is less agreement is on the form that such a theoretical recognition of the syllable must take, and that is the issue to which the present paper is devoted. After a brief review of the kinds of argument which have caused this change of heart, we proceed to a comparison of 'linear' versus 'hierarchical' models of syllable structure, concluding in favour of the latter. The remainder of the paper is devoted to questions relating to the internal constituency of the syllable, in particular the rhyme and the interlude.

Let us begin, then, with the arguments that can be used in

support of the syllable, which Selkirk (1982) suggests fall into three main types. In the first place, following Hooper (1972) — though see Fischer-Jørgensen (1972: Ch. 12.10) for a good discussion of the background to this idea — there is good evidence for the view that the syllable is the natural domain for the statement of phonotactic patterns; in other words, the converse of the view advocated by O'Connor & Trim (1953) that the syllable should be defined in terms of the distribution of phonemes. Two subtypes of this argument exist. The first involves showing that a certain grouping of segments is sensitive to or can be predicted on the basis of a division into syllables. For example, notice that the cluster /tl/ does not occur in English in word-initial position, but it is found medially: *atlas, cutlass, fetlock*, etc. We can avoid making a special statement to this effect in the grammar if we say that English words are made up of sequences of possible English syllables. Since /tl/ is not a possible syllable-initial cluster, it will never be found word-initially, but since /t/ is possible syllable-finally and /l/ syllable-initially, the medial sequence /-tl-/ is to be expected. The other variant of this argument involves the circumstance in which a given sound or sounds have limited distribution within a language. Thus, Henderson (1949) gives the following two inventories of segments for Thai:

> *Syllable-initial*
>
> | | | | |
> |----|-----|----|---|
> | p | t | k | ʔ |
> | ph | th | kh | |
> | b | d | | |
> | | tɕ | | |
> | | tɕh | | |
> | f | s | | h |
> | m | n | ŋ | |
> | | l | | |
> | | r | | |
> | | j | w | |
>
> *Syllable-final*
>
> | | | | | |
> |----|----|----|----|-----|
> | p′ | t′ | k′ | ʔ′ | (i.e. unreleased stops) |
> | m | n | ŋ | | |

Clearly, it would be an inordinately and unnecessarily difficult task to give an account of the phonology of a language of this type without making reference to the syllable. Jacques Durand has pointed out to me that the above argument is weakened to the extent that in Thai there is a coincidence between syllables and morphemes and/or words, since such a state of affairs would always allow the alternative of stating the distributions of the two sets of consonants in terms of the grammatical boundaries. I refer the reader to Henderson (1949) for discussion of the phonology of Thai polysyllables, but even supposing that Thai (or some other language) did exhibit a perfect coincidence between morpheme and syllable, it would still be a moot point which was the proper unit for the statement of the phonological distribution. On the fairly widely held view that, where possible, phonological generalisations should always be made in terms of phonetically relevant parameters (the 'naturalness' condition), the case for the syllable would still be supported by data of the kind we have adduced. Numerous other examples where distributional arguments favour the syllable are to be found both in the present volume and in the phonological literature, so we will not discuss this question further here. We will simply assume in what follows that the syllable is the natural unit for the statement of phonotactic patterns, and to that extent the syllable is required as a unit in phonological theory.

The second type of argument which may be used in defence of the syllable is to show that it is required as an environment in the statement of phonological processes. S.R. Anderson (1974: Ch. 14) contains a lucid discussion of several such situations, while Kahn (1976) is usually acknowledged as having begun the task of reconstructing the theoretical edifice of generative phonology in order to allow the syllable to act as a conditioning environment for phonological rules. A simple but instructive case in point is to be found in Vennemann (1972), who discusses the import of those German dialects in which *Adler* 'eagle', *radle* 'I cycle', etc. are pronounced [atlə], [ra:tlə], etc. rather than [adlə], [ra:dlə], etc. as in the standard language. It seems clear that what has happened here is that the standard rule of word-final devoicing has generalised to become a rule of syllable-final devoicing. Just as the spread of sound changes through classes of segments may be taken as evidence that those classes are natural ones (cf. King 1969: 58ff), so the generalisation from word to syllable boundary suggests that both must be recognised within phonological theory.

If the syllable is not recognised in the foregoing example, then the rule for the dialects in question will have to be stated as in (1):

(1)

$$C \implies [-\text{voice}] \ / \ - \ \left\{ \begin{matrix} C \\ \# \end{matrix} \right\}$$

The disjunction of C and # is forced to do duty for the single statement — $ (where $ = syllable boundary), and is thus a useful diagnostic for other cases where the influence of syllable structure is suspected. Indeed, if we are to believe Harris (1983: 5),

> every linguistic description that contains either an explicit boundary symbol or the cryptic notation / — {C,#} thus constitutes a challenge: either it must be reformulable with equal or greater descriptive adequacy in terms of internal syllabic organisation, or the more restrictive (and hence a priori more desirable) theory that eschews the allegedly functionless machinery must be abandoned.

A typical instance concerns the distribution of [ŋ] in a number of Northern Italian dialects (and corresponding pronunciations of the standard language). Compare the forms set out in (2) below:

(2)

	Standard Italian		*Ligurian*	*Gloss*
	campo	[kampo]	[kaŋpu]	field
	vendere	[vendere]	[veŋde]	to sell
	pungere	[pundʒere]	[puŋze]	to prick
	cinque	[tʃiŋkwe]	[siŋkwe]	five
	vino	[vino]	[viŋ]	wine
	pane	[pane]	[paˀŋ]	bread
	non	[non]	[noŋ]	not

(Ligurian forms from Azaretti 1977)

Two points are to be noted here. First, the Standard Italian forms clearly exhibit the familiar pattern of assimilation of a nasal to the place of articulation of a following obstruent, whereas Ligurian regularly has [ŋ] in preconsonantal position. Second, with the exception of the negative particle *non* and the prepositions *in* and *con*, which are in any case never utterance final, Standard Italian words never end in a nasal. In Ligurian, on the other hand, vowel truncation produces any number of final nasals, which are then regularly [ŋ], as the last three examples in (2) indicate. It is not difficult to see, therefore, that the relevant rule/sound change should be stated as in (3):

(3)   C $\Longrightarrow$ [ŋ] / — $
       [+ nasal]

Such a formulation has the added advantage of explicitly connecting the presence of the velar nasal to syllable-final position, a
connection for which there is considerable cross-linguistic evidence. Thus, in a number of languages, even though /ŋ/ has
phonemic status, it nevertheless has a distribution limited to
syllable-final position — English, Mandarin Chinese (Kratochvil
1968: 33-4) and Kobon (Davis 1981: 219) are but three examples.
Indeed, it is possible to state a typological universal to the effect
that if a language has initial [ŋ], it will also have syllable-final [ŋ],
but not vice versa. What is particularly striking about this example
is the way it runs counter to the normal Italian tendency for NC
clusters to agree in place of articulation. Whereas a rule of
homorganic nasal assimilation has the effect of uniting the two segments in a single articulatory gesture, the change in (3) seems
deliberately to throw the two segments (or syllables) apart. We
shall return below to the further theoretical consequences of such a
state of affairs.[2]

Both the preceding types of argument relate to the way in which
segments group together into the higher-order construct of
syllable. A third kind of evidence is to be found in the way syllables, in turn, may group into larger units for the purposes of rules
of stress and intonation. Consider, for example, the following
statement about the Australian language Watjarri by Douglas
(1981, p. 206-7)

> Primary stress falls on the first syllable of each word except in a
> few borrowings ... In three-syllable words, secondary stress falls
> on the second syllable. In four-syllable words, secondary stress
> falls on the third syllable. In words of more than four syllables,
> secondary stress falls on the penultimate.

These generalisations are straightforwardly captured by the rules in
(4) together with a constraint to block assignment of stress to both
syllables of a disyllabic word.

(4)   (a) $ $\Longrightarrow$ [1 stress] / # —
       (b) $ $\Longrightarrow$ [2 stress] / — $ #

Any attempt to restate these rules without reference to the syllable would require cumbersome use of variables to allow for all the possible consonant strings which could intervene between the vowels which are the standard recipients of stress in SPE-type formulations. On the question of the role of syllable in English prosodic structure, see Selkirk (1980a, b) and Giegerich (this vol.). For more general and very valuable discussion of the relation between syllables and higher-order phonological categories, see Allen (1973).

Other types of rules which may require reference to syllables are those involved in morphological processes such as reduplication and infixation — see Vincent (in prep.) for an interesting case of the former kind. All in all, then, the case for admitting the syllable into the theoretical fold seems fairly overwhelming. We turn our attention now to exactly what kind of animal it is that we are obliged to harbour!

Two general views of syllable structure may be identified in the recent literature, which we will dub 'linear' and 'hierarchical'. Under the former view, held principally by natural generative phonologists such as Vennemann (1972, 1974) and Hooper (1972, 1976), phonological representations start out as unstructured linear sequences of segments, much as in SPE, which are then at an early stage in the derivation broken down into smaller sequences by a combination of universal and language-particular rules of syllabification. Such rules assign syllable boundaries according to universally determined hierarchies of phonological strength like the one displayed in (5) below (after Hooper 1976: 206), so that syllables consist of a nucleus flanked by segments of increasing strength as one moves out towards the margins.

(5)

glides	liquids	nasals	voiced continuants	voiceless continuants voiced stops	voiceless stops
1	2	3	4	5	6

Furthermore, within this overall framework, the syllable-initial position is treated as inherently strong and the syllable-final position as inherently weak, while a phonological law of the jungle asserts that the strong will tend to get stronger and the weak weaker. In addition to specifying the maximal sequences in either direction, language particular grammars may interfere with this optimal pattern in one of two ways. First, they may permit certain syllable types which violate the hierarchy as it stands. Thus, in English there are initial clusters of the form /Cl-/ as in *blue, click,* etc., and there are final clusters of the form /-lC/ as in *belt, bulb,* etc. This is exactly in accord with the scale (5) since liquids are weaker than stops and therefore should occur nearer the nucleus. In French, on the other hand, although the initial clusters behave as in English — *bleu, clair,* etc., final clusters of the form /-Cl/ are found — *peuple, boucle,* etc. Hence the rules of French syllable structure will have to have the power to override the scale (5) at this point. Secondly, a language may exhibit a characteristic perturbation of the general scale. Thus, Vennemann (1972) argues that for Icelandic the segment /v/ behaves in the same way as /j/ and therefore needs to be treated as of strength 1 rather than 4. Clearly, there are also respects in which the universal scale needs to be extended and refined — for example, there is the problem of affricates (are they stronger or weaker than stops?) and the probably not unconnected difficulty of /s/, which despite being a fricative seems to occur more commonly before rather than after a stop in a syllable-initial cluster (cf. Kiparsky 1979). Place of articulation, too, is a factor which ought to be taken into account (cf. Lass 1984: Ch. 8.3.3 for some discussion).

In fact, the literature on the hierarchical patterning of phonetico-phonological features is by now quite extensive (see Lass 1984: Ch. 8.3, for a convenient survey; and Foley 1977, for a large collection of (somewhat idiosyncratically interpreted) examples), and there are obviously a number of genuine phenomena there to be explored. Nor does it seem initially implausible to connect this patterning to the question of the syllable. At the same time, it is clear that the particular model of the syllable that Hooper, Vennemann and others in this tradition work with is unjustifiably impoverished. We must turn our attention, therefore, to the evidence for hierarchical organisation of another kind, namely the grouping together of subparts of the syllable into units very like constituents in syntax.

The first such division for which there is widespread (though not total — cf. Clements & Keyser 1983) support in the literature is that between the onset and the rhyme, so that the English monosyllable *cat* should be represented not as /$kæt$/ but as:

(6)

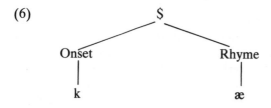

Arguments in favour of this division are of various kinds. First, it is often the case that the 'weight' of the syllable for metrical purposes is calculable solely by reference to the components of the rhyme. Thus, it is traditional in Latin metrics and accentology to distinguish between light and heavy syllables, with the former containing a short vowel, and the latter either a short vowel and a following consonant or a long vowel. On closer inspection, however, it is clear that what matters is the weight of the rhyme, since the nature of the onset is irrelevant. Thus, *ă, fĭ, brŏ, splĕ* are all light, while ē, *ĭt, ŏk, ăb* are all heavy. In other words, a short vowel cannot be compensated for by any number of consonants in the onset, but a consonant in the rhyme automatically contributes the necessary unit of weight. In the same vein, consider the notion of strong and weak clusters as exploited in SPE. To the extent that Chomsky & Halle's principles for assigning stress are valid they provide an argument for the recognition of the 'cluster' as a proper unit of linguistic analysis, and when we come to ask what exactly the 'cluster' is we find that it is no less (and no more) than the rhyme portion of the syllable. Another type of justification for the rhyme as a constituent is offered by Harris (1983: 9-10), where it is argued that the proper generalisations regarding syllable size in Spanish can only be made by independently computing the size of the onset and the rhyme. He writes:

> If these constituent groupings are not recognised, a statement like this becomes necessary: Spanish syllables have a maximum length of five segments if the initial string of consonants contains two segments, but a maximum length of four segments if there is one initial consonant, and three segments if there is no initial consonant. One has only to formulate this (non)alternative to see its inadequacy: in fact, rhymes are maximally three segments long independently of onset length.

A third kind of argument consists in showing that the rhyme is a proper domain for the assignment of phonological features. Consider, for example, the three diphthongal rhymes [ei, ou, øy] in Cantonese (see Hashimoto 1972: 90-1), the only ones in the language where the first element is a lax vowel. The phonological generalisation seems clear: diphthongs of this type contain any one of three mid vowels followed by a homorganic glide. Furthermore, they cannot be followed by a consonant. An obvious solution would seem to be to argue that the diphthongs constitute fully-fledged rhymes rather than syllable nuclei, and hence there is no room for a following consonant. The properties common to both segments can then be specified at the level of the rhyme, while those which change from segment to segment can be attached to lower nodes. In other words, for the syllable *tou* we get:

(7)

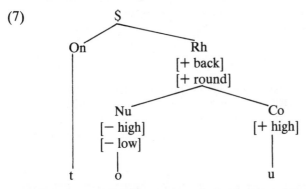

Against this view, it may be argued, following Clements & Keyser (1983), that all we strictly need to do is split the features as shown and assign them directly to the elements of the phonological skeleton thus:

(8)

Under such a view, it becomes an accident that there are no features which spread over the first two elements, but not over the last one. Nor is this difference simply attributable to the fact that positions one and two are occupied by a consonant and a vowel, but positions two and three are both occupied by vocalic elements:

similar distributional facts obtain even when the rhyme is made up of a vowel and a consonant. Thus, [i:, u:, y:, ø] only occur before [n, t] ([i:] also occurs before [m, p], but this doesn't affect the argument). On the other hand, [ι, ʋ, ε:, œ:] are only to be found before [ŋ, k]. Following Hashimoto's suggestion (1972: 159) that the relevant phonological feature is [diffuse], we can represent the two rhymes [øt] and [œ:k] as:

(9)

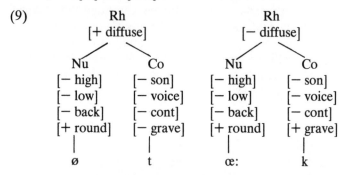

Fourthly, an argument can be made from the need to recognise differences of grouping amongst elements of apparently similar, or even identical, phonetic composition. Thus, in a classic study, Fudge (1969) observes that English monosyllables can end in either of the following sequences:

(10)   (a)   V   C   C (b)   V   C   C
                [− long] [+ son]   [+ long] [+ son] [+ cor]

Hence, we find *health, limp, gulf, singe, silk, film*, etc. and *mind, sound, yield*, etc. but no **soump, *bailge*, or the like. On the assumption that the second half of a long vowel or a diphthong is also a sonorant element, this pattern can be explained in terms of a difference in constituent structure in the two cases, viz.:

(10)   (a′)   (b′)

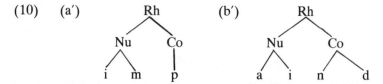

Overall, therefore, the evidence in support of constituent structure inside the syllable seems inescapably strong. So too, incidentally, does the case for the recognition of a rhyme constituent, and thus we side with recent theorists such as Selkirk

(1982) and Harris (1983) as against Clements & Keyser (1983). In fact, the essence of our argument with regard to Cantonese was that the rhyme serves as a single domain for the assignment of phonological properties. Consider now what follows for a language, such as Italian, which requires intervocalic clusters of nasal plus obstruent to be homorganic. This is tantamount to saying that there is a single domain -NC- which is relevant for the assignment of place-of-articulation features. But it would appear that such a domain cannot be a constituent since it is made up of the coda of the first syllable followed by the onset of the second syllable thus:

(11)

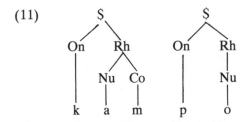

Either the tree in (11) is incorrect or else phonological properties can spread over stretches which are not constituents, in which case the argument from Cantonese is greatly, if not totally, undermined. I will try to argue here for the former conclusion. Consider first the claim that a representation such as (11) makes, namely that a word in Italian may consist of at least two independently well-formed syllables. While true, such a generalisation seriously understates the position: /pan, kol, sep, kur, gof, fred, muŋ, bir, *etc.*/ are all possible syllables of Italian, but only in words such as /panno, kolpo, seppi, kurva, goffo, freddo, muŋgo, birra, *etc.*/. Words such as */panpo, septi, gofta, fredgo, muŋbo, *etc.*/ are not possible in Italian: only clusters of the type liquid + obstruent may violate the constraint on homorganicity. Furthermore, in the case of sequences of obstruents (except where one is /s/), there must be total identity of the two segments, so that not even */-fp-, -vb-, -pf-, -bv-/ are to be found. Let us see how such a state of affairs could be handled in the notation of Clements & Keyser (1983). Their position on geminates is clear enough — they receive a representation as in (12):

(12)

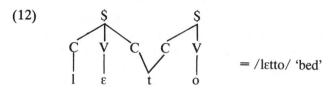

= /lɛtto/ 'bed'

If we now dissociate the nasal and the place of articulation features, we have:

(13)

```
            +N   −N
             |    |
    C   V   C    C    V
    |   |    \   /    |
    l   ε     t       φ
```

= /lɛnto/ 'slow'

While both the representations in (12) and (13) are adequate to represent the observational facts of Italian, they fail in so far as they do not rule out any number of other possible patterns of association between melodic properties and members of the CV tier. Yet it is precisely a characteristic of standard Italian *vis-à-vis* dialects of the kind exemplified in (2) above that these special constraints exist on intervocalic sequences. In order to capture the facts in the two types of pronunciation, we propose the following two patterns of constituency:

(14)   Standard Italian   Dialects and regional Italian in
                            the North
        [ka [Np] o]   [kaN][po]

The nasal element, here symbolised N, gets two very different interpretations. In the standard language it assimilates to the following obstruent: in the Northern dialects it either becomes [ŋ] or it associates to the nucleus and gives rise to nasal vowels.

To sum up, therefore, we have argued for a representation of the syllable in which there is internal constituent organisation. We have also suggested that when two syllables come together, they may in some instances simply sit side by side, but they may also be, as it were, welded together by the creation of an intervocalic constituent which acts as the domain for the assignment of features which are shared between the coda of one syllable and the onset of the next. In order to achieve such a representation, we must allow for the existence of a rhyme constituent. Somewhat more controversially, we must also allow for the creation of a special kind of ambisyllabic constituent — essentially a reconstruction in a modern guise of the concept of 'interlude' discussed by Hockett (1955: 52). Thus, a full representation of Italian *campo* 'field' will be as in (15):

(15)

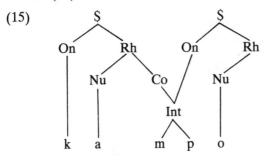

A crucial property of such a notation is that features or feature bundles may be assigned to non-terminal nodes — indeed, they must be so assigned if the maximally general statements are to be made. The full details of such a system remain to be worked out, and may well involve phonological features other than the rather standard ones that have been used, principally for reasons of expository convenience, in this article. What will also be required is a percolation mechanism whereby features can 'trickle' from non-terminal to terminal nodes (cf. Gazdar (1982: 135ff) for a similar concept in syntax). Once again, the details remain to be elaborated. In the meantime, I will list a series of questions that the full working out of such a system will need to face:

(a) How are features from different levels of the tree to be combined?

(b) How are major class features to be represented? (cf. here particularly the very interesting suggestion of Selkirk (1984) that such features can be dispensed with in favour of sonority indices attached to terminal nodes. Unfortunately, I was only able to consult Selkirk's article when the present paper was almost complete — and already long overdue!)

(c) To what extent is the syntactic notion of 'head' (cf. Zwicky 1985) reconstructible in phonology, possibly via an X' representation of the syllable, where the nucleus is represented as N, the rhyme as N' and the syllable as N''?

(d) To what extent is such a system rendered obsolete by an entirely dependency-based phonology, such as is argued for by a number of other contributors to this volume? Once again compare the situation in syntax, and the arguments set out in Matthews (1981: Ch. 4). This last issue is a complex one and certainly needs more extensive discussion. One point, however, that is worth making is that perhaps the strongest objection to pure constituency representations in syntax comes from those circumstances in which one wants to state a relation without also stating a linear order. On the other hand, the one thing that is always fixed in phonology is the order of elements in a constituent, and of constituents with respect to one another. Put another way, there are no phonological scrambling rules.[3]

Notes

1. I would like to thank Jacques Durand both for his comments on an earlier version of this paper, and for his superhuman editorial patience and tolerance!

2. See now Harris (1984) for a discussion of some similar developments in syllable-final nasals in certain dialects of Spanish and their theoretical import.

3. The obvious phenomenon which springs to mind in this connection is metathesis, but this (a) is much more restricted than the kinds of word order rearrangements that one finds in the syntax of certain languages; and (b) usually involves precisely a switching of position of segments to match some canonical syllable structure for the language in question.

BIBLIOGRAPHY

Abercrombie, D. (1965a). *Studies in Phonetics and Linguistics.* London: Oxford University Press.
—— (1965b). 'A Phonetician's View of Verse Structure'. In Abercrombie, D. (1965a).
—— (1965c). 'Syllable Quantity and Enclitics in English'. In Abercrombie, D. (1965a).
—— (1971). 'Some Functions of Silent Stress'. In Aitken, A.J., McIntosh, A. & Pàlsson, H. (eds.), *Edinburgh Studies in English and Scots.* London: Longman.
Ågren, J. (1973). *Etude sur quelques liaisons facultatives dans le français de la conversation téléphonique.* Uppsala: Ka-We Tryck.
Aitchison, J. (1981). *Language Change: Progress or Decay?* London: Fontana.
Allen, G.D. (1975). 'Speech Rhythm: its Relation to Performance Universals and Articulatory Timing. *Journal of Phonetics* 3. 75-86.
Allen, W.S. (1973). *Accent and Rhythm.* Cambridge: Cambridge University Press.
Anderson, J.M. (1969). 'Syllabic or Non-syllabic Phonology?' *Journal of Linguistics* 5. 136-42.
—— (1971). 'Outline of a Proposal for the Lexicalisation of Complex Structures'. *Studia Linguistica* 25. 1-8.
—— (1975). 'Principles of Syllabification'. *York Papers in Linguistics* 5. 7-20.
—— (1976). *On Serialisation in English Syntax. Ludwigsburg Studies in Language and Linguistics* 1.
—— (1980). 'On the Internal Structure of Phonological Segments: Evidence from English and its History'. *Folia Linguistica Historica* 1. 165-91.
—— (this volume). 'Suprasegmental Dependencies'.
—— (to appear a). 'Structural Analogy and Dependency Phonology'. *Acta Linguistica Hafniensia.*
—— (to appear b). 'The Lexical Head Hypothesis'.
—— (to appear c). 'Old English Ablaut again: the Essentially Concrete Character of Dependency Phonology'. In Festschrift X.
—— (to appear d). 'The English Prosody /h/'. In Festschrift Y.
—— & Durand, J. (this volume). 'Dependency Phonology'.
—— & Ewen, C.J. (1980a). 'Introduction: a Sketch of Dependency Phonology'. In Anderson, J.M. & Ewen, C.J. (eds.), (1980b). 9-40.
—— (1980b) (eds.) *Studies in Dependency Phonology. Ludwigsburg Studies in Language and Linguistics* 4.
—— (1981). 'The Representation of Neutralisation in Universal Phonology'. *Phonologica* 1980. 15-22.
—— (to appear). *Principles of Dependency Phonology.* Cambridge: Cambridge University Press.
—— & Jones, C. (1974). 'Three Theses Concerning Phonological Representations'. *Journal of Linguistics* 10. 1-26.
—— (1977). *Phonological Structure and the History of English.* Amsterdam: North-Holland.
Anderson, S.R. (1974). *The Organization of Phonology.* New York & London: Academic Press.
—— (1976). 'Nasal Consonants and the Internal Structure of Segments'. *Language* 52. 326-44.

—— (1980). 'Problems and Perspectives in the Description of Vowel Harmony'. In Vago, R.M. (ed.). 1-48.

—— (1982). 'The Analysis of French Schwa: or, How to Get Something for Nothing'. *Language* 58. 535-71.

Armstrong, L.E. (1955). *The Phonetics of French.* London: G. Bell & Sons.

Aronoff, M. (1979). 'A Reply to Moody'. *Glossa* 13. 115-18.

—— & Oehrle, R.T. (eds.), (1984). *Language Sound Structure. Studies in Phonology Presented to Morris Halle by his Teacher and Students.* Cambridge, Mass.: M.I.T. Press.

—— & Schvaneveldt, R. (1978). 'Testing Morphological Productivity'. *Annals of the New York Academy of Sciences* 318. 106-14.

Azaretti, E. (1977). *L'evoluzione dei dialetti liguri.* San Remo: Casabianca.

Basbøll, H. (1974). 'The Phonological Syllable, with Special Reference to Danish'. *ARIPUC* 8.

—— (1978). 'Boundaries and Ranking of Rules in French Phonology'. In de Cornulier, B. & Dell, F. (eds.) 3-18.

Beddor, P.S. (1983). 'Phonological and Phonetic Effects of Nasalization on Vowel Height'. *Indiana University Linguistics Club.* Bloomington: Indiana.

Bell, A. & Hooper, J.B. (eds.) (1978). *Syllables and Segments.* Amsterdam: North-Holland.

Booij, G. (1983). 'Principles and Parameters in Prosodic Phonology'. *Linguistics* 21. 249-80.

Brown, G. (1970). 'Syllables and Redundancy Rules in Generative Phonology'. *Journal of Linguistics* 6. 1-17.

—— (1977). *Listening to Spoken English.* London: Longman.

Cairns, C.E. & Feinstein, M. (1982). 'Markedness and the Theory of Syllable Structure'. *Linguistic Inquiry* 13. 193-255.

Campbell, A. (1959). *Old English Grammar.* London: Oxford University Press.

Catford, J.C.(1977). *Fundamental Problems in Phonetics.* Edinburgh: Edinburgh University Press.

Chomsky, N. (1964). *Current Issues in Linguistic Theory.* The Hague: Mouton.

—— (1965). *Aspects of the Theory of Syntax.* Cambridge, Mass.: M.I.T. Press.

—— & Halle, M. (1968). *The Sound Pattern of English.* New York: Harper & Row.

Clements, G.N. (1981). 'Akan Vowel Harmony: a Non-linear Analysis'. In Clements, G.N. (ed.), *Harvard Studies in Phonology* II. 107-77.

Clements, G.N. & Keyser, S.J. (1981). 'A Three-tiered Theory of the Syllable'. *Occasional Papers No 19,* The Center for Cognitive Studies, M.I.T.

—— (1983). *CV Phonology: A Generative Theory of the Syllable.* Cambridge, Mass.: M.I.T. Press.

Clements, G.N. & Sezer, E. (1982). 'Vowel and Consonant Disharmony in Turkish'. In van der Hulst, H. & Smith, N. (eds.), (1982b). 213-55.

Colman, F. (to appear). '*ie* Dependency'. In Anderson, J.M. & Durand, J. (eds.), *Explorations in Dependency Phonology.*

Comrie, B. (1978). 'Morphology and Word Order Reconstruction: Problems and Prospects'. In Fisiak, J. (ed.) *Historical Morphology.* The Hague: Mouton. 83-96.

de Cornulier, B. (1978). 'H aspirée et la syllabation. Expressions disjonctives'. In Goyvaerts, D.L. (ed.), *Phonology in the 1970's.* Ghent: Story-Scientia.

—— & Dell, F. (eds.), (1978). *Etudes de phonologie française.* Paris: Editions du C.N.R.S.

Crothers, J. (1978). 'Typology and Universals of Vowel Systems'. In Greenberg, J.B. (ed.), *Universals of Human Language Vol 2: Phonology.* Stanford: Stanford University Press.

—— & Shibatani, M. (1980). 'Issues in the Description of Turkish Vowel Harmony'. In Vago, R.M. (ed.). 63-88.
Cutler, A. (1980). 'Productivity in Word Formation'. *Chicago Linguistic Society* 16. 45-51
Dauer, R. (1983). 'Stress-timing and Syllable-timing Reanalyzed'. *Journal of Phonetics* 11. 51-62.
Davenport, M. & Staun, J. (this volume). 'Sequence, Segment and Configuration: Two Problems for Dependency Phonology'.
Davis, J. (1981). *Kobon*. (Lingua Descriptive Series.) Amsterdam: North-Holland.
Davis, S. (1982). 'Rhyme, or Reason? A Look at Syllable-internal Constituents'. *Berkeley Linguistic Society* 8. 525-32.
Dell, F. (1970). 'Les règles phonologiques tardives et la morphologie dérivationnelle du français'. Unpublished M.I.T. PhD Dissertation.
—— (1973a/1980). *Les règles et les sons*. Paris: Hermann, 1973. Translated as *Generative Phonology and French Phonology*. Cambridge: Cambridge University Press, 1980.
—— (1973b). 'Two Cases of Exceptional Rule Ordering'. In Kiefer, F. & Ruwet, N. (eds.), *Generative Grammar in Europe*. Dordrecht: Reidel
—— (1977). 'Schwa précédé d'un groupe obstruante-liquide'. *Recherches Linguistiques* 4.
—— (1978). 'Certains corrélats de la distinction entre morphologie dérivationnelle et morphologie flexionnelle dans la phonologie du français'. *Recherches Linguistiques à Montréal* 10. 1-10.
—— & Selkirk, E.O. (1978). 'On *French Phonology and Morphology* and some Vowel Alternations in French'. In Keyser, S.J. (ed.), *Recent Transformational Studies in European Languages*. Cambridge, Mass.: M.I.T. Press.
Dogil, G. (1981). 'Elementary Accent Systems'. *Phonologica 1980*. 89-99.
[Donegan] Miller, P.J. (1973). 'Bleaching and Coloring'. *Chicago Linguistic Society* 9. 386-97.
Donegan, P.J. (1978). 'On the Natural Phonology of Vowels'. *Ohio State University Working Papers in Linguistics* 23.
Douglas, W.H. (1981). 'Watjarri'. In Dixon, R.M. & Blake, B. (eds.) *Handbook of Australian Languages* II. Amsterdam: John Benjamins. 197-272.
Drachman, G. (1969). 'Twana Phonology'. *Ohio State University Working Papers in Linguistics* 5.
Dresher, B.E. (1981). 'Abstractness and Explanation in Phonology'. In Hornstein, N. & Lightfoot, D. (eds.), *Explanation in Linguistics*. London: Longman.
Dressler, W.U. (1975). 'Zentrifugale und Zentripetale phonologische Prozesse'. *Wiener Linguistische Gazette* 8. 32-41.
—— (1977). 'Morphophonological Disturbances in Aphasia'. *Wiener Linguistische Gazette* 14. 3-10.
—— (1979). 'Remarks on the Typology of Segmental Process Phonologies'. *Wiener Linguistische Gazette* 20. 3-13.
——, Luschützky, H.C., Pfeiffer, O.E. & Rennison, J.R. (eds.), (1985). *Phonologica 1984*. Cambridge: Cambridge University Press.
——, Pfeiffer, O.E. & Rennison J.R. (eds.), (1981). *Phonologica 1980*. Innsbruck: Innsbrucker Beiträge zur Sprachwissenschaft.
Durand, J. (1976). 'Generative Phonology, Dependency Phonology and Southern French'. *Lingua e Stile* XI-1. 3-23.
—— (1980). 'Esquisse d'une théorie de la syllabe en phonologie de dépendance'. *Modèles linguistiques* Tome III, fasc. 2: 147-71.
—— (this volume). 'French Liaison, Floating Segments and Other Matters in a Dependency Framework'.
—— (1985). 'On a Recent Tridimensional Analysis of French Liaison. Encrevé and

322   *Bibliography*

Liaison non-enchaînée'. *Sheffield Working Papers in Language and Linguistics.* Vol. 2. 50-65. Also to appear in *Folia Linguistica.*
Encrevé, P. (1983). 'La liaison sans enchaînement'. *Actes de la recherche en sciences sociales* 46. 39-66.
Ewen, C.J. (1977). 'Aitken's Law and the Phonatory Gesture in Dependency Phonology'. *Lingua* 41. 307-29.
—— (1978). 'The Phonology of the Diminutive in Dutch: a Dependency Account'. *Lingua* 45. 141-73.
—— (1980a). 'Aspects of Phonological, Structure, with Particular Reference to English and Dutch'. PhD thesis, University of Edinburgh.
—— (1980b). 'Segment or Sequence? Problems in the Analysis of Some Consonantal Phenomena'. In Anderson, J.M. & Ewen, C.J. (eds.). 157-204.
—— (1981). 'Phonological Notation and Foreign Language Teaching'. In James, A. & Westney, P. (eds.), *New Linguistic Impulses in Foreign Language Teaching.* Tübingen: Narr.
—— (1982). 'The Internal Structure of Complex Segments'. In van der Hulst, H. & Smith, N. (eds.), (1982b). 27-67.
—— (this volume). 'Segmental and Suprasegmental Structure'.
—— & van der Hulst (1985). 'Single-valued Features and the Nonlinear Analysis of Vowel Harmony'. In Beukema, F.H. & Bennis, H. (eds.), *Linguistics in the Netherlands 1985.* Dordrect: Foris. 39-48.
Fallows, D. (1981). 'Experimental Evidence for English Syllabification and Syllable Structure'. *Journal of Linguistics* 17. 309-17.
de Félice, Th. (1950). *Eléments de grammaire morphologique.* Paris: Didier.
Fischer-Jørgensen, E. (1975). *Trends in Phonological Theory.* Copenhagen: Akademisk Forlag.
Foley, J. (1977). *Foundations of Theoretical Phonology.* Cambridge: Cambridge University Press.
Fouché, P. (1956). *Traité de prononciation française.* Paris: Klincksieck.
Fudge, E.C. (1969). 'Syllables'. *Journal of Linguistics* 5. 253-86.
—— (1970). 'Phonological Structure and Expressiveness'. *Journal of Linguistics* 6. 161-88.
Fujimura, O. & Lovins, J.B. (1978). 'Syllables as Concatenative Phonetic Units'. In Bell, A. & Hooper, J.B. (eds.). 107-20.
Gazdar, G. (1982). 'Phrase Structure Grammar'. In Jacobson, P. & Pullum, G.K. (eds.), *The Nature of Syntactic Representation.* Dordrecht: Reidel. 131-86.
Giegerich, H.J. (1979). 'On Stress-timing in English Phonology'. Linguistic Agency, University of Trier. Revised version: *Lingua* 51 (1980). 187-221.
—— (1981). 'Zero Syllables in Metrical Theory'. In Dressler, W.U., Pfeiffer, O.E. & Rennison, J.R. (eds.). 153-9.
—— (1983a). 'Metrische Phonologie und Kompositionsakzent im Deutschen'. *Papiere zur Linguistik* 28. 3-25.
—— (1983b). 'On English Sentence Stress and the Nature of Metrical Structure'. *Journal of Linguistics* 19. 1-28.
—— (1984). 'Glottal Stop, Syllable Structure and Gmc. Vowel Alliteration'. MS.
—— (1985). *Metrical Phonology and Phonological Structure: German and English.* Cambridge: Cambridge University Press.
—— (this volume). 'Relating to Metrical Structure'.
Goldsmith, J. (1976). *Autosegmental Phonology.* PhD thesis, reproduced by Indiana University Linguistics Club.
—— (to appear). 'Vowel Harmony in Khalkha Mongolian, Yaka, Finnish and Hungarian'. *Phonology Yearbook* 2.
Gougenheim, G. (1938). *Le système grammatical de la langue française.* Paris: Bibliothèque du français moderne.

Goyvaerts, D.L. & Pullum, G.K. (eds.), (1975). *Essays on the Sound Pattern of English*. Ghent: Story-Scientia.

Grevisse, M. (1964). *Le bon usage*. 8th edn, Gembloux: Duculot.

Gussenhoven, C. (1983). 'Focus, Mode and the Nucleus'. *Journal of Linguistics* 19. 377-417.

Halle, M. (1977). 'Tenseness, Vowel Shift, and the Phonology of the Back Vowels in Modern English'. *Linguistic Inquiry* 8. 611-25.

—— & Clements, G.N. (1983). *Problem Book in Phonology*. Cambridge, Mass.: M.I.T. Press.

Halliday, M.A.K. (1967). *Intonation and Grammar in British English*. The Hague: Mouton.

Harris, J.W. (1983). *Syllable Structure and Stress in Spanish. A Non-linear Analysis*. Linguistic Inquiry Monograph 8. Cambridge, Mass.: M.I.T. Press.

—— (1984). 'Autosegmental Phonology, Lexical Phonology and Spanish Nasals', In Aronoff, M. & Oehrle, R.T. (eds.) 67-82.

Hashimoto, O.Y. (1972). *Phonology of Cantonese*. Cambridge: Cambridge University Press.

Hayes, B. (1980). 'A Metrical Theory of Stress Rules'. PhD dissertation, M.I.T.

—— (1982). 'Extrametricality and English Stress'. *Linguistic Inquiry* 13. 227-76.

—— (1984). 'The Phonology of Rhythm in English'. *Linguistic Inquiry* 15. 33-74.

Heger, S. (1975). *Tal og Tegn*. Copenhagen: Gjellerup.

Henderson, E. (1949). 'Prosodies in Siamese. A Study in Synthesis'. In Palmer, F.R. (eds.), 27-53.

Herbert, R.K. (1977). 'Language Universals, Markedness Theory, and Natural Phonetic Processes: the Interaction of Nasal and Oral Consonants'. PhD dissertation, Ohio State University.

Higginbottom, E. (1964). 'Glottal Reinforcement in English'. *Transactions of the Philological Society*. 129-42.

Hirst, D. (1983). 'Linearisation and the Single Segment Hypothesis'. MS. CNRS, Institut de Phonétique, Aix-en-Provence.

Hockett, C.F. (1955). *A Manual of Phonology*. International Journal of American Linguistics Memoir 11. Baltimore: Waverly Press.

Hooper, J.B. (1972). 'The Syllable in Phonological Theory'. *Language* 48. 525-40.

—— (1976). *An Introduction to Natural Generative Phonology*. New York: Academic Press.

van der Hulst, H. (1984). *Syllable Structure and Stress in Dutch*. Dordrecht: Foris.

—— and Smith, N. (eds.), (1982a). *The Structure of Phonological Representations* (Part I). Dordrecht: Foris.

—— (eds.), (1982b). *The Structure of Phonological Representations* (Part II). Dordrecht: Foris.

—— (1982c). 'An Overview of Autosegmental and Metrical Phonology'. In van der Hulst, H. & Smith, N. (eds.), (1982a). 1-45.

Hyman, L. M. (1975). *Phonology: Theory and Analysis*. New York: Holt, Rinehart & Winston.

—— (1985). *A Theory of Phonological Weight*. Dordrecht: Foris.

Iverson, G.K. (1983). 'The Elsewhere Condition and *h*-aspiré'. *Journal of Linguistics* 19. 369-76.

Jakobson, R. (1968). *Child Language, Aphasia, and Phonological Universals*. The Hague: Mouton. (Translation of *Kindersprache, Aphasie und allgemeine Lautgesetze*, 1941, Uppsala: Almqvist & Wiksell.)

—— & Waugh, L. (1979). *The Sound Shape of Language*. Brighton, Sussex: Harvester Press.

—— Fant, C.G.M. & Halle, M. (1952). *Preliminaries to Speech Analysis*. Cambridge, Mass.: M.I.T. Press.

Jespersen, O. (1969). *English Phonetics*, 8th edn. Copenhagen: Gyldendal.

Job, D.M. (1981). 'Circassian Vowels: One, Two, Three'. In Dressler *et al.* (eds.). 231-6.

Jones, C. (1976). 'Some Constraints on Medial Consonant Clusters'. *Language* 52. 121-30.

—— (1978a). 'Rounding and Fronting in Old English Phonology'. *Lingua* 46. 157-68.

—— (1978b). 'Segment Gemination and Syllable Shape'. *Studies in English Linguistics* 6.

—— (this volume). 'A Dependency Approach to some Well-known Features of English Phonology'.

—— & Nakao, T. (to appear). *English Phonology to 1450: a Dependency Approach.*

Jordan, R. (1974). *Handbuch der Mittelenglischen Grammatik*, I. Translated by Cook, E.J. The Hague: Mouton.

Kahn, D. (1976). *Syllable-based Generalisations in English Phonology.* Bloomington: Indiana University Linguistics Club.

Kim, C.-W. (1970). 'A Theory of Aspiration'. *Phonetica* 21. 107-16.

King, R.D. (1969). *Historical Linguistics and Generative Grammar.* Englewood Cliffs, N.J.: Prentice-Hall.

Kiparsky, P. (1973). 'How Abstract is Phonology?' In Fujimura, O. (ed.), *Three Dimensions of Linguistic Theory.* Tokyo: TEC Company Ltd.

—— (1979). 'Metrical Structure Assignment is Cyclic'. *Linguistic Inquiry* 10. 421-42.

—— (1981). 'Remarks on the Metrical Structure of the Syllable'. In Dressler *et al.* (eds.). 245-56.

—— (1982). 'Lexical Morphology and Phonology'. *Linguistics in the Morning Calm.* Seoul: Hansin. 3-91.

Klatt, D.H. (1976). 'Linguistic Uses of Segmental Duration in English: Acoustic and Perceptual Evidence'. *The Journal of the Acoustical Society of America* 59.

Klausenburger, J. (1977). 'Deletion vs. Epenthesis: Intra- vs. Inter- paradigmatic Arguments in Linguistics'. *Lingua* 42. 153-60.

—— (1978a). 'French Linking Phenomena: a Natural Generative Analysis'. *Language* 54. 21-40.

—— (1978b). 'Liaison 1977: the Case for Epenthesis'. *Studies in French Linguistics* 1-2. 1-20.

Kratochvil, P. (1968). *The Chinese Language Today.* London: Hutchinson.

Krech, E.-M. (1968). *Sprechwissenschaftlich-phonetische Untersuchungen zum Gebrauch des Glottisschlageinsatzes in der allgemeinen deutschen Hochlautung.* Basel: Karger.

Ladd, D.R. (1978). *The Structure of Intonational Meaning: Evidence from English.* Bloomington: Indiana University Press.

Ladefoged, P. (1968). *A Phonetic Study of West African Languages. An Auditory-instrumental Study.* Cambridge: Cambridge University Press.

—— (1971). *Preliminaries to Linguistic Phonetics.* Chicago: University of Chicago Press.

—— (1975/1982). *A Course in Phonetics.* New York: Harcourt, Brace, Jovanovich. First edition, 1975. Revised edition, 1982.

Langendoen, T. (1975). 'Finite-state Parsing of Phrase-structure Languages and the Status of Readjustment Rules in Grammar'. *Linguistic Inquiry* 6. 533-54.

Lass, R. (1976). *English Phonology and Phonological Theory.* Cambridge: Cambridge University Press.

—— (1983). 'Glottal Stop and Syllable Structure in South African English; with a Note on Germanic Alliteration'. MS.

—— (1984). *Phonology*. Cambridge: Cambridge University Press.
—— & Anderson, J.M. (1975). *Old English Phonology*. Cambridge: Cambridge University Press.
Leben, W. (1982). 'Metrical or Autosegmental'. In van der Hulst, H. & Smith, N. (eds.), (1982a). 177-90.
Lehiste, I. (1977). 'Isochrony Reconsidered'. *Journal of Phonetics* 5. 253-63.
Liberman, M. (1975). 'The Intonational System of English'. PhD dissertation, M.I.T. Published 1979. New York: Garland.
—— & Prince, A. (1977). 'On Stress and Linguistic Rhythm'. *Linguistic Inquiry* 8. 249-336.
Lieberman, P. (1975). *On the Origins of Language. An Introduction to the Evolution of Human Speech.* New York: Macmillan Publishing Co., Inc.
—— (1984). *The Biology and Evolution of Language*. Cambridge, Mass.: Harvard University Press.
Lindau, M.E. (1975). 'Features for Vowels'. PhD thesis. University of California, Los Angeles.
—— (1978). 'Vowel Features'. *Language* 54. 541-63.
Lodge, K.R. (1973). 'Stockport Revisited'. *Journal of the International Phonetic Association* 3. 81-7.
—— (1981). 'English Consonants and Dependency Phonology'. *Lingua* 54. 19-39.
—— (1984). *Studies in the Phonology of Colloquial English.* London: Croom Helm.
—— (this volume). 'The English Velar Fricative, Dialect Variation and Dependency Phonology'.
Love, N. (1981). *Generative Phonology: A Case-Study from French.* Amsterdam: John Benjamins.
Lowenstamm, J. (1981). 'On the Maximal Cluster Approach to Syllable Structure'. *Linguistic Inquiry* 12:4. 575-604.
McCawley, J.D. (1973). 'On the Role of Notation in Generative Phonology'. In Gross, M., Halle, M. & Schutzenberger, M. (eds.), *The Formal Analysis of Natural Language.* The Hague: Mouton.
Malécot, (1975). 'French Liaison as a Function of Grammatical, Phonetic and Paralinguistic Variables'. *Phonetica* 32. 161-79.
Malsch, D.L. & Fulcher, R. (1975). 'Tensing and Syllabification in Middle English'. *Language* 51.
Matthews, P.H. (1981). *Syntax*. Cambridge: Cambridge University Press.
Milner, J.-C. (1973). *Arguments Linguistiques*. Paris: Mame.
Moody, M. (1978). 'Some Preliminaries to a Theory of Morphology'. *Glossa* 12. 16-38.
Morin, Y.-C. (1978). 'The Status of Mute "e".' *Studies in French Linguistics* 1-2. 79-140.
—— (1983). 'Quelques observations sur la chute du e muet dans le français régional de Saint-Etienne'. *La linguistique* 19:I. 71-93.
—— & Kaye, J.C. (1982). 'The Syntactic Bases for French Liaison'. *Journal of Linguistics* 18. 291-330.
Nespor, M. & Vogel, I. (1982). 'Prosodic Domains of External Sandhi Rules'. In van der Hulst, H. & Smith, N. (eds.) (1982a). 225-55.
Noske, R. (1982). 'Syllabification and Syllable Changing Rules in French'. In van der Hulst, H. & Smith, N. (eds.) (1982b). 257-310.
O'Connor, J.D. & Trim, J.L.M. (1953). 'Vowel, Consonant, Syllable — a Phonological Definition'. *Word* 9. 103-22.
Ó Dochartaigh, C. (1981). 'Vowel Strengthening in Gaelic'. *Scottish Gaelic Studies.* 219-40.
Ohala, J.J. & Kawasaki, H. (1984). 'Prosodic Phonology and Phonetics'.

326   *Bibliography*

Phonology Yearbook 1. 113-27.
Orton, H. & Halliday, W.J. (1962-3). *Survey of English Dialects* I. Leeds: E.J. Arnold.
—— & Barry, M.V. (1967-71). *Survey of English Dialects* II. Leeds: E.J. Arnold.
Palmer, F.R. (ed.), (1970). *Prosodic Analysis.* London: Oxford University Press.
Pike, K.L. & Pike, E.V. (1947). 'Immediate Constituents of Mazatec Syllables'. *International Journal of American Linguistics* 13. 78-91.
Pope, E. (1972). 'Gh-words'. *Linguistic Inquiry* 3. 125-30.
Prince, A. (1983). 'Relating to the Grid'. *Linguistic Inquiry* 14. 19-100.
Prost, A. (1980). *La langue des KOUROUMBA ou akurumfe.* Vienna: Schendl.
Quirk, R. & Wrenn, C.L. (1959). *An Old English Grammar.* London: Methuen & Co. Ltd.
Rennison, J.R. (1979). 'Schwierigkeiten bei der monodialektalen Beschreibung österreichischer Stadtmundarten: zur Homogenität der bidialektalen Phonologie'. *Grazer Linguistische Studien* 9. 152-61.
—— (1981). 'Bidialektale Phonologie'. *Die Kompetenz zweier Salzburger Sprecher.* Wiesbaden: Steiner.
—— (1985). 'On the Vowel Harmonies of Koromfe (Burkina Faso, West Africa)'. In Dressler *et al.* (eds.).
—— (this volume). 'On Tridirectional Feature Systems for Vowels'.
Ringen, C. (1980). 'A Concrete Analysis of Hungarian Vowel Harmony'. In Vago (ed.), 135-54.
Roach, P. (1982). 'On the Distinction Between "Stress-timed" and "Syllable-timed" Languages'. In Crystal, D. (ed.), *Linguistic Controversies: Essays in Linguistic Theory and Practice in Honour of F.R. Palmer.* London: Edward Arnold.
Robinson, J.J. (1970). 'Dependency Structures and Transformational Rules'. *Language* 46. 259-85.
Romaine, S. (1978). 'Postvocalic /r/ in Scottish English: Sound Change in Progress?' In Trudgill, P.J. (ed.), *Sociolinguistic Patterns in British English.* London: Edward Arnold.
Ross, J.R. (1972). 'A Reanalysis of English Word Stress'. In Brame, M.K. (ed.), *Contributions to Generative Phonology.* Austin: Texas University Press. 229-323.
Ruhlen, M. (1975). 'A Guide to the Languages of the World'. Language Universals Project, Stanford University.
Saib, F. (1978). 'Segment Organization and the Syllable in Tamazight Berber'. In Bell, A. & Hooper, J.B. (eds.). 93-104.
Schane, S.A. (1968). *French Phonology and Morphology.* Cambridge, Mass.: M.I.T. Press.
—— (1973). 'The Formalisation of Exceptions in Phonology'. In Gross, M., Halle, M. & Schutzenberger, M. (eds.), *The Formal Analysis of Natural Languages.* The Hague: Mouton. 63-72.
—— (1974). 'There is No French Truncation Rule'. In Campbell, R. *et al.* (eds.), *Linguistic Studies in Romance Languages.* Washington: Georgetown University Press. 89-99.
—— (1979). 'Rhythm, Accent, and Stress in English'. *Linguistic Inquiry* 10. 483-502.
—— (1984a). 'The Fundamentals of Particle Phonology'. *Phonology Yearbook* 1. 129-55.
—— (1984b). 'Two English Vowel Movements: a Particle Analysis'. In Aronoff, M. & Oehrle, R.T. (eds.). 32-51.
Schenker, A.M. (1966). *Beginning Polish* 1. New Haven: Yale University Press.
Selkirk, E.O. (1972/81). 'The Phrase Phonology of English and French'. M.I.T.

PhD Dissertation, 1972. Indiana University Linguistics Club, 1981.

—— (1974). 'French Liaison and the X̄ Notation'. *Linguistic Inquiry* 5. 573-90.

—— (1978). 'The French Foot: on the Status of "Mute" *e*'. *Studies in French Linguistics* 1.2. 141-50.

—— (1980a). *On Prosodic Structure and its Relation to Syntactic Structure.* Bloomington: Indiana University Linguistics Club.

—— (1980b). 'The Role of Prosodic Categories in English Word Stress. *Linguistic Inquiry* 11. 563-605.

—— (1982). 'The Syllable'. In van der Hulst, H. & Smith, N. (eds.) (1982b). 337-83.

—— (1984a). 'On the Major Class Features and Syllable Theory'. In Aronoff, M. & Oehrle, R.T. (eds.). 107-36.

—— (1984b). *Phonology and Syntax: the Relation between Sound and Structure.* Cambridge, Mass.: M.I.T. Press.

Sievers, E. & Brunner, K. (1965). *Abriss der Altenglischen Grammatik.* Niemeyer: Halle.

Sommerstein, A. (1977). *Modern Phonology.* London: Edward Arnold.

Stampe, D. (1969). 'The Acquisition of Phonetic Representation'. *Chicago Linguistic Society* 5.

Stanley, R. (1967). 'Redundancy Rules in Phonology'. *Language* 43: 1. 393-436.

Stevens, K. (1972). 'The Quantal Nature of Speech'. In David, E.E. & Denes, P.B. (eds.), *Human Communication: a Unified View.* New York: McGraw Hill.

Thorsen, N. & Thorsen, O.M. (1978). *Fonetik for Sprogstuderende.* Copenhagen University Phonetics Department.

Thráinsson, H. (1978). 'On the Phonology of Icelandic Preaspiration'. *Nordic Journal of Linguistics* 1. 3-54.

Trager, G.L. & Smith, H.L. (1951). *An Outline of English Structure.* Norman, Oklahoma: Battenburg Press.

Tranel, B. (1974). 'The Phonology of Nasal Vowels in Modern French'. PhD Dissertation, University of California, San Diego.

—— (1981). *Concreteness in Generative Phonology: Evidence from French.* Berkeley: University of California Press.

—— (1984). 'Closed Syllable Adjustment and the Representation of Schwa in French'. In Brugman, C. & Macaulay, M. (eds.) *Proceedings of the Tenth Annual Meeting of the Berkeley Linguistics Society.* Berkeley: Berkeley Linguistics Society, University of California.

—— (to appear a). 'French Liaison and Extrasyllabicity'. *Proceedings of the 14th Linguistic Symposium on Romance Languages* (USC — February 1984).

—— (to appear b). 'Floating Schwas and Closed Syllable Adjustment in French'. To appear in *Phonologica 1984.*

—— (to appear c). 'On Closed Syllable Adjustment in French'. In King, L.D. & Maley, C.A. (eds.), *Selected Papers from the 13th Linguistic Symposium on Romance Languages.* Amsterdam: John Benjamins.

Trudgill, P.J. (1983). *On Dialect.* Oxford: Basil Blackwell.

—— & Foxcroft, T. (1978). 'On the Sociolinguistics of Vocalic Mergers: Transfer and Approximation in East Anglia'. In Trudgill, P.J. (ed.), *Sociolinguistic Patterns in British English.* London: Edward Arnold.

UPSID: 'UCLA Phonological Segment Inventory Database'. *UCLA Working papers in phonetics,* 53 (1981).

Vago, R.M. (1980a). *The Sound Pattern of Hungarian.* Washington: Georgetown University Press.

—— (1980b). 'A Critique of Suprasegmental Theories of Vowel Harmony'. In Vago, R.M. (ed.) 155-81.

—— (ed.), (1980c). *Issues in Vowel Harmony.* Amsterdam: John Benjamins.

Vennemann, T., (1972). 'On the Theory of Syllabic Phonology'. *Linguistische Berichte* 18. 1-18.

—— (1974). 'Words and Syllables in Natural Generative Grammar'. In Bruck, A., Fox, R.A. & La Galy, M.W. (eds.) *Papers from the Parasession on Natural Phonology*. Chicago: Chicago Linguistic Society. 346-74.

Vergnaud, J.-R. (1980). 'A Formal Theory of Vowel Harmony'. In Vago, R.M. (ed.), 49-62.

—— (1982). [no title.] Oral presentation at the Phonology Symposium, GLOW Colloquium, March 1982, Paris.

Vincent, N. (this volume). 'Constituency and Syllable Structure'.

—— (in prep.). 'Segment and Syllable in Ponapean Reduplication'.

Warnant, L. (1973). *Dictionnaire des rimes orales et écrites.* Paris: Larousse.

Werth, P. (1983). 'Contrastivity'. Paper presented to the English language Society of Edinburgh, Oct. 31, 1983.

Wunderlich, D. (1979). *Foundations of Linguistics.* Cambridge: Cambridge University Press.

Zabrocki, L. (1951). *Usilnienie i lenicja w językach Indoeuropejskich i w Ugrofińskim.* Poznań: Nakładem Poznańskiego Towarzystwa Przyjaciół Nauk z Zasiłkiem Ministerstwa Szkół Wyższych i Nauki..

Zwicky, A. (1985). 'Heads'. *Journal of Linguistics* 21. 1-29.

NAME INDEX

Abercrombie 58, 109, 233, 255-6
Ågren 168
Allen, G.D. 254
Allen, W.S. 310
Anderson, J.M. 3, 6, 7, 9, 15, 17-19,
  24, 50, 53-4, 77, 86, 96, 127-8,
  136, 139, 142, 157, 215-16, 225,
  229, 274, 305
Anderson, S.R. 130, 162, 183, 195-6,
  200, 303, 307
Anderson and Durand 55, 173, 187,
  191, 200, 219, 258, 273
Anderson and Ewen 3, 6, 7, 14, 21,
  24, 29, 37, 40, 51, 55, 56-7, 68,
  76, 97, 127, 129-31, 142, 179,
  191-2, 195, 203-6, 209, 210, 216,
  219, 224, 283, 286, 297, 303
Anderson and Jones 14, 32, 47, 55,
  67, 86, 99-100, 135, 140, 205,
  223, 225, 227, 231, 257, 272,
  261, 267, 285, 298
Armstrong 196
Aronoff 186
Aronoff and Schvaneveldt 279
Azaretti 308

Basbøll 139, 166, 192
Beddor 265
Bloomfield 183
Booij 231, 254
Brown 58, 305

Cairns and Feinstein 77, 130
Campbell 131
Catford 40, 41, 137, 153-6
Chomsky 129, 243
Chomsky and Halle 7, 19-20, 23, 36,
  120, 203, 223, 231, 236, 259,
  269-70, 277-8, 281, 312
Clements 281, 286-8
Clements and Keyser 10, 14, 44, 161,
  172, 181, 199, 201, 207-8, 311,
  313, 315
Clements and Sezer 289
Colman 34
Comrie 58
de Cornulier 201

Crothers 26, 28
Crothers and Shibatani 293, 297
Cutler 279

Dauer 254
Davenport and Staun 21, 39, 42-3,
  278
Davis 127, 309
Dell 162, 164, 176, 181, 187-9, 193,
  195, 200
Dell and Selkirk 200
Dogil 66
Donegan 24, 282
[Donegan] Miller 26
Douglas 309
Drachman 282
Dresher 278
Dressler 282, 286, 288, 291, 300
Durand 14, 23, 127, 189, 199

Encrevé 168, 182, 199
Ewen 21, 28, 39, 40, 42-3, 49, 67,
  100, 131, 136-41, 145-8, 150-5,
  158-9, 205, 206, 209-10, 225,
  273
Ewen and van der Hulst 34

Fallows 95-6, 255
de Félice 185
Fischer-Jørgensen 306
Foley 36, 192, 197, 311
Fouché 162, 166
Fudge 72, 314
Fujimura and Lovins 72

Gazdar 317
Giegerich 9, 46, 123, 125, 130, 133,
  213, 217-20, 224, 227, 230, 232,
  235, 241, 256, 310
Goldsmith 46, 53, 206
Gougenheim 177-8
Goyvaerts and Pullum 282
Grammont 166
Grevisse 162
Gussenhoven 119, 128

329

SUBJECT INDEX